POWER

POWER

A POLITICAL HISTORY OF
THE TWENTIETH CENTURY

EDITED BY
C. S. NICHOLLS

New York
OXFORD UNIVERSITY PRESS
1990

Volume editor Mike March
Art editor Ayala Kingsley
Designers Frankie Macmillan,
  Wolfgang Mezger, Gill Mouqué,
  Tony de Saulles, Rita Wütrych
Picture research Christine
  Vincent
**Senior cartographic
  editor** Olive Pearson
Cartographic editor Zoë
  Goodwin
Project editor Peter Furtado

AN EQUINOX BOOK

Planned and produced by
Equinox (Oxford) Ltd
Musterlin House
Jordan Hill Road
Oxford
England

Copyright © Equinox (Oxford) Ltd
1990

Published in the United States of
America by Oxford University
Press Inc., 200 Madison Avenue,
New York NY 10016

Oxford is a registered trademark of
Oxford University Press

Library of Congress
Cataloguing-in-Publication Data

  Power: a political history of
  the twentieth century/edited
  by C.S. Nicholls.
    p. cm.
  "An Equinox book" – T.p.
  verso.
  Includes bibliographical
  references..
  ISBN 0-19-520793-9
  1. World politics – 20th
  century. I. Nicholls, C. S.
  (Christine Stephanie)
D443.P67 1990
909.82–dc20   89-36858
                                  CIP

Printed in Yugoslavia by
Gorenjski Tisk, Kranj,
by arrangement with Papirografika

ADVISORY EDITORS

William McNeill
University of Chicago

Peter Pulzer
All Souls College, Oxford

CONTRIBUTORS

Sir Julian Bullard All Souls College, Oxford
Peter Carey Trinity College, Oxford
Christine Collette St Hugh's College, Oxford
Malcolm Cooper Formerly of the University of
  Newfoundland
Michael Geyer University of Chicago
Robert Gildea Merton College, Oxford
Anthony Glees Brunel University
Roger Griffin Oxford Polytechnic
Matthew Jones St Antony's College, Oxford
Paul Kennedy Yale University
Wolfgang Krieger Munich University
Dermot MacCann Brunel University
Roger Morgan London School of Economics
A.J. Nicholls St Antony's College, Oxford
Gowher Rizvi University of Warwick
Harry Shukman St Antony's College, Oxford
Stanley Trapido St Antony's College, Oxford
Paul Wilkinson University of Aberdeen
Roger Zetter Oxford Polytechnic

CONTENTS

PREFACE

Political history is something we should all understand; it is the background to all current political activity, and we know (from the study of history) that if politicians wish to win control of our hearts and minds, then they try to rewrite history to tell us only the things they wish us to know.

As a result (especially in an age when governments are able to control the information flow to their peoples as never before) it is important that we all have access to the facts of political history, as discovered by professional historians.

Nevertheless, even the most professional history cannot be valuefree; the questions historians ask, and the emphases they put on events, themselves shape the story that they are trying to unfold. History is therefore a continual redefinition of the terms of the debate, and a reappraisal of the past in terms of the concerns of the present. It therefore has continually to be rewritten, and the past re-evaluated, as historians discover more about what happened, and as the questions of primary concern themselves change.

This book sets out to cover the background to the most momentous conflicts, the most horrific events and the most cheering developments in the world in our century, with a coverage selected and presented by a team of professional historians. It begins by setting out the main terms within which political change has occurred, starting from the underlying concepts of state and power, and the fundamental assumptions such as left and right, democracy and authority, fascism and socialism. While the main thrust of the book is to give a concise and primarily chronological account of the power conflicts between and within the major states, the history of smaller nations is not forgotten. Meanwhile broad themes of the history of the century, such as the role of young people, of unions or of art are given special coverage; as are archetypically 20th-century problems such as forms of dictatorship and the sufferings of large numbers of refugees or victims of mass extermination.

Whereas the history of the early years of the century was primarily that of the European Powers and their empires, as the century has continued the emergence of the authentic voice of the rest of the world, with its own problems and attempted solutions, has become more and more insistent; and the relationship between First and Third Worlds has become a central issue. Similarly, the emergence of weapons capable of destroying the world in its entirety, and, less dramatic but equally ominous, of a social and economic system that threatens to destroy the environment within which life and human society exists, have brought new topics to the attention of historians, as of the rest of us. While this book cannot hope to provide a complete re-evaluation of the history of the world since 1900, it offers itself as a contribution both to general knowledge of the events of the past, and of the issues that confront past, present and future.

C.S. Nicholls   Oxford 1989

INTRODUCTION

Why study history? What do the politics of the past matter to men and women in the 1990s? What relevance have Czar Nicholas II, Woodrow Wilson, Hitler, Stalin or Churchill to children who have grown up in the 1970s and 1980s? Nowadays it is fashionable in many circles to deny that there is any intrinsic value in historical study. Yet, whenever statesmen, administrators, educationalists or journalists wish to convince us of the rightness of their actions, they appeal to history. It is important, therefore, how history is written and who writes it. We need reliable and accurate guides to the world of the past.

It has been claimed that "the past is a foreign country". Certainly the attitudes and behavior of people in the past – even the recent past – are often alien to us. On the other hand we should remember that the past was also peopled with foreigners – in the sense that most people lived in closely-knit national, regional or even tribal communities – with access to much less information about events and conditions elsewhere in the globe than we have today. To these people the world outside their communities often looked exotic and strange. It was simultaneously menacing and enticing. At one level this distance from foreigners could give people a romantic zeal for exploration; at another it could encourage xenophobic resentment and murderous hatred. The 20th century saw the occupants of the planet Earth come to know more about each other than ever before. It also witnessed genocide and mass destruction. It is important that the facts as to how these two, contradictory developments came about are widely known.

The world in 1900

When the century began, the industrialized nations of the world – those in Europe, north America and Australasia – were bursting with confidence. Their leaders and, by and large, their peoples believed that Western civilization had established itself as clearly superior to other world lifestyles. This belief even affected the newly emerging industrial power of Japan, where determination to retain independence in the face of Western predators was coupled with a willingness to take over the most important advantages of the West: its technical know-how and its political organization.

Westerners believed they had an unassailable position with regard to the rest of the world because they were blessed with the Christian religion and the enlightenment of reason. The former had given them moral strength and powerful organizations reaching centuries back into the past. The latter, celebrated particularly in northern Europe and north America since the 18th century, encouraged scientific methods, a utilitarian attitude towards the economy and rational forms of human administration. In the face of this combination all other civilizations seemed doomed to subjection.

From the 17th century the West had swept aside its Muslim, Hindu, Buddhist, Confucian or Shinto rivals. In some cases, as with the great Moghul empire of India or the ancient communities of the East Indies, formal subjection to European imperial rulers was well established by 1900. In others, such as the colonial areas of sub-Saharan Africa, Western control was recent and sometimes still contested. The great civilization of China remained nominally independent, but its territorial integrity had already been chipped away by successive losses to Western powers – not to mention its Westernized Japanese neighbor – and China's sovereignty was undermined by humiliating treaties which gave foreigners a privileged existence within its own borders.

It was symbolic that the arrival of the 20th century was heralded by the Boxer rising, in a large part a desperate revolt of the Chinese people against their Western tormentors. Without coherent organization or effective military equipment, the rising itself had little chance of success. Its suppression, accompanied by an orgy of atrocity, reinforced the West's view of its own superiority and, more important, of its own mission. No less symbolic was the fact that the German Kaiser, himself the ruler of a new and thrusting industrial state, should create a sensation by urging his troops to cast aside all pity when crushing the Boxers and behave like "the Huns" of old. This phrase was to dog him and his countrymen for decades. It helped to illustrate the uneasy relationship between self-consciously Christian, or at least "enlightened", values in the West and a power-worshipping belief in "the survival of the fittest" – an unscientific but immensely appealing application of Darwinian theories about natural selection within animal populations to the history of nations.

These notions were associated with other pseudo-scientific concepts based on theories of race. In many Christian societies antisemitism – the term itself was first used in the 1880s – had reappeared. Ancient prejudices against the Jews took on a modern form. The enlightened liberalism which had apparently characterized the rise of nation-states in Europe in the nineteenth century had not pleased everybody. Many groups which had formerly been privileged, whether they were landowners, clergy, craftsmen or small traders, felt that they were losing out in a world of free trade and careers open to talent. The section of society apparently most favored by the new liberal attitudes was the Jews, a repressed minority who could now claim equal rights with others. For those who hated liberalism the Jew was a useful stick with which to beat the modern world. How could life be just if the hated Jews were flourishing? Though the old Christian enmity towards the Jews might have seemed old fashioned or obscurantist in the new liberal and scientific world, new racialist theories were conceived according to which Jews were members of a different and alien species which the European peoples should drive from their midst. Parallel with this venomous hatred for the Jews, and reinforcing it, were half-baked genetic and anthropological concepts which divided the human family into different races, with the "Nordic" or white race superior to all the others. The exact character of racialism varied from country to country – a German might take a different view from a Briton or a citizen of the United States of America. But the fundamental belief in the "white man's burden" characterized the Western civilized world at the turn of the century.

Certainly by 1900 most Europeans were convinced that white supremacy was the natural order of things and that other races would have to make way for white rule. The vast extent of European colonial empires – particularly the British, upon

► **The image of empire – a puzzle showing Britain's George V.**

ROYAL REVIEW AT DELHI

ICH DIEN

THE ROYAL PROCESSION ON ITS WAY TO THE SHAMIANA - DELHI

which the sun literally never set – were seen as proof of that fact. Overseas possessions became to some excited nationalist minds the touchstone of a country's success; hence the enthusiasm with which countries like Germany or Italy pursued colonial conquests of little or no intrinsic value. Hence also the opposition Germany encountered from an established colonial power like Britain, which feared loss of influence if its own colonial predominance was threatened. The fact that colonial empires were usually as much a source of weakness as of strength to the mother country was ignored. Entrenched vested interests in colonies received vociferous support from rabble-rousing newspapers eager for circulation and nationalist groups seeking support among the masses by stressing the boundless opportunities presented to their people by colonial expansion.

Furthermore, the experience of the last decades of the 19th century seemed to reinforce this confidence. Everywhere the white "races" were carrying all before them. It is true that in 1905 the Japanese sprung a surprise by defeating the Russians but even this could be reconciled. To many Westerners the Russians were regarded as partly Asiatic anyhow, and since the 1860s the Japanese had imitated Western civilization so assiduously that they could be considered honorary – if second-class – whites.

In fact, however, the dominance of the Western world was not due to cultural or racial superiority, but to the development of technical expertise in a manner which bestowed tremendous military advantages on the colonizing powers. The machine gun, the steamship and the telegraph, in particular, gave the West the initiative in every colonial conflict.

adapt to new techniques, even if their achievements were not quite so impressive. Czarist Russia, commonly regarded as a symbol of backwardness and reaction, produced spectacular industrial growth rates between 1890 and the outbreak of World War I. Across the Atlantic the United States of America, arguably the most favored environment for free enterprise capitalism, developed even more powerfully as an industrial nation. It too had overtaken Britain by the early years of the 20th century, even if in some areas of financial services such as banking and insurance the City of London still outranked Wall Street.

These economic developments had a crucial impact on power politics. Wealth and power have always gone hand in hand. But in previous eras, when agriculture was the predominant source of income for most people the world over, power fluctuations depended as much upon dynastic conflicts, religious affiliations or population movements as upon industrial strength. By 1900 it had become clear that only those nations that could create a sufficiently sophisticated industrial infrastructure to maintain modern armed forces would be able to preserve their independence very far into the 20th century. This infrastructure was not just a matter of coal mines or textile mills. It required banking systems, communications networks, public education and scientific research. These were not to be acquired overnight. The attempt to create an effective industrial base was destined to involve many countries in agonizing social conflicts, some of which have lasted until our own time. Russia is an obvious example; Iran is another. Much environmental devastation and human misery in the so-called "Third World" has been caused by misplaced attempts to "modernize" societies which were unready for such dubious experiments, even assuming that they needed them in the first place. At the root of such developments lay the arrogant assumption that the Western national state was bound to be superior to any other form of human organization.

Nations, states and power conflicts

By the onset of the 20th century most people expected that power struggles would take the form of conflicts between nation states. This was a relatively new idea. Before the French revolution of 1789, wars had been as much about dynastic interests or religious conflicts as about national aggrandizement. Many nationalities – such as the Czechs, the Germans, the Italians, the Poles, the Romanians and the South Slavs – were not organized into national states. When, in 1815, Napoleon was defeated, the settlement of Europe at the Congress of Vienna was a deliberate denial of the principle of national self-determination, even though the concept of nationalism had received a great boost in the course of the previous 20 years. The settlement was to be maintained by great multinational empires such as those of Russia and Austria, or by the king of Prussia, whose subjects included Poles as well as Germans. Many European peoples were still contained within the Muslim Empire of the Ottoman Turks. Nationalists were regarded as tiresome cranks or upstarts among the growing urban intelligentsia, whose activities should be repressed wherever possible.

The turbulent history of Europe in the 19th century was to see all that transformed, with the liberation of Bulgars, Greeks, Romanians and Serbs from Turkish rule, and the defeats of Habsburg Austria, which led to the unification of both Germany and Italy. The future now seemed to belong to nations organized along homogenous ethnic lines, buttressed by

However misleading the term "industrial revolution" may be, it could not be denied that in the 19th century Western nations had outstripped all their rivals so far as technical development and industrial growth were concerned. By the mid-Victorian era Britain could regard itself as the "workshop of the world", its exports of manufactures flowing into all parts of the globe. Traditional methods of production were no match for new techniques based on steam power and the division of labor. Yet just as the British achieved mushrooming growth in the manufacturing sector in the first half of the 19th century, so their neighbors in Europe quickly made up for lost time in the second half. By 1914 Germany had outstripped Britain in the production of coal and steel, and was leading in newly developed industries such as chemicals and electrical engineering. Other European countries showed similar readiness to various forms of nationalist ideology. Multinational states, such as the Austro-Hungarian Empire whose authority extended over a confused patchwork of Germans, Magyars, Poles, Czechs, South Slavs and Romanians, or the Ottoman Turkish empire which still ruled Christian Slavs in the Balkans and Muslim Arabs in the Middle East, were perceived even in 1900 as threatened by decadence and decline. By 1918 both were in ruins. The future evidently belonged to Great Powers like the British, the French, the Germans, the Russians or the Japanese, whose core strength lay in a numerous and economically efficient population sharing the same language and culture. The one apparent exception to this was the United States of America, a nation created from a variety of immigrant populations. Yet even there the predominant opinion was that the great American democracy was a "melting pot" in which under-privileged refugees from various forms of autocracy were able to adapt themselves to a homogenous form of Anglo-Saxon culture claiming to offer political and economic freedom. Before the 1960s the elites that dominated Washington were white, Anglo-Saxon and Protestant. To all intents and purposes the United States was a nation state.

Despite all the arrogance of Western elites and their sycophantic intelligensia, they faced serious internal problems which generated feelings of insecurity. Nationalism itself created its own insecurities because very few states actually were homogenous. National minorities like the Irish in Britain or the Poles in Russia disturbed the complacency of "master races". The Paris peace settlement in 1919, which redrew the map of Europe, granted national self-determination to more people in Europe than ever before but it created new problems by leaving German and Hungarian minorities, who habitually though of themselves as superior, to be ruled by Poles, Czechs, Yugoslavs and Romanians.

The rights of the people
There was also the awkward problem of democracy. It was clear that power could no longer be exercised by a privileged elite based on gentle birth, but that technical progress, even from the narrowest military viewpoint, demanded an educated labor force. Governments needed mass support if they were to wage modern war. That meant pandering to nationalist demagogues such as jingoist imperialists, Pan-Germans or Pan-Slavs. But it might also mean making concessions to popular demands for political rights. Few of the Great Powers were real democracies in 1900. The United States and France were in that category; they were not regarded as models to follow by many of their neighbors. Britain and Italy were "liberal" states, in that they had regimes responsive to Parliament. They did not, however, possess properly democratic electoral systems. Many of their citizens did not possess the vote. Austria and Germany elected their parliaments on a wider franchise but gave them much less power over essentially authoritarian governments. In Russia the political system was neither liberal nor democratic, although a weak parliamentary constitution had been established after an abortive revolution in 1905.

What authoritarian rulers in Berlin and St Petersburg hoped to do was to achieve the technical superiority associated with industrialization without surrendering their authority to popularly elected governments. Although many liberals believed that a modern economy required a liberal form of political organization, there seemed no necessary connexion between these two phenomena. The old elites could also take comfort from the fact that liberal reformers were now becoming increasingly nervous of a growing socialist movement which was threatening to attract mass support more effectively than they had ever been able to do.

The fact was that national self-assertion and parliamentary constitutions were not the only issues which exercised peoples' minds at the turn of the century. Just as important was the "social question".

Nationalists regarded the real community of interests between people as stemming from some kind of ethnic brotherhood, based on common language or shared history, or both. In fact the languages were often artificially revived during the 19th century and the history had to be "rediscovered" for nationalist purposes. A different way of viewing the human family was to divide it horizontally into rich and poor, working people and employers. There was nothing new in this, but the social changes brought about by increased labor mobility, the division of labor in factories and the breakdown of traditional patterns of craft production made such an interpretation attractive to those who felt themselves to be exploited by economic forces beyond their control.

Industrial workers tried to develop organizations to protect themselves against the immense power of capitalist employers. These trade unions, as they were called, faced victimization everywhere and outright repression in many countries. Nevertheless they grew in numbers and membership, and the years before 1914 saw increasing labor militancy in most industrial countries. This in turn encouraged industrial workers to think of themselves as a separate class engaged in a war with the better off.

The most celebrated prophet of social conflict was Karl Marx who, with his colleague Friedrich Engels, in the 30 years after 1850, developed the view that the development of capitalism was polarizing society into an ever more wealthy minority of those who owned the "means of production" and an ever-increasing and more impoverished mass of workers or "proletariat". Just as investment capital knew no boundaries in its search for profit, so the proletariat should recognize no national differences, but should seek salvation in common action against its wealthy exploiters. The class struggle which modern economic developments inevitably produced was therefore bound to be an international conflict. The ultimate goal should be a revolution in which the exploited masses would seize the property of the capitalists (referred to rather misleadingly as the *bourgeoisie* or middle class, to distinguish them from the older feudal elites of pre-industrial society) and administer it for the good of all. The state, which Marx conceived of as an agent of class oppression, would then wither away since it would no longer be needed. The fact that in many countries industrial workers had no chance of influencing government behavior and were treated as social outcasts by the "respectable" classes made Marx's apocalyptic vision of revolutionary change very attractive to them.

Marx was by no means the only apostle of socialism in the 19th and 20th centuries. But in the years before 1914 Marxism had achieved a commanding status amongst working class movements in Europe. The German Social Democratic party, the largest of its kind, was formally committed to a Marxist program, even if in practice its leaders were men of pragmatism and common sense, not to mention national pride. In their hands, Marxist theory was subordinated to a policy of seeking gradual reform within the context of the nation state. The prestige of German views made this approach attractive to socialists in other, more backward, societies such as czarist Russia. In 1903 the Marxist Social Democrats there were split by V. I. Lenin to establish his radically revolutionary Bolshevik party as separate from the reformist Mensheviks.

UHP
JURAD SOBRE ESTAS LETRAS HERMA
ANTES MORIR QUE CONSENTIR TIRAM

In the first decade of the century there already existed a forum for socialist parties in the second "Socialist International", with its offices in Brussels. At conferences of the International its members were exhorted to renounce participation in capitalist wars of aggression. It was confidently believed that a war between the European powers could be stopped by working class opposition. Yet, when the call came in August 1914, industrial workers everywhere flocked to the colors. Lenin, in exile in Switzerland, was outraged and determined to establish a genuinely revolutionary socialist international purged of "revisionists" and prepared to accept revolutionary discipline. Another radical socialist, Benito Mussolini in Italy, drew a very different conclusion. He decided that international working class solidarity was a sham and that

nationalism was the real driving force behind human actions. From these men stemmed two of the most powerful – and frequently the most destructive – forces in 20th-century history – Communism (or, more accurately, Marxism-Leninism) and fascism.

It should not be thought, however, that social conflict in the 20th century was just a matter of industrial workers versus capitalists. As literacy became more widespread and communications improved, as tax burdens were imposed on even the most underdeveloped areas, and as obligations like compulsory military service affected increasingly large numbers of people, so there appeared the political mobilization of peasant

▲ Volunteers for the fight against fascism in Spain in 1936.

proprietors, craftsmen, small shopkeepers and the growing numbers of white-collar employees associated with state bureaucracies and large-scale private enterprises. The political aspirations and economic grievances of such groups were articulated very clearly. Their exact position in the political spectrum was less obvious. In some cases they would be attracted by extreme nationalism, in others by a moderate form of liberalism and elsewhere they might even move towards socialism. Matters were complicated by the appearance of powerful Roman Catholic parties in countries such as Austria, Germany and Italy. Religious fervor was by no means dead, and division between different creeds or denominations were still very important within Western countries. Lastly, another section of society which had awoken to demand its rights consisted of that half of the population which was female. Women's emancipation became an issue throughout the developed world. On the whole it was supported by socialists and radical liberals, opposed by nationalists and conservatives.

The rise of internationalism

World War I seemed to mark a decisive stage in the development of international power struggles and domestic social conflict. It certainly was a decisive defeat for traditional dynastic power elites. The Prussian and Russian emperors were driven from power. The Habsburgs not only lost their thrones in Austria-Hungary but saw their empire disintegrate into independent nation-states. The outcome of the war, which had itself required massive sacrifices from all the peoples involved, was hailed as a victory for democracy over the old hereditary political order. The victory for democracy proved short-lived, but the deposed monarchs were not able to reassert themselves.

The years 1917 to 1919 saw the appearance on the world stage of two types of internationalism. Neither was successful initially, but both were significant for the future. The first was the intervention, in April 1917, of the United States in the European conflict and the determined attempt by President Wilson to create a new form of international organization which would supplant the secret diplomacy he held responsible for the evils of war. "Open covenants of peace openly arrived at" was the slogan which underlay the new League of Nations that was established by the Versailles peace treaty under the sponsorship of Wilson. Public opinion, by nature good-hearted and fair, would prevent rapacious political groups from leading their peoples into war. The fact that the United States Congress rejected both the treaty and the League was not the only reason for its failure, but it certainly blighted it from the outset. Even so, the principle of international cooperation to resolve tensions and conflicts between states was established as worthwhile.

In March 1919 meanwhile, Lenin, by then the ruler of Russia, established the so-called Third International or Comintern, the aim of which was to subordinate all radical socialist movements throughout the world to his own Communist discipline with the intention of fomenting revolution, especially in industrialized countries like Germany and colonial territories which he perceived as especial objects of capitalist exploitation. By 1921 he had successfully split many major socialist parties, including those of Germany, Italy and France, into national reformist and international revolutionary wings. Henceforth most Western countries played host to Communist parties whose first loyalty was to Moscow. Yet the aim of world revolution proved a chimera. By Lenin's death it was becoming increasingly obvious that socialism in Russia would have to shift for itself, a fact which helped the aspirations of Joseph

Stalin. As leader of the Soviet Union from 1926 to his death in 1953 he successfully manipulated the international Communist movement as an instrument for his own personal aggrandizement and as a weapon in the armoury of Soviet foreign policy.

The two apparently incompatible strands of internationalist thinking came together in 1943, when Stalin abolished the Comintern and United States president Franklin D. Roosefelt outlined a new form of international organization in which the peace would be kept by four "world policemen" – Soviet Russia, the United States, Britain and China. Of these four the first two were obviously going to be much more powerful than the others, especially as China had been riven by civil war since the 1920s. The era of competing nation states and imperial rivalries had given way to the hegemony of the "superpowers" each representing a different ideology.

It should not be thought, however, that any such development seemed probable – or even possible – earlier in the century. The 1920s and 1930s were the high-water mark of European imperialism. National self-assertion with Europe became ever more strident. As liberal parliamentary systems collapsed in Central and Eastern Europe, and were increasingly called in question elsewhere, they were replaced by protectionist, militarist and often xenophobic regimes pandering to the mass appeal of nationalism. Fascist regimes abandoned the right of the individual and suppressed free unionism to create a collectivist society in which the interests of the state were supreme. The economic crisis of the early 1930s exacerbated this tendency by encouraging states to put their own commercial interests before those of the international trading community.

In the 1920s parliamentary democracy had failed in countries like Italy and Germany because propertied elites (on whose involvement everything depended) feared that a mass electorate might try to redistribute wealth and that party conflicts might lead to social chaos. These fears were not entirely groundless, but the solution chosen – to put power into the hands of fascist dictators, who ruthlessly abandoned humanitarian values together with political liberalism – was misguided and immoral. As the 1930s progressed, those who hoped to find a middle way between Marxist Communism and fascism seemed increasingly outmoded. In fact, many democratic countries such as those in Scandinavia, the British Dominions (such as Canada or Australia) and the United States emerged from the Slump battered but with more effective economic systems than before. American leaders pressed for a renewal of free trade as the basis of international commerce, whilst accepting responsibility for domestic social harmony. This combination of free market principles and state intervention to redistribute wealth or combat poverty was the hallmark of successful Western societies in the years which followed.

The turning point – 1941

In 1939, however, with Hitler rampant in Germany and enjoying the support of both Mussolini and a militarist Japanese regime which had established itself in the 1930s, the future seemed to belong to some form of tyrannical collectivism. The defeat of France at the hands of Hitler in 1940 and Hitler's success in overrunning much of Europe only confirmed such a gloomy outlook. The turning point in the history of the century arrived in the second half of 1941, when Hitler attacked the Soviet Union and the Japanese invaded both Southeast Asia and the south Pacific. The first of these acts of aggression marked the attempt to implement a racialist ideology in its purest

▶ The Berlin Wall dwarfed the inhabitants of East Germany.

form, by providing the Germans with huge tracts of settlement land at the expense of the Slavs. The second sounded the death knell of Western imperialism, since peoples used to white rule in Asia now found that their British, Dutch, and French masters could be swept away in humiliating defeat by Asiatic Japanese. The American defeat in the Philippines was of less importance in this respect because the United States had already promised independence to the area.

In fact the Western empires were defeated as much in Europe as in the Far East. By the time the imperial nations had overcome the Rome–Berlin Axis powers, they were economically enfeebled and dependent on their American allies for food and dollars. The two major victors of the war were the Soviet Union and the United States. Neither were enthusiastic for a revival of colonial empires, and by the mid-1950s, when the rivalry between the two had built up into the tensions of the Cold War, the movement towards decolonization was too powerful to be stopped.

World War II had far-reaching consequences both for the international power structure and the nature of society in the Western world. Since the two most important powers in the victory over Hitler were the United States and the Soviet Union, the international system after the war would depend on the relationship established between them. At meetings between the leaders of the new superpowers at Tehran in 1943 and Yalta early in 1945, Europe was effectively divided into Soviet and Western spheres of influence. Asia was assumed to be largely a Chinese sphere, but in 1949 the nationalist Guomindang government finally fell to Mao Zedong's Communist forces, giving rise to a lengthy power conflict in east Asia generally. The Guomindang government established itself on the island of Formosa (Taiwan), but attempts by former colonial powers to reestablish their influence on the mainland largely failed.

The postwar world
The domestic political and social consequences of the war were also far-reaching. Before 1941 democracy had been a sickly plant in most European states, with the exception of Scandinavia and the Low Countries. France had a long democratic tradition, but her defeat in 1940 was erroneously presented as a consequence of political decadence and confusion. Britain had only possessed a truly democratic electoral system since 1929 (when women were given the vote on the same terms as men), and even then it had made little impact on her elitist class system. Once Hitler overran France, however, attitudes changed. The new prime minister, Churchill, was a genuinely national leader who cared little for sectional privilege. Even more important was the fact that, if Hitler overwhelmed Britain, all classes, and not just the poor, stood to lose heavily. The mass of the population was needed for the war effort. In order to motivate them, political and economic concessions had to be made. Full employment appeared as a consequence of the war, and politicians committed themselves to try to maintain it. In 1944 Britain's notoriously backward public education system was reformed to create a genuine ladder for talent for the first time in the nation's history. Further social benefits were promised in the controversial Beveridge Report of 1942, which pledged the state to wage war on insecurity and want.

There was nothing new about promises being made to the masses in wartime only to be forgotten once peace was restored. This had happened in Britain itself after the Napoleonic wars and after World War I, when Lloyd George's "homes fit

for heroes" promise soon had a hollow ring. But with the defeat of Hitler there appeared a new and even more frightening possibility. A major victor in the war had been Stalin's Soviet regime in Russia. The Red Army was on the Elbe and looked poised to overrun Western Europe. Soviet Communism had reached what was probably the peak of its prestige. Both from the military and the political point of view, the social elites in Western Europe seemed vulnerable. It was therefore necessary for them to make concessions to their own people if they were to survive.

This process was aided by the eclipse of the European power system which had existed since 1871. Germany was occupied and effectively divided. France and Italy had suffered humiliation and defeat. Aggressive nationalism, especially in its fascist manifestation, was discredited. Parliamentary democracy seemed the safest form of political system to many in Western Europe, since at least it would secure American support and encourage resistance to Communism. Even the Vatican, which had always opposed both liberalism and democracy and had thereby given tacit support to both Mussolini and Hitler, came round to accepting these evils when faced with the threat of Stalinist encroachment. Christian Democratic parties became important in Western Europe, especially in Italy and the Federal Republic of Germany (West Germany), where they presided over postwar recoveries. Socially conservative in many respects, the Christian parties nevertheless combined acceptance of the democratic system with a commitment to social welfare for the poorest sections of the community.

The war also finally eclipsed the European financial power which had seemed so impressive at the turn of the century. New York's Wall Street, and not the City of London, could now call the tune in financial affairs; the US dollar became the key currency in world trade. The Americans pressed for the removal of tariff barriers and especially of colonial preferences. They also established a stable system of exchange values based on parity with the dollar in order to prevent a recurrence of the economic chaos of the 1920s and 1930s. The intensification of the Cold War after 1947 enabled the American government to justify large-scale expenditure on helping economic recovery. The most spectacular example of this was the Marshall Plan which poured money in to rebuild the shattered economies of western Europe and, despite continuing controversy, was undoubtedly crucial in boosting confidence at a time when economic and political problems seemed very grave.

The Cold War also made it easier for Western European nations to bury their old differences and seek a new form of co-operation. This was an objective of American policy, and was explicit in the terms of the Marshall Plan. With Western security underpinned by a prolonged American presence in Germany – exemplified by the defeat of the Berlin blockade and the establishment of the North Atlantic Treaty Organization (NATO) – the French and the Germans had a mutual interest in improving relations, an interest shared by smaller European countries. The result was the European Coal and Steel Community, Euratom and finally the European Common Market (EEC) in 1957. The result of all this collective effort – combined as it was with a progressive liberation of trade from wartime controls – was an enormous growth of economic output throughout the Western world and a level of mass prosperity unparalleled in history.

East, West and Third World
But if the peoples of the West gained from the Cold War, the price was paid by the nations of Eastern Europe. Prevented from receiving Marshall Aid by the Soviet Union and controlled

by puppet Communist regimes, the East Germans, Poles, Czechs, Hungarians, Albanians, Bulgars and Romanians not only saw their own market economies emasculated and the political liberties they had hoped for denied to them, but also had to contribute largely to the reconstruction of the Soviet Union. What they did gain was peace. Many of these states had never enjoyed a parliamentary system, and had been devastated by war on several occasions in the 20th century. Until 1953, when Stalin died, they were the objects of totalitarian terror, but as the Soviet system itself gradually became less repressive, so many of the regimes in Eastern Europe took on a somewhat less arbitrary appearance. Nevertheless, political freedom was still denied to the East Europeans, as the ruthless suppression of attempts at independent action in East Germany (1953), Hungary (1956) and Czechoslovakia (1968) were to show. Even in the late 1980s, when the Soviet system itself was belatedly undergoing change, Eastern Europe remained partly under Stalinist domination. Even while Poland was voting the Communist party out of government in 1989, repression was continuing on an unprecedented scale in Romania, and liberalization was proceeding most cautiously in other countries.

The power balance between the United States and the Soviet Union seemed to create a stalemate in Europe. Prospects for change receded, especially after the building of the Berlin Wall (1961) and the Cuban missile crisis the following year, both expressive of the extreme distrust prevailing between the two superpowers. Yet unexpected developments were occurring elsewhere in the world. The United Nations – an international forum for peace-keeping which, it had been assumed, would be dominated by the victor powers in the war, was itself divided by the Cold War. The appearance of a Communist regime in China, which horrified the United States and soon stressed its independence from the Soviet Union was only one symptom of the loss of European/American domination over the rest of the world. In the Middle East, destabilization, partly caused by the establishment of the state of Israel as a national home for the Jews, weakened Western influence in a region controlled by colonial powers since 1918. Indian independence encouraged the emergence in the United Nations of a growing bloc of non-aligned countries which were able to play off East and West to encourage the rapidly snowballing movement of decolonization and to demand economic aid from industrially developed countries.

Competition for the favors of Third World countries had some impact on the domestic politics of developed countries, especially the United States. The Americans could not be seen to be overtly practising racial discrimination within their own borders if they were trying to win friends for democracy in Africa. The 1960s presented a unique opportunity for civil rights activists in the United States: economic prosperity helped the blacks to argue for a fairer slice of the cake, whilst the international situation pushed federal governments towards helping the blacks. Had the opportunity not been seized it might never have reappeared; by 1980, political interest in Africa was waning and confidence in the American economy was no longer self-evident.

The period from 1948 to 1970 was marked by a long and almost uninterrupted economic expansion in the industrialized countries of the world. This enabled many previously underprivileged groups – young people, women, racial minorities – to articulate political grievances and to question the authority of established elites. The result was a sense of political instability in the West; this was exacerbated by the loss of financial hegemony on the part of the United States. Embroiled in a debilitating and divisive war in Vietnam, the Americans began to find that the dollar was no longer as powerful as it had been in the immediate post-war years. In 1973 the Western world – and many poorer nations – suffered a grievous economic shock as Arab states reduced oil supplies and set up a temporarily effective oil cartel which trebled oil prices within a year. The result was predictable, though rarely predicted by economists. The high price of oil forced a sharp reduction in industrial expansion and severe limitations on the consumption of oil. It also generated a huge burden of debt, particularly in poorer countries. The confidence which had characterized the postwar era began to evaporate.

An unplanned and largely irrational redistribution of wealth occurred, with oil producers suddenly flooded with money they were in no position to spend effectively. Grandiose attempts to force the pace of modernization – as in Iran or Nigeria – usually failed miserably. The main beneficiaries were corrupt politicians. In developed countries dissatisfaction with materialist consumerism manifested itself in the ecological or "Green" movement, which combined with longer-standing opposition to the proliferation of nuclear weapons. Although this movement has never achieved power at national level, it influenced public opinion in a number of countries.

By the 1980s equilibrium was beginning to return to the industrialized world, but the burden of debt still had a destabilizing influence on poorer countries, and this had even spread to the Communist bloc, where countries like Poland and Hungary had borrowed heavily in the hopes that subsequent industrial expansion would repay their creditors. Whereas in the early 1970s the future of the capitalist world had been called in question, firstly by the radical libertarian student movement and secondly by the oil crisis, by the end of the 1980s Marxist-Leninist regimes seemed to be intellectually and economically bankrupt. The Chinese government openly welcomed market forces, though it was less enthusiastic about political freedom for its subjects. The Soviet Union, unable to win the arms race with Reagan's United States and humiliated by its defeat at the hands of numerically and logistically weaker forces in Afghanistan, sought to implement fundamental and economic and political reforms, their scope and pace being such that military spending was much reduced and internal tensions – including nationalist risings – threatened the unity of the country. With Communism no longer perceived as a threat, political forces which had been eclipsed in 1945 began to reappear in Europe and elsewhere – fundamentalist religious movements in the Middle East, fascist parties in Western Europe, nationalist resentments in Eastern Europe.

In the late 1980s the world was in a state of flux unprecedented since 1945. The disintegration of the monolithic Communist empire continued on apace. In China attempts to democratize the country ended in tragic failure with a massacre in Tiananmen Square, raising many doubts as to the longterm nature of the Chinese regime. In the Soviet Union disaffection amongst non-Russian nationalities became more strident, threatening to compromise the reformist *perestroika* policy of President Gorbachev. The Poles, East Germans and Hungarians demonstrated – albeit in different ways – that they were no longer willing to tolerate subservience to Soviet Communism. In Hungary and Poland, substantial progress was made toward a multiparty system, with the formation of a non-Communist government in Poland in 1989. Emigration from the Eastern bloc resumed in the late 1980s for the first time since the building of the Berlin Wall, and some commentators predicted the imminent collapse of Soviet control in Eastern Europe.

Ideologies and Key Terms of Political History

All beliefs, values and goals form part of an ideology when they help to condition the way an issue is interpreted or contribute to the stability or transformation of a social situation. The interplay of ideologies is crucial to an understanding of modern history, yet political ideologies – such as socialism, fascism or liberalism – are hard to define since they can be interpreted differently even within a single party. Opinion may cluster around opposites such as "radical/conservative", "democratic/authoritarian", "universalist/nationalist".

The *radical* wing of a party seeks to transform the standard interpretation of the ideology to accommodate new cultural forces, address new problems or realize previously neglected aspects of the original ideology. The *conservative* position accentuates organic change, emphasizing traditional institutions to ensure stability and cohesion. In the early 20th century conservatism was antisocialist and antiliberal; in recent years the "new conservatism" has, paradoxically, denoted a radical form of economic liberalism.

Democracy is the principle of power exercised by and for the people as a whole rather than by and for any sectional interest. There are differing interpretations as to which institutions are most appropriate, so that anarchism, revolutionary socialism and fascism all claim to be more truly democratic than liberalism. The *authoritarian* view is that power must "descend" from a small elite or natural leader, rather than "ascend" from the populace. Yet authoritarianism is often justified by an appeal to democracy.

Ideologies such as liberalism and socialism, which postulate political principles valid for all human beings, are theoretically *universalist*, but they can become dominated by the principle of *nationalism*, according to which the achievement of goals within a nation state takes precedence over their realization globally. Nationalism may acquire even greater emotional charge in conjunction with forces such as imperialism or religious fundamentalism.

Left and *right* are terms that grossly simplify complex ideological positions by locating them on a single axis with two extremes. Left is associated with radical, democratic and universalist aspects of an ideology, and right with the conservative, authoritarian and nationalist ones. Thus, in the context of liberalism, "left" can refer to socialistic, egalitarian, interventionist views; within fascism it applies to those who argued for a greater degree of democracy and socialism within the national community. In socialism, a movement which threatens the party leadership's monopoly of power can be considered leftwing (radical and democratic); yet it may be denounced as rightwing (liberal) by orthodox socialists.

▼ The Ayatollah Khomeini acknowledges the cheers of his Iranian supporters in the early 1980s. His Islamic fundamentalist revolution challenged the conventional political idiom of left- and rightwing; but it can be usefully considered as involving unusual tensions between conservative and radical tendencies. It was undoubtedly authoritarian in nature, and universalist in intent.

THE
IMPERIAL
AGE

Time Chart

	1900	1901	1902	1903	1904	1905	1906	1907
Europe/Mediterranean	● Start of armaments race in Europe, as construction of 38 new battleships approved in Germany to double navy within 20 years ● Feb: Labour Representative committee formed in UK with Ramsay MacDonald as secretary (1906, Labour Party) ● May: 1st trial of proportional representation in Belgian general election	● 22 Jan: Death of Queen Victoria and accession of Edward VII to UK throne ● May: Limited franchise in local elections extended to Norwegian women ● Jul, Taff Vale case: UK House of Lords ruled that trade unions could be sued for members' actions during strikes	● Sinn Féin (Irish republican party) founded by Arthur Griffith ● Anglo–Japanese alliance broke UK's policy of "splendid isolation" ● Jan: Protests in Malta at replacement of Italian by English as official language ● 28 Jun: Renewal of Triple Alliance (Ger, Aut-Hung, Ita)	● Meeting in London, the Russian Social Democratic Party split into Bolsheviks (led by Lenin) and Mensheviks ● Denmark granted Iceland responsible government ● Worker's Educational Association (WEA) founded in UK by Albert Mansbridge ● 10 Oct: Women's Social and Political Union founded (UK) by Emmeline Pankhurst	● 8 Apr: Anglo–French Entente Cordiale signed, ending overseas territorial rivalry	● 22 Jan (Old Style 9 Jan), Bloody Sunday: Demonstrators marching on the Russian Tsar's Winter Palace killed by Cossack troops ● 7 Jun: Norway dissolved union with Sweden ● Dec: French law decreed separation of Church and State	● May–Jul: 1st Russian *Duma* (parliament); dissolved by Tsar ● Dec: UK Trades Dispute Act reversed 1901 Taff Vale ruling	● Mar: World's 1st women MPs elected, in Finland ● Jun: Limited female suffrage introduced in Norway ● Sep: Signature of Anglo–Russian agreement on Asia, aligning Russia in Triple Entente with France, against Triple Alliance powers
The Middle East	● Dec: Secret Italo–French agreement over respective interests in Tripolitania and Morocco	● Persian oil concession granted to William Knox D'Arcy (later, Anglo–Persian Oil Co.) ● Jul: Franco–Moroccan agreement, fixing frontier with French colony of Algeria and regulating police and trade policies		● Jan: UK King Edward VII proclaimed Emperor of India, in Delhi	● Apr: Anglo–French agreement over respective interests in Egypt and Morocco ● Oct: Secret Franco–Spanish agreement on eventual partition of Morocco	● 31 Mar: German Kaiser's visit to Morocco perceived as threat to European interests in N Africa	● Muslim League founded in India ● Jan–Apr, Algeciras Conference: Morocco's independence agreed ● Protests led to convening of 1st Persian parliament (Oct) and authorization of constitution (30 Dec) by Persian Shah	● Aug: Following local uprisings, French troops occupied coastal areas (Mor) ● Aug: Anglo–Russian Entente divided Persia into UK and Russian spheres of influence
Africa	● 24 May, Boer War: Britain annexed Orange River Colony (S Afr) ● 25 Oct: Boer Republic of S Africa annexed by UK and renamed Transvaal	● Nov: Anglo–Italian agreement on frontier between respective colonies of Sudan and Eritrea (E Afr)	● 31 May: Peace of Vereeniging ended Boer War; Boers accepted British sovereignty; pledged representative government	● Jul: Uganda (E Afr) offered by UK government as site for Jewish homeland	● Beginning of Herero uprising in German SW Africa (to 1907)	● Beginning of Maji Maji rising in German E Africa (to 1907)	● 21 Mar: UK agreed to £9.5 million damages for Boer War ● Apr: UK troops fought Zulu uprising (S Afr) ● 6 Dec: Transvaal (S Afr) granted self-government by UK	● Mar: Indian immigration restricted in Transvaal; Mohandas Gandhi opened civil disobedience drive (*satyagraha*) ● 1 Jul: Orange River Colony (S Afr) granted self-government by UK
The Americas	● 6 Mar: Social Democratic party (1901, Socialist Party) formed in US ● 16 Dec: National Civic Federation formed in US, for arbitration of labor disputes	● 12 Jun: Cuba took on Platt Amendment; US right to military intervention confirmed ● 6 Sep: US President William McKinley shot dead; succeeded by Theodore Roosevelt ● 22 Oct (to Jan 1902): 2nd Pan-American Conference ● 18 Nov: 2nd Hay–Pauncefoote treaty recognized US right to build C American shipping canal	● Dec: UK, Germany and Italy blockaded Venezuelan coast to procure payment for damage incurred during 1899 revolution	● Mar: US Congress moved to restrict immigration, imposing $2 per head tax ● 3 Nov: Revolution in Panama and proclamation of independence from Colombia ● 18 Nov: Treaty between US and Panama allowed for construction of Panama Canal, and US occupation and control of canal zone	● Dec: By Roosevelt Corollary to Monroe Doctrine, US claimed right to intervene in Latin American affairs	● Sep: Canadian provinces of Alberta and Saskatchewan established	● May: Last UK troops left Canada ● 29 Sep: Following uprisings and invoking Platt Amendment, US proclaimed provisional government in Cuba (to Jan 1909)	● Feb: US Immigration Act limited entry of Japanese laborers ● Feb–Dec: Conference of C American States, after war between Honduras and Nicaragua threatened regional stability ● 1 Aug: 1st US military air force formed ● 16 Dec: US Battle Fleet began round-the-world cruise
Asia and Pacific	● Russia occupied S Manchuria (Chn) ● May: Tonga (formerly Friendly Is) annexed by UK ● Jun–Aug, Boxer Rising (Chn): Foreign legations in Peking besieged; relieved by expeditionary force from 6 nations	● Australian Labor Party founded ● 1 Jan: Federal constitution of new Commonwealth of Australia in force ● Mar: Capture of Filipino rebel leader marked tougher US rule in Philippines. William H Taft installed as 1st US civil governor (Jul) ● Sep: Peking Protocol marked end of Boxer Rising	● Australian women granted federal vote ● Reforms in China of judiciary, government and education ● 30 Jan, Anglo–Japanese Alliance: to protect interests in China and Korea ● 8 Apr: Russo–Chinese accord to evacuate Manchuria ● 7 Oct: French agreement with Siam on Indochinese frontier	● Jul–Aug: Japanese and UK protests at Russian failure to evacuate Manchuria	● 8 Feb: Outbreak of Russo–Japanese War, with Japanese naval attack on Russian fleet at Port Arthur, Manchuria, then invasion of Korea ● Mar–Sep: 100s of Tibetans killed before UK military expedition forced trade treaty ● 27 Apr: Australia's 1st (minority) Labor government	● New parliamentary government pledged by Chinese rulers ● 27–8 May: Russian Baltic Squadron destroyed by Japanese navy ● End of Russo–Japanese War. Pres. Roosevelt led way to peace talks in US (Aug) and signature of Treaty of Portsmouth (5 Sep): Manchuria to return to China; Russia recognized Japanese rights in Korea	● 1 Sep: British New Guinea declared an Australian federal possession and renamed Papua	● 26 Sep: New Zealand constituted a dominion within Commonwealth of Nations ● 16 Oct: Philippines' 1st elected legislature opened ● 8 Nov: Harvester decision of Australian Arbitration Court established concept of basic wage
World	● Sep: 5th congress of 2nd International, Paris (Fr)	● International Federation of Trade Unions established	● 14 Oct: 1st decision by International Court of Arbitration at The Hague (Neth)	● Policy of prefential trading adopted within Commonwealth	● Aug: International Miners' Congress called for 8-hour day and minimum wage	● Industrial Workers of the World (IWW) founded in US		● 15 Jun: 2nd international peace conference opened at The Hague (Neth)

1908	1909	1910	1911	1912	1913	1914
• 23 Apr: Signature of Baltic Conventions (Ger, Swe, Den, Rus) and North Sea Conventions (Ger, Swe, Den, UK, Neth, Fr) • 5 Oct: Bulgaria declared independence from Turkey • 7 Oct, Bosnian Crisis: Austria-Hungary annexed Turkey's Balkan provinces of Bosnia-Herzegovina	• 1-month general strike in Sweden, over economic conditions • Graduated rates of income tax introduced in UK • 30 Nov: Rejection by UK House of Lords of "people's budget", shifting taxation burden to wealthy, forced election on Liberal government	• Eleutherios Venizelos became Greek prime minister, beginning program of financial, administrative and constitutional reform • 6 May: Death of King Edward VII; George V succeeded to UK throne • 5 Oct: Portuguese monarchy overthrown; democratic republic proclaimed	• Assassination of Russian prime minister, P.A. Stolypin • Aug: Parliament Bill restricting power of House of Lords enacted (UK)	• Mar: Principle of minimum wage established in UK • Jul: UK decided to transfer Mediterranean warships to North Sea, to counteract German naval build-up • Oct: Outbreak of 1st Balkan War between Balkan League (Bulg, Serb, Gre, Montenegro) and Turkey	• Apr: UK suffragette leader Emmeline Pankhurst sentenced to 3 years' imprisonment • 30 May: 1st Balkan War ended by Treaty of London; Turkey surrendered most of its European empire • 29 Jun: Outbreak of 2nd Balkan War, between Bulgaria and Romania, Greece, Serbia and Turkey • Aug, Treaty of Bucharest: 2nd Balkan War ended, with loss of territory by Bulgaria	• 28 Jun: Assassination of Austro-Hungarian heir, Archduke Franz Ferdinand, at Sarajevo (Bosnia); Serbs suspected of plot • 28 Jul: Austria-Hungary declared war on Serbia • 1–3 Aug: Germany declared war on Russia and France, and invaded Belgium • 4 Aug: UK and Commonwealth declared war on Germany
• Jun: Successful counter-revolution by new Persian shah, Mohammad Ali, who ordered bombing of majlis (parliament) • Young Turk Revolution: Army rebellion (Jul) forced Ottoman sultan to restore 1876 constitution and convene parliament (Dec) • Aug: In Morocco, Sultan Abdel Aziz overthrown by brother, Mulay Abdel Hafid	• India Act (Morley–Minto Reforms) gave Indians share in legislative councils of British India • Jul: Persian shah deposed by nationalist forces • Nov: Attempted assassination of UK viceroy, Lord Minto, in India	• Feb: Egypt's Coptic Christian premier, Butros Ghali, assassinated by nationalist	• Jul–Nov, Agadir Crisis: Franco–German rivalry over Morocco threatened to erupt into war • 29 Sep: Italy began war with Turkey over latter's N African provinces of Tripolitania and Cyrenaica • Nov: Franco–German agreement, recognizing French rights in Morocco; French Togoland (W Afr) given to Germany	• Protectorates set up by French in S Morocco (Mar), Spain in N Morocco (Nov) • Aug: Abdication of Moroccan sultan in protest at French rule • 15 Oct, Treaty of Ouchy: Italo–Turkish war ended with Turkey ceding Tripolitania and Cyrenaica	• Jun: Young Turks formed cabinet and assumed power over Turkish empire	• Nov: Turkey entered war on side of Central Powers (Ger, Aut-Hung) • 17 Dec: Egypt declared a UK protectorate
• 15 Nov: Congo (C Afr) formally annexed by Belgium	• Aug: S Africa Act passed in UK, approving union of Cape Colony, Natal, Orange River Colony (renamed Orange Free State), Transvaal	• Gabon, Middle Congo and Ubangi-Shari-Chad federated as French Equatorial Africa • 1 Jul: Union of S Africa became dominion within Commonwealth under Louis Botha (Sep)		• African National Congress (ANC) formed in S Africa	• Afrikaner Nationalist Party formed by James Hertzog (S Afr)	• 1 Jan: Union of N and S Nigeria as UK protectorate and colony • Aug: Anglo–French colonial troops invaded German protectorate of Togoland (W Afr) and forced German surrender
• In US, Federal Employers' Liability Act covered industrial injury on interstate carriers • 25 May: C American Court of Justice established, in Chile	• General Juan Gómez established dictatorship in Venezuela (until 1935) • Jun: National Negro Committee founded in US (from 1910, National Association for the Advancement of Colored People, NAACP)	• Revolutionary movement instituted in Mexico by Francisco Madero; supported by Emiliano Zapata and Pancho Villa	• 25 May: Mexican dictator Porfiro Díaz forced to resign, ending 35-year rule	• Jul–Oct: Civil war in Nicaragua; beginning of US military intervention (to 1933), as US forces intervened to support President Adolfo Díaz • 5 Nov: Woodrow Wilson elected 1st Democrat president of US in 20 years	• 25 Feb: Collection of income tax constituted in US, by 16th Amendment • Feb: Overthrow of Mexico's President Madero heralded military dictatorship of Victoriano Huerta and civil war • 31 May: Election of US senators instituted, by 17th Amendment	• Clayton Act legalized US trade unions • US took military control of Haiti • Apr: US support for restoration of constitutional government in Mexico implemented by landing of troops and capture of Veracruz • 4 Aug, WWI: US President Wilson issued proclamation of neutrality • 15 Aug: Panama Canal opened to shipping
• Foundation of Indonesian cultural society Budi Utomo gave focus to early nationalism (Dutch E Indies) • Nationalist movement in French Indochina began with rising in Tonking • Invalid and Old-Age Pensions Act passed by Australian federal government • 14 Nov: Death of Chinese Empress Tzu Hsi and succession of boy emperor, Pu Yi	• Assassination of Japanese resident-general in Korea • Mar: Anglo–Siamese treaty placed unfederated states in north of Malay peninsula under UK control	• 1st national assembly met in China; half members elected, half appointed by throne • Feb: Chinese army occupied Lhasa (Tib); Dalai Lama fled to India • Aug: Korea annexed by Japan	• 10 Oct: Revolution began in China; led to overthrow of Manchu dynasty • Dec: Sun Yat-sen elected president of provisional Chinese government (to Feb 1912)	• In New Zealand, new Reform Party gained power under leadership of W. Ferguson Massey, ending 42 years of Liberal government • 12 Feb: Emperor Pu Yi forced to abdicate; provisional republic of China declared • Jul: Death of Meiji emperor, Mutsuhito; accession of his son Yoshihito began Taishō era in Japan	• Dalai Lama returned to Tibet, following withdrawal of Chinese occupying force • 8 Apr: 1st Chinese elected parliament	• Following outbreak of WWI, German possessions of New Guinea captured by Australia, W Samoa by New Zealand, Pacific Is (Marianas, Carolines, Marshalls) and territory in Shandong province (China) by Japan (all formally ceded as mandates by League of Nations after 1919) • Aug: Japan, Australia and New Zealand declared war on Germany
• Nov: World's 1st aerial bombing raid, by Italians in N Africa					• Apr: International Women's Peace Conference, The Hague (Neth)	

Datafile

The pursuit of power has always been closely linked with economic development. Growth in industry, agriculture and transportation supports an expanding population, creates trade opportunities and provides the economic surplus necessary for expansion and war. The wars of the early 20th century drew their rationale and their economic support from the industrializing economies of the Great Powers, and their outcome was determined as much by economic strength as by military prowess. At the turn of the century, the rapid industrial growth of Germany was the most important factor in the upsetting of the European balance of power, while in the Far East Japan emerged as the dominant industrial power.

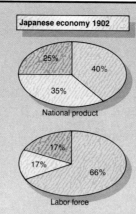

Japanese economy 1902

National product

Labor force

☐ Agriculture
☐ Services
▨ Manufacturing

◀ In the mid-19th century, the Japanese economy was almost entirely agricultural. Some 50 years later, the manufacturing and service sectors together accounted for more than half the national product while employing only a third of the labor force – evidence that Japan was developing into a well-articulated industrial state with the economic strength to make an impact on the world political scene.

▼ Russia entered the 20th century with an overwhelmingly agricultural economy. Industrialization was beginning to gather momentum in the western cities, deriving strength from the development of a national rail network to bring food and raw materials to the cities and distribute goods around the huge but largely unexploited domestic market. The predominance of the railway sector is clear – levels of employment in other industries were low compared to both the total Russian population and other European industrial Powers.

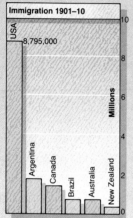

Immigration 1901–10

USA 8,795,000

Argentina
Canada
Brazil
Australia
New Zealand

Millions

▶ By 1900 the United States had already emerged as the largest industrial nation in the world. Within Europe the UK still maintained a lead over Germany, but the latter's far greater rate of growth was fast eroding that advantage. The other four major European Powers could match neither the UK nor Germany, and excepting possibly Russia, did not possess the resources to close the gap. Economic competition in Europe was a matter of Anglo-German rivalry, but both were threatened on the world scene by the United States.

Manufacturing output 1900

24%
22%
18%
13%
9%
7%
7%
2%

☐ USA
☐ Other
☐ UK
☐ Germany
▨ Russia
▨ France
▨ Austria–Hungary
▨ Italy

Employment in Russia 1904

Rail transport
Other factories
Cotton
Metallurgy
Other textiles
Other metalworking
Water transport
Mineral mining
Sugar
Coal mining

Thousands

▲ World industrialization was attended by a mass migration – largely from Europe to the Americas. Early industrialization in western Europe produced a surplus working population, while agricultural improvement to the east produced a whole generation of unemployed people with no factories into which to move. The huge underdeveloped hinterlands of the Americas and Australasia served as a magnet for these jobless millions. In economic terms, the major beneficiary was the United States.

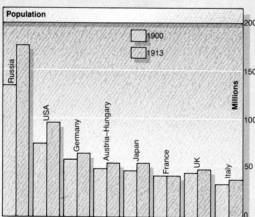

Population

☐ 1900
☐ 1913

Russia
USA
Germany
Austria–Hungary
Japan
France
UK
Italy

Millions

◀ Population growth was essential to economic growth at this stage of industialization, and in an era when military might depended upon the ability to mobilize mass conscript armies, the birth rate was also a matter of strategic importance. With the exception of France, all the Great Powers were experiencing dynamic population growth, although in the case of Russia, Italy and Austria-Hungary, retarded industrial development made it difficult to translate people into economic or military power.

▼ Railway development provided the support system for economic growth, transporting raw materials and produce to industrial cities, and manufactured goods to inland markets or to ports for export overseas. It was also critical to the development of military capacity, through the mass mobilization of armies and the ability to supply those armies at the front. The effectiveness of Russian rail development is distorted by the geographical scale of the nation; of the major powers Germany had the most advanced rail network.

▶ Industrialization was attended by the large-scale movement of population from the countryside to the factories of the city. At the turn of the century, well over half the populations of the Great Powers still lived in the country, but the proportion of city dwellers was steadily rising, giving a useful indication of industrial might. One other aspect of urbanization was soon to play a central role – the collection of workers into factories and industrial slums would accelerate the emergence of class consciousness.

Urban population

Total population (percent)

☐ 1900
☐ 1913

Russia
USA
Germany
Austria–Hungary
Japan
France
UK
Italy

Building railroads

☐ 1890
☐ 1910

Russia
Germany
France
UK
Italy
Spain
Belgium
Switzerland

Kilometers (thousands)

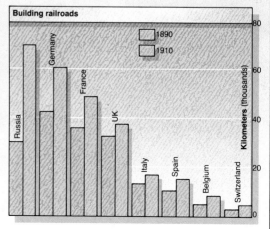

POWERS AND EMPIRES

Colonial empire builders

Great-power alliances of convenience

Anti-imperialist revolt in China

Russia's defeat by Japan

1905, the year of revolution

Franco-British alignment and the isolation of Germany

Imperialist propaganda

The Boxer rising

The first years of the 20th century were marked by the scramble for colonial possessions. In the previous decades new imperial states, such as Germany and Italy, had emerged to rival the traditional colonial powers of Britain, France and Russia. They were soon followed by the United States and Japan. By 1900 sub-Saharan Africa and many of the Pacific regions had been conquered.

Except for Russia, whose armies marched across Asia, the Great Powers of Europe gained access to their colonies by sea. Accordingly, this was a period in which the major instrument of national power was seen to be the navy. Each country with imperial ambitions strove to build large fleets of battleships and, especially in the Far East, to secure coaling stations and naval bases.

Increases in the armies of Europe were comparatively insignificant and considered far less urgent. Earlier rivalries between military blocs – the Dual Alliance of France and Russia on the one hand and the Triple Alliance of Germany, Austria-Hungary and Italy on the other – still existed, but the tension was much less than it had been a decade earlier. The great-power states could thus afford to direct their attention largely outside Europe, in pursuit of what the Germans called *Weltpolitik*, or world politics. Only Austria-Hungary did not take part in the race for the colonies and seek "a place in the sun".

How effectively a government pursued its colonial ambitions became important for electoral success at the national polls. Canvassing in the British general elections of 1900 focused on the war in South Africa to quell the Boers, while the American election of the same year dwelled on the conquest of the Philippines. In Germany, the 1907 election was dubbed the "Hottentot election" because the government's handling of uprisings by Hottentot tribes in German-controlled southwest and east Africa was a major electoral issue. Later, colonial clashes in Morocco, annexations of Bosnia and Tripoli and the race to build battlefleets to safeguard or further imperial ambitions colored the domestic politics of the great-power states.

▼ European sovereigns gathered for the funeral of Britain's King Edward VII in 1910. The period before the World War I represented an Indian summer for Europe's royalty, who ruled vast empires in grand style, but within a decade war and revolution would destroy their power for ever.

▶ The idyllic face of imperialism – George V of Britain on an Indian tiger shoot. To many eyes, the European imperial experience was a great endeavor, at once romantic and worthy. Exotic lands provided a playground for the wealthy and a challenge to civilized nations intent on shouldering the "white man's burden" and bringing enlightenment and improvement to the "uncivilized" and (hopefully) grateful natives.

▲ The darker side of imperialism – a Congolese child mutilated by Belgian colonial soldiers. Everywhere in Africa and Asia the imposition of European rule destroyed traditional patterns of life and was backed by the brutal suppression of any form of resistance.

▶▶ A poster advertising a French colonial exhibition. European governments used imperialist propaganda to distract their people from domestic problems. The government of France, a country defeated in the Franco-Prussian war, beset by political instability, and fearful of the rising power of Germany on its frontier, tried to foster national pride in colonial expansion in Africa. Imperial policies undoubtedly brought short-term political gains, but did little to strengthen the nation and involved an already unstable Europe in a furious competition for overseas influence that heightened the risk of war.

Imperialist Propaganda

In the industrial age of mass-production and increasing literacy, the press played an important part in swaying public opinion to support colonial expansionism. Imperial enthusiasts described the "opening up" of the nation's latest overseas acquisitions in glowing terms. Some colonial territories were said to be important as future markets, or as sources of raw materials or precious metals. Others – especially those that adjoined existing colonies or lay along major sea routes – had "strategic value". Sometimes protecting the lives of missionaries or explorers was given as a justification for intervention or conquest. Often more emotional arguments were used, although wrapped up in pseudo-scientific language. The Social-Darwinists, who analyzed historical trends in terms that derived from Charles Darwin's theory of natural evolution, claimed that any country that did not expand its power beyond its frontiers would face decline.

Imperial rivalries also produced nationalist arguments. The British referred to the Anglo-Saxon genius for colonial rule. The French had a "civilizing mission" to perform, the Americans a "manifest destiny" in Latin America and the Pacific, and the Russians something similar in the Balkans and in Asia.

The arguments from ethnic and cultural identity used to justify imperial expansion were, however, double-edged. They also aroused passions among the peoples who had been conquered. In Ireland, for instance, a culturally-driven "Celtic revival" was under way. Similar movements were stirring among the Czechs, Poles, Finns, and Balkan peoples, and nationalist circles were growing up in Egypt and India. In Budapest, Theodor Herzl (1860–1904) began promoting Zionism, an ideological movement calling for the return of Jews to a national, territorial homeland in Palestine.

▲ German cartoon of imperial growth.

Patterns of colonialism

By far the richest and most powerful of the colonial empires was the British Empire. It sprawled over almost a quarter of the Earth's land mass and included about a quarter of the world's population. Some parts of it were made up of self-governing Dominions like Canada and Australia. Others included the British Raj in India – the "jewel in the imperial crown" – and an array of older Crown Colonies and naval bases as well as newer acquisitions in northeast, central and southern Africa. In effect, there were really four British empires under the Crown, each governed differently.

France's colonial empire, occupying some ten million square kilometers (four million square miles), was administered much more uniformly. Heavily centered upon northwest and equatorial Africa, it also included territories in the West Indies, southeast Asia, and the Pacific. Germany held territories in Africa and the Pacific covering an area about a quarter the size of France's colonies. However, as a latecomer Germany had acquired chiefly tracts of jungle and desert. Italy, Portugal and Belgium also had colonies in Africa. Russia's colonial expansion had been achieved by a persistent push eastward across Asia. Of the

China, the Near East or North Africa, the colonizer risked provoking rivals to join forces in opposition.

Even Britain, the greatest of the traditional world powers, began to experience the strain of maintaining its erstwhile policy of "splendid isolation". While the bulk of the British army was pinned down in South Africa in the war against the Boers (1899–1902), it could not intervene to settle any dispute that might arise in the colonies. Moreover, foreign battlefleets presented a growing challenge to Britain's naval power, increasing the pressure in areas of the world such as China and Persia where Britain had important commercial or strategic interests. Consequently, the foreign secretary, the Marquess of Lansdowne and his colleague A.J. Balfour (who became prime minister in 1902) were forced to reconsider the question of making regional agreements, or forming alliances, with other countries.

In 1901 Britain conceded to the United States its rights to a half-share in the control of the future Panama Canal, and two years later accepted American territorial claims along the Alaska-British Columbia border. Britain reasoned that it was better to secure American goodwill through concessions than to risk a quarrel when so many serious interests were at stake elsewhere.

Similar considerations prompted other deals throughout Europe. The French and the Italians were secretly beginning to sink their differences over colonial territories in North Africa, while at the same time some of the French politicians hoped to secure British agreement to a takeover of Morocco. German entrepreneurs also looked to Britain for financial and diplomatic aid to develop the Baghdad railway. With international relations in an unusual state of flux, European foreign ministries warily watched each other for potential rivals or potential partners.

Powers outside Europe, Japan had acquired overseas territories in the Pacific and Far East following a victorious war with China 1894–95, as had the United States after the Spanish-American war of 1898.

Despite the jingoism of the age, many radicals and liberals in Europe were opposed to this imperialism. They believed that annexing other peoples' territories was morally indefensible, and the arms race a waste of the nation's resources. Colonial policies, they argued, served the interests of the armed forces, the financiers, the munitions manufacturers and the press barons, not the people – a view that found support among the rising forces of organized labor. Trade union leaders contended that passions over empires were being aroused to divert attention and resources away from pressing domestic issues. Opponents of imperialism in the United States also stressed that colonization opposed the country's own heritage of being born out of an anti-imperial revolt.

Great-power alliances

As the jostling for colonies and spheres of influence increased, it became harder for any of the powers involved to act alone. Whether in

Trouble in the Far East

A crisis looming in the Far East brought about changes in the diplomatic scene. In China, irregular nationalist groups known as the Boxers rose up against foreign missionaries and diplomats, prompting the dispatch of an international army to Peking in 1900. These events seriously weakened the Manchu empire and left foreign forces in charge of key areas. Britain, worried by Russia's desire to maintain its grip on Manchuria and northern China, sought the cooperation of Germany to uphold the territorial status quo in the region. The government in Berlin, however, wanted neither to antagonize Russia nor to help Britain out of a jam, and the Anglo-German alliance talks of 1901 petered out by the end of the year.

The Japanese, on the other hand, were keen to help to check Russian expansion into Manchuria and especially Korea. Under the terms of the Anglo-Japanese alliance signed in January 1902, Britain and Japan agreed to come to each other's aid if its ally was at war with more than one enemy over Far Eastern issues, but to stay neutral if its ally was fighting only one foe. This treaty, which commited Britain, under certain circumstances, to fight for another Power, virtually ended the country's policy of "splendid isolation". It also reduced the need for an alliance with Germany, which was emerging as an ever more dangerous rival. By 1902–03 an Anglo-German press war was raging and many Britons viewed with alarm the massive expansion of Admiral Alfred von Tirpitz's High Seas Fleet in the North Sea.

The French too were worried about the German buildup. After the British King Edward VII's highly successful visit to Paris in May 1903, voices in both Britain and France urged an end to their countries' long-standing colonial quarrels in Africa, stressing the need to hold together against Germany. The new mood suited the ambitions of the able French foreign minister Théophile Delcassé to gain a free hand for his country in Morocco by befriending Britain and at the same time detaching Italy from the Triple Alliance. The German chancellor von Bülow proved to be no match for Delcassé, and his bungled attempts to play off the powers against each other, coupled with Kaiser Wilhelm II's impulsiveness, only further compromised German diplomatic efforts.

The Russo-Japanese war

Japan had sought to contain Russian expansion in the Far East by diplomacy, but influential circles around Czar Nicholas II seemed more determined to make Russia the dominant power in the Orient than to negotiate seriously. In February 1904 the Japanese, unable to ignore Russian actions in the Far East any longer, launched a preemptive strike at Russian warships anchored in Port Arthur.

At the outset of the Russo-Japanese war, many believed that Russia would be the eventual victor. It had the largest army in the world and a mighty fleet too. Moreover, a European Power would allegedly always be superior to an Asiatic one. Realistically, however, Japan had an important strategic advantage in being much closer to the

The Boxer Rising

The Chinese Boxer rising of 1900 was both the long-term result of progressive European penetration of the Chinese economy together with the steady disintegration of the corrupt and inefficient Qing dynasty, and the short-term consequence of the Chinese government's attempt to use popular unrest to oppose colonial settlements.

Colonial exploitation of China gained momentum in the 1890s. In the same decade a feeble modernization program of the Chinese government received a serious blow when its forces were crushed in the Sino-Japanese war (1894–95). Losing power to mount direct opposition, the regime of the dowager-empress Cixi secretly encouraged the growth of a popular resistance movement, The Society of Harmonious Fists (popularly known as the Boxers), and helped to whip up anti-European feeling among its youthful members. The Boxer movement was fired by a hatred of anything foreign, particularly the Christian religion being preached by missionaries, and developed a semi-mystical ideology which included the belief that its members were imune to foreign bullets. Small-scale attacks on foreign nationals and their

▲ US soldiers at the foot of China's Great Wall. After the rebellion the imperial government were unable to prevent foreign troops from moving at will throughout the country.

▲◀ European governments used graphic accounts of Boxer atrocities to whip up popular support for intervention.

◀ The foreign powers collaborated against the Boxer rebellion – the soldiers and marines in this photograph represent eight different fighting forces.

Chinese associates grew in number all over north China, and even British reinforcements on their way to Beijing to protect resident nationals came under fire.

On 14 June 1900 a government-inspired uprising broke out in Beijing. The German minister was assassinated, European property sacked and foreign legations besieged as frenzied mobs ran riot. As a result, six foreign nations, in a rare exercise, collaborated in a joint military relief mission to Beijing. The Boxers fought bravely to oppose the march, but, lightly armed and poorly organized, they succumbed to superior firepower and the legations were relieved in mid-August. A wave of brutal repression followed all over the affected area, until resistance finally collapsed. In 1901 the

foreign powers imposed the Peking Protocol, forcing China to pay an annual indemnity, accept the stationing of troops in its territory and submit to foreign control of the capital's diplomatic quarter. This settlement intensified antiforeign feeling and totally discredited the old Qing dynasty. Anti-imperial nationalist and republican movements attracted scores of new recruits, and when fresh unrest broke out in 1912 it rapidly developed into a full-scale revolution which destroyed the Chinese imperial government in a matter of months. A republic was set up, and a National Assembly met in February 1913, at which the Nationalists (Guomindang) were the majority party. Yuan Shikai was appointed president, and forced through a new constitution in 1914.

combat zones. To reach the Far East, Russia had to send its troops along the 10,000-kilometer (6,000-mile) single-track trans-Siberian railway, and its reserve fleet had to steam from the Baltic and around Africa and the East Indies. Japan also enjoyed superior organization. The Japanese navy was especially highly trained in gunnery, and the army drilled in making fearless assaults on enemy machine-gun posts, trenches and barbed wire. The Russian troops fought hard, but suffered from poor leadership and at home the war became increasingly unpopular.

Eventually, at the end of 1904, Port Arthur fell to the besieging Japanese, who advanced irresistibly on to Mukden. Worse was to follow. The Russian Baltic fleet, after an epic round-the-world voyage around the world full of incidents (including firing on British trawlers on the Dogger Bank, which almost sparked off an Anglo-Russian war), sailed into the straits of Tsushima in May 1905, to be annihilated by the Japanese navy.

In Russia itself, the hardships caused by the war and the increasing unpopularity of the czarist regime led to widespread riots, strikes and demands for reform. Moreover, the government could no longer count on the loyalty of the armed forces to quell unrest. Throughout 1905 the whole country trembled on the brink of a full-scale revolution. Russia had lost its status as a Great Power, the treasury was bankrupt, and it had become impossible to raise the huge foreign loans needed to continue the war.

Following mediation by the US president

▼ Japanese soldiers survey the sunken Russian warships in Port Arthur. The Russian loss of the harbor was the product of Japanese superiority on land and sea. The Russian fleet was unable to break the blockade imposed by the better-trained Japanese navy while the heroic resistance of the Port Arthur garrison could only delay defeat, because the Japanese army blocked the way for any military relief force. Unwilling to face certain loss at sea, Russian warships were eventually sunk at their mooring by land-based siege artillery.

The 1905 Revolution

As Russia faced defeat by Japan, public opinion voiced open criticism of the government and political parties expressed sectional discontents. The workers were partly organized by Marxists as the Russian Social Democratic Labor party, the Socialist Revolutionaries claimed to represent the peasants, and the Constitutional Democrats (Kadets) called for democratic reform.

Matters came to a head with the "Bloody Sunday" episode of 22 January 1905. A strike in St Petersburg begun in December 1904 gave rise to a demonstration in which the priest Father Gapon (himself a police agent) was persuaded by socialists to present a political petition to the czar. The huge crowds that amassed were fired on by troops, causing about 200 deaths. Strikes and demonstrations ensued throughout the year. The humiliating Portsmouth Treaty, which ended hostilities with Japan, sustained the dual mood of protest and nationalist outrage. In October 1905 the czar was forced to concede a national assembly (Duma).

Basic freedoms were introduced and gradually the opposition parties, including the Kadets, who had boycotted the elections, and the socialist Soviet of Workers' Deputies, who had called for an armed uprising, took part in the Duma. Having divided the forces of revolution, the government, under prime minister Stolypin, proceeded to carry out a dual policy of reform and repression.

▶ Bloody Sunday, 1905, at St Petersburg.

▼ Crude imagery to glorify Japanese success. The blockade of Port Arthur and the role of Russia's navy are parodied here as stakes are driven in to seal Russian mouths and render them toothless. Such propaganda made a direct appeal to a susceptibly bellicose public.

▲ Racist imagery to bolster Russian resistance. The depiction of the noble, upright Russian, beleaguered by a host of subhuman Asiatics typified European incredulity at the successful expansion of an Eastern culture hitherto seen as barbarous and backward.

Theodore Roosevelt, in August 1905 Russia and Japan signed the Treaty of Portsmouth, under which Japan gained a protectorate over Korea and southern Manchuria. The war had launched Japan as a great power, but had been a profound humiliation for Russia. The outcome was ideal for Britain, whose interests in China were safeguarded by Japan's victory. The British could now recall their Far Eastern battleships to join the growing force being assembled to keep watch on Germany's powerful High Seas Fleet nearer home. Not surprisingly, Britain hastened to renew its 1902 alliance with Japan.

The Franco-British settlement
During the Russo-Japanese war the great fear of Britain and France, as respective allies of Japan and Russia, was that they might be drawn in to fight on opposite sides, just at a time when relations between them were improving. This fear grew with suspicions of intrigue by Germany to escalate the war in order to enhance its own position and weaken that of the combatants.

Thus, in 1904, in a move to resolve their outstanding differences and seek closer cooperation, the governments of London and Paris announced a wide-ranging colonial settlement. The French agreed to recognize Britain's claims in Egypt and the Nile valley in exchange for British support for France's position in Morocco. The agreement also committed the signatories to helping each other to achieve their aims. The French foreign minister, Delcassé, anticipating problems with Germany over Morocco, was keen that the new

entente cordiale should have an anti-German thrust, but his British counterpart, Lansdowne, was less enthusiastic about this. Delcassé also managed to secure the Spaniards' support for his country's policy, by offering them a sphere of influence in Morocco.

The collapse of Russia in 1905, however, represented a serious setback to France's plans. Since the early 1890s there had been a power balance in Europe between the Dual Alliance (France and Russia) and the Triple Alliance (Germany, Austria-Hungary and Italy). While Italy's commitment to the alliance was half-hearted, and Austria-Hungary was riven with internal conflict between ethnic groups, imperial Germany more than made up for the weaknesses of the other two member states. The industrial powerhouse of Europe, it had a modern battlefleet and a large, efficient army, and was growing stronger year by year.

Before 1905 Germany's ability to dominate Europe had been checked by the military and economic expansion of Russia. But with its ally now weakened by war and revolution, France alone was not strong enough to oppose Germany. Kaiser Wilhelm II and his advisers, many of whom had a diplomatic score to settle with Delcassé, read the situation only too well. In a move to thwart French efforts to take over Morocco, the German foreign ministry first encouraged the kaiser to pay a symbolic visit to Tangiers in March 1905, and then backed this up by making veiled threats to settle the dispute with France by force. How serious a threat this was remains unclear, but in military terms it would have been an opportune time for Germany to attack France. Fearing the worst, the French premier dismissed Delcassé in June 1905 and agreed to attend an international conference to settle Morocco's future. On the German side, Chancellor von Bülow was made a prince for his great diplomatic victory.

Anglo-German rivalry

Germany's diplomatic successes were, however, short-lived. In July 1905 the kaiser met the czar in Björkö, Sweden, to seek a new German–Russian alliance, but the proposal was rejected by the Russian government, who preferred to maintain the older ties with France. Germany's diplomatic initiatives and naval policies were the cause of growing concern to Britain, which already suspected that ministers in Berlin had been secretly plotting to involve the British Empire in the war in the Far East. Any agreement that the Germans made with the Russians, Britain believed, would be directed against British interests. Moreover, under Admiral von Tirpitz Germany was building a battlefleet, apparently to challenge the Royal Navy's control of the North Sea.

In late 1904 and early 1905 some extreme politicians in Britain had argued that the German High Seas Fleet should be "copenhagened" – sunk in port before it could grow any bigger. The British government dismissed the idea as absurd but the possibility still alarmed the kaiser. In this atmosphere of growing suspicion and mistrust, some British officials drew up contingency plans to help France in the event of an attack by Germany over the Morocco dispute. For almost a century Britain had avoided a policy of what it called "the continental commitment", since any military intervention in Europe would break with Britain's liberal traditions and be unpopular at home.

Now, voices within the newly formed Imperial General Staff argued that, if Britain did nothing while Germany overran France, then Britain too would suffer a serious strategic setback. How to support the French without involving unacceptable levels of commitment was a problem that

▲ Colonial postage stamps reflect the scale and variety of the imperial experience. European rule was underpinned by a massive colonial bureaucracy and a communications system in which the steamship and the mail service were central.

▼ The German kaiser leads his troops through Tangiers in 1905. Colonial rivalries reflected more deep-set European antagonisms, and the series of diplomatic crises away from the European continent increased the likelihood of war in Europe.

Imperial Powers in 1900

ALASKA (US)

CANADA

NEWFO

UNITED STATES
OF AMERICA

BAHAMAS (Br)

CUBA US occ

BRITISH
HONDURAS   JAMAICA   *Leeward Islands*

Windward Island

TRINIDAD

PACIFIC

OCEAN

BRITISH GUIAN
DUTCH GU
FRENC

European empires
- Belgian
- British
- Dutch
- French
- German
- Italian
- Portuguese
- Spanish
- Other important power

Scale 1:115 000 000

0 ———————— 3000 km

0 ———————— 2000 mi

Falk

Balfour's Conservative government bequeathed to its Liberal successor at the end of 1905.

The Moroccan and Persian settlements

An international conference held at the Spanish town of Algeciras early in 1906 decided the future of Morocco. The settlement gave France and its junior partner Spain effective control of the Moroccan police and finances, and was a bitter diplomatic blow to the Germans. Only Austria-Hungary supported the German claim, and did so reluctantly. Britain strongly backed the French, and was determined to improve Anglo-Russian relations in Asia, a move much encouraged by the French, who sought to bring together its new entente partner, Britain, and its old ally, Russia, in an alliance that would hold Germany in check.

After tough, difficult negotiations, Britain and Russia concluded an agreement in August 1907. Sometimes referred to as the Asian entente, it

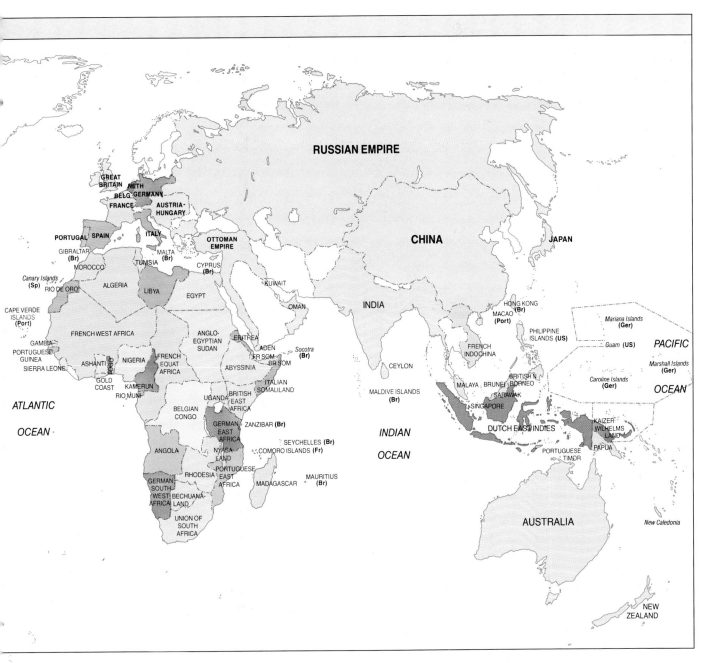

RUSSIAN EMPIRE

GREAT
BRITAIN
NETH
BELG GERMANY
FRANCE AUSTRIA-
HUNGARY

PORTUGAL SPAIN ITALY OTTOMAN
EMPIRE

CHINA JAPAN

GIBRALTAR
(Br) MALTA
(Br)
MOROCCO TUNISIA CYPRUS
(Br)
Canary Islands
(Sp) ALGERIA LIBYA
RIO DE ORO EGYPT KUWAIT OMAN
CAPE VERDE
ISLANDS
(Port) INDIA HONG KONG
(Br)
MACAO
(Port) Mariana Islands
(Ger)
GAMBIA FRENCH WEST AFRICA ANGLO-
EGYPTIAN
SUDAN ERITREA PHILIPPINE
ISLANDS (US) PACIFIC
PORTUGUESE
GUINEA ADEN
FR SOM Socotra
(Br) FRENCH
INDOCHINA Guam (US)
SIERRA LEONE ASHANTI NIGERIA FRENCH
EQUAT
AFRICA BR SOM
ABYSSINIA Marshall Islands
(Ger)
GOLD
COAST KAMERUN
RIO MUNI UGANDA ITALIAN
SOMALILAND CEYLON MALAYA BRUNEI BRITISH N
BORNEO Caroline Islands
(Ger) OCEAN
BRITISH
EAST
AFRICA MALDIVE ISLANDS
(Br) SARAWAK
SINGAPORE KAIZER
WILHELMS
LAND
ATLANTIC BELGIAN
CONGO
OCEAN GERMAN
EAST
AFRICA ZANZIBAR (Br) DUTCH EAST INDIES PAPUA
ANGOLA NYASA-
LAND SEYCHELLES (Br) INDIAN PORTUGUESE
TIMOR
COMORO ISLANDS (Fr) OCEAN
RHODESIA PORTUGUESE
EAST
AFRICA MADAGASCAR MAURITIUS
(Br)
GERMAN
SOUTH
WEST BECHUANA-
AFRICA LAND
UNION OF
SOUTH
AFRICA AUSTRALIA New Caledonia

NEW
ZEALAND

divided Persia into spheres of Russian and British influence in the north and south respectively, with a neutral "buffer zone" in the middle. The treaty also stabilized the status of the Indian border territories of Tibet and Afghanistan and marked the end of a century of Anglo-Russian rivalry in central Asia.

The end of _Weltpolitik_
The year 1907 also marked the end of the era of "world policy" and a return to the European political arena. After Roosevelt's energetic presidency, in which the United States had helped to end the Russo-Japanese war and participated in the Algeciras conference, the country returned to a more isolationist diplomacy under President William H. Taft. By then, the position of the United States as the strongest power in the Western Hemisphere was unchallengeable.

Affairs in the Far East had also stabilized, Japan and Russia having secretly agreed, in 1907, on

zones of influence in Manchuria. The "scramble for Africa" too seemed virtually complete, and Britain's fears over the defense of India were partly allayed by its Asian entente with Russia.

As for Germany, events had dealt a series of blows to its colonial ambitions and hopes of achieving the status of a great world power. The United States blocked any German expansion in Latin America, and Japan did the same in the Far East. France and Britain held the initiative in Morocco and Egypt. Russia and Britain exercised joint influence in Persia, and opposed the Germans' Baghdad railway project in Mesopotamia. It seemed to Germany that Britain, France and Russia, despite their ideological differences, were drawing closer together and eyeing Germany with hostile intent. The cry arose that the Fatherland was being "encircled" by jealous foes, and the time had come, Prussian conservatives argued, to forget about distant colonies and to prepare to engage enemies much closer to home.

▲ The map of the world in 1900 shows the effects of several decades of frenetic imperial expansion. Africa and large parts of Asia were either under direct imperial rule or had been heavily penetrated by foreign economic interests. The export of European rivalries to a wider stage had carried the flags of Britain, France, Germany, Russia and others across the desert, jungle and mountains with little regard for economic or political rationality. Many colonies were unstable, underdeveloped hinterlands which cost more to maintain than they returned to European treasuries – and whose very existence threatened the stability of the international political order.

POWERS AND GREAT POWERS

The Great Powers were the states around which the deadly game of international diplomacy revolved in the years before 1900. They were not necessarily large in size. China, though an enormous country, was not considered a Great Power while Japan, a group of small islands, was. Another group of small islands, the United Kingdom, was arguably the world's leading Power for most of the 19th century.

There were five main conditions of great-power status. First, military strength. A Great Power required land armies to ensure continental dominance and naval power to gain and defend overseas colonies. Second, an industrial base. Guns and battleships presupposed coal, iron, steel and engineering industries. A railway network was needed for the swift mobilization of troops. Third, colonies. These provided raw materials such as oil, rubber and metals, markets for exports and investment opportunities for capital. They were also training-grounds and garrisons for troops. Areas such as China or the Ottoman Empire, which were themselves being colonized, were "sick men" rather than Great Powers. Fourth, a certain degree of social cohesion. One way to check social unrest and the progress of socialism was social reform; another, and commoner, way was the official encouragement of nationalism by mass education, jingoistic organizations and the popular press. Politicians and generals could not expect to mobilize men and resources for war without the services of nationalism. Fifth, national cohesion. States with one dominant nationality tended to be in a strong position. Those possessing numerous national minorities, or evenly balancing national minorities, were nstable, with the conflict of loyalties and confusion of languages extending into the army itself.

In the mid-19th century, when Britain was evidently the most powerful nation, there was a certain tranquility on the international scene. Then came serious challenges for great-power status, particularly from Germany, Russia, the United States and Japan, and immense rivalry for recognition as the greatest Power. Worst of all, there was the fear of demotion from the "league-table" of Powers, and of annihilation in the event of war. No effective European or global organizations existed to keep the peace; the Powers were driven into a relentless arms race. There was a scramble for colonies, first in Africa, then in the Far East and Middle East, to win extra points for the league-table, but the scramble multiplied instances of contact between powers and possibilities of conflict. Safety was sought in numbers. Ententes and alliances were formed to isolate enemies and increase military strength by proxy. But the effect was to divide the world into two armed camps, from which before 1917 only the United States stood aloof. The system was unstable, the stakes were repeatedly raised, and in the end national honor excluded any kind of retreat, the only alternative to fullscale war.

◀ Theodore Roosevelt inspecting progress on the construction of the Panama Canal. Even at the turn of the century such "photo opportunities" generated symbols of state power: advanced technology plus political authority.

▶ When "your country needs you" the abstract forces of state authority and military might are transformed into the expendable flesh and blood of able-bodied men. Here young Russians undergo medical examination before being sent to the front in 1905.

▶ At the level of international diplomacy states act as individuals writ large as well as having a unique cultural and political history which give them a mythical personality. This French cartoon vividly expresses the natural tendency for European nations to be stereotyped in various states of passivity, submission or aggression. It also dramatizes the dynamic, precarious nature of the balance of power.

▲ The Great War dramatically exposed the sinister relationship between military might and productive capacity at the heart of modern state power. This accumulation of army stores was needed to sustain the "war of attrition" of 1914–18.

▼ Military hardware, formed by an alliance between state and industry, underpins the political initiatives of modern states. Without the guns rolling off the Krupp assembly lines, Wilhelmine Germany could never have behaved as a "Great Power".

Datafile

The decade and a half before the outbreak of World War I witnessed an unprecedented build-up of armaments. As alliances and antagonisms hardened, and as commercial competition added heat to existing political rivalries, governments devoted larger amounts of economic output to expanding armies and navies. Europe was experiencing a huge arms race, and as much attention was paid to the numbers of men under military training and warships under construction as to industrial output or social welfare.

Germany was a military threat to its European neighbors because it could exploit its coal and iron resources and efficiently mobilize a growing population. Britain remained predominant at sea because the government could justify heavy expenditure on warship construction to a population which equated maritime supremacy with national greatness. The other Powers, however, could only maintain the pace at the cost of putting great strain on their weaker economies.

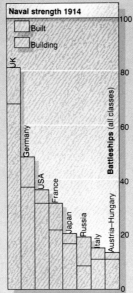

Naval strength 1914

◀ Britain was unusual among the European powers in devoting the bulk of defense expenditure to the navy. Because it did not maintain a huge conscript army, Britain never lost the lead in the naval building race, despite German efforts to create a rival battlefleet. The US fleet emerged as the third largest but was not yet a factor in world politics.

▶ By 1910 the European Powers were maintaining large armies and had the capacity to call up many more trained reservists. The bare figures distort the reality of the situation, as the Russian army could not be efficiently deployed and the French army was maintained at too great a cost – the German army was more effective than either.

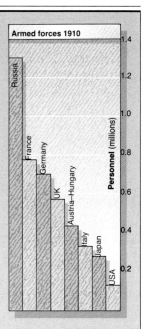

Armed forces 1910

Growth rates 1870–1913

◀ Growth rates, which show how the economic balance was changing, were in many ways more significant than annual output figures. The US was continuing to get stronger, while Germany was outstripping France and overtaking a flagging UK – Japan was a rising force in the East, but in Europe itself Russia, Austria and Italy were sluggish performers.

▶ Arms expenditure varied only over a spread of about 15 million pounds equivalent among the five major spenders, but the relationship between that expenditure and total mobilizable resources showed the US, UK and Germany to be stronger than France or Russia, who would have severe problems in continuing the war.

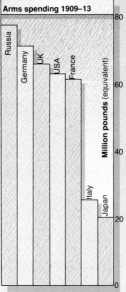

Arms spending 1909–13

▼ While it is extremely difficult to measure an "industrialization coefficient" of the rival Powers, the key manufacturing outputs, available horsepower and railway mileage in relation to population give a fair idea of overall economic strength. The US, UK and Germany had achieved a relatively high level of industrial resources in terms of their available human resources, but the other Powers lagged well behind. Even if the latter could find the men to send into the field in time of war, they did not have the raw materials, the manufacturing capacity or the transportation infrastructure to arm and supply them. The war would show that in Europe only the UK and Germany could sustain the effort of prolonged warfare.

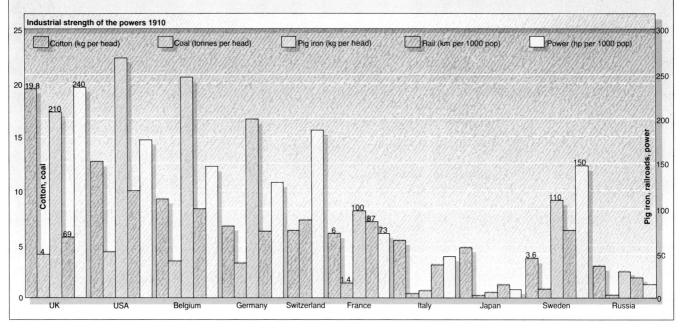

Industrial strength of the powers 1910

GREAT POWER RIVALRIES

The rivalries among the Great Powers of Europe over colonial possessions had for the most part been settled diplomatically, without the need to resort to war. The situation within Europe itself, however, proved to be less tractable. Germany's imperial aspirations abroad had been thwarted, largely by Anglo-French cooperation, and now Germany looked to the power struggle within Europe as a means of reasserting itself and restoring German pride.

From 1907 the political climate of Europe steadily worsened. At the second Hague Peace Conference of that year the Great Powers failed to agree on any substantial reduction in armaments or on the control of their use in war. Each of the participants supported proposals that would bring advantage to themselves, but fiercely resisted schemes that would hamper their freedom of action. Thus the British Liberal government's proposal for all-round cuts in naval expenditure and for a freeze on building new warships was opposed by Germany because it would leave Britain's Royal Navy with an unapproachable

▼ A banner at the Hague Peace Conference of 1907 proclaims "Down with War". Intensifying political rivalries and rearmament programs alarmed many, but the failure of the Hague conference proved that nationalism remained a more potent force than pacifism.

superiority over the German High Seas Fleet.

Germany also rejected plans to enforce binding arbitration upon quarreling states, which it regarded as a ploy to neutralize the logistical advantages the German army enjoyed over its neighbors. The kaiser's government gained a particular notoriety by its opposition to proposals to limit war, but, despite appearances, it was not alone in preferring to defend national interests by force rather than by negotiation. The imperialist fervor, which in earlier decades had focused upon colonial disputes in Africa and the Pacific, now concentrated increasingly upon naval and military rivalries in Europe. Rightwing organizations such as naval and national-service leagues, who sought to mobilize public opinion behind larger armament expenditures, issued grim warnings about the evil intentions of jealous enemies. The press, appealing to patriotic emotions, fanned the flames of hostility. Against the barrage of nationalist propaganda, the opposition of peace societies, churchmen, left-liberals and socialists could make little headway.

The Anglo-German naval race

Britain and Germany were not alone in investing more and more money in battlefleets. Following its losses in the war with Japan, Russia plunged itself into a costly shipbuilding program, while in the Mediterranean, Italy and Austria-Hungary both sought to create modern navies, provoking a similar response from France. Outside Europe, Japan and the United States already possessed powerful navies.

By 1908 Britain and Germany, urged on by their naval lobbies, were building warships faster than anyone else. Admiral von Tirpitz, the head of the German navy, was making a determined bid to challenge the world's number-one maritime power in its own home waters.

The rivalry had sharpened after 1906, when the British Admiralty unveiled a new and much more powerful Dreadnought-class battleship, which made all earlier types obsolete. The Germans responded by announcing in their 1908 fleet program that, from then on, they would launch four Dreadnought-class vessels each year. Britain's Liberal government had hoped to hold down defence spending, but by early 1909 the allegation – vigorously denied by von Tirpitz – that Germany was laying down ships faster than permited by its own Navy Law – caused such outrage in Britain that H.H. Asquith's government was forced to order eight new battleships in one year.

By this time, too, almost all of the major warships of the Royal Navy, apart from a Mediter-

Early 20th-century Nationalism

Nationalism had become a powerful political force in the 19th century, drawing its inspiration from the French Revolution and the experience of Napoleonic conquest in Europe. Initially it was regarded as subversive, aiming at the overthrow of conservative dynasties, but by 1900 – after the successful unification of Germany and Italy – the nation state seemed to be the most successful form of political organization. Multinational empires, such as those of the Habsburgs or the Ottoman Turks, were in decline, at least within Europe. By this time nationalism had lost some of its revolutionary edge and become associated with conservative social forces – a useful cement binding different classes together in a national community, in opposition to the divisive influences of Marxist socialism, which emphasized class conflict. Nationalism stressed the importance of linguistic and historic communities, implying an organic connection between their members.

Nationalism appealed to large nations trying to eliminate the nationhood of smaller ones, for example the Germans and the Russians in their attitude towards the Poles, as well as to separatist movements within smaller nationalities rebelling against hegemony, such as the Irish or the Norwegians. During World War I nationalism received a strong boost as the result of the damage done to large central and east European empires. The defeat of czarist Russia paved the way for independence for the Poles, the Finns and the Baltic peoples. The Ukrainians also emerged as a nationality, although their attempts to gain political independence from their Russian masters failed.

After the United States entered the war, President Wilson announced, early in 1918, that he wished to see a peace based on the principle of national self-determination. This was encouraged at the negotiations to produce a postwar settlement, which reinforced disintegrating tendencies in the Habsburg monarchy, and in 1918 the Czechs and Slovaks gained national independence, as did the peoples of Yugoslavia. Hungary and Austria became small but independent states. The Ottoman Empire collapsed and a new, nationalistic Turkish state emerged under the charismatic leader Atatürk.

▶ Military training in Russia in the 1900s.

▲ A British postcard asserting that the *Pax Britannica* still prevailed in 1906.

▶ The German navy firing a ceremonial salute during a British royal visit. Britain had enjoyed unchallenged naval supremacy since the Napoleonic wars, and it was on the might of the Royal Navy that the security of the empire rested. German naval expansion threatened this security, pulling Britain directly into the highly-charged alliance politics of the continent. To Britain, the new German navy was a weapon purpose-built for use against it.

ranean fleet much reduced in size, were concentrated in the North Sea to shadow the German navy. Moreover, in accordance with Admiral J.A. Fisher's drastic reforms, dozens of small cruisers and gunboats deployed overseas – the naval symbol of a former age of *Pax Britannica* – were scrapped to release crews for the North Sea squadrons.

Crisis in the Balkans

A renewal of trouble in the Balkans, the scene of so many international disputes in the 19th century, was a further cause of rising tension in Europe. However, with the exception of spasmodic interest in reforming Turkish rule in Macedonia, the regions had been relatively peaceful since 1897, when Russia and Austria-Hungary had agreed that they would put Balkan issues "on ice".

That situation changed, beginning with a coup d'état in Serbia in 1903, which put into power a strongly nationalistic faction who looked to St Petersburg for guidance rather than to Vienna. These events encouraged many southern Slavs in Austria-Hungary, especially those suffering under the harsh rule of the Magyars. The overthrow of the regime of Sultan Abdul Hamid by the "Young Turks" in 1908 further stimulated Balkan nationalism, causing concern among other states that a reinvigorated Turkey might thwart their ambitions in the Balkans.

Russia, halted in its far-eastern drive, now showed renewed interest in the Balkans, though its military weakness forced it to proceed with caution. The Austrians were the first to make a move. Politicians and generals in Vienna, unable to solve the problem of the differences between

the Hungarians and the southern Slavs, feared that the Habsburg Empire might disintegrate unless the Serbian threat was checked. Foreign minister Alois von Aehrenthal tried to warn off the Serbs by threatening to annex the provinces of Bosnia and Herzegovina, which were already governed by the Empire. In exchange for granting this concession, the Russian foreign minister, Alexander Isvolsky, hoped to secure Vienna's support for Russian claims in the Black Sea Straits, the lifeline of its southern and western trade.

In October 1908, however, Austria-Hungary annexed Bosnia and Herzegovina without further warning. The Serbs were taken by surprise, but so too were the Russians, who now felt forced to defend the Slavic cause. Russia received only token support from its allies Britain and France, both of whom opposed Russian claims in the Straits, whereas Austria-Hungary had the strong backing of Germany. Given the state of its own armed forces, Russia had little choice but to concede without a fight. In fact, the Austro-

German action did not solve the problem of the south Slavs. It succeeded only in temporarily driving the opposition underground.

The repercussions of the Balkan crisis were felt across Europe. Italy was alarmed by Austria-Hungary's aggression, as was Britain by Germany's habit of diplomatic blackmail. When, over the next two years, the new German chancellor Bethmann Hollweg tried to make a neutrality treaty with Britain in exchange for slowing down the naval race, the government in London was unresponsive. Although, generally, the Liberal government favored arms reductions, it did not want to give Germany a free hand in Europe by committing itself not to intervene in any continental conflict.

The second Moroccan crisis
In 1911, a new crisis flared up in Morocco. In response to a rebellion by the Berbers, France dispatched a military expedition to Fez, then Morocco's capital. The Germans, fearing for their own colonial ambitions, sent a a warship to the Moroccan port of Agadir, to warn off the French from taking over the whole of the country. France and its prime minister Joseph Caillaux were eager to compromise. Britain, however, was alarmed at what it perceived to be a further example of Germany's browbeating diplomatic tactics.

In his famous "Mansion House" speech of 21 July 1911, the British Chancellor of the Exchequer, David Lloyd George, sent what was widely seen as a warning to Germany and a message of support to France. The speech infuriated German nationalists, who regarded it as another example of Britain jealously blocking Germany's legitimate overseas claims. However, the Berlin government was not prepared to go to war over the issue, and later that year accepted a compromise settlement that included part of the French Congo. French patriotism was so revived that, in January 1912, Caillaux was swept out of office and replaced by the strongly nationalistic Raymond Poincaré. The Moroccan crisis, though soon forgotten, added to the overall international tension.

Preparing for war
Until the Balkan and Moroccan crises the existence of rival alliance blocs had little direct influence on military or naval planning. Now, diplomacy and operations plans began to interact. At the time of the annexation of Bosnia and Herzegovina, the German and Austro-Hungarian general staffs had each found that the other had a plan that complicated its own operational scheme. Conrad, the Austrian chief of staff, hoped to eliminate Serbia early in the war, at the same time as Germany tied down the Russian armies. The Germans, however, were committed to the Schlieffen plan. This involved three-quarters of the German army launching a swift westwards strike, across Belgium, against France while Austria-Hungary kept Russia busy.

Since then the two general staffs had moved towards a closer cooperation, and had made contingency plans for a coalition war. Moreover, Germany, unlike in Chancellor Otto von Bismarck's time, was prepared to give the Habsburg Empire

unconditional support. Thus, if Austria-Hungary went to war in the Balkans and Russia responded, German troops would be marching over the Belgian frontier a few days later.

In the other camp, too, military arrangements were being strengthened. France was pouring loans into Russia's strategic railway network to facilitate the transportation of the enormous Russian army towards the German and Austro-Hungarian borders. France had also replaced its earlier defensive war-plan with a scheme to launch assaults into Alsace-Lorraine (but keeping its armies out of Belgium). The Moroccan crisis had caused British defence planners to reconsider how best to assist France and Belgium in the event of a European war and a German push westwards. They rejected the idea of using naval operations alone, but favored, in principle, sending an expeditionary force across the Channel. All these decisions further strained international relations and increased the prospect of war.

The French government, encouraged by the nationalist revival, forced through a law extending the period of compulsory military service from two years to three, in a bid to create an army as large as Germany's. Russia, too, by 1912, had announced enormous increases in its armed forces for the following few years, provoking Germany to draw up its own army expansion plan of 1913. Moreover, the German Admiral von Tirpitz, despite opposition from the chancellor and army, managed to increase the size of the High Seas Fleet and its preparedness for battle.

When the British admiralty learned how many German warships would be kept in a state of readiness on the other side of the North Sea, it decided that, to meet the German challenge, there was no alternative but to withdraw the remainder of its large vessels from the Mediterranean. In

▲ The Balkan wars of 1912–13 were a curtain-raiser for the far larger war to follow. The Bulgarian capture of the Turkish fortress of Adrianople was an example of the heavy casualties that modern weaponry could inflict.

◀ The cost borne by the civilian population through brutality and requisition showed that war endangered the lives of not only soldiers.

▶ Cartoon showing the Russian and Austrian emperors wrenching possessions from a sullen and helpless Turkish sultan. The Great Powers came into direct and dangerous rivalry for influence in the unstable patchwork of small states left behind by the collapse of Ottoman power in an area controlled from Constantinople since the Middle Ages.

LE REVEIL DE LA QUESTION D'ORIENT
La Bulgarie proclame son indépendance. — L'Autriche prend la Bosnie et l'Herzégovine

▶▶ **The Balkan wars of 1912–13 saw a jockeying for position among the new states of the region that left a legacy of bitterness quite apart from the dangers implicit in great-power involvement.**

▼ **Military failure and political corruption produced a nationalist revolution in Turkey, which transformed the country into an important player in the European diplomatic game. The Young Turks ruthlessly swept aside the discredited old regime, executed opponents and turned to Germany for military and economic assistance. The presence of another dynamic political force in an unstable area posed a further threat to peace because it suggested an extension of German power into the Entente Powers' areas of interest in the Middle East.**

view of Britain's imperial interests in the region, and the presence of Italian and Austro-Hungarian Dreadnought fleets, it was a very controversial decision to take. After much hesitation, Britain made an agreement with France in November 1912, whereby the French navy would protect British interests in the Mediterranean in exchange for British guarantees of French maritime security in the Channel and southern North Sea. Although there was still no formal military alliance between Britain and France, moral, political and strategic ties drew them closer together.

The Balkan wars
The wars that broke out in the Balkans in 1912 and 1913 represented the most serious consequence of the Morocco crisis. In September 1911, Italy, envious of French colonial gains in Morocco, but powerless to press its own territorial claims in the region, declared war on Turkey with a view to seizing Tripoli as compensation. When this attempt failed, Italy set its sights on the Dode-

canese, bringing the conflict nearer to the Balkans and causing the Turks to close the Straits.

These events worried the Russians and excited the Balkan states – Serbia, Montenegro, Bulgaria, Greece – which for a long time had wished to drive Turkey out of Europe altogether. By October 1912 the Balkan states were at war with Turkey. Austria-Hungary feared that Serbia would expand as far as the Adriatic, while Russia was afraid that Bulgaria would reach Constantinople. Both Great Powers were concerned at the volatility of the small Balkan states and resolved to settle the issue diplomatically. The first Balkan war formally ended at a conference in London in May 1913, with neither Serbia nor Bulgaria achieving its distant objective.

Within a month, however, war broke out again. Bulgaria quarreled with Serbia and Greece over territorial gains, and was in turn attacked by Romania and Turkey. The second Balkan war, which ended in October 1913, stripped Bulgaria of all that it had won earlier. The animosity

The Balkan Wars

▲ **Enver Pasha (1881–1922),** a leader of the Young Turks, with a a key role in modernizing the army and forging links with Germany.

Scale 1 : 10 000 000

- - - International boundary 1912

—— Balkan League

Ottoman lands gained to 1914 by
- Albania
- Bulgaria
- Greece
- Montenegro
- Serbia

Ottoman Empire 1914

1912

March
Bulgaria and Serbia form alliance against Ottoman Empire; Greece and Montenegro join in October, to form Balkan League.

October 8
Montenegro declares war on Ottoman Empire

October 17
Ottoman Empire declares war on Serbia and Bulgaria, after refusing to make reforms in its Balkan territories, as proposed by the Great Powers.

December 3
After Ottoman defeats at the hands of Bulgaria (Kirk Kilisse), and Serbia (Kumanovo), an armistice is called.

1913

May 30
Treaty of London ends first Balkan war; an independent Albania is formed, chiefly to deny Serbia access to the Adriatic. The next day Serbia and Greece sign a secret pact against Bulgaria.

June 29
Serbia and Greece attack Bulgaria. Ottoman Empire separately attack Bulgaria.

August 10
Balkan states sign Treaty of Bucharest.

September 30
Ottoman Empire and Bulgaria sign Treaty of Constantinople.

between Austria-Hungary and Serbia was greater than ever before, and they had come close to the brink of war. Politicians in Berlin felt obliged to stand by their allies in Vienna, but were eager to avoid a war with others of the Great Powers, at least until the summer of 1914. By then, the widening of the Kiel Canal to take Dreadnought-sized battleships would be complete, and the 1913 army increases would have taken effect.

Meanwhile, the news that a German military mission was reorganizing the Turkish armed forces, and a German general was to take command at Constantinople, greatly disturbed the Russians. After extreme tension, both sides accepted a compromise solution in 1914, but the St Petersburg government concluded from the incident that, from then on, not only Austria-Hungary but also Germany would oppose Russia's Balkan interests.

War or peace

Anglo-German relations improved publicly after 1912. Liberals in the British cabinet and Parliament were eager to head off a war, and Britain renegotiated an old agreement about the future disposal of Portugal's colonies in Africa.

However, any similarities to the earlier period of *Weltpolitik* were only superficial. In reality, all non-European controversies were of marginal im-

portance. Despite Britain's discussions with Germany over colonial issues, the two powers could never properly restore harmonious relations so long as the naval race in the North Sea continued unabated and British worries about a German attack upon France and Belgium persisted. Earlier colonial hotspots such as the Far East, Venezuela, the south Pacific, the Transvaal, and the upper Nile, had all faded from the headlines. As both Britain and Germany and their respective allies increased their armaments and streamlined their mobilization schedules, they concentrated their attention on the traditional cockpits of Europe – the Belgian plain, Lorraine and the Balkans.

Of course, a major war was by no means inevitable. The Great Powers had already avoided being drawn into the two earlier Balkan crises, while at home attention focused on domestic issues, such as taxation, social reform and, in Britain, the troubles in Ulster. Diplomatic relations between states proceeded as normal and many felt that the prospects for peace had actually improved. However, it was clear that if there were to be a war in Europe it would involve many countries. The tightening alliance system, the joint military plans, and a plethora of national rivalries would convert any single clash of arms into a massive coalition war, with large and small powers ranged on either side.

THE MISSIONARY MOVEMENT

Reflecting a belief that "the white man" was in the vanguard of history spiritually as well as materially, the 19th century saw a revival of the missionary movement. Organizations both Protestant and Catholic operated from the United States, Britain, Holland, Scandinavia, Germany, Switzerland, France, Belgium and Portugal and competed to turn vast areas of Southeast Asia and Central and southern Africa into parishes of their national churches. The "scramble" for foreign possessions went hand in hand with the contest for the souls and minds of their inhabitants, so that by the turn of the century the missionary movement was well established as a integral part of the "development" of colonies, and was given an international dimension by the setting up in 1910 of the World Missionary Conference (superseded in 1921 by the International Council of Missionaries).

Many missions provided elementary medical services and rudimentary social welfare which from a humanitarian perspective were essential; but the imposition of an alien religion had profoundly disruptive consequences on the integrity of the subject peoples. This was especially the case when it was accompanied by the imposition of an alien language in both spoken and written form. Most devastating of all, Christian evangelism might undermine the basis of the complex ritual and symbolism through which tribes and nations had evolved and maintained their identity, their sense of place and origins.

The cultural imperialism of the missionaries, unwittingly or otherwise, prepared for or colluded with the depredations wrought by commercial and military imperialism. The Ethiopian Emperor Theodore was prompted to comment wryly, "First it's traders and missionaries. Then its ambassadors. After that, they bring the guns. We shall do better to go straight to the guns." The contamination of colonial cultures, generally carried out within artificially imposed territorial boundaries, was perpetuated by the attempts of the more "enlightened" nations to fill minor bureaucratic positions with officials recruited from the indigenous population. In practice this meant the formation of an elite indoctrinated with the Eurocentric vision of history which underpinned imperialism, so that the very people best placed to help their own societies develop autonomously complied with the unraveling of the fine tissue of their native history.

▶▶ The colonizer as a blend of Christ and doctor. It was widely assumed by 19th-century Europeans that as the alleged incarnation of a superior culture "the white man" had a mission to bring spiritual and physical succour to "primitive" peoples.

▶ A white teacher in an African missionary school looks sternly but benignly over her black "flock". Only in the recent decades have anthropologists come to recognize the extraordinary complexity, richness and ecological sanity which tribal cultures possessed before being forcibly "educated" into adopting Western notions of "progress".

▼ Devout missionaries were sufficiently blinded by their own religious convictions to reject native belief systems wholesale and seek to replace them with European creeds and icons.

▶ Even after decolonization the states created by Europeans have generally been retained, along with the alien religion they implanted. Though the stamp with the "present cathedral" is of lower numismatic value than the earlier one, it is presented as more "modern".

◄ Zimbabwe is another nation-state superimposed over existing tribal territories. Though the remaining settlers eventually submitted to black majority, the ceremonial opening of its parliament still celebrates the continuity with British legal institutions, and indirectly the superiority of "white" civilization.

▲ Natives were taught to read and write, ostensibly for philanthropic purposes, but primarily to be more susceptible to European rule. Recently, however, gifted writers have emerged using the colonial *lingua franca* they learned to express instead the unique history of their "ethnic" culture.

Datafile

Behind the growth of the industrial economies and the build-up of national armories, another development was unfolding which would have an equally dramatic effect on 20th-century politics. Economic, demographic and social trends had combined to produce a large, politically-aware industrial workforce that was beginning to articulate its desire for full political representation and a fair share in the general rise in prosperity.

British electorate 1914

30%

70%

Total population (20+) 24,969,210

- Non-eligible
- Electorate

US representation 1901-13

- Republican
- Democrat

Seats (percent)

House of Representatives
Senate

100
75
50
25
0

1901 1903 1905 1907 1909 1911 1913

▲ In almost undisputed control since the end of the American Civil War, the Republicans began to lose ground as new working class voters, many of them recent arrivals, sought a new kind of government.

US Presidents

1901	T H Roosevelt	R
1905	T H Roosevelt	R
1909	W H Taft	R
1913	W Wilson	D

▼ As the new century unfolded, working-class protest began to manifest itself in increasing industrial radicalism. The number of hours lost through strikes rose steeply as workforces sought better pay and conditions, and a larger say in their destinies. Britain suffered the most dramatic rise in strike activity.

UK elections 1900-10

- Conserv & Unionist
- Liberal & Lib Union
- Irish Nationalist
- Labour

Seats in Commons (percent)

100
75
50
25
0

Oct | Jan | Jan | Dec
1900 | 1906 | 1910 | 1910

▲ A slow process of electoral reform had given a proportion of the British working class the vote by 1914, but the majority of the population remained unenfranchised. Despite the rising tide of working class protest, the established political parties maintained their power, though each was forced to adopt social reform policies.

Days lost through industrial militancy 1901-15

- 1901-05
- 1906-10
- 1911-15

Millions

16
12
8
4
0

UK   Germany   France   Belgium

Trade union membership

- 1904
- 1910
- 1914

Millions

3
2
1
0

UK   Germany   France   Italy

▲ High levels of trade union membership in Britain and German were reflections of both the spread of working-class consciousness and the high level of industrialization. In France and Italy forms of working-class association remained smaller and more traditional, and radicalism manifested itself in different forms.

▶ In Russia, the connection between politics and industrial action was more profound than elsewhere in Europe. With its relatively small workforce clustered in the western cities, Russia experienced a rapid politicization of the working class. This manifested itself in high strike activity in times of national crisis.

Strikes in Russia

Thousands

Total strikes

Hundreds

Political strikes

Tens

1905   1908   1911   1914

Apart from Russia, Turkey and tiny Montenegro, all the European nations had some form of parliamentary system. However, the workings of that institution varied from country to country and did not fit any overall democratic pattern. By 1900 the German empire had universal adult male suffrage, whereas in Britain voting was still limited by complicated residence qualifications, so that many working-class men (and, of course, all women) could not vote. On the other hand, the British Parliament had far greater powers than the German Reichstag; and Britons considered their system much more liberal in regard to the freedom of the press, police actions, monarchical privileges, conscription, state controls over the economy, and so on.

In France and the United States, professional, middle-class politicians, once elected, had total control of the country. whereas in Britain, Italy, Germany and Austria-Hungary that power was shared, to different degrees, with a nonelected upper house and the monarchy. In Russia, even after the Duma was set up in 1905 as a consultative-legislative body, control still rested very firmly with the czarist autocracy.

From about the beginning of the century, however, all of these systems came under pressure for changes, which could not easily be effected by constitutional means. While women suffragettes, non-Magyar elements in Hungary, and other groups disadvantaged by the restricted franchises of the day still agitated for electoral reform, newer pressures for social and economic reform from organized labor joined, and often overshadowed, this traditional concern about political rights.

Russia

In 1900 czarist Russia represented the bastion of autocracy. Nicholas II's power was supported by a reactionary aristocracy (who were almost absolute monarchs on their own estates) and mediated by an elaborate array of government inspectors, judicial officials, tax-collectors, and the police. Dissenters either fled abroad or were punished with death or deportation to Siberia. Ethnic minorities were "russified", Jews were persecuted, and the press and intelligentsia came under the constant scrutiny of the secret police.

The widespread unrest and revolutionary upheaval of 1905 shook the regime to its very foundations. Never before had there been so much united opposition and so much pressure for change from so many different groups, including liberal parliamentarians, the St Petersburg workers' soviet (council), peasants, and ethnic minorities in the Baltic states and in Finland, Poland, and Georgia. Yet, despite the concession of a national legislative assembly (Duma) and

POLITICS AND PEOPLE

some civil liberties, within a few years the autocracy had reasserted itself. By 1914, Russia seethed with discontent.

Germany

The unification of Germany had taken place with the support of many of the middle classes, who had been rewarded with a national constitution, a code of laws, and a legislative assembly. However, Bismarck deliberately widened the franchise to include all males over 25 in order to curb the influence of liberal intellectuals and businessmen. Moreover, the individual German states still retained their own very considerable prerogatives and, in Prussia and other states, a restricted three-class franchise ensured that real power remained with the traditional elites. The German parliament, the Reichstag, had no control over the Kaiser or his ministers in matters of

▼ The Russian royal family in the early years of the century exemplified the world of inherited privilege.

foreign policy, military affairs, or war and peace. Frustrated critics termed Prussia-Germany a *Scheindemokratie* ("bogus democracy"). In fact, the Reichstag did possess the power to vote taxes, and included different political parties, even if it was a very restricted form of parliamentary rule, and came under growing pressure from below as Germany became more industrialized. In the few years before 1914, the chancellor, Bethmann Hollweg, found it increasingly difficult to form a coalition of pro-government parties in the Reichstag because of the intransigence of the conservative right and the stated policy of having no dealings with the large Social Democratic party.

Austria-Hungary

Compared with the Habsburg monarchy, Germany was a model of constitutional efficiency. Austria-Hungary was a great conglomeration of

The Duma, Russia's concession to parliament, failed to make the czarist autocracy more democratic

◄ The British House of Commons was often presented as the most successful democratic institution. Its virtues were considered to be its combination of tradition and innovation. In the early 20th century the House of Commons asserted its supremacy over the hereditary House of Lords, and the government was formed by the party that commanded a majority in the Commons.

territories and ethnic groups sharing allegiance to a "common monarchy" but with little else in common. When war came, the mobilization posters had to be prepared in 15 languages.

Pressure from the Magyars in 1867 had forced the government in Vienna to make widespread concessions to the kingdom of Hungary, which, as its price for not breaking up the Austro-Hungarian duocracy, opposed both centralization of the empire and the granting of rights to other nationalities. Whereas in Hungary a ruthless "Magyarization" policy continued to deny representation to ethnic minorities, the *Reichsrat*, the constitutional assembly of Austria (and, in effect, of all the other lands in the empire) was multinational and included Poles, Czechs, Ruthenes and others, as well as Germans. The emperor, his ministers and the imperial bureaucracy had overall charge of Austria-Hungary, including the powers of war and peace, albeit with the need to secure Hungarian support.

Italy

Italy had a monarchy with very considerable powers of appointment, both of ministers and of life-members of the Senate, the upper house. However, central government could not function without control of the Chamber of Deputies, the lower house, whose members were elected on a limited suffrage, though this rose as literacy increased. The most successful prime ministers, such as Giuseppe Zenardelli and Giovanni Giolitti, used widespread bribery and political favors to "oil" the electoral system, and preferred to work with the various factions in the Chamber rather than challenge parliamentary powers, as Luigi Pelloux had tried to do in 1899–1900.

The political malaise that, despite Giolitti's reforms, prevailed in Italy during this period was

caused not so much by constitutional idiosyncrasies, as by cynicism at the overt jobbery and electoral corruption, and, in particular, by economic failure and the widening gap between the north and the south. Loyalty to the Italian state was less deep-rooted than loyalties to the family, church, village or region.

Britain

In contrast to Italy, Britain, another constitutional monarchy, possessed a strong sense of national unity (except in Ireland) that dated back hundreds of years. The king's role was much more honorific, and the complex relationships between the political parties and the executive and legislature were well established. General elections were free of corruption, and victory in them by one or other of the two major parties, Liberals or Conservatives, allowed the administration to carry out, unhindered, its electoral pledges. Politics centered very tightly upon Westminster, and was an honored profession. The British constitution (which was never committed to paper) was widely praised for its balance and utility, which was why Britons felt justified in passing it on to the self-governing Dominions. Whether, however, its delicate mechanisms and gradual adjustment to change could easily withstand new social and fiscal pressures, or a revived Irish nationalism, was still not clear.

The years 1909–14, in particular, placed great strains upon Britain's traditional Parliament-based solutions to problems. For example, in 1910 Asquith's Liberal government called two general elections over the question of the House of Lords' unprecedented obstruction of a money bill. In theory, Britain's unwritten constitution was intended to be very flexible, but in practice, it did not always prove to be so.

The Birth of Bolshevism

By the late 1890s some German Social Democrats, inspired by Eduard Bernstein, had begun to question Marxist predictions about revolution in capitalist society. This so-called "revisionist" school of thought was formally denounced at party conferences, but in fact many Social Democratic politicians leaned towards compromise with the institutions of the German empire. Such apparent backsliding disgusted more radical figures like Rosa Luxemburg, a refugee from czarist oppression and a passionate believer in proletarian revolution.

Inside Russia, gradual progress toward democracy – let alone socialism – seemed unlikely. In 1903 V.I. Lenin split the Russian Social Democratic Labor party by insisting on the need for a highly disciplined revolutionary organization rather than a mass membership movement modeled on those in the west. Lenin's breakaway party, which received majority support, were called Bolsheviks, from the Russian for "more". The other faction were known as Mensheviks (from the Russian for "less"). The Bolshevik party schooled a cadre of professional revolutionaries who were to be the future rulers of the Soviet Union.

◄ Russian poster of Karl Marx, c. 1920.

France and the United States

Constitutionally, France and the United States distinguished themselves by being democratic republics, which had universal male suffrage. (Few countries in the world at that time gave the vote to women.) There were significant differences between the two constitutions, however. Fundamentally, the United States exercised a much stricter division of powers between the executive and the legislature. Compared with the powers of the US Senate, the rights of the upper house in France were limited, as in Britain's House of Lords. The center of politics in France was the Chamber of Deputies, elected from single-member constituencies. Both houses chose the president, but government ministers felt responsible to the Deputies, where voting numbers were really significant.

In both France and the United States the lack of strong party discipline helped to produce individual senators or deputies who were powerful independent figures who had to be wooed by governments that needed their vote. Ideology did affect politics in the legislative assembly (especially, in France, over church–state relations or social issues), but it was very much the place where regional and sectoral interest groups struggled for influence and hammered out compromises over such issues as tariffs. As in Italy or Austria, the effective political figures were those who could, whether by patronage or concession, get together a majority to vote on the matters of the day.

The labor movement

The root cause of the pressure for social and economic reform was industrialization. It had herded workers into factories, steel-mills and shipyards, created mushrooming urban slums close to the workplaces, and given rise to the formation of organizational bodies to protect the interests of the new urban proletariat.

By far the most important of these organizations was the trade union. Trade unions brought together workers of a particular skill into a body to negotiate improvements in wages, hours and working conditions, and which, by the concerted action of withdrawal of labor – the strike – could threaten to bring industrial production to a halt. Such combinations clearly challenged the industrialists' *laissez-faire* creed, as well as their profits, and many factory owners fought to suppress them. The setting up of trade unions was often accompanied by strikes, lockouts, street violence, clashes with the police and legislation, which generally favored the established orders.

In Russia, trade unions were outlawed and strikes were put down by force. In the United States, where some ferocious industrial struggles occurred, trade unions were restrained by the sheer power of the factory owners, as well as the size of the country and the mobility of labor. Italy and France were predominantly agrarian societies in which the unions were really only significant in the industrialized towns and cities of the north. There, they developed syndicalist ideas of using trade unions as a revolutionary force. In Britain and Germany, which were more industrialized, trade-union membership grew rapidly in the

▲ An American socialist delivers an unequivocal message to his government. In the decades before the Great War, the rise of international socialism and other working-class movements seemed to threaten the international political order. Socialists and syndicalists, with their tens of thousands of members, possessed the power to halt the arms race and deny conscript armies the mass manpower needed for war. When war occurred, however, national pride proved stronger than international class consciousness, and the workers of the world shouldered arms to fight against each other.

Votes for Women

The motives of women campaigners for the vote were complex and varied. Some wanted the vote to achieve social reform. Others demanded the vote for working women to bargain for pay and conditions and the right to work. Women of liberal persuasion sought to extend the traditional quest for political democracy to women, and in so doing they came into conflict with intransigent male politicians. Even emergent socialist movements campaigned only for the enfranchisement of the working classes. In the United States women suffragists became distanced from the antislavery movement, which concentrated on registering the black vote.

Means were as varied as motive. Suffragists, such as the 50,000 strong membership of the British National Union of Women's Suffrage Societies, formed the largest groups and followed constitutional means such as non-payment of taxes and extensive lobbying. Much smaller, but better publicized, were the groups of militant suffragettes who used violence against property in their cause; these included the 5,000-member Women's Social and Political Union run by Emmeline and Christabel Pankhurst in Britain and the National Women's Suffrage Association led by Susan Anthony in the United States.

Much of the international contact between these groups was loosely based in the international labor movement, whose priority was working-class emancipation, rather than votes for women. At the 1910 Labor and Socialist International meeting at Copenhagen. British women were condemned for supporting the enfranchisement of propertied women. Yet, the eventual winning of the parliamentary vote owed much to these contacts, as socialists pressed for electoral reform, which included the enfranchisement of women.

New Zealand led the way with a new constitution and women's franchise in 1893; Australia followed in 1901. Finland was the European pioneer (1906) when a new diet was empowered; then Norway (1907). Revolutions in the Soviet Union (1917), Germany and Austria (1918) and China (1925) enfranchised women. British women over 30 gained the vote in 1918, but 21–30-year-olds had to wait till 1928. By 1920 American women had been enfranchised, but out of 20 European states, six (including France) still partially or wholly denied women the vote.

▲ A British suffragette is led away by police in 1914 after participating in an attack on Buckingham Palace. Such militant tactics alienated some liberal support for the cause of women's suffrage, but the sense of crisis generated, together with changes wrought by the impact of the World War, led to a consensus for change in 1918.

► British suffragettes endured prison and forcible feeding while on hunger strike for their cause. After the election of a Liberal government in 1906, seven suffrage bills failed in Parliament and tactics such as hunger-strikes became more common and won a degree of public support, despite male fears about the rationality of women.

◄ A Hungarian suffragist puts her cause to men in a Budapest street in the early 1900s. Women's suffrage was a worldwide cause during this period; in Hungary, too, women won the vote in the new republic set up in 1918.

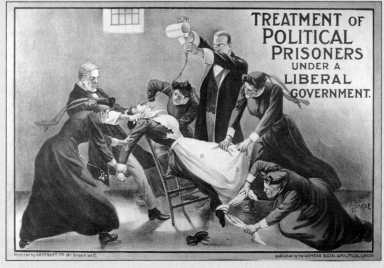

TREATMENT OF POLITICAL PRISONERS UNDER A LIBERAL GOVERNMENT.

published by the WOMEN'S SOCIAL & POLITICAL UNION

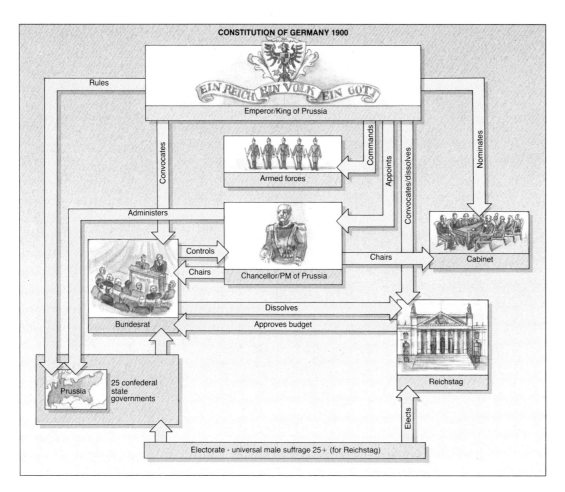

CONSTITUTION OF GERMANY 1900

EIN REICH EIN VOLK EIN GOTT

Emperor/King of Prussia

Rules
Convocates
Administers
Controls
Chairs
Chairs
Commands
Appoints
Convocates/dissolves
Nominates
Armed forces
Chancellor/PM of Prussia
Cabinet
Chairs
Dissolves
Approves budget
Bundesrat
Reichstag
Prussia
25 confederal state governments
Elects
Electorate - universal male suffrage 25+ (for Reichstag)

◄ The German empire was a classic example of a constitution that sought to provide a strong central authority by focusing power in the hands of two men – the emperor (president) and his chancellor. Both men usually held equivalent positions within Prussia, and the dominance of that state within Germany assured their authority throughout the empire. The crucial role of chairmanship of the Bundesrat (federal council), at which members of all the German states approved imperial policy. The Reichstag had been set up in 1871 as a concession to democracy, and could vote on legislation and exercised a degree of budgetary control over the Bundesrat. Some of the state governments also included a small democratic element within them. By the early 1900s opposition in the Reichstag was growing more effective with the development of liberal and socialist parties. This constitution was swept away in 1918.

years before 1914, among both unskilled and skilled workers, making them a new, if uncertain force in national politics.

The reaction of the aristocratic or middle-class governing elites to the rise of trade unionism, and to the industrial proletariat as a whole, was usually hostile. The movement received some support, however, from among French radicals, American Democrats and certain British Liberals, who argued for social and economic reforms and regarded the growing workforce as a potential source of electoral support. By broadening the political agenda to include socioeconomic issues, they hoped to absorb this new class within the system and so preserve its essential stability.

In many countries of Europe (less so in Britain and the United States) organized labor had long been influenced by the socialist ideas of Karl Marx and Friedrich Engels, and by their vision of a complete transformation of political and economic relationships along egalitarian lines. Such programs (and even more, the anarchist doctrines of Pierre Proudhon and Mikhail Bakunin) called for the revolutionary overthrow of the existing order. Nevertheless, many trade-union leaders began to accept the utility of electing working-class representatives into their national assemblies, to influence legislation.

The newly formed Labour party in Britain gained 29 members of parliament in the 1906 election, while its counterpart in Germany, the Social Democratic party, though professedly revolutionary Marxist, worked through the existing quasi-democratic structures to become the largest

single party in the Reichstag at the 1912 elections.

To many among the older elites, the growth of trade unions and socialist parties posed the greatest threat to the internal order of the country. Even more alarming to them was the fact that the various national organizations were also members of the International, committed to the advance of the working classes everywhere. On their side, the labor movements encountered enormous difficulties, quite apart from harassment by the police and tough measures by employers to resist their influence. Most trade unionists, in fact, wanted improved pay and conditions, not social revolution. Many were strongly patriotic, and unlikely to join in any international strike that might be called to oppose a war. Moreover, socialist programs did not appeal to peasant smallholders across Europe or to the American farmer, and they were attacked by anarchists and other revolutionaries. Neither did they win the support of ethnic minorities to whom they seemed irrelevant.

Some of the more desperate and reactionary elites wanted to imitate the czarist regime by using force to quash trade union and socialist movements. Most governments, however, looked for more subtle ways to keep them in check and reduce their revolutionary appeal. Significantly, in many Western countries, state spending on education and health, and in other domestic areas, rose steadily in this period, as did taxes. Labor's rise had brought social issues to the fore, and greatly added to the problems that confronted politicians in the decade after 1900.

▲ US president Theodore Roosevelt on the campaign trail in 1903. The growth of democracy meant that politicians were increasingly forced to defend their actions to the public; Roosevelt in particular brought a fresh populism to the US political scene.

CONSTITUTION OF UNITED KINGDOM 1900

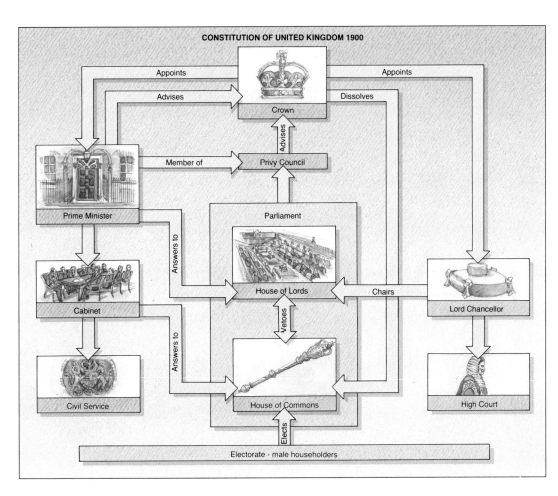

◀ The British system has never been formalized in the same way as the German or US constitutions, and the division of power between the branches of government is more pragmatic than theoretical. By the early 20th century the power of the Crown played a role that was advisory and ceremonial, with most power in the hands of Parliament. The prime minister, though appointed by the Crown, was the person, usually leader of the majority party in the Commons, who could command a majority in the Commons. The House of Lords retained a veto over decisions of the Commons until 1911, when its powers were limited to delaying legislation. From the same date, the maximum term of a Parliament before fresh elections were called was reduced from seven years to five. Universal male suffrage was introduced in 1918, with women given identical voting rights in 1928.

CONSTITUTION OF UNITED STATES 1900

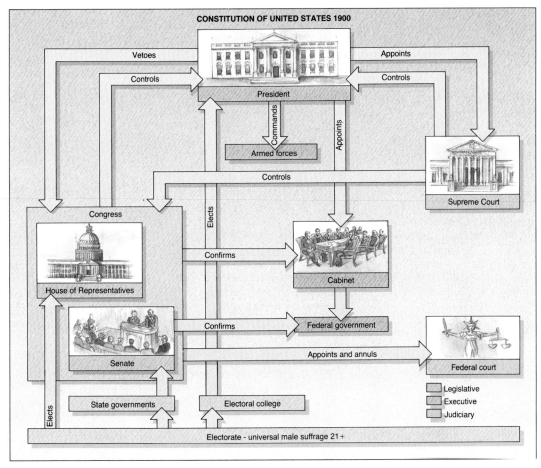

◀ The constitution of the United States was established by the Founding Fathers in 1787, and has been modified only 26 times since. It is based on the classic division of powers between the executive, legislature and judiciary, and seeks to impose a set of checks and balances to ensure that central government does not impose itself on the rights of individuals or of the individual states. Congress, the supreme legislative body, is made up of two houses, with direct elections to the House of Representatives. Until 1913, the members of the Senate were selected by the state governments; thereafter direct elections were introduced. The Supreme Court has the power to declare any act of the president, or decision of Congress, illegal.

1914 · 1929

THE REVOLUTIONARY FLOOD

Time Chart

	1915	1916	1917	1918	1919	1920	1921
Europe/Mediterranean	• 18 Mar, Dardanelles Straits: Attempted naval attack on Turkish defenses by Allies • 26 Apr: Secret treaty between Allies and Italy, breaking Triple Alliance (Ger, Aut-Hung, Ita) • 10 May: 1st Zeppelin raid on London (UK) • 5 Sep: Tsar Nicholas II took personal command of Russian forces	• 21 Feb – 18 Dec, Battle of Verdun (Fr): Heavy French and German casualties • 24 – 29 Apr: Easter uprising in Dublin (Ire), seeking immediate independence from UK • 31 May – 1 Jun, Battle of Jutland: Principal naval engagement of WWI • 1 Jul – 19 Nov, Battle of the Somme (Fr): 600,000 Allied deaths	• 15 Mar: Abdication of Nicholas II, following March Revolution • 27 Jun: Prime Minister Venizelos' government brought Greece into WWI on side of the Allies • 29 Jul: Finland declared independence from Russia • 31 Jul – 10 Nov, 3rd Battle of Ypres (Bel): Combined UK, Australian and Canadian offensive • 6 – 8 Nov (Old Style: 24 – 26 Oct): Bolshevik Revolution in Russia	• Married women over 30 given vote in UK • 3 Mar: Treaty of Brest-Litovsk: Central Powers (Ger, Aut-Hung, Tur, Bulg) and Russia • Jun: Civil war in Russia between opposing armies • Jul: Execution of Russian royal family • 9 – 10 Nov: Kaiser Wilhelm II forced to abdicate and exiled • 11 Nov: WWI ended, with signature of armistice by Germany and Allies • 12 – 16 Nov: Separate republics of Austria and Hungary proclaimed	• 12 Jan: Socialist uprising, Berlin (Ger) • Jan: Irish Republic declared, Dublin; start of Anglo–Irish War • 18 Jan: Opening of Paris Peace Conference (PPC) • 23 Mar: Formation of Italian fascist party • 28 Jun: Germany signed Treaty of Versailles • 31 Jul: German Weimar Republic established • 10 Sep: Treaty of St Germain: Austrian republic and Allies • 27 Nov: Treaty of Neuilly: Bulgaria and Allies	• Foundation of UK Communist Party • Mar: UK parliament's Home Rule Act passed, dividing Ireland into N (6 counties) and S (26 counties) • 1 Mar: Miklós Horthy became regent of Hungary (ruling for 24 years) • 4 Jun: Hungary cut to ⅓ pre-war size by Treaty of Trianon • Nov: Defeat of White armies in Crimea ended Russian civil war	• Italian Communist Party founded by Antonio Gramsci • Feb: UK unemployment exceeded 1,000,000 • Apr: German war reparations fixed at £6600 million plus interest • 14 May: Fascists gained 29 seats in Italian parliament • 16 Dec: UK parliament ratified peace agreement ending Anglo–Irish war and recognizing Irish Free State (S Ire) as a dominion within Commonwealth
The Middle East	• 25 Apr: 1st Allied landing on Gallipoli Peninsula; Australian and New Zealand troops at Anzac Cove • 6 Nov: Indian Division landed on Persian Gulf beginning successful occupation of region • 22 Nov: Mohandas Gandhi returned to India from S Africa	• 16 May: By Sykes–Picot Agreement, UK and France secretly planned partition of Turkish empire • Jun: Start of Arab Revolt against Turkish rule in the Hejaz (Arabia) • Nov: Lucknow Pact between Indian Hindus and Muslims • Dec: UK recognized Emir Hussein as king of the Hejaz	• 2 Nov, Balfour Declaration: UK stated support for establishment of Jewish homeland in Palestine • Dec: Allied capture of Jerusalem (Pal)	• Imam Yahya became king of Yemen • Sep–Oct: Allies captured Beirut and Aleppo (Syria) • 1 Oct: Arab forces entered Damascus (Syria) • 30 Oct: Signature of armistice by Turkey and Allies • UK rejection of Egyptian nationalist delegation led to formation of *Wafd* (delegation) Party	• 13 Apr: Unarmed protesters massacred by UK troops at Amritsar (Ind) • May: Mustafa Kemal (Atatürk) began nationalist revolution in Turkey • 10 Aug: Turkish empire dismembered by Treaty of Sèvres • Nov: Egypt granted constitution by UK • Dec: UK's India Act set up elected bicameral parliament	• Apr: Syria and Lebanon became French mandates; Mesopotamia (Irq) and Palestine, UK mandates • 23 Apr: In Turkey, Mustafa Kemal (Atatürk) became 1st president of provisional republican government • Sep: Indian Congress Party adopted Gandhi's program of non-violent noncooperation (*satyagraha*)	• Coup in Persia led by Colonel Reza Khan • May: Nationalist riots in Egypt suppressed by UK troops • Jul: Start of rebellion in Spanish Morocco; Riff Arabs led by nationalist Abdel Krim • 23 Aug: Emir Faisal crowned king of Iraq (Faisal I)
Africa	• Jun: Start of main Allied campaign in Cameroons (to Jan 1916) • 9 Jul: German SW Africa surrendered to forces led by S African Prime Minister Botha	• 4 Sep: Allied capture of Dar Es Salaam, seat of government of German E Africa			• Anglo–French partition of Cameroons and Togoland (former German W African protectorates); mandates later issued by League of Nations • SW Africa mandated to Union of S Africa	• League of Nations mandate divided German E Africa between UK and Belgium, creating Tanganyika and Ruanda-Urundi • Jul: Kenya (E Afr) made a UK crown colony	• Formation of Kikuyu Association in Kenya (E Afr)
The Americas	• Ku Klux Klan revival (US) • 7 May: Sinking of UK passenger liner *Lusitania* by German U-boat; loss of 128 US lives • Jun: League to Enforce Peace founded in US • 27–8 Jul: Assassination of Haitian president then US marine occupation invoking Monroe Doctrine (to Aug 1934)	• Punitive US expedition into Mexico after rebel forces killed 17 Americans • Sep, Adamson Act: 8-hour working day on US interstate railroads • 7 Nov: Jeannette Rankin became 1st female member of US Congress • 29 Nov: US military rule in Dominican Republic	• US marine guard in Nicaragua (to 1933) • Feb: US broke diplomatic ties with Germany • Feb: Mexico adopted new constitution • Mar: Puerto Ricans made US citizens • 6 Apr: US declared war against Germany		• Founding of US Communist Party, under William Foster • 29 Jan: Prohibition constituted in US (to 1933), by 18th Amendment • 19 Nov: US Senate voted against ratifying Treaty of Versailles, thereby excluding US from League of Nations	• Jan: 1000s arrested in US Communist scare • 26 Aug: US women enfranchised, by 19th Amendment • 1 Dec: Alvaro Obregón elected president of Mexico	• 18 Oct: US Senate ratified peace treaties with Germany, Austria and Hungary
Asia and Pacific	• 18 Jan: Japan presented its 21 Demands to China, in attempt to establish virtual protectorate	• New Zealand's 1st Labour Party formed	• Siam declared war on Germany • Aug: China declared war on Germany • Dec: Australians rejected conscription in their 2nd referendum; nearly half million volunteered during WWI	• Sep: Nationalists (Kuomintang), under leadership of Sun Yat-sen, organized provisional Chinese government at Canton, in opposition to official government in Peking	• By Treaty of Versailles, control of Shandong province (Chn) officially transferred from Germany to Japan	• Australian Communist and Country parties founded	• Jul: Foundation of Chinese Communist Party by Chen Tu-hsiu and Li Ta-chao • 5 Nov: Crown Prince Hirohito became regent of Japan
World	• 22 Apr: Germany was 1st country to use poison gas, on Western Front	• Sep: 1st use of tanks in warfare, on Western Front		• 8 Jan: US President Wilson outlined his 14 Points for world peace	• International Labor Organization formed • Feb: League of Nations pledged support at PPC • Mar: Founding of 3rd International (Komintern)	• Dec: 1st full meeting of League of Nations Assembly, in Geneva (Sui), attended by 41 nations	• 12 Nov (to Feb 1922): Washington Conference on naval disarmament and the Pacific (US, UK, Fr, Ita, Neth, Bel, Port, Chn, Jap)

1922	1923	1924	1925	1926	1927	1928	1929
16 Apr: Treaty [of] Rapallo between [Ge]rmany and USSR, [r]establishing [di]plomatic and [ec]onomic relations 24 Jun: [as]sassination of [Ge]rman foreign [mi]nister Walther [Ra]thenau, a Jew, by [ri]ghtwing nationalists 30 Oct: Mussolini [in]vited to become [pri]me minister by [Vi]ctor Emmanuel III 30 Dec: Russia [be]came Union of [So]viet Socialist [Re]publics (USSR)	• 11 Jan: Occupation of Ruhr (Ger) by French and Belgian troops • Apr: Josef Stalin became head of USSR Communist Party • 10 Jul: All nonfascist parties abolished (Ita) • 13 Sep: General Miguel Primo de Rivera became dictator of Spain • 8–9 Nov, Munich Putsch: Hitler's failure to overthrow Bavarian state government (Ger) • 20 Nov: Introduction of *Rentenmark*, to curb inflation (Ger)	• Republican Party founded in Spain by Manuel Azaña • Jan–Oct: UK's 1st Labour goverment, under Ramsay MacDonald • 21 Jan: Death of Lenin (USSR) • 25 Mar: Greek republic proclaimed • Apr: Fascist party victory in Italian general election • 16 Aug: Dawes Plan on reparation payments agreed by Germany and Allies • 30 Aug: Introduction of *Reichsmark* (Ger)	• 25 Apr: Field Marshal von Hindenburg became Germany's 1st elected president • Oct: Arrests after police raid on UK Communist Party HQ • Nov: Foundation of SS by Nazis (Ger) • 1 Dec, Locarno Pact: Treaties signed by European powers (Ger, Bel, Fr, UK, Ita); French and Belgian borders with Germany confirmed; Rhineland made a demilitarized zone	• Jan: Mussolini assumed power to rule by decree (Ita) • Jan–Aug: Theodoros Pangalos ruled Greece as a dictator • May: UK's 1st General Strike, in support of coal miners' dispute • May: Military coup in Poland, led by Józef Pilsudski (effective dictator to 1935)	• UK Trades Disputes Act outlawed general strikes and compulsory political levying by trade unions • Jan: End of Allied military control of Germany • Jul: Clashes between *Heimwehr* (fascist) and *Schutzbund* (socialist) private armies in Vienna (Aut) • Oct: Norway's 1st Labor government elected • Dec: Trotsky expelled from Communist Party (USSR)	• Launch of Stalin's 1st Five–year Plan in USSR; beginning of land collectivization • Italian Communist Party leader, Antonio Gramsci, sentenced to 20 years' imprisonment • May: In UK, suffrage extended to women over 21	• Liquidation of *kulaks* (farmers) ordered by Stalin (USSR) • Jan: Alexander I of the Serbo-Croat-Slovenes (3 Oct, Yugoslavia) set up a royal dictatorship • Jan: 7-hour working day introduced (USSR) • 11 Feb: Lateran Treaty established Vatican as City State, ruled by Pope • May: Little Entente signed (Tch, Yugo, Rom) • Aug: Germany accepted Young Plan for war reparations
[UK] protectorate [over] Egypt ended [Feb]: Suppression [of] 6-month Muslim [re]bellion in Indian [pr]ovince of Malabar; [be]ginning of renewed [Hi]ndu–Muslim tension [Mar]: Gandhi sen[te]nced to 6 years in [pri]son for sedition (Ind) [Sep]: Turkish capture [of] Smyrna ended Greek [pr]esence in Asia Minor	• Tangier (Mor) declared an international free port • 15 Mar: Sultan Ahmed Fuad proclaimed King Fuad I of Egypt • 24 Jul: Treaty of Lausanne between Turkey and Allies, renegotiating 1920 Treaty of Sèvres • 29 Oct: Turkish republic proclaimed, with Mustafa Kemal (Atatürk) as president	• Mecca (Arabia) captured by forces of Emir Ibn Saud • Feb: Gandhi released from prison (Ind) • Mar: Caliphate (spiritual leadership of Islam) abolished in Turkey • 15 Mar: Opening of 1st Egyptian parliament	• Riff rebels under Abdel Krim pushed south into French Morocco, having expelled Spanish from north • Jul: Opening of Iraq's 1st parliament, in Baghdad • Druse uprising began in Syria, against French military presence (to Jun 1927)	• Lebanon proclaimed a republic • 8 Jan: Ibn Saud declared himself king of Hejaz and Nejd (Arabia), overthrowing King Hussein • Apr: Pahlevi dynasty founded in Persia, as Reza Khan crowned shah in Tehran • May: Moroccan nationalist Abdel Krim surrendered to Franco–Spanish army led by Marshal Pétain	• May: King Ibn Saud of Hejaz and Nejd (Arabia) recognized by UK		• Jan–Oct: Civil war in Afghanistan, led by Habibullah, resulted in election of Nadir Khan as king • Aug: Arab–Jewish clashes in Jerusalem (Pal) led to 250 deaths • Dec: Turkish women enfranchised
12 Sep: UK formally [an]nexed S Rhodesia as [s]elf-governing colony	• Segregationalist Nationalist Party in coalition government with Labor Party; James Hertzog as prime minister (S Afr) • N Rhodesia formally made a UK protectorate	• Afrikaans made official language of Union of S Africa	• Joint Front set up between ANC and Indian community (S Afr)	• Friendship and arbitration treaty signed by Ethiopia (Abyssinia) and Italy			
[Central] American [C]onference met, in [W]ashington (US); [Pan-]American Court of [Ju]stice reinstituted	• 3 Aug: Calvin Coolidge sworn in as US president, on death of Warren Harding • Dec: US support for President Obregón of Mexico against right-wing military uprising	• Johnson–Reed Act set US immigration at 2% of each nationality as 1890 census • General Plutarcho Calles elected Mexican president • Jul: End of US military occupation of Dominican Republic; constitutional government set up under Pres. Horacio Vázquez	• 170-day miners' strike in US • 5 Mar – 3 May: 5th Pan-American Conference, Santiago (Chi); Gondra Treaty on prevention of conflict • Aug: 1st national congress of Ku Klux Klan (US)	• 31 Jul: Mexican priests began a strike (to 1929), after enforcement of anti-clerical clauses of 1917 constitution	• Canadian autonomy within Commonwealth reaffirmed by opening of embassy in Washington, DC (US) • Escalation of dispute between Paraguay and Bolivia over Chaco Boreal • Beginning of guerrilla resistance to US intervention in Nicaragua	• Jun: US Agricultural Marketing Act encouraged establishment of farming cooperative associations • 7 Nov: Republican Herbert Hoover elected US president	• May: Revised US tariff legislation increased duties payable; led to retaliation by overseas nations • Aug: League of Nations arbitration convention rejected by Paraguay and Bolivia
			• Vietnamese Nationalist (1931, Indochinese Communist) Party founded by Nguyen Ai Quoc (Ho Chi Minh) • 12 Mar: In China, death of Sun Yat-sen; Jiang Jieshi made leader of Kuomintang	• Start of Communist-led nationalist uprising in Dutch E Indies (until 1927) • 25 Dec: Hirohito became emperor of Japan on death of father	• Mar: US/UK shelling of Nanking (Chn) after Nationalist capture • 12 Apr: Communist purge in Shanghai (Chn) • Jun: Indonesian Nationalist Party (PNI) founded	• Apr: Japanese troops began year-long occupation of China's Shandong province • Oct: Jiang Jieshi established Nationalist government at Nanking, claiming control of unified China	• Indonesian nationalist leaders, including Achmed Sukarno, gaoled (Dutch E Indies)
15 Feb: 1st sitting [of] Permanent Inter[na]tional Court of [Ju]stice, at The [Ha]gue (Neth)	• Sep: Dominions' right to make foreign treaties recognized by UK at Imperial conference in London			• Germany joined League of Nations		• 27 Aug: Kellogg–Briand Pact (renouncing war as an instrument of national policy) signed by 15 nations in Paris (Fr)	• 24 Oct, Black Thursday: Depression ushered in by panic selling of 13 million shares on Wall Street (US)

Datafile

The Great War was a vast struggle of attrition in which industrial and military mobilization held the key to success. The major combatants maintained mass armies in the field for four years, supplying them with thousands of tonnes of shells, food and other supplies. The naval powers also maintained large battlefleets, with extensive requirements for fuel, ammunition and manpower. And as the war developed, every combatant was forced to devote resources to the development of a third arm, capable of taking the war to the enemy by air. The human and material cost of this effort was immense. Mass war produces mass casualties, and advances in military technology – particularly in the form of the high explosive shell and the machine-gun – reduced land warfare to a grim struggle of attrition in which victory went to the army which could sustain huge losses the longest. The human slaughter was underpinned by an equally great economic effort. The highly developed industrial economies of the Great Powers were mobilized to produce vast quantities of military equipment.

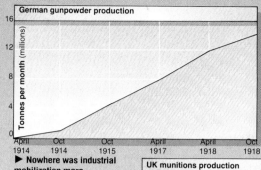

◄ The economies of the combatant powers were restructured to meet the increasing demands of the war. Factories and workers were switched away from their normal peacetime activities to produce the materials of war. The effects are made clear by statistics for German gunpowder production which increased fourteenfold in four years.

► Nowhere was industrial mobilization more impressive than in Britain. UK munitions production increased by factors varying between 500 and 1000 percent – an achievement which allowed Britain to expand its volunteer army to match the much larger conscript forces of its continental allies and enemies.

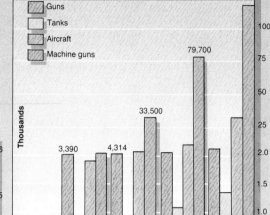

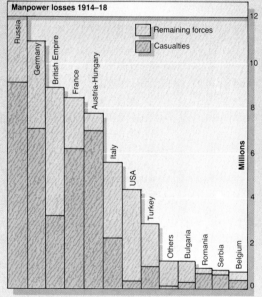

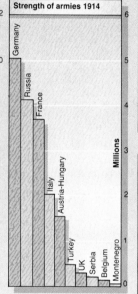

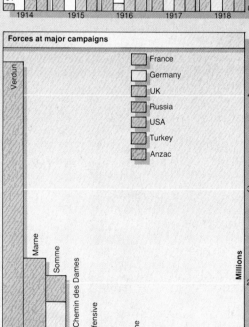

▲ Europe became a continent in arms, with millions of young men donning the uniforms of their countries and serving in the trenches. The scale and duration of the fighting produced an inevitably heavy toll in casualties – the dead, wounded and prisoners were also numbered in millions, accounting in many cases for over half the total mobilized.

◄ The failure of Germany's surface fleet to make an impact on the war placed the U-boats (submarines) in the forefront of the naval struggle. While German submarines sank millions of tonnes of Allied merchantmen, the cost was high – well over half of the U-boats deployed were lost to mines, marine hazard and anti-submarine weapons.

▲ Superior German organization and economic mobilization produced the largest army to take the field in 1914 with 5 million men marching to the guns. Only Russia and France fielded forces on the same scale. Of the other original combatants, only Britain had the capacity to produce a force of equivalent size under wartime conditions.

► The large battles fought on the Western and Eastern Fronts were bloody, sprawling engagements which dragged on for weeks and sometimes months, drawing in millions of men. Verdun, the epic battle for the strategic center of France's defenses, dwarfed all others in scale, but everywhere the scale of the fighting was immense.

THE GREAT WAR

▼ French reservists on their way to a military depot to join the colors in 1914. When war broke out, the Great Powers mobilized millions of working-class conscripts, the vast majority of whom reported to their units without protest.

By the spring and early summer of 1914 the international situation seemed to have entered a period of relative calm. The Balkan wars had been settled, Anglo-German naval rivalry had diminished, and there were no crises looming in colonial affairs. This gave rise to the view, which became popular after World War I, that the Great Powers stumbled into a global conflict by a series of accidents. Lloyd George, British prime minister from 1916 to 1922, later said that the belligerents "slithered over the edge into war".

In reality most of the major European governments felt that the need to protect their vital interests could justify a war. The Germans had prepared themselves for a showdown with Russia and the Austrian government yearned to assert itself in the Balkans. President Poincaré was determined not to give the Russians a chance to renege on their alliance with France while the czar could not afford to ignore the strength of nationalist feelings at home.

The apparent cause of the war was the assas-sination of the heir to the Habsburg throne the archduke Franz-Ferdinand during a visit to Sarajevo on 28 June 1914. The culprits were Bosnian Serbs who had some links with the Serbian military but not, as the Austrians claimed, with the Serbian government. Austria used the affair as an excuse to demand a settlement of accounts with Serbia. Significantly the German kaiser and his ministers, rather than hold the Austrians back, encouraged this aggressive design. On 23 July politicians in Vienna presented Belgrade with an ultimatum drawn up in collusion with the Germans. The Serbs' unexpectedly soft reply, combined with British and Russian attempts to urge conciliation, might have caused the kaiser to waver had it not been for the determination of his generals. Thus Austria-Hungary declared war on Serbia on 28 July. Two days later the Russian government, unable to stand by and let Serbia be crushed, ordered mobilization. The Germans' war plan depended on speed. Their intended campaign – the famous Schlieffen plan – required

The Italian people were divided in their attitude to the war from the outset

World War I in Europe

1914	**1915**	**1916**	**1917**	**1918**
August 3 Germany invades Belgium, intending to march on Paris.	**February 8–22** Russians are forced to retreat on the Eastern Front.	**February 21–December 18** Germans launch a massive but unsuccessful attack on Verdun.	**April 6** USA enters war on Allied side.	**March 21** Germany launches Spring offensive on Western Front.
August 26–30 Germany defeats a Russian advance at Tannenberg.	**March 10–13** Battle of Neuve Chapelle.	**May 31–June 1** Decisive sea battle at Jutland.	**April 16–29** French offensive on Western Front bringing little gain.	**July 18–November 10** Allied counteroffensive drives Western Front eastwards, and peace initiatives by Germany lead to the signing of the Armistice on November 11.
September 5–10 Westward German advance halted by French and British in early September, leading to trench warfare.	**April 25** Allied offensive at Gallipoli, abandoned January 1916.	**June 4–October 10** Brusilov offensive by Russia drives back Austria-Hungary	**July 31–November 10** Allies make minor advance at Third Battle of Ypres.	
	September 25–October 6 French offensive on Western Front, with limited results.	**July 1–November 19** Little gain after costly British offensive on Western Front.	**October 24–November 10** Central Powers defeat Italy at Caporetto.	

▲ **The Great War involved continuous military operations on four fronts around the Central Powers alliance of Germany and Austria-Hungary. On the Western Front, stretching from Switzerland north to the English Channel, the Germans confronted the British, French and Belgians, while on the Eastern Front the two Central Powers stood together against Russia until revolution took Russia out of the war. In the Balkans, operations centered first on Serbia and then in Salonika, with Bulgaria joining the Central Powers in 1915 and Romania joining briefly the Allies in 1916. Italy entered the war on the Allied side in 1915.**

them to knock France out of the fight first, enabling them to deal at leisure with Russia. It also involved a massive drive through Belgium in an attempt to encircle Paris. The day after the Russians announced general mobilization the Germans issued an ultimatum to St Petersburg, before declaring war on Russia on 1 August. The French faced a German demand to remain neutral. When they refused to comply, the Germans also declared war on France on 3 August, having on the previous day demanded that Belgium give free passage to their troops. This last action tipped the balance in Britain, where the Liberal cabinet had been divided in its attitude to the conflict. Germany had wanted Britain to stay neutral but such hopes were dashed when Britain too entered the fray, declaring war on Germany on 4 August 1914.

Early deadlock in the fighting
Early on the French embarked on offensives in Alsace-Lorraine and the Ardennes but these failed. The German sweep through Belgium looked as if it would succeed until the French commander, General Joseph Joffre, halted the Germans north of Paris and forced them back at the battle of the Marne, which began on 6 September 1914. By 10 September the Germans realized that the rapid victory they had sought would be denied them. The German commander Helmuth von Moltke was held responsible for the failure and replaced by Erich von Falkenhayn. On the Eastern Front the Germans were more successful. They repulsed a brief Russian assault on the provinces of Prussia and inflicted a massive defeat on the Russian army at the battle of Tannenberg on 27 August. Meanwhile Allied supply routes to

southern Russia had been cut after the Germans had forced Turkey into an alliance on 2 August. The Turks also closed the Dardanelles straits at the end of September. On 1 November the Entente powers, as Russia, France and Britain were known, declared war on Turkey.

In the west a line of trenches and dugouts now extended from Switzerland to the Belgian coast. The losses on both sides were running into hundreds of thousands of men. Ammunition was used up so fast and so much of it was wasted that offensives sometimes petered out altogether. In 1915 the Entente powers attacked Turkey to break the deadlock and to reopen the Black Sea link with Russia. They also aimed to bring Italy into the war on their side. Both attempts failed. The British expedition to the Dardanelles proved too costly and was abandoned in the summer of 1915. Those supplies that the Allies could spare for Russia had to go through the ports of Archangel and Murmansk and did not greatly affect the the war on the Eastern Front.

As a price for their support the Italians were promised Albania, northern Dalmatia, Istria and the Tyrol by the Treaty of London of 26 April 1915. Italy entered the war against Germany and Austria on 23 May. In November 1917 the Italian army was heavily defeated by Austro-German forces at Caporetto and did not take the offensive again until October 1918 when the Austro-Hungarian empire was already in a state of collapse.

Fighting on land and by sea

In the east the Germans did well in 1915. On 4 May they and the Austrians broke the Russian

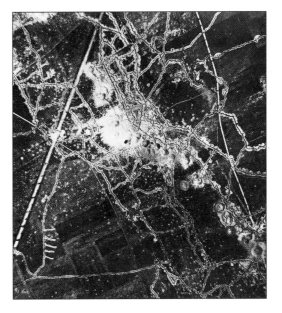

◀ The spider's web of stalemate – an aerial view of trench networks on the Western Front. These entrenchments were continuous defensive lines, supported by a network of trenches and strongpoints over several miles and protected by thick barbed wire barriers. For four years, massed artillery bombardment and infantry attack proved incapable of breaking cleanly through these lines, and the armies of the Western Front fought back and forth across a narrow zone, losing millions of men in the process.

▼ A British tank with supporting infantry. Introduced by the British in 1916, the tank was to prove one of the most influential weapons of World War II. Early tanks were slow, unreliable and vulnerable to artillery fire, and often they operated over terrain that was so waterlogged that their cross-country performance was of little benefit. Used in close cooperation with other arms, they could take local objectives with minimal losses, but these successes were insufficient for a decisive breakthrough.

line at Gorlice. By September Russia had lost Poland and Lithuania. Bulgaria came into the war on Germany's side on 14 October and overran Serbia. Yet Russia remained in the war and even took the offensive again in May 1916, inflicting defeats on the Austrian army.

In the west the German commander Erich von Falkenhayn tried to wear the French down by launching an offensive at Verdun. This lasted from 21 February 1916 until the middle of July 1916, proving a dismal failure and resulting in a loss of almost 300,000 men on each side. An Anglo-French offensive launched on the Somme on 1 July 1916 was also hideously profligate of

human lives. Other offensives by the French general Robert Nivelle and by Sir Douglas Haig, the British commander-in-chief, in the spring and summer of 1917, were equally futile and costly in lives. Indeed, after the April offensive some of the French army mutinied.

By sea the Entente forces were more successful. One of their most effective weapons was the naval blockade, organized by the British to cut off trade from overseas. At the same time, the Entente benefited from supplies purchased and financed (largely on credit) from the United States, since the German navy was too weak to challenge this traffic. Its only major excursion on to the high seas resulted in the battle of Jutland on 31 May 1916, in which the British sustained heavy losses but drove the Germans back to home ports (from where they did not re-emerge until 1919 when they sailed to Scapa Flow and scuttled their fleet to avoid capture).

Consequently, the Germans decided to blockade Britain by means of U-boat warfare against Entente shipping lanes. The attempted blockade began in February 1917 despite the grave misgivings of civilian German political leaders, who feared that it would bring the United States into the war. In fact the German submarine fleet was not large enough to blockade Britain effectively. The British, on Lloyd George's insistence, adopted the convoy system which, despite heavy losses, enabled them to survive the onslaught.

In the United States President Woodrow Wilson's government, infuriated by attacks on American nationals and irritated by German intrigue in Mexico, declared war on Germany on 6 April 1917. The fact that revolution had broken out in Russia in March and the czar had been deposed spared the Americans the embarrassment of fighting shoulder-to-shoulder with an autocracy. The decision to enter the war could thus be justified as defending democracy against militarism and authoritarian Germanic regimes.

The end of the Great War
In the Far East the Allies received valuable support from the Japanese, who had entered the war on 23 August 1914. Japan gave naval assistance to Britain in the Pacific and Indian Oceans and at one point in the war Japanese naval vessels patrolled the Red Sea. Japan's status as an allied power encouraged it to seek greater influence outside its borders, particularly in China, after the Japanese had driven the Germans from the Shantung Peninsula on 18 January 1915.

By the early summer of 1918 it was clear that the Germans were running out of steam. A combination of fresh US troops, improved Anglo-French tactics, air superiority and the use of tanks made the German's prospects hopeless. On 8 August the British broke through on the Marne and on 28 September Ludendorff admitted to the civilian politicians in Germany that victory was no longer possible. Germany's allies also faced defeat. Austria-Hungary's renewed offensive against Italy petered out with heavy losses on 24 June 1918 and desertions from the Habsburg

▼ Military planning in the Great War was often uninspired and out of touch with the real situation at the front. Despite repeated failures and horrendous casualties commanders clung to the idea of the decisive breakthrough and many (but by no means all) were unaware of the daily horrors that their men had to face. However, the deadlock and heavy loss of life were not due solely to a failure of command; technological developments and the sheer scale of the military endeavor were also to blame.

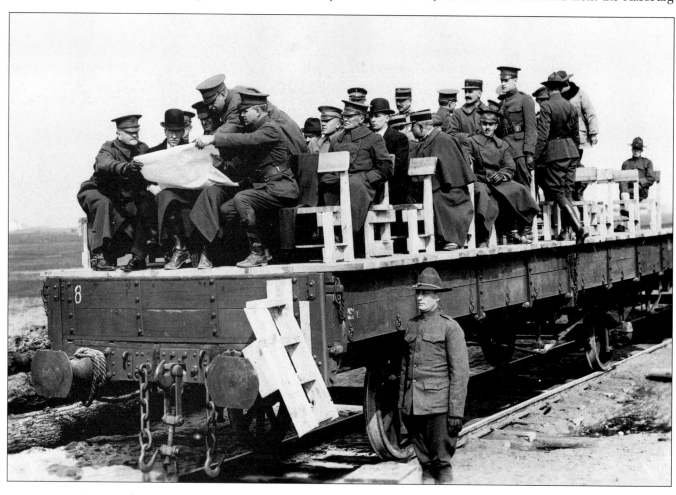

24 June 1918 and desertions from the Habsburg armies became a serious problem. Entente forces in Salonika broke through the Bulgarian front on 19 September 1918 and on 26 September Bulgaria sued for peace. On 3 October Germany, Austria and Turkey sent messages to President Wilson asking for an armistice. In the weeks that followed the subject nationalities of the Habsburg monarchy – Czechs, Croats, Serbs, Slovenes, Poles and Romanians – prepared to establish their own states or to join fellow nationals outside the Habsburg empire. On 21 October the German-Austrian deputies in the Viennese Reichsrat voted to establish an independent German–Austrian state. A Czecho-Slovak republic was formed in Prague on 28 October, followed on 1 November by an independent Hungarian state

proclaimed in Budapest. On 3 November Austrian armies on the Italian front surrendered.

In Germany too the will to resist collapsed. The High Command ordered the parliamentary government, headed by Prince Max of Baden, to make peace. However on 23 October Wilson informed the Germans that the Kaiser would have to abdicate before hostilities could cease. On the morning of 8 November the Bavarian monarchy was overthrown and on the next day socialist parties declared a republic in Berlin. Eventually, on 11 November, the German center party politician Matthias Erzberger signed an armistice with Marshal Ferdinand Foch, the leader of the Allied forces. Earlier, on 30 October 1918, Germany's ally Ottoman Turkey had capitulated, heralding the dismemberment of its empire.

▲ The grim reality of trench warfare, portrayed by the German artist Otto Dix. Men spent days on end in muddy trenches and airless dugouts, surrounded by the dead, tormented by rats and lice, assailed by a constant barrage of noise and exposed to random danger from exploding shells, snipers' bullets and sometimes even the waterlogged terrain itself. Even those fortunate enough to escape death or mutilation were often scarred mentally for the rest of their lives.

Datafile

The war efforts of the European combatants were only sustained by the mass mobilization of industry and the civilian population. At the beginning of the war, tension and political protest were submerged by patriotic fervor, but as the war dragged on, economies began to show signs of strain and the sacrifices demanded of the people increased. The result was that the fighting nations faced rises in leftwing political opposition – some faced revolution as well.

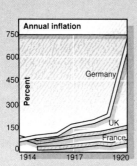

Socialist representation 1914

▶ One sign of economic strain was a rising inflation rate. By the middle of the war inflation was moving steadily upwards all over Europe, and in Germany, in particular, the problem was beginning to reach disastrous proportions. Defeat dealt the final blow to the German economy, and by 1920 inflation was running out of control.

Annual inflation

▲ Socialism had made steady progress in Europe prior to 1914. Although patriotism stifled political protest in the early years of the conflict, the presence of many leftwing representatives in Europe's parliaments provided a focus for a radical challenge to authority when the economic and social costs of the fighting began to bite.

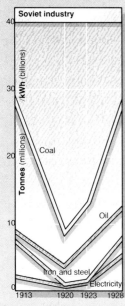

Soviet industry

▶ While levels of labor unrest fluctuated in different fashions, the general trend in all the major combatants was upwards, with the workforce increasingly resorting to strike action in response to the demands of war. Continuing economic problems pushed the trend up even more steeply after peace came in 1918.

Labour unrest

◀ Gradual wearing down under the strain of the war effort, and widespread socio-political disruption after the shock of revolution, combined to push the Russian economy into crisis. Industrial production fell sharply until 1920 – after that, the corner was turned by state coercion, at heavy cost to the workforce.

▼ Russian industrial workers were politically aware and made a clearer identification between economic and political grievances than elsewhere in Europe. As the crisis of 1917 approached, huge rises in political strikes showed that the Russian industrial worker no longer considered his rulers fit to rule.

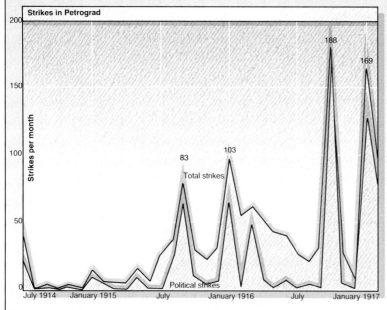

Strikes in Petrograd

The outbreak of World War I was greeted with rapturous enthusiasm in the belligerent states and with horror elsewhere. In Berlin, Paris and other cities, soldiers rushed to the colors to the accompaniment of cheering crowds. Britain sent a small expeditionary force to France and volunteers hastened to enlist. War also suppressed internal political conflicts such as Britain's problems over Ireland.

At the same time, it had a divisive effect on the international labor movement. At its congress in Stuttgart in 1907 the International had condemned war and committed itself to opposing it. Yet during the first week of war in August 1914 the Belgian, French and German social democrats agreed to support their countries' war efforts. The German Social Democrats saw their country threatened by czarist autocracy. The French were afraid of Prussian militarism. Fear of defeat at the hands of a tyrannical foreign power outweighed any feelings of solidarity with workers abroad, while socialist leaders were afraid of alienating their own rank-and-file membership who had been carried away by patriotism when the war broke out. There were socialist demonstrations for peace in Germany and elsewhere, but socialist leaders who tried to resist the war were overwhelmed by nationalist fervor. In France the socialist leader Jean Jaurès was assassinated on 3 July 1914 and in Germany Hugo Haase, the antiwar parliamentary spokesman of the Social Democrats, was forced by weight of numbers to support the voting of German war credits in the Reichstag on 4 August 1914. In the belligerent countries only two socialist parties – the Serbian Social Democrats and Lenin's Bolsheviks – rejected outright any participation in the war.

Disillusion in Europe

As the war dragged on, and its privations increased, the working classes of Germany became more skeptical about their government's attempts to blame Russia for everything. Among the parties of the left a struggle ensued between those socialists who refused to continue to support the war effort and those who, like Friedrich Ebert and Philipp Scheidemann, believed it was in the best interests of their party to do so. In April 1917 the antiwar dissidents, having been expelled from their own party, set up the new and more radical Independent Social Democratic party (USPD) dedicated to opposing the war. Some radical elements within it, such as the Spartacists led by Rosa Luxemburg and Karl Liebknecht, were actively trying to foment revolution.

The Italian social democrats had traditionally been radical and Italy's neutrality in 1914 made it easy for most of them to assert their commitment to peace. Even so, a minority were impressed by

WAR AND REVOLUTION

the power of nationalism, among them Benito Mussolini, then a socialist newspaper editor in Milan, who became committed to Italian intervention in the war. August 1914 proved that international working-class solidarity was a myth and that tribal loyalties were the real force in world affairs.

When Italy joined the war on the Entente side on 24 May 1915 it was clearly for territorial gain, and met with bitter opposition from the left. The "maximalist" or revolutionary wing of the Italian socialist party gained in strength. Defeats and hardships during the war deepened the cleavage in Italian politics between its supporters and opponents. The political system came under particular strain at a time when it was having to adjust to a broadening of the franchise in 1911 which gave organized labor and the Roman Catholic peasantry greater political opportunities. Before 1915, a skilful liberal politician such as Giovanni Giolitti might have been able to integrate these disparate elements into the parliamentary system, but the conflicts over the war made that almost impossible.

▼ A people's war – women workers in a British aircraft factory. During the Great War, with so many young men in uniform, industry could only reach the high targets it was set by bringing thousands of women into the factories.

In Austria-Hungary too, the appalling levels of casualties at the front, as well as shortages of food and consumer goods at home, damaged civilian morale. The hardships further exacerbated the relationships between the different nationalities within the empire. Hungary was fairly able to provide for itself, but was not generous to other areas. In the German-speaking provinces, and especially the large towns such as Vienna, food was very scarce.

Politically, the empire was on the verge of breakdown. The Reichsrat (imperial parliament) was suspended and all criticism muzzled. On 21 October 1916 the Austrian head of government, Count Carl Stürgkh, was assassinated by a young socialist, and on 21 November the aged Emperor of Austria-Hungary, Franz-Josef, died. His successor, Charles, lacked the prestige to halt the impending disintegration. The United States' entry into the war in April 1917 further encouraged those political groups – such as the Czechoslovakian National Committee in Paris – who were working for the liberation of the subject nationalities. President Wilson was known to

The Partition of Ireland

◄ The Irish republican flag raised above the Dublin post office during the Easter rebellion of 1916. With British attention concentrated on the Great War, several thousand armed Irish insurgents surprised the authorities by seizing strategic buildings in Dublin. After some considerable confusion, the British recovered to surround the isolated rebel outposts with forces greatly superior in number. The Irish leaders were executed.

In 1912, after pressure from the Irish parliamentary party, a British Liberal government introduced a Home Rule bill, involving the ceding of power, in almost everything except foreign affairs and defense, to a parliament in Ireland, which became law in 1914, though it was never implemented. The bill was fiercely opposed by the Unionist (and predominantly Protestant) minority, concentrated in the six industrialized northeastern counties of Ireland.

As it was, the intervention of World War I delayed the bill's implementation, during which time the character of the nationalists' demands changed. In the first postwar election, in 1918, Sinn Fein, the party of separatist nationalists, supplanted the Irish parliamentary party as the major nationalist party. Negotiations began in the autumn of 1921 between the British government under pressure from the United States and international opinion and Sinn Fein, culminating in the establishment of an independent Irish state within the framework of the British Commonwealth. Ireland was partitioned so the northern six counties with their Protestant majority remained within the United Kingdom. While the Unionists reluctantly accepted the settlement, it divided the nationalists into pro- and antitreaty factions of Sinn Fein and started a civil war.

▼ A makeshift barricade erected during the 1916 rebellion. A lack of public support for the uprising allowed the British to restore order and force the outnumbered rebel garrisons to surrender. Harsh repressive action, including the execution of many of the insurgent leaders, hardened public opinion and, transformed the rebels into martyrs for the cause of Irish independence.

favor self-determination for national minorities, while the length and severity of the war gave them hope, in that, if both the Russian and the Habsburg empires collapsed, nationalities like the Czechs or Poles would not have to choose between them.

The last of the Russian czars

By 1917 the situation in Russia was dire. Despite some notable victories, particularly against the Austrians in eastern Galicia in September 1914 and General Brusilov's offensive at Bukovina in 1916, the czar's armies were largely defeated. They had been forced back out of Russian Poland and suffered enormous casualties. The logistical support for the Russian army at the front was lacking, and the severe losses of manpower and horses were damaging agriculture. Privation and war-weariness became widespread.

On 10 March 1917 bread riots in Petrograd (renamed from "St Petersburg" after the outbreak of war) led to a mutiny amongst garrison troops. The government proved powerless to act. A soviet of workers and soldiers was established, while at the same time politicians in the Duma assumed that the authority in the state had passed to them. On 15 March (old style, 2 March) Czar Nicholas II was persuaded to abdicate and a Provisional Government of Duma politicians was established, led at first by Prince Lvov and later by Alexander Kerensky, a liberal lawyer and member of the Socialist Revolutionary party.

Everywhere the "February revolution" was hailed as a great act of liberation. In Germany the newly formed Independent Socialists welcomed it at their founding congress. In France and Britain concern over Russian instability mingled with hope that the new liberal regime might wage war against Germany more effectively (a hope shared by many of the Duma politicians). Even inside Russia revolutionary parties (like the Marxist Mensheviks and populist Socialist Revolutionaries who wanted a socialist society based on the peasantry) agreed not to oppose the new Provisional Government for fear of provoking counterrevolution.

This consensus was shattered by Lenin, who arrived from Switzerland on 15 April 1917. He announced that the Bolshevik party would attack the new regime root and branch and demanded an immediate end to the war, land for the peasants, and bread for the people. The Germans welcomed Lenin's agitation because it damaged Russia's war effort. Indeed they had allowed Lenin's party to travel through their territory and even provided the Bolsheviks with funds to develop their organization.

By contrast the Russian Provisional Government led by Kerensky and his colleagues was committed to national defence and constitutional reform. No major steps towards social change would be taken, however, until a constituent assembly had been elected. Already in the villages peasant communes were seizing landlords' land while the relaxation of harsh military discipline in the army after the czar's abdication encouraged desertion and sometimes mutinies. Agitation by the soviets and mistrust of the

government by the officers at the front, many of whom regarded Kerensky as the embodiment of treason, undermined troop morale.

After a further military setback in early July 1917, General Kornilov, the commander of the troops at the front, staged an unsuccessful coup in Petrograd in September, with the intention of establishing a military regime. This led to the arming of workers' militias or Red Guards loyal to the Petrograd soviet, which increasingly came under the influence of the Bolshevik party. On 4 October 1917 Leon Trotsky became chairman of the soviet as the Bolsheviks made final plans to seize power. By then the administrative system and military command structure in Russia were beginning to disintegrate.

The Bolshevik revolution
The Petrograd soviet established a military revolutionary committee whose stated purpose was to resist counterrevolution. Dominated by Bolsheviks, this body gained the support of most of the soldiers in the city's garrison. Despite the nervousness of Zinoviev, Kamenev and others among his colleagues, Lenin pressed ahead and seized power in Petrograd on 7 November 1917 (old style, 27 October). The provisional government offered little resistance. Kerensky fled. The Bolsheviks set up a Council of People's Commissars to run the revolution and in December established the Cheka, a security police force headed by a Pole, Felix Dzerdzhinsky.

The democratically elected constituent assembly in which the Socialist Revolutionaries, not the Bolsheviks, were the largest party met on

5 January 1918 but was prevented from continuing by Bolshevik soldiers. Liberals and other "enemies of the people" were arrested by the Cheka. Although there was resistance to the Bolshevik seizure of power in many parts of Russia, often the opposition was patchy and uncoordinated. The Socialist Revolutionaries split and their left wing worked for a time with the Bolshevik government. Meanwhile the provisional government's supporters who wanted to overthrow Lenin often found they could not easily cooperate with reactionary army officers to achieve their objective. Only in areas where there were non-Russian nationalities such as Finland and the Ukraine were the Bolsheviks checked.

One of the first measures taken by the Bolsheviks, on 8 November 1917, was to abolish the

▲ Massacre on the streets of Petrograd in July 1917. During the overthrow of the czarist regime and the prolonged power struggle that followed such scenes were repeated all over the country. The toppling of the statue of Alexander III in Moscow symbolized the end of czarism. Economic and social problems bequeathed by the feudal autocracy were not so easily solved.

◄ Russian peasants starving by their hut. Torn by revolution and war, the new Soviet regime was also beset by famine.

▶ Lenin addressing troops in Sverdlov Square, Moscow, in 1920. Lenin and Trotsky (standing beside rostrom) were chiefly responsible for the Bolshevik rise to power and the successful defence of the party's position in the subsequent civil war. A brilliant theorist and persuasive orator, Lenin was also a master of political tactics. He was ably supported by Trotsky, one of the most brilliant military organizers of modern times.

▲ Revolutionary art – the new Soviet state often used posters to spread its message – the appeal to the work ethic was a common theme. Here the message is, "We destroyed our enemy with weapons, we'll earn our bread with labor – comrades, roll up your sleeves for work!"

private ownership of land and to redistribute it amongst the peasantry. Although the Bolsheviks' authority was not established in the countryside this land policy and the fact that they were not associated with the landlords in the eyes of the peasants gave them an advantage over their "white" opponents in the civil war that followed.

Civil war and intervention in Russia

Against the wishes of the left Socialist Revolutionaries and many of his own party Lenin made a separate peace with the Germans. Under the treaty of Brest-Litovsk, signed on 3 March 1918, the Bolsheviks conceded large areas of western Russia, with the creation of puppet states in the Baltic, in Poland and in the rich wheat-growing region of the Ukraine. The treaty gave the Bolsheviks breathing-space from German pressure but encouraged intervention against them by the western powers after a variety of White forces sought aid from the allies of the former provisional government. For three years a bitter civil war raged across Russia, bringing with it famine, economic dislocation and refugee problems.

Allied support for the Whites was substantial but sporadic and ill-organized. Early in March 1918 the British landed near Murmansk, hoping to prevent arms dumps and enemy prisoners-of-war falling into the hands of the Germans. US, British and Italian troops were sent to the Archangel area for the same purposes, though once established it was clear that they were also engaged in a political war to help overthrow the Bolsheviks. In southern Russia British forces invaded the Baku oilfields on the Caspian Sea and established themselves in the western Caucasus, while the French occupied part of the northern coast of the Black Sea around Odessa.

In Siberia the Japanese sent more than 70,000 troops to Siberia to occupy the area from Lake Baikal to Vladivostok. President Wilson had grave inhibitions about this extension of Japanese power although the Japanese forces were joined in the area by over 10,000 British and Canadian troops, 7,000 Americans and token forces from France and Italy.

As the civil war progressed the dictatorship of the Bolshevik party under Lenin became more repressive. The Red Army, which was organized by Leon Trotsky, used former czarist officers closely supervised by Bolshevik party commissars. Sometimes those who proved disloyal or laggardly were shot. In July 1918 an attempted rising against Lenin's regime by Socialist Revolutionaries was suppressed with great ferocity. Terror became commonplace, and news of Red atrocities was played up in the Western press. Particularly shocking to many was the murder of Czar Nicholas II and his family at Ekaterinburg on 16 July 1918.

Until the autumn of 1918 the aim of the intervention was to keep the Russian front alive against the Germans despite the Bolshevik–German peace treaty of earlier that year. But as the German threat receded, Allied leaders became more concerned with the politics of intervention. The French were anxious to chastise a Bolshevik government that had repudiated czarist debts while some, like Foch and Churchill, regarded Lenin's doctrines as a menace to civilization itself. Britain was interested in the control of Russia's oil supplies and some of the Japanese military were attracted by the possibility of dominating Siberia.

Disagreements over these objectives, fatigue among the troops and the public's reluctance to

The Russian Revolution and Civil War

1917

November
Bolsheviks seize power in Petrograd and Moscow.

December
Armistice signed by Germans and Bolsheviks.

1918

January–February
Cossack armies defeated by Red Guard.

February–May
Germans occupy the Causasus and Crimea.

March 3
Treaty of Brest-Litovsk signed between Germany and Russia.

March 5
British forces disembark at Murmansk to support Whites.

April 6
Japanese forces disembark at Vladivostok; the Whites set up a government there in July.

June
White governments are set up in Samara and Omsk.

August
The British set up a White government in Archangel. Allied forces land at Vladivostok.

November 28
French troops land at Odessa; the British occupy Baku and Georgia.

1919

April
Red Army expels Allies from Ukraine and enters Crimea.

September–October
Allies evacuate Archangel and Murmansk.

October 22
White attack on Petrograd is repulsed.

1920

May 6
Kiev occupied by Poles and Ukrainian nationalists.

June 11
Kiev retaken by Red Army, who then advance into Poland, only to be repulsed in August by Poles near Warsaw.

1921

March 1
Sailors mutiny at Kronstadt, but are quelled two weeks later.

March 18
Treaty of Riga defines the frontier with Poland.

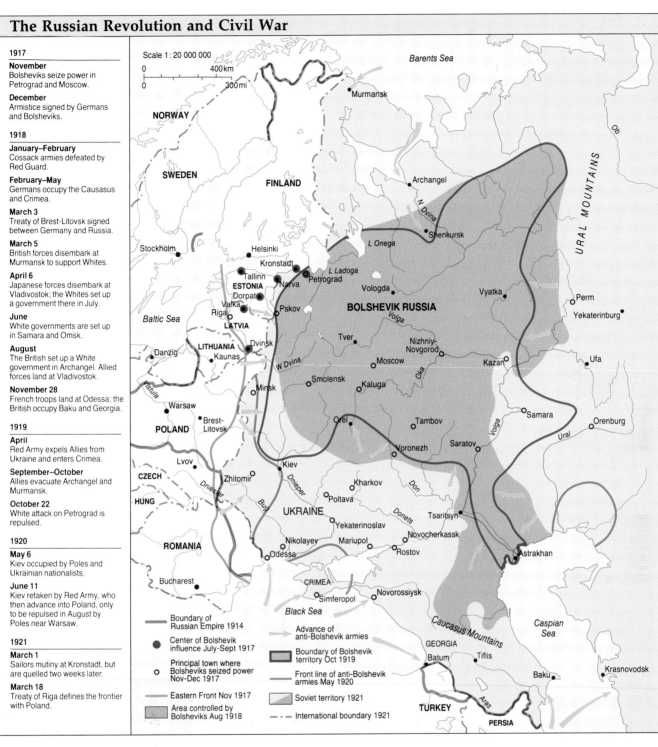

Scale 1 : 20 000 000

Boundary of Russian Empire 1914

● Center of Bolshevik influence July-Sept 1917

○ Principal town where Bolsheviks seized power Nov-Dec 1917

Eastern Front Nov 1917

Area controlled by Bolsheviks Aug 1918

Advance of anti-Bolshevik armies

Boundary of Bolshevik territory Oct 1919

Front line of anti-Bolshevik armies May 1920

Soviet territory 1921

International boundary 1921

▲ After withdrawing from World War I in March 1918, the Bolshevik state faced a grave new challenge in the form of Western intervention. Together White and Allied forces make deep incursions all round Russia's borders. Drastic action by Lenin and Trotsky created a new Red Army, which repelled these invaders and launched a brief invasion of Poland. The Bolshevik cause was aided by lack of coordination or agreement among the White forces and the war-weariness of Allied governments.

continue intervention in Russia once the war with Germany had come to an end brought the campaign to a halt. By the spring of 1920 Allied forces had been withdrawn from European Russia. The Americans left Siberia in January 1920, quickly followed by the European contingents. The Japanese continued to occupy the area but came under strong American pressure to evacuate it. In 1922 they complied and Soviet control was established over the whole of Siberia. Only northern Sakhalin remained under Japanese occupation until 1925 by which time the Union of Soviet Socialist Republics (a name that had been adopted two years earlier) had established itself in a new Europe.

Russo-Polish war

At the end of the Russian civil war in May 1920, Polish forces had advanced into Russia and taken Kiev. However the Red Army counterattacked so successfully that by the end of July they were nearly at the gates of Warsaw. Aided by French arms and advisers the Poles managed to fight back and the war ended in September with the Poles obtaining a generous frontier in the Pripet marshes east of Pinsk. This was several hundred kilometers to the east of a demarcation settlement proposed by Britain as Poland's eastern boundary in December 1919, and that frontier remained a bone of contention between Poles and Russians until the end of World War II.

ART AND REVOLUTION

The upheavals of the early decades of the 20th century left no sphere of human activity untouched. The art of the period both reflected the demise of the old order and in its own way contributed to it. Cubism and Futurism were, according to the Russian artist Kasimir Malevich, the "revolutionary form of art that foreshadowed the revolution in political and economic life in 1917". To Lenin, Russia was the weakest link of the capitalist chain; once that link broke, capitalism would collapse, leaving the world ready for socialism. Likewise, to contemporary Russian artists Cubism signaled the end of the bourgeois era in art: an era which, they believed, Russia would – uniquely – be able to bypass as a stage in its own development.

Foremost among the movements that grew out of Russian Cubo-Futurism in the post-Revolutionary period were the Constructivists. They and others sought to eliminate the differences between art and engineering, between painting and music, between poetry and design and between fine art and propaganda. Rejecting the world of nature and false nostalgia, they championed urban culture, the machine and the language of the street. Artists now aspired to change reality rather than simply mirror it. Traditional easel painting was abandoned in favor of utilitarian design (of everything from boiler suits to the abortive Monument to the Third International by Vladimir Tatlin) and public spectacles such as the reenactment of the Bolshevik revolution on the occasion of its first anniversary. "The streets our brushes, the squares our palettes", proclaimed the Futurist poet Vladimir Mayakovsky.

One of the earliest post-Revolutionary art forms was poster design. Often, but not always, political, the posters featured combinations of abstract shapes (showing the influence of Malevich's Suprematist movement), bold experimental typography (Lissitsky's contribution) and photomontage (Rodchenko's innovation). During the Russian civil war "agitprop" (agitational propaganda) trains and ships, brightly decorated with political slogans, carried artists, poets and politicians around the battlefronts to reinforce the revolutionary message among the troops. Artists at this time were under no compulsion to produce or agitate for the state; many genuinely believed in the revolution and the possibilities it offered for the future.

This period, one of the most creative in the history of art, also had an impact outside Russia, giving the world, among other things, Vsevolod Meyerhold's "theater in the round", the films of Sergei Eisenstein, and the German Bauhaus school, in which the Russian painter Vassili Kandinsky was a major force. In Mexico the ideals of the Bolshevik revolution inspired artists to produce art for the public, in the form of murals. This "great Renaissance" in Mexican art began around 1920, a decade after the national revolution that deposed the Diaz dictatorship, and lasted until the fall of the Obregon government in 1925.

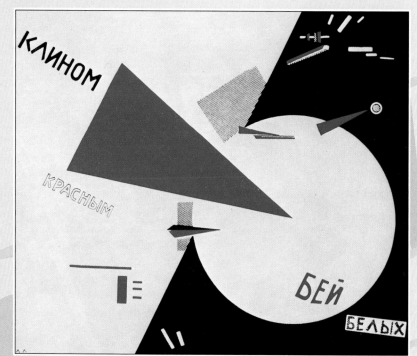

◄ The Soviet artist El Lissitzky's poster *Beat the Whites with the Red Wedge* (1919–20) combines an urgent political message with realistic exploration. Designed in the Constructivist style which sought a new art for the revolutionary and machine age. By the early 1930s the Communist party rejected Constructivism in favor of an esthetically more conservative style.

► The Agitprop trains, covered in revolutionary imagery and spreading revolutionary leaflets, were an important element in bringing the Bolshevik revolution from its urban heartlands to the Russian country as a whole. On a larger scale, the dramatist Nathan Altman had staged a futurist reconstruction of the storming of the Winter Palace in Petrograd itself on the first anniversary of the October Revolution.

◄ Lenin was closely associated with the new art, appearing here on a plate of 1921. Stalin, on the other hand, was no friend of the avant garde, seeing its work as decadent and bourgeois; it was firmly repressed under Zhdanov.

◄ The theater director Vsevolod Meyerhold (1874–1940) developed another revolutionary version of an old art form, putting Constructivism on the stage, as in this production of "The Bathhouse", put on in Moscow in collaboration with Mayakovsky. It was a satirical work attacking the lifestyle of the bourgeois.

▲ The heroic art of Socialist Realism was adopted not only by the Soviet Union after its initial years, but in Communist China too. The official "art of the state" maintained an educative role – celebrating the ideals of work and community service, while the figures on posters always marched to the left.

◄ The art of rival artists such as Diego Rivera and José Clemente Orozco formed an important element in the popularization of the Mexican Revolution. Although each approached the concept of "socialized art" differently, they were untied by a "native tradition" of the Aztecs and Mayans.

Datafile

The Paris peace conference was spoiled from the outset by the distrust between the Allied leaders that had built up over the course of the war. Though there was a pressing need to redraw the map of Europe to prevent future disputes, the French and the British had each felt that they had had to shoulder too high a proportion of the burden of the war effort, and neither wished to see the United States take over a leading role in world affairs. For his part, President Wilson disliked all power politics and was determined not to be a tool of European imperialism. He pressed for the establishment of the League of Nations to help replace the old world of secret diplomacy, which he saw as a major contributing factor to the outbreak of war.

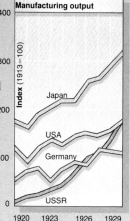

Manufacturing output

Index (1913=100)

Japan

USA

Germany

USSR

1920 1923 1926 1929

▲ The economy of Japan, barely affected by the war, grew more significantly between 1913 and 1920 than that of any other Power. By 1920, Russian output, ravaged by revolution and civil war, was only 12 percent of the 1913 figure.

◄ Of all the clauses in the Versailles treaty, clause 6, in which the Germans were forced to accept blame for the war and pay reparations for the damage done, proved the most unacceptable to the German people.

◄ The covenant of the League of Nations was the first major attempt to set up an international organization for dealing with political conflict between nations by rational and public means. Although it proved ineffectual in the face of irrational forces such as fascism, and was disbanded in 1946, its agencies did much useful work, including in the collection of international data such as the manufacturing output statistics (top).

▼ Energy consumption statistics bear out the great predominance of the United States economy through the 1920s, as the main European Powers struggled to make up for the losses incurred during the war.

The Treaty of Versailles 28 June 1919

1. The signatories accept the Covenant of the League of Nations, which includes guarantees of their territories.

2. Germany to lose certain territories. Provisions include the return of Alsace-Lorraine to France and the loss of German colonies to Allied powers as mandated territories of the League of Nations. The Rhineland is to be demilitarized.

3. Limits are imposed on German military power: army limited to 100,000 men (all volunteers); navy limited to 36 major ships, 15,000 men and 1,500 officers (no submarines and replacements capital ships); no air services allowed.

4. Former Kaiser and German military leaders to be tried for violations of laws of war.

5. Germany accepts responsibility for damage caused by war and will pay reparations (to be determined by Allies).

6. Allied forces to occupy the Rhineland for 15 years.

7. Germany abrogates the Treaty of Brest-Litovsk.

Covenant of the League of Nations

1. Original members are Allied signatories of the postwar peace treaties.

2. Assembly to contain representatives of all members; Council to consist of representatives of permanent members (USA, UK, France, Italy and Japan) and of four others elected by the Assembly.

3. All members to reduce armaments to lowest possible levels.

4. Principles of collective security. Each member to respect the security of all others. All disputes to be referred to the Council. No member to go to war until the Council's procedures have been implemented.

5. Procedures for arbitration, including the establishment of a permanent Court of International Justice.

6. All members to join action against a member who violated the Covenant. First course would be economic sanctions, then military intervention. Provision made for nonmembers to join action.

7. Colonies of defeated powers to become mandates of the League and administered by selected powers.

8. Members to cooperate on other matters, such as transport, commerce, labor. Other international organizations to be brought under League direction. Red Cross to be encouraged.

9. Provisions for amending the Covenant.

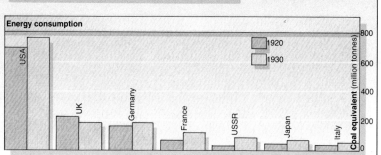

Energy consumption

USA   UK   Germany   France   USSR   Japan   Italy

☐ 1920
☐ 1930

Coal equivalent (million tonnes)

The end of World War I came suddenly and left the victors with enormous problems. Germany as defeated, Austria-Hungary was disintegrating, the Ottoman Empire was in ruins and the future of Russia was uncertain. Had the western Powers been united in purpose and coordinated in their actions, the peacemakers would still have faced a daunting task. In fact they were badly organized and mistrusted one another.

The Paris Peace Conference

France's major problem was security against its more powerful German neighbor. Before the war its safety had rested on the alliance with Russia, but the Bolshevik revolution of 1917 had replaced a friendly regime with a hostile one. Even if Bolshevik rule was shortlived – and in November 1917 there were few who thought it would last long – its successor was an unknown quantity. The British wanted a peace that would establish their empire as the leading world Power while preserving Germany as a sound trading partner and a useful counterweight to France. President Wilson of the United States pressed for a new system of international relations. His Fourteen Points declaration called for a peace based on national self-determination, an end to old-style secret diplomacy; and the establishment of a League of Nations to help to resolve international conflicts. The Germans claimed that Wilson's principles implied a settlement based on self-determination, no punitive indemnities and an international system in which they would be permitted to play a full part.

The peace conference met in Paris for the first time on 18 January 1919, with the most important decisions taken by the "big four" representing Britain, France, Italy and the United States. The Italians soon realized that they were to be denied the territories promised to them under the 1915 Treaty of London, and their premier, Vittorio Orlando, withdrew in protest on 24 April 1919, thus leaving matters firmly in the hands of Clemenceau (the French premier), Lloyd George (prime minister of Britain) and President Wilson.

Founding of the League of Nations

France's security problem with her German neighbor was to be overcome by a guarantee of protection from Britain and the United States. The League of Nations organization was to be set up and its covenant adopted on 14 February 1919. The left bank of the Rhine was not to be annexed by France, as Clemenceau had demanded but, occupied by allied forces for 15 years and then demilitarized permanently.

However the Germans were forced to concede the provinces of Alsace and Lorraine to France, as well as surrendering frontier districts to Belgium

REBUILDING EUROPE

and Schleswig to Denmark. More serious were the substantial losses of eastern territories in Posen, West Prussia and Poland along with the port of Danzig. At the same time, the Germans were forbidden to unite with German-speaking populations of the Habsburg monarchy which would have given them control of the Danube basin making the new state of Czechoslovakia, which was crucial to the allied settlement proposed for central Europe, economically and strategically unviable. To the Germans such an application of the self-determination principle seemed grossly one-sided.

Germany also surrendered its colonies, which were parceled out among the victors under the doubtful authority of the League of Nations to whom their new proprietors were responsible for their trusteeship. Germany also lost its battle fleet and most of its mercantile marine and was ordered to reduce its army to 100,000 long-serving professional soldiers and abolish its airforce al-

► British troops sporting German helmets as trophies in November 1918.

▼ US president Wilson was fêted in Europe, but his own people did not support his League of Nations.

together. Most controversially of all, the Germans were required to pay compensation for all damages caused by the war including the costs of pensions for the dependents of war victims. Although this demand did not conform with Wilson's original rejection of the idea of punitive indemnities, without it Britain would have been left with almost no compensation and the French would never had been able to repay their war debts to the British and Americans.

The articles of the treaty articulating the reparations settlement held the Germans solely responsible for the war, an assertion which together with a demand for the surrender of war criminals was seen by German politicians as an affront to national honor. The Germans also resented being excluded from the League of Nations organization.

The draft treaty was presented to the Germans on 7 May 1919 and aroused immediate public outrage, fanned by the German Republican government. A list of German objections was sent to the Allies. Lloyd George, who was already uneasy over some aspects of the settlements urged conciliation. He did not want to damage Germany too much economically and was skeptical of the new Poland, which the French saw as a counterweight to both Germany and Bolshevik Russia. In common with others at Paris in 1919, Lloyd George also perceived a threat of Communist subversion in Europe.

Far from collapsing, the Bolsheviks were beginning to extend their influence outside Russia. On 4 March 1919 a new Communist International – the Comintern or Third International – was founded in Moscow, aimed at creating a worldwide and truly revolutionary socialist movement.

Under its influence Bela Kun, on 21 March, set up a Communist regime in Hungary, and on 7 April Bavaria declared itself a Soviet Republic.

Although these revolutions were abortive and soon suppressed, Austria still seemed threatened by subversion and there were disturbances in the Ruhr. The Allies, naturally, did not want to see central Europe in chaos and Lloyd George, among others, feared public reaction at home if the Germans rejected the treaty and resumed the war. They therefore agreed to make certain concessions to Germany over its eastern frontier. Upper Silesia would not go to Poland until a plebiscite had been held to decide its future and Danzig was to be a "free city" under the supervision of the League of Nations. In effect, this meant that it was administered by the Germans but the Poles could use it as a trade outlet. These concessions did not satisfy the Germans but they were given an ultimatum to accept the terms of the treaty or face invasion. They eventually agreed to sign the treaty at the Palace of Versailles on 28 June 1919.

Eastern Europe after the war

So far as Germany's major allies were concerned World War I ended in catastrophe. Austria-Hungary disintegrated and was replaced by the independent states of Austria, Czechoslovakia and Hungary. The Southern Slav element in the old monarchy joined with Serbia and Montenegro to become the new state of Yugoslavia. Galicia went to the new Polish state while Transylvania was annexed by Romania. Whereas before, the Germans and the Magyars had been the dominant nationalities in the Habsburg monarchy, their rule was now confined to rump states with substantial German and Hungarian minorities having come under Slav control. There was a significant German-speaking population in the Sudeten region of Czechoslovakia, and Magyar minorities in Czechoslovakia, Yugoslavia and Romania.

The settlement of the successor states of the Habsburg monarchy was finalized in two treaties made with Austria at St Germain on 10 September 1919 and with Hungary at Trianon on 4 June 1920. Initially the succession states were parliamentary democracies, guaranteeing individual rights, press freedom and political liberty. The Czechs, in particular, wanted to create a new balance of power in east–central Europe, and in August 1920 organized a mutual defense treaty with the Yugoslavs. In April and June 1921 Romania concluded similar treaties with Czechoslovakia and Yugoslavia. Described as the "little entente", this tripartite grouping aimed to prevent a Habsburg restoration and to defend the new states against reactionary intrigues by former elites. Despite the fanatical hostility of the Magyars and the resentment of the Austrians, the postwar settlement in Central Europe remained relatively stable until it was shattered by Hitler's aggression in 1938.

In some countries, however, a multiplicity of parties reflecting cultural, social, regional and even linguistic divisions made constructive leadership almost impossible. In 1925, the Sejm, the Polish parliament, contained 32 parties or-

ganized into 18 groups. Incapable of supporting a stable government, on 26 May 1921 it suffered a military coup launched by Josef Pilsudski. Parliament was formally retained and the press remained relatively free but the move presaged the end of Polish democracy in the longer term.

The Middle East after the Ottomans

The Ottoman empire, like Austria-Hungary, had also failed to survive the war intact. Turkey's Asian provinces, which were either under occupation or in revolt, were divided up as spheres of influence between the French and the British under the auspices of the League of Nations. The British became responsible for Palestine, Iraq and Saudi Arabia; the French for Syria and the Lebanon. Under the Treaty of Sèvres of 10 August 1920 Turkey lost western Armenia and also had to give up western Thrace and part of western Anatolia, including the important port of Smyrna, to Greece. By this time the Ottoman regime faced a serious challenge from a nationalist movement centered on Ankara. It was led by General Mustafa Kemal, who later became Turkish dictator under the name of Atatürk ("father of the Turks"). Encouraged by the British and French, the Greeks tried to suppress Atatürk's movement in 1922 but they were defeated, and in September of that year driven out of Smyrna.

With Sèvres a dead letter, the Allies contracted a new treaty with Atatürk's government at Lausanne, Switzerland, on 24 July 1923. This restored western Thrace, Smyrna and western Armenia to Turkey. So bad had relations between Turks and Greeks become, however, with massacres on both sides, that the two states agreed on a transfer of populations. In the period after the Greek defeat in 1922, 1,377,000 Greeks were expelled from Turkey and 410,000 Turks left Greece.

Formerly part of the Ottoman empire, Palestine passed to the British under the League of Nations mandate presented on 3 June 1922 which was seen as the legitimation of Zionist claims in the area. Earlier, on 2 November 1917, the British Foreign Secretary Arthur Balfour, promised Lord Rothschild that Britain would support a "national home for the Jewish people in Palestine". The "Balfour declaration", which was influenced by the Zionist Chaim Weizmann and Nahum Sokolow further stated that "nothing shall be done to prejudice the civil and religious rights of

▲ British cartoon patronizing the League of Nations' impotence in the face of war. Western democratic governments, struggling with severe economic problems and aware that their people did not want another war, were not prepared to use force to maintain peace or deter aggressive dictators.

▲ Kemal Atatürk, Turkey's most successful soldier, capitalized on his country's defeat in 1918 by mobilizing support for a national uprising. He ejected Greek occupation forces and, overturning Turkey's Islamic tradition, built a modern secular state.

◄ The signing of the Treaty of Versailles brought the Great War to its formal conclusion, but the settlement did not provide a basis for lasting peace in Europe.

existing non-Jewish communities in Palestine".

The Balfour declaration formed part of the preamble of the League of Nations mandate. By 1925 there were just over 100,000 Jewish settlers in Palestine, many of whom had arrived before 1917, but their presence and the claims of the Zionists to bring in more aroused the lasting resentment of the indigenous Arab population.

Friction in Western Europe

From the beginning, the Paris peace treaties were a source of major dissatisfaction among the parties concerned. Not only the vanquished objected to them; many of the victors were also unhappy. In particular, the Italians, despite their modest military performance in the war, now complained of their "mutilated victory", for which they blamed their allies.

Most significant of all was President Wilson's failure to convince the United States Congress that it should accept the Versailles peace treaty.

The American public, suspicious of European rapacity, saw no reason why they should shoulder any more responsibilities for the Europeans. Consequently, the United States did not become a member of the League of Nations of which President Wilson had been the architect. Still more important, the United States' guarantee of France's security lapsed, leaving the French unprotected when Britain did not renew its guarantee in the light of American withdrawal. To make matters worse for France, the American presidential election produced a victory for the isolationist Republican Warren G. Harding, eliminating any further possibility of a collective security system that would involve the United States.

The League of Nations, despite the absence of the Americans, the Russians and, until 1926, the Germans, began to function in November 1920 from its headquarters in Geneva. Although it became a useful forum for international dip-

► The peace settlement of 1919 redrew the map of Europe and the Middle East, creating new states in the vacuum left by the collapse of the Austro-Hungarian and German empires as well as large European mandates in the former territories of the Ottoman empire. Although plebiscites were held in some regions to determine the will of the people, the new Europe was an unstable creation.

▼ French troops in the Rhineland. France was the staunchest advocate of imposing harsh peace terms on Germany. When the economically troubled Weimar Republic failed to maintain the reparation payments, France ordered the occupation of the Rhineland.

Europe in the 1920s

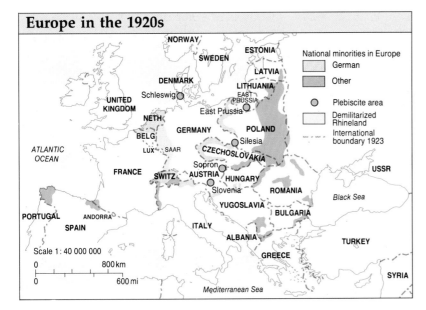

National minorities in Europe
German
Other
○ Plebiscite area
Demilitarized Rhineland
--- International boundary 1923

Scale 1 : 40 000 000
0 — 800 km
0 — 600 mi

lomacy during the 1920s, the member states could not agree on how to solve the problem of disarmament themselves. In particular the French, after the United States self-imposed isolation, decided that they would have to look after themselves by adopting a rigid attitude to Germans fulfilment of the peace treaty terms.

On 27 April 1921 the Allied reparations commission set a figure of 132,000 million gold marks as Germany's debt to her former enemies. The German government finally accepted this after receiving an ultimatum on 5 May, but stressed that they believed the burden was economically impossible. The German mark, already seriously weakened by wartime government borrowing and increased postwar expenditure, declined sharply on the exchanges. On 10 January 1923 the Germans were declared in default, having failed to deliver telegraph poles which formed part of the reparations commitment. French and Belgian troops marched into the Ruhr and the German government announced a policy of passive resistance. These actions resulted in domestic German instability, increased Franco-German bitterness.

By 13 August 1923, when Gustav Stresemann took over the chancellorship in Germany at the head of a broadly based coalition, the German currency had become worthless. On 26 September the Germans called off passive resistance and the French, who had also suffered financially from the operation, expressed a willingness to negotiate. With the help of American mediation, the parties met in London and agreed a new and milder schedule of reparations payments. The new scheme, accepted on 16 August 1924, was called the Dawes Plan after its American architect General Charles G. Dawes.

The League of Nations suffered an ominous reverse when Italy seized the Greek island of Corfu on 31 August 1923 and refused to give it back. Unable to act directly, the League entrusted the matter to a conference of ambassadors who agreed that Greece should pay an indemnity for the alleged assassination of Italian officials. Only afterwards, on 27 September 1923, did the Italians evacuate Corfu. This incident illustrated the

The Weimar Republic

After the flight of Kaiser Wilhelm II, a republic was proclaimed in Berlin on 9 November 1918. The following January, elections were held for a constituent national assembly. Since Berlin was insecure after an attempted leftwing uprising, the assembly met in the small town of Weimar, famous for its associations with the poet Goethe.

From the outset the Weimar Republic faced serious problems. Blamed for Germany's defeat in the war and saddled with the harsh peace settlement imposed by the Treaty of Versailles, it faced further economic dislocation caused by demobilization and labor unrest. Inflation, inherited from the Kaiser's government, worsened during the early 1920s as the result of high public spending, reparations payments and loss of confidence among foreign investors.

In 1923 the French occupied the Ruhr to force Germany to comply with reparations demands, precipitating total collapse of the currency and internal unrest. In the years that followed, the republic enjoyed something of a recovery. A new currency, the Reichsmark, was introduced, reparations payments were rescheduled under the Dawes Plan (1924), and in 1926 Germany was admitted to the League of Nations. Soon industrial production had recovered to prewar levels, and in 1928 parliamentary elections produced gains for the Social Democrats, who strongly supported the republic. However, the American stock market crash of October 1929 plunged the country into another economic crisis. The situation grew worse and by January 1932 six million Germans were out of work. Exploiting the crisis, Hitler's Nazi party became the biggest in Germany. On 30 January 1933 Hitler took up office as chancellor, replacing democracy with a Nazi dictatorship – the so-called Third Reich.

▲ German currency in 1923 was cheaper than firewood.

fundamental weakness of the League and fore-shadowed further humiliations in the 1930s.

Following the Corfu incident the League considered the question of how to prevent war if nations were determined to embark on hostilities. The British Labour government headed by Ramsay MacDonald suggested that the acid test for responsible international behavior should be a willingness to submit disputes to arbitration. On 24 October 1924 the League assembly drewup the Geneva Protocol, committing signatories to accept arbitration in international disputes. Those who refused arbitration could expect to be regarded as aggressors and sanctions might be applied against them. Although initially received with enthusiasm, these proposals were soon rejected first and foremost by Britain and her dominions. Governments were jealous of their sovereignty and reluctant to be drawn into other peoples' disputes.

Nevertheless, by 1928 the international scene appeared more promising than for many years. The Kellogg–Briand pact, an American initiative for a general renunciation of war, further encouraged this mood of optimism. Almost all self-governing nations signed the pact in Paris on 27 August 1928.

Locarno – the era of optimism

In May 1924 the emergence of a more moderate left-wing government in France under Edouard Herriot and Aristide Briand assisted Stresemann, the German chancellor, and Austen Chamberlain, the British foreign secretary, to work towards a détente in Western Europe. The resulting Locarno pact of 15 October 1925 consisted of a number of treaties designed to prevent further frontier violations and to create an atmosphere of stability. The Germans agreed to confirm acceptance of their western frontier, which Britain and Italy said they would guarantee. This agreement furnished the French with some of the security they had been seeking since 1918 but was far from ideal. Since the guarantee was to both France and Germany, it would not be supported by military force. Instead, the French had to put their trust in the demilitarized zone on the left bank of the Rhine, which was specifically protected by the Locarno agreement. To improve relations in Western Europe, Germany was admitted to the League of Nations in September 1926. The French still had occupation troops in the area but as a further gesture of goodwill, French and British troops withdrew completely in 1930.

By comparison with the immediate postwar years the international climate had apparently undergone a remarkable change. The spirit of Locarno gave cause for optimism. Briand, Chamberlain, Dawes and Stresemann all received the Nobel Peace Prize for their achievements. However, nationalist resentments were never far beneath the surface, especially in Germany.

At Locarno the Germans had given no guarantee to accept their frontiers with Poland and Czechoslovakia though they did agree to arbitration treaties with those countries. The French for their part balanced their pact at Locarno with treaties of mutual assistance against German

aggression that they signed with the Poles and Czechs.

The Poles were uncomfortably aware that both their Soviet and their German neighbors – perhaps in concert – had designs on their territory. On 16 April 1922 the Germans had made a pact with the Soviet Union at Rapallo, whereby the two countries agreed to cooperate economically. The also began – more covertly – to engage in joint military training and armaments production. The Rapallo agreement helped the Germans to overcome some of the military restrictions that the Versailles treaty placed upon them, although militarily, they still remained very weak.

The rise of Japan

At the Paris peace conference the Japanese had insisted that they be allowed to keep the concessions in China's Shandong province that they had wrested from the Germans during the war. President Wilson opposed this plan, but unsuccessfully, and this became a focus of criticism in the US Senate when Washington rejected the peace settlement. At first China refused to be a signatory to the peace settlement, but in February 1922 the Chinese signed a treaty with Japan, Belgium, Britain, France, the Netherlands, Portugal and the United States. However, Japan and the European Powers, with the exception of Germany, retained many commercial and legal privileges in China, whose independence was largely illusory.

Japan also gained control of German islands in the Pacific under League of Nations' mandate and became a member of the League Council. However, Japan's attempt to insert a clause in the League Covenant asserting racial equality was unsuccessful. Both Australia and the United States opposed the move because they wanted to limit Japanese migration.

Further tension between the Japanese and the Americans arose over naval activity in the Pacific. However, at a naval conference held in Washington late in 1921, Japan, Britain and the United States agreed to limit the number of naval vessels in the Pacific to the satisfaction of all parties and

▲ Chinese prisoners of war during the civil war await their fate. The Chinese revolution of 1912 failed to provide viable government or answers to the country's social and political problems. By the early 1920s central power had broken down entirely and the country was ruled by a number of local warlords who competed with nationalist forces in an uneasy alliance with Chinese communities.

▲ The new Japanese emperor Hirohito photographed in 1926 in his court robes. Behind the majesty of the imperial throne, Japan had an unstable political system in which a small military elite exercised undue influence. Japanese economic growth provided the stimulus for the buildup of military power and the development of an imperialistic foreign policy. Chaos in China provided the opportunity for quick expansion.

allowed the Japanese to confirm their status as the leading naval power in the western Pacific.

When the last Chinese emperor abdicated, President Sun Yat-sen established the republic of China in 1912. However, there was no strong central Chinese government and conflicts between Sun Yat-sen's nationalist Guomindang party and former imperialist warlords ravaged the country. The nationalists established one regime in Guangzhou while a more conservative government, recognized by foreign powers, held sway in Beijing. Chinese resentment at foreign, and particularly Japanese, influence over the country grew. On 4 May 1919 students demonstrated in the streets of Beijing to protest at the failure of the Paris peace conference to guarantee China's rights in Shantung. This "May 4th movement" led to more radical anti-imperialist attitudes and in July 1921 the Chinese Communist party was established with the help of the Comintern. Moscow encouraged the Chinese Communists to collaborate with and strengthen the Guomindang as an anti-colonialist movement while building Communist influence within it. Jiang Jieshi who became the Guomindang's military leader on the death of Sun Yat-sen on 12 March 1925, began a march to the north in 1926, threatening Western colonial interests in Shanghai and Guangzhou. Initially the Communists had directed their efforts towards urban workers and intellectuals but the policy foundered and an attempt to set up a Communist regime at Guangzhou, 11–12 December 1927 was crushed with much blood-

shed. Already Mao Zedong had been trying to rally peasants in the Hunan province to the communist cause and from 1927 his rural guerrilla army was a significant force. Nevertheless in 1928 Jiang's Guomindang seemed poised to take over control in China.

During World War I, China's neighbor India had supported Britain with soldiers and money and looked to Britain for some relaxation of its colonial rule in return. When Britain made no move, the Congress party put forward demands for self-government, and in March 1919 Mahatma Gandhi, a new, charismatic leader of Indian nationalism, began a campaign of civil disobedience. Widespread violence followed, culminating in the massacre at Amritsar on 13 April 1919, when British troops fired on and killed Indian demonstrators.

To try to appease nationalist opinion, the British passed the Government of India Act on 23 December 1919, giving provincial assemblies control of some areas of government and establishing a central legislature. However the British governor-general remained in overall control and the central executive was responsible to London. The legislature opened in February 1921, but failed to satisfy the Congress party which continued to press for home rule and made the provincial assemblies unworkable. In November 1927 an all-British parliamentary commission was set up in London to examine Indian grievances but it failed to meet nationalist demands for greater autonomy.

▼ A mass demonstration in Bombay in 1930 to promote a boycott of British goods. During the postwar period Indian nationalist opposition to British rule increased sharply. The movement, which was notable for its high level of female participation, found a charismatic leader in Gandhi, whose nonviolent forms of protest presented the colonial administration with insoluble problems.

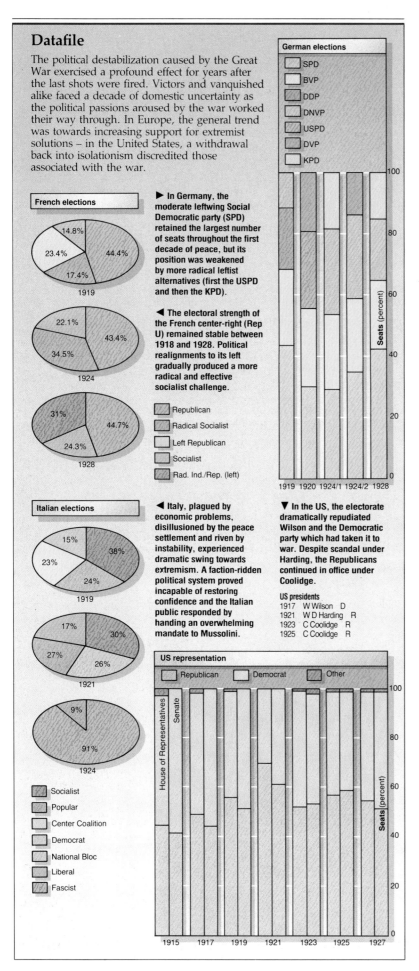

Datafile

The political destabilization caused by the Great War exercised a profound effect for years after the last shots were fired. Victors and vanquished alike faced a decade of domestic uncertainty as the political passions aroused by the war worked their way through. In Europe, the general trend was towards increasing support for extremist solutions – in the United States, a withdrawal back into isolationism discredited those associated with the war.

French elections

1919
- 14.8%
- 44.4%
- 23.4%
- 17.4%

1924
- 22.1%
- 43.4%
- 34.5%

1928
- 31%
- 44.7%
- 24.3%

- Republican
- Radical Socialist
- Left Republican
- Socialist
- Rad. Ind./Rep. (left)

Italian elections

1919
- 15%
- 38%
- 23%
- 24%

1921
- 17%
- 30%
- 27%
- 26%

1924
- 9%
- 91%

- Socialist
- Popular
- Center Coalition
- Democrat
- National Bloc
- Liberal
- Fascist

German elections

- SPD
- BVP
- DDP
- DNVP
- USPD
- DVP
- KPD

Seats (percent)

1919 1920 1924/1 1924/2 1928

▶ In Germany, the moderate leftwing Social Democratic party (SPD) retained the largest number of seats throughout the first decade of peace, but its position was weakened by more radical leftist alternatives (first the USPD and then the KPD).

◀ The electoral strength of the French center-right (Rep U) remained stable between 1918 and 1928. Political realignments to its left gradually produced a more radical and effective socialist challenge.

◀ Italy, plagued by economic problems, disillusioned by the peace settlement and riven by instability, experienced dramatic swing towards extremism. A faction-ridden political system proved incapable of restoring confidence and the Italian public responded by handing an overwhelming mandate to Mussolini.

▼ In the US, the electorate dramatically repudiated Wilson and the Democratic party which had taken it to war. Despite scandal under Harding, the Republicans continued in office under Coolidge.

US presidents
1917	W Wilson	D
1921	W D Harding	R
1923	C Coolidge	R
1925	C Coolidge	R

US representation

- Republican
- Democrat
- Other

House of Representatives / Senate

Seats (percent)

1915 1917 1919 1921 1923 1925 1927

During the postwar period, Western liberal democracy was challenged by two opposing ideologies – Communism and fascism. Of the two, Communism was perceived as the greater threat. Yet, while Soviet Communism was professedly international in outlook, arousing fears in the West of world revolution, it became more isolated and introverted as the decade wore on. By contrast, fascism, as it grew in strength, became increasingly aggressive at home and expansionist abroad.

The retreat from Communist ideals

During the Russian civil war private firms were abolished and the market economy ceased to exist in all but the most primitive form. Food supplies were requisitioned from peasants, if necessary by force, to feed the starving townspeople. Many left the towns where there was no food, and returned to family villages in which the peasantry had seized what remained of the landlords' land. Between 1917 and 1927 the number of peasant farms increased from about 18 million to 25 million though the holdings decreased in size and per capita production fell.

By the end of 1920 the Bolsheviks were triumphant in the civil war but the country was economically in ruins. Discontent and hardship led to strikes in Petrograd and Moscow at the end of February 1921. A mutiny that broke out among the naval garrison at Kronstadt on 17 March was severely put down. Lenin tackled the problem of economic reform while imposing more rigorous controls on political opposition.

To encourage more food deliveries, the peasants were permitted to sell part of their produce on the free market. The government also allowed small retailers to operate again and tried to encourage the investment of foreign capital to help expand industrial output. Lenin described this New Economic Policy (NEP) as a "retreat" necessary to consolidate the Bolshevik system before pressing ahead with the realization of a socialist society. It never really succeeded because the peasants had little incentive to increase their sales. Urban production was so low that there was little for the farmers to buy with the money they earned. Arguments arose within the Communist party as to the best way to overcome these problems and foreshadowed the power struggle within the party that followed Lenin's death in January 1824.

Power struggle in the Kremlin

Leon Trotsky, the People's Commissar for War and architect of the Red Army, strongly advocated taking a tough line with the "*petit bourgeois*" peasants. He had emerged as the strongest Bolshevik leader besides Lenin, and

THE TRIUMPH OF IDEOLOGY

The task facing the
Bolsheviks

Russia after Lenin

Socialism in Western
Europe

Fascism in Italy

The rise of National
Socialism

Democracy under threat

What is Communism?

What is fascism?

many in the party – especially Zinoviev and Kamenev – saw him as a potential Napoleon. His eventual rival, Joseph Stalin, was not a leading member of the prewar revolutionary intelligentsia like Lenin or Trotsky, but he was a more successful intriguer. Appointed General Secretary of the Communist party's Central Committee on 3 April 1922, he packed the party apparatus with men loyal to himself. When, in 1923, Trotsky complained of the high levels of bureaucracy in the party and its comparative lack of genuine workers, Stalin increased the number of 'proletarians' by 500,000, making sure that they knew whom to thank for their preferment.

At the time of Lenin's death on 21 January 1924, Trotsky still seemed to be the most likely leader. Partly in order to block Trotsky's taking power, Zinoviev, Kamenev and Stalin established a triumvirate to dominate the Politburo, the inner cabinet of the Communist party. Trotsky remained People's Commissar for war, but was otherwise isolated.

Like Lenin, Trotsky and Zinoviev, who was the first president of the Comintern's executive committee, were internationalists, who believed that socialism could not succeed in Russia unless the revolution spread to more advanced capitalist societies. However, by 1923, this prospect had receded. On 6 July 1923 the constitution of the Union of Soviet Socialist Republics was promulgated, which, while apparently giving autonomy to non-Russian areas, effectively ensured centralized control from Moscow. In December 1924 Stalin published an article claiming that it was possible to achieve "socialism in one country", even one as backward as Russia. This view was endorsed by the 14th Communist party Congress of 1925, dealing a further blow to Trotsky, who had already been deprived of his war commissariat in January of that year. Kamenev and Zinoviev, having served their purpose, were also stripped of their power bases in Moscow and Leningrad. Too late they tried to form a united opposition with Trotsky. In December 1927 Stalin denounced this group as an illegal faction and Trotsky and his colleagues were expelled from the party. Zinoviev and Kamenev recanted their "Trotskyite deviation" while Trotsky was exiled to Soviet Asia. Stalin's reign as the dictator of Russia had begun.

The Comintern and European socialism

The experience of war had radicalized many socialist movements, especially in Germany, Austria and Hungary, where defeat encouraged those on the far left to try to emulate the Bolsheviks. Even the victor countries were ripe for socialist propaganda in the postwar era, with labor unrest existing on a wide scale. Shortages of food and capital created hardships, and often inflation made the situation still worse. Demobilized soldiers were being decanted onto a depressed labor market which had· to reorient itself towards peacetime production.

At the second Congress of the Comintern in July 1920, Lenin set out 21 conditions that socialist parties would neéd to fulfil in order to affiliate to the new International. Among them were the acceptance of strict revolutionary discipline and the purging of so-called revisionists who had supported national defense in the war. These conditions effectively meant that the new International would be controlled by Moscow.

At its Bologna congress in October 1919 the Italian Socialist party committed itself to achieving the dictatorship of the proletariat but did not reject its parliamentary role. The general election of 16 November 1919 trebled the number of Socialists in parliament making them the largest single party. During the following months strikes and disturbances wracked the country,

▼ The writing was on the wall for Western middle classes: in the Soviet poster the name of the Third International strikes fear into the heart of a fat capitalist. But capitalism struck back – by encouraging the right wing.

What is Communism?

In 1848 Karl Marx published the *Communist Manifesto* in which he stressed the belief in class conflict as the central tenet of communism. Accordingly, human beings are not divided by nationality or tribal loyalty, but by to their relationship to the means of production. Those who own wealth try to exploit those who do not. Government agencies, law courts, police and even the educational system are designed, in practice if not in theory, to further the interests of the ruling classes. In a feudal, agrarian society land was "the means of production" and the ruling class was made up of landowners. As the "bourgeoisie" grew in economic power, they ousted the landowners, revolutionized production methods and, in their turn exploited the newly-created industrial proletariat. By collaborating with workers in other countries, the proletariat dispossess the wealth and create a classless society. According to Marx, the role of Communists is to take the lead in developing class consciousness among the masses in order to foment revolution when the time is ripe. Lenin developed Marx's teaching by emphasizing the importance of the party as the revolutionary vanguard. When he came to power in Russia in 1917 it was to replace a weak nascent democracy with a working-class dictatorship. Changing his party's name from Bolshevik to Communist, he proposed global revolution, with the creation, in 1919, of the Third International or Comintern.

SOCIALISM

Affirmations

Rationality, humanism, progress

Dignity of work

Internationalism and pacifism

Rejections

Violations of human rights: despotism, militarism, imperialism, fascism, racism, torture

Custom-based societies

Capitalism, liberal individualism; inequality

Ideal of society

Based on human capacity for interdependence, solidarity and cooperativeness and their ability to abolish injustice and achieve substantive equality for all

Permutations and factions

Revolutionary socialism may be Marxist or Leninist, based on ideas of Marx's critique of capitalism, or as amended by Lenin; utopian (retaining liberal strains); anarchist, rejecting the necessity of the state; anarcho-syndicalist, encouraging anarchism through revolutionary trade union activity

Reformist socialism seeks socialist goals through reform of liberal and capitalist structures

Dilemmas

Scientific or utopian vision of harmony; gradualism or revolution; voluntarism or determinism; nationalism or internationalism; state power or radical decentralization

Historical blind spots

Premodern and non-European societies; ecology; militarism; bureaucracy; totalitarian dangers of elite-run state

Revolutionary organizations and tactics

Political parties based on highly ●ware activists

Political activity in workplace; trade unions; strikes

Broadly-based parties working for electoral success

Military or economic challenge to authority

State structures and official policies

Identification of state with interests of working classes, through medium of political party

Removal of old institutions and laws redolent of privilege

State direction of economic activity in interests of equal distribution of wealth and opportunity

◀ A Communist party reading room in 1920s Moscow with portraits of Lenin and Marx on prominent display. The Soviet state prompted universal literacy but exercised control over the press and other media. Political education, a concept inherited from earlier socialists, became a powerful propaganda weapon in the hands of the Soviets. Growth in the state-sponsored media and in education gave greater access to the public consciousness, while a strict central control of the information ensured that this consciousness reflected the values of the Soviet system.

▼ A scene from a 1925 Soviet movie evokes the Communist state's role as the bringer of progress to the huge peasant population. Behind the awe-struck peasant worthies is a picture of Mikhail Frunze who preceded Trotsky as commissar for war in 1924. In fact, the one-party state's impact on rural communities was less impressive. New peasant landholders resisted attempts to break down private production, while underinvestment in agricultural improvement led to sector-wide stagnation and profound food shortages in developing industrial centers.

culminating in workers' occupations of factories in Milan and Turin at the end of August. The unrest spread to other parts of Italy and soon affected half a million workers. The Socialist party however, instead of trying to turn these events into a political attack on the state, negotiated a compromise settlement, and the possibility of establishing a workers' state receded.

Italian socialism received another setback when the party split on the question of the Comintern. The majority of the party only accepted Lenin's 21 conditions with reservations. The sizable minority of hardliners who agreed with Lenin left the congress to form the Italian Communist party. The Italian socialist movement, increasingly torn by dissent, became an easy prey for its Fascist enemies in the years that followed.

In Germany too the split in the socialist movement begun in the war widened with the experience of revolution and the activities of the Comintern. After the collapse of the monarchy in 1918, government passed to a coalition of Majority Socialists (SPD) and Independent Socialists (USPD). However, the tendency of Friedrich Ebert, the SPD head of government, to collaborate with officers in the old Imperial army caused the coalition to break up on 27 December 1918. After elections on 19 January 1919, SPD, the largest party in the constituent assembly, shunned the USPD and collaborated with nonsocialist parties like the Roman Catholic Center and the liberal Democratic party. The government's crackdown of radical left-wing stirrings in Berlin in January 1919 and Bavaria in April and May of the same year added to the bitterness.

In the Reichstag elections of June 1920 Ebert's

SPD lost substantial ground to the much more radical Independent Socialists. At the USPD's Halle Congress in October 1920 a majority of the delegates voted to accept Lenin's 21 conditions and join the Comintern and, in effect, the small German Communist party (KPD).

The new Communist recruits were eager for revolutionary action despite the caution of more experienced comrades. Inspired by Soviet Comintern leaders, especially Trotsky, their revolutionary adventurism culminated at the end of October 1923 in attempts to seize power in Saxony and Thuringia and in an abortive coup in Hamburg. These failures made the KPD depend still more on the Comintern leadership and transformed it into an instrument of Soviet policy. The German Social Democrats – whom it described as "social fascists" – became its main target. The KPD attracted young workers, particularly those not already members of trade unions, and its representation in the Reichstag grew steadily, though it never achieved the same amount of popular support as the SPD.

In France, the postwar labor unrest and the repressive policies of rightwing governments towards labor unions encouraged a radical response amongst socialists and trade unionists, especially those who had earlier been attracted to anarcho-syndicalism. At the Congress of Tours, in December 1920, the French Socialist party voted by a large majority to join the Comintern, setting themselves up as the French Communist party and controlling both the Socialist party apparatus and its newspaper. Later, many converts who rebelled against control from Moscow, left and joined a re-established French Socialist party under Léon Blum. In France, as in Italy and Germany, the working-class socialist movement remained divided, but its class-war rhetoric still frightened the propertied classes.

Mussolini and Italian fascism
On 23 March 1919 Benito Mussolini established the Fasci Italiani di Combattimento in Milan, a movement standing for a mixture of populist extremism – demanding a capital levy, land for peasants and the confiscation of ecclesiastical property – and violent nationalism. Fascist squads, distinctive in their black shirts, stormed the headquarters of trade unions and rural co-operatives and assaulted socialist and Christian Democratic functionaries as well as German or Slav minorities in border areas. These actions were applauded by Italian middle classes, including landowners and industrial employers, who feared that a socialist revolution would overwhelm Italy, and the police often turned a blind eye to fascist excesses.

Even the veteran Liberal politician Giolitti, who headed the government from June 1920 to June 1921, regarded fascist activities with complacency and even welcomed Mussolini into an electoral alliance in May 1920. With the socialists' Roman Catholic people's party and liberal groups divided and in disarray, Italy's political crisis deepened and support for the fascists grew rapidly. After many acts of fascist violence against political opponents during the summer of 1922,

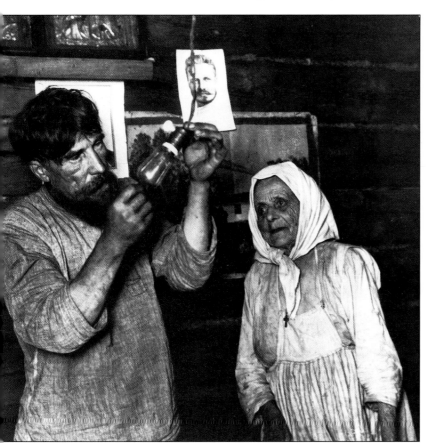

▼ Mussolini's demagogic antics made him appear ridiculous to many people, but his message of national renewal, strong government and overseas expansion struck a vibrant chord in Italy. Denied promised territorial gains by the 1919 peace setlement and demoralized by economic stagnation and the near paralysis of government, many Italians were ready to turn to a strong man with a simple message promising to restore the glory of ancient Rome.

some of the leaders of the Catholic People's party attempted to form an alliance with the socialists to oppose fascism. However, the Vatican publicly distanced itself from any such move, causing a split in the People's party.

During the night of 27/28 October 1922 Fascist squads took over most cities in northern and central Italy and thousands of "blackshirts" began to converge on Rome. Army units and police blocked the path of the insurgents, and having gained the upper hand, began preparing to recapture the provincial cities. The prime minister Luigi Facta asked the king to declare a state of siege but when Victor Emmanuel refused, Facta resigned, enabling Mussolini to demand the right to form a government, and on 31 October 1922 he did so.

At first Mussolini led his government as an orthodox prime minister, including in his government members of other parties. The chastened, but not altogether unsympathetic, parliament gave him a year's plenary powers to carry out reforms. During that time he extended fascist control over the judiciary and civil administration and intimidated working-class opposition. He appeased the business community by cutting taxes, privatizing state enterprises, dropping plans for unemployment insurance and replacing trade unions with a system of class collaboration in which industrialists were well represented.

In November 1923 Mussolini put through an electoral reform to give the largest party in parliament two-thirds of the seats. The elections of April 1924 returned an enormous Fascist majority after a violent campaign of intimidation against its political opponents. One Socialist deputy, Giacomo Matteotti, who denounced the violence was kidnapped on 10 June 1924 and murdered. A wave of popular revulsion followed and on 13 June the opposition walked out of parliament in protest in the Aventine secession. Moreover, they failed to agree on what positive action to take and Mussolini's confidence recovered. On 31 December 1924 he suppressed all opposition newspapers and arrested opponents. Two years later, in November 1926, the Fascists excluded opposition deputies from the chamber and established a one-party dictatorship.

Military takeover in Spain

The emergence of mass parties on the left, particularly the socialists and anarchists, and labor unrest troubled the Spanish parliamentary monarchy. Liberal elites too who had supported a constitution to modernize the country were dismayed by social disruption, while the army, traditionally an important factor in Spanish politics was dissatisfied by the government's neglect of military needs and by its weakness in dealing with colonial insurrection in Morocco. Matters came to a head when, in September 1923, General Primo de Rivera overthrew parliamentary government and established a military dictatorship. Like Mussolini, he retained the monarchy. De Rivera had no political party, but he shared Mussolini's contempt for conventional politics and imported Fascist rhetoric into Spain. His regime was welcomed by similar social groups to those who supported Mussolini.

Nazism and the decline of Weimar

The most virulent form of fascism characterized the Nazi movement, established in Munich in 1919 by Adolf Hitler. Hitler was born in Braunau, in Austria on 20 April 1889. Footloose art student in Vienna and Munich, he joined the German army in August 1914 and served as a front soldier throughout the war. He was also employed by the army as a propagandist against Bolshevism.

In the autumn of 1919 Hitler joined an obscure nationalist group called the German Workers' party, at that time being led by Anton Drexler. He quickly became the party's chief propagandist and spokesman, whose skills helped to win recruits to the cause. On 24 February 1920 the party changed its name to the National Socialist German Workers' party (NSDAP, or Nazis for short). Its aim was to win working people away from class war to support the cause of German nationalism. Its chief targets were Marxists, the Weimar Republic and the Jews.

Hitler inherited a virulent antisemitism, which had existed in Germany and Austria before the war, and exaggerated it to suit his own purposes. The international conspiracy of the Jews could be blamed for everything, from Germany's military defeat to the Bolshevik revolution, and from stock-exchange speculations to crippling strikes.

The Nazis established a paramilitary formation, the brown-shirted SA, (*Sturmabteilungen*), to protect their meetings and to break up those held by their opponents. As such they were not alone. In the years 1920-23 the antirepublican Bavarian government encouraged the existence of nationalist paramilitary groups, hoping that they might form the basis of an army of liberation from both the Versailles treaty and the Weimar system.

In 1923 Germany's massive inflation ruined many of the middle classes and created a crisis of confidence in the Weimar Republic. When in August of that year Chancellor Stresemann suspended passive resistance against the French occupation troops in the Ruhr, the Bavarian government encouraged a military revolt against the republican regime. However the army, headed by General Hans von Seeckt, was too cautious and the Bavarian government also wavered. Hitler, seizing the initiative, carried out a coup in Munich on the night of 8 November 1923. Although it failed, Hitler gained a personal victory, using his trial to proclaim his own responsibility for the coup, in contrast to other nationalist figures who tried to deny their complicity. A sympathetic court sentenced him to a brief period of comfortable imprisonment, during which he wrote *Mein Kampf*, a testimony to his hatred of the Jews and his geopolitical objective of expanding German "living space" (*Lebensraum*) by attacking Bolshevik Russia.

Democracy under threat

On the surface, the years that followed Hitler's putsch, 1924-28, were the most stable in the short history of the Weimar Republic. Political violence declined, the currency was stabilized and Germany's international situation improved. In the Reichstag elections of May 1928 the Nazis fared

What is Fascism?

The rise of Mussolini began a long debate into the nature of fascism as a political movement or ideology. Conventionally, fascism has been seen as a virulently destructive display of irrational politics attributable to perverse social or cultural processes at work in the evolution of particular nation states. Marxists, on the other hand, have interpreted fascism as a preemptive strike on the part of "late" capitalism to combat the threat posed by revolutionary socialism.

On a third interpretation, a highly politicized nationalism was dedicated to realizing the vision of a new order born out of the ashes of the old one. In this idea, only the rejuvenated nation can restore to human life the value and intensity eroded by "decadent" forces such as liberalism, communism, individualism, materialism, pacifism or cosmopolitanism. The urge to found a strong, healthy national community, and even create a new type of human being, is common to most forms of fascism.

Historically, fascism embraced a number of interwar movements, including the Falange (Spain), the Iron Guard (Romania), Rex (Belgium), as well as British and French Fascist parties. The most virulent forms of fascism were those of Mussolini and Hitler. The atrocities committed under Nazism were the consequence of a sustained effort to eradicate all alleged enemies of the German people so as to make way for the reborn nation the Third Reich. Following the third definition, fascism, though outlawed after World War II, has since reappeared in Latin America and in some of the new right movements in Europe.

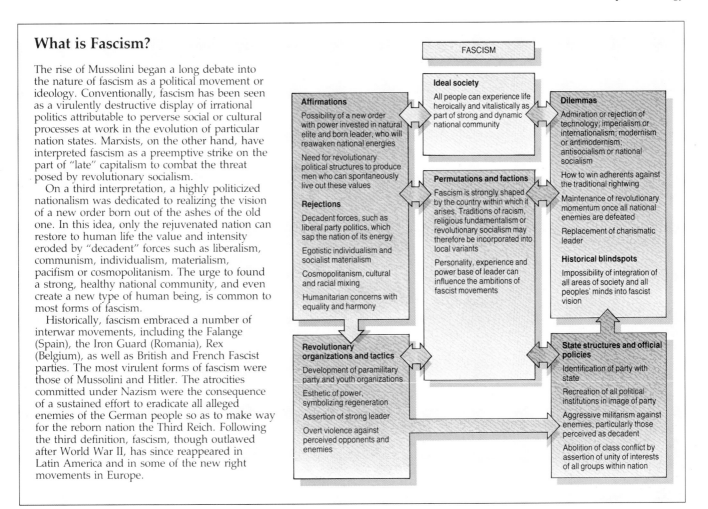

FASCISM

Ideal society
All people can experience life heroically and vitalistically as part of strong and dynamic national community

Affirmations
Possibility of a new order with power invested in natural elite and born leader, who will reawaken national energies

Need for revolutionary political structures to produce men who can spontaneously live out these values

Rejections
Decadent forces, such as liberal party politics, which sap the nation of its energy

Egotistic individualism and socialist materialism

Cosmopolitanism, cultural and racial mixing

Humanitarian concerns with equality and harmony

Permutations and factions
Fascism is strongly shaped by the country within which it arises. Traditions of racism, religious fundamentalism or revolutionary socialism may therefore be incorporated into local variants.

Personality, experience and power base of leader can influence the ambitions of fascist movements

Dilemmas
Admiration or rejection of technology; imperialism or internationalism; modernism or antimodernism; antisocialism or national socialism

How to win adherents against the traditional rightwing

Maintenance of revolutionary momentum once all national enemies are defeated

Replacement of charismatic leader

Historical blindspots
Impossibility of integration of all areas of society and all peoples' minds into fascist vision

Revolutionary organizations and tactics
Development of paramilitary party and youth organizations

Esthetic of power, symbolizing regeneration

Assertion of strong leader

Overt violence against perceived opponents and enemies

State structures and official policies
Identification of party with state

Recreation of all political institutions in image of party

Aggressive militarism against enemies, particularly those perceived as decadent

Abolition of class conflict by assertion of unity of interests of all groups within nation

badly getting only 2.1 percent of the vote and 12 parliamentary seats. They had, however, extended their organization into northern and central Germany. The party attracted the young and, though it was predominantly middle-class, it appealed to a broader social cross-section than most of the established parties.

In both Italy and Germany the enemies of democracy were helped by parliamentary systems that did not produce powerful governments able to maintain clearcut policies and generate business confidence. Any hopes of fundamental reforms in institutions such as education or the civil service evaporated and all the economic problems were blamed on the system. Even so, by 1925 fascism had only taken root in Italy and Spain. Elsewhere in Europe parliamentary government, albeit in many countries weak and often attenuated, had so far managed to survive.

In Japan, democracy was extended to give universal suffrage for men over 25 in 1925. But a wave of strikes in the economic slump experienced in Japan through the 1920s resulted in an increase in leftwing parties until Communist party leaders were arrested *en masse* in 1928. Culturally and politically, the country osillated between an international and westernizing attitude and a militaristic and imperialist one.

However, the United States, the strongest of all the democracies, was less concerned with the state of European democracy than with domestic matters such as the prohibition of the sale of al-

cohol, which became law in December 1919, and laws restricting immigration passed in 1922. The alliance to defend democracy during the war ran counter to the thinking of the time.

The period between 1923 and 1929 was one of unparalleled American prosperity despite some regional backwardness and growing discrimination against the nation's black population. The wage output increased by 13 percent and manufacturing by 50 percent. As President Calvin Coolidge remarked on 4 December 1928 the country could "regard the present with satisfaction and the future with optimism".

▼ The Nazi party of the early 1920s was a small and loosely organized group of rightwing nationalists embracing several different visions of Germany's future. It grew in strength by exploiting discontent with the Versailles peace settlement and the failure of the Weimar Republic to deal with the country's severe economic problems. Only when he achieved a substantial level of electoral support did Hitler assert himself as the party's sole leader.

TRADE UNIONISM AND SOCIALISM

The task of trade unions was either to improve the conditions of the working classes within capitalist society, or to help to build a new socialist order. Within capitalist society the main aim was to bargain collectively for better wages and conditions for the whole workforce; socialism required the nationalization of industries, transport and banks. The main weapon of trade unions was strike action, its highest form the general strike of all industries. Workers tended to vote (if they had the vote) for socialist parties, but trade unions themselves were often distrustful of party politics, because even socialist politicians were seen as seeking power for themselves.

Four broad strategies were tried. The first was revolutionary. The revolutions of 1917 in Russia began as an explosion of strikes, by the mastering of which the Bolshevik party came to power. The Bolsheviks then claimed that the new state took care of workers' interests, and labor organizations lost their independence.

The second strategy prevailed in countries which remained capitalist. The war effort had obliged capitalist governments to bring labor organizations into partnership. The example of the Bolsheviks and a postwar boom in the economy provoked a wave of strikes in 1919–20, with one of its demands nationalization. But as the economic situation worsened in the 1920s employers regained the whip hand. In Britain, a strike of miners against wage-cuts in 1926 was escalated by the Trade Union Congress (TUC) into a general strike of three million workers. The political complexion of the government was all-important to the success of this strategy. A victory of the socialist-led Popular Front in France in 1936 ushered in a festival of sit-down strikes and factory occupations. The government forced employers to make major concessions.

The third option was that imposed on unions in fascist regimes. In Italy – as in Germany after 1933 – strikes were banned as only fascist trade unions were permitted, regimented into a corporative system which gave the state and employers a free hand to fix wages and conditions. Fourthly, there was the anarcho-syndicalist vision, briefly realized during the Spanish Civil War. A military coup of 1936 knocked out the government, but the unions took the argument into their own hands. They formed popular militias and collectivized farms and factories behind their lines. The anarchists saw unions as organizing cells of a new stateless society.

▶ A meeting of factory workers in Petrograd electing members to the local soviet in 1920. The system whereby elected workers councils or soviets took responsibility for local and central government, was a theoretical high point in the translation of unionism into socialist practice, but in reality unions became mere "transmission belts" for decisions taken by the Communist party.

▶▶ One of the prime targets of unionism was to campaign against dangerous working conditions such as these boys working looms in North Carolina in the early years of the century.

▶ Union solidarity and political ideals were frequently promoted by colorful and graphic banners such as this British example of 1921.

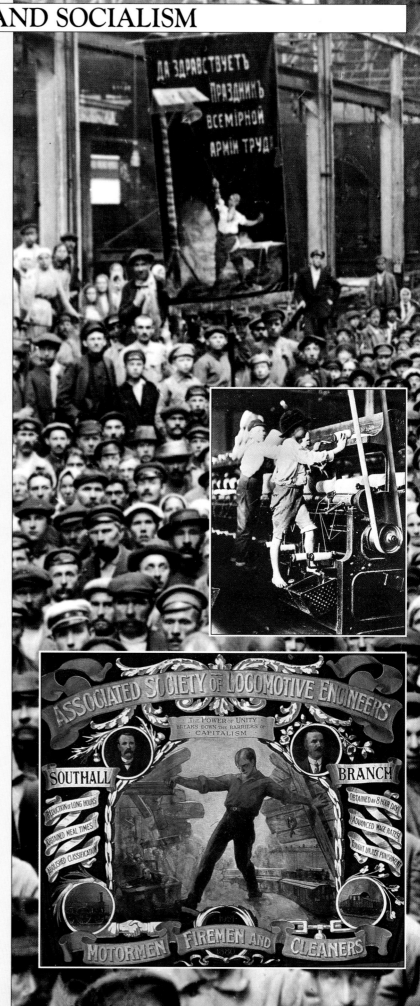

Починить один паровоз значит приблизить голода и нищеты добить окончательно капитализм

ROT FRONT

ARRIBA ESPAÑA

RUSSIA

▲ Politicians such as Jean Jaurès in France campaigned democratically for socialism, opposing revolutionary socialism in the Second International. He also argued for the resolution of international conflict through arbitration and moderation.

▼ ◄ The clenched fist symbolised socialist opposition to capitalism and fascism in the interwar years.

▼ The socialists and communists played a major role in the defense of the Spanish republic against Franco in the 1930s. Here a republican replaces the falangist (rightist) symbol with the hammer and sickle.

1929 · 1945

THE TOTALITARIAN THREAT

Time Chart

	1930	1931	1932	1933	1934	1935	1936	1937
Europe/Mediterranean	• Jan: End of Primo de Rivera's dictatorship in Spain • 1 Jul: Last Allied troops withdrew from German Rhineland	• 14 Apr: King Alfonso XIII left Spain, in face of rising Republicanism • Sep: Yugoslavia adopted new constitution, ending King Alexander's royal dictatorship • Dec: Spain became a republic, with Alcalá Zamora as its 1st president, Manuel Azaña as prime minister	• Feb: Protective tariffs introduced in UK, ending free trade • May: Assassination of French president, Paul Doumer • Jul: Elections made Nazi Party largest in German *Reichstag* (parliament) • 5 Jul: António de Oliveira Salazar made Portuguese prime minister, with virtual dictatorial powers	• Spanish Fascist party, Falange, founded by José Antonio Primo de Rivera (son of former dictator) • 30 Jan: Hitler became German chancellor, at request of President von Hindenburg • Mar: Parliamentary government suspended in Austria, by Chancellor Engelbert Dollfuss • 14 Jul: Germany became 1-party state	• Feb: Signature of Balkan Pact • 17 Mar: Rome Protocols signed • 29–30 Jun: Night of the Long Knives (Ger) • 25 Jul: Assassination of Chancellor Dollfuss by Austrian Nazis • Aug: Adopting title of *Führer*, Hitler abolished German presidency • Dec: Start of Stalinist purges in USSR	• Mar: Saar Basin returned to Germany; Hitler announced German rearmament, repudiating disarmament clauses of Treaty of Versailles • 15 Sep: Nuremberg Laws in Germany, legitimizing anti-semitism • Nov: Restoration of Greek monarchy by plebiscite (King George II)	• Mar: Germany reoccupied Rhineland • Jun: 1st Popular Front government (Fr) • 18 Jul: Start of Spanish Civil War. Oct: General Francisco Franco led provisional Nationalist government • Aug: Gen. Joannis Metaxas, dictator of Greece (to Jan 1941) • October: Berlin–Rome Axis established • 10 Dec: Abdication of King Edward VIII (UK)	• 1 Jan: Public Order Act came into force in UK, banning political uniforms and private armies • 27 Apr: Undefended Basque capital of Guernica destroyed by Nazi aerial bombing (Sp) • Jun: Irish Free State renamed Eire, when new constitution as dominion within Commonwealth came into force
The Middle East	• Mar: Beginning of active civil disobedience campaign by Gandhi in India, with breaking of salt tax laws • May: Syria granted constitution by France	• Universal suffrage introduced in UK colony of Ceylon • Sep–Dec: 2nd Round Table talks on India held in UK; attended by Gandhi • Dec: Conference in Jerusalem (Pal) attended by 22 Muslim nations; warning against Zionism issued	• Sep: Imprisoned in India, Gandhi fasted to improve political status of *Harijans* (untouchables) • 20 Sep: King Ibn Saud created Saudi Arabia from his lands of Nejd and Hejaz • Oct: Iraq achieved full independence from UK on entry to League of Nations	• First Saudi Arabian oil concession made, to Standard Oil Co. of California (US) • Murder of Afghan king, Nadir Khan; succeeded by son, Mohammed Zahir	• Mohammed Ali Jinnah returned to India, to lead new Muslim League Party • Jan: Libya formed by union of Cyrenaica and Tripolitania, with Fezza • Nov: French rejected Young Moroccan nationalists' reforms • Dec: Turkish women granted vote	• Persia officially renamed Iran • 2 Aug: UK Government of India Act proposed federation and provincial autonomy • Nov: Arab parties in Palestine demanded end to Jewish immigration (from 30,000 in 1933 to 61,000 in 1935)	• Apr: King Farouk succeeded his father to Egyptian throne • Apr: Start of Arab rebellion in Palestine (to 1939); formation of secret Jewish force, *Hagannah* • Aug: Anglo–Egyptian Treaty agreed withdrawal of UK forces, except from Suez Canal Zone	• Jan–Feb: 1st general elections in India • 7 Jul: Peel Report in UK recommended partition of Palestine into Arab and Jewish states • 9 Jul: Pact of Saadabad (Tur, Irq, Irn, Afg) for nonaggression
Africa	• May: White women given vote in S Africa • 2 Nov: Makonnen Tafari crowned Emperor Haile Selassie of Ethiopia			• Coalition government formed in S Africa by Hertzog's segregationalist Nationalist Party and Smuts' S African Party	• DF Malan formed Purified Nationalist Party (S Afr) • 5 Dec: Clashes on borders of Ethiopia and Italian Somaliland	• 3 Oct: Ethiopia invaded by Italian troops	• Segregation extended (S Afr) • May: Addis Ababa captured: Ethiopia merged with Italian Somaliland and Eritrea to form Italian E Africa	•
The Americas	• Getúlio Vargas came to power after revolt in Brazil (to 1945) • Feb: General Rafael Trujillo began 31-year dictatorship, Dominican Republic • Jul: Richard Bennett became prime minister of Conservative government in Canada • Dec: US President Hoover presented unemployment relief program to Congress		• Jul: War broke out between Paraguay and Bolivia over Chaco Boreal	• US marines withdrawn from Nicaragua (since 1917) • Mar–Jun, New Deal program: Creation of numerous welfare and unemployment agencies by Franklin D Roosevelt, following his inauguration as 32nd US president • Nov: US–USSR diplomatic and trade relations resumed, after 14 years	• General Lázaro Cárdenas became president of Mexico, instituting program of social reform (to 1940) • Jun: Reciprocal Tariff Act improved US overseas trade relations • Jun: US–Cuban treaty abrogated enforcement of Platt Amendment	• Start of Roosevelt's 2nd New Deal program • Jun: Armistice ended Chaco War between Bolivia and Paraguay • Oct: Liberal Party reelected in Canada • 17 Dec: Death of General Gómez in Venezuela, ending 26-year dictatorship	• 1–23 Dec: Inter-American Conference for Maintenance of Peace	• 1 Jan: General Anastazio Garcia became president of Nicaragua; start of family's dictatorship
Asia and Pacific	• Nov: Assassination of Japanese prime minister, Hamaguchi • Dec: Launch of 1st Kuomintang campaign against Chinese communist bases (Soviets)	• New Zealand National Party formed, from United and Reform parties • 18 Sep: Start of Japanese occupation of Manchuria (NE China) • Oct: Chinese Soviet republic proclaimed by Mao Zedong, in Kiangsi province	• 18 Feb: Japanese puppet state of Manchukuo established in Manchuria • May: End to party government in Japan after assassination of Prime Minister Inukai • Jun: Coup in Siam led to constitutional government	• Feb: League of Nations' censureship over Manchukuo led to Japan's withdrawal from organization • Apr: Western Australians voted 2:1 to secede from Commonwealth; move rejected by UK government	• Mar: Philippines granted autonomy and president by US Tydings–McDuffie Act, with US high commissioner retaining some rights • Oct: Long March began, as Communists broke through Nationalist encirclement of Kiangsi Soviet (China)	• 1st New Zealand Labor government elected • Oct: End of Long March, as Communists reached Yenan, N Shensi (China) • Nov: Manuel Quezon became 1st president of Commonwealth of Philippines	• Feb: Failure of coup by military extremists in Japan; power of central faction consolidated • Dec: In China, Jiang Jieshi kidnapped by communists to force nationalist–communist front against Japan	• China signed nonaggression pact with USSR • 7 Jul–23 Nov: Japanese occupation of NE and E China
World	• Worldwide unemployment as Depression took effect • 21 Jan–22 Apr: London Naval Conference; treaty limited size and number of warships and submarines (UK, US, Jap)	• 11 Dec, Statute of Westminster: Dominions (Can, Aus, NZ, S Afr, Irish Free State, Newfoundland) defined as autonomous and equal in status within Commonwealth of Nations	• Feb: League of Nations disarmament talks, Geneva (Sui); no agreement reached • 21 Jul–20 Aug: Imperial Economic Conference in Ottawa (Can)	• Jun–Jul: World Monetary and Economic Conference held in UK; no consensus reached • Oct: Germany withdrew from Geneva disarmament talks and League of Nations	• Sep: USSR joined League of Nations	• 18 Nov: League of Nations imposed economic sanctions on Italy following its invasion of Ethiopia	• Jul: League's sanctions against Italy suspended, despite its annexation of Ethiopia • 25 Nov: German–Japanese Anti-Comintern Pact against international communism	• Nov: Italy joined Anti-Comintern Pact • 11 Nov: Italy withdrew from League of Nations

1938	1939	1940	1941	1942	1943	1944	1945
13 Mar: German ...ry occupation ...stria; *Anschluss* ...) proclaimed ...Sep: Munich ...ment (UK, Ger, ...); led to German ...xation of Sudeten ...n (Tch) 10 Nov: ...allnacht pogrom ...rmany	• Mar: End of Spanish civil war • 6 Apr: Mutual assistance pact (Pol, Fr, UK) • 22 May: Italo–German Pact of Steel • 24 Aug: Non-aggression pact between USSR and Germany • 1 Sep: German invasion of Poland. • 3 Sep: UK and France declared war on Germany: start of World War II	• 13 Mar: Russo–Finnish armistice • 10 May: Winston Churchill became UK prime minister • 10 Jun: Italy entered war on German side • 22 Jun: French Pétain government signed armistice with Germany following invasion (5 Jun). Jun: Free French movement established by Gen. de Gaulle in UK • 27 Sep: Signature of Tripartite Pact (Ger, Ita, Jap)	• Yugoslav resistance movements organized • Apr: German invasion of Yugoslavia and Greece • 7 May: Stalin became USSR prime minister • 22 Jun: Start of German invasion of USSR • 6 Sep: In German-occupied territory, ordered to wear Star of David • 11 Dec: Italy and Germany declared war on US	• 50,000 Jews killed in Warsaw, as SS "purged" ghettos (Pol) • 26 May: 20-year mutual aid treaty signed by UK and USSR • 1 Dec: Publication of Beveridge Report, basis for Welfare State in postwar UK	• Jun: French Committee of National Liberation set up in Algiers (Mor) under De Gaulle and Giraud • 25 Jul: Resignation and arrest of Mussolini (Ita) • Sep–Oct: Italy forced to make peace with Allies and declare war on Germany • 29–30 Nov: Jajce Congress announced Yugoslav republic; partisan leader Tito given title of Marshal	• French women enfranchised • 6 Jun, D-Day: Launch of 2nd Front, with Allied invasion of France • 17 Jun: Iceland became an independent republic • 25 Aug: Liberation of Paris (Fr) • 23 Oct: De Gaulle's government (Fr) recognized by Allies • Dec: Civil war between rival resistance groups in liberated Greece	• 28 Apr: Execution of Mussolini by Italian partisans • 30 Apr: Hitler committed suicide (Ger) • 7–8 May: Surrender of Germany • 29 Nov: Federal People's Republic of Yugoslavia proclaimed, under President Tito • Dec: 2nd Austrian republic established, under President Karl Renner
...afd government of ...s Pasha ousted by ...Farouk (Egy) ...v: Death of ...afa Kemal ...ürk); Ismet Inönü ...eeded him as ...dent of Turkey	• Oct: Turkey signed mutual assistance pact with UK and France	• Spanish troops occupied free port of Tangier throughout war • Mar: Muslim League called for split of India and a new "Pakistan" • Sep: Beginning of Italy's N African campaign • 9 Dec: Start of 1st major UK land offensive in Western Desert	• Feb: Reinstatement of Egypt's *Wafd* government by UK authorities • May: UK occupation of Iraq • Aug: Joint UK–USSR invasion of Iran • 16 Sep: Abdication of Reza Shah in favour of his son, Mohammad Reza Pahlavi (Iran)	• 8 Aug: Indian Congress passed a Quit India resolution • 24 Oct–4 Nov: 2nd Battle of Alamein opened Allies' final N African offensive; Italian and German armies forced into retreat • 8 Nov: Allied troops landed in French NW Africa	• Feb: Independence manifesto presented by Algerian nationalist leader Ferhat Abbas to French and Allied authorities • 12–13 May: Surrender of Italian and German armies in N Africa	• French citizenship extended to certain Muslim categories in N African colonies • 1 Jan: Syria and Lebanon proclaimed independence from France	• 24 Feb: Egyptian premier, Ahmed Maher Pasha, assassinated, after declaring war on Germany and Japan • 22 Mar: Arab League established (Egy, Syr, Irq, Leb, Sau Ar, Transj, Yem, Arab Pal) • May: Start of anti-French uprising by Algerian nationalists
		• Aug: Italian forces invaded British Somaliland	• 5 May: Haile Selassie returned to Addis Ababa to resume Ethiopian throne • Nov: Allied conquest of Italian E Africa completed			• Jan, Brazzaville Declaration: France's postwar colonial policy in Africa outlined; autonomy and independence rejected	
...pular Front ...rnment in Chile ...blished by ...dent Aguirre ...a (to 1941); led ...cial reform ...r: In Mexico, ...opriation of US ...UK oil companies, ...spute over wages ...conditions 27 Dec, ...aration of Lima: ...an-American ...erence confirmed ...–South solidarity	• 5 Sep: US neutrality announced at outbreak of WWII	• Beginning of long period of military dictatorship in Paraguay • 26 Jan: US abrogated 1911 commercial treaty with Japan	• 11 Mar: Lend–Lease Act authorized President Roosevelt to aid countries vital to US interests (to Aug 1945) • 8 Dec: US declared war on Japan following attack on fleet at Pearl Harbor	• Jan: Meeting in Rio de Janeiro, 21 American republics pledged to end relations with Axis powers; 9 had already declared war	• Alexander Bustamente founded Jamaican Labor Party • 4 Jun: Coup in Argentina led to establishment of provisional military dictatorship	• Oct–Dec: Revolution led to 1st free elections in Guatemala • 7 Nov: Franklin D. Roosevelt elected US president for an unprecedented 4th term	• 12 Apr: Death of President Roosevelt; Harry S. Truman succeeded him • 29 Oct: Revolution in Brazil overthrew President Vargas; led to adoption of new constitution (in 1946), strengthening civil liberties
...New Zealand, ...al Security Act ...ided state medical ...ce	• National conscription ordinance in Japan • Jun: Siam officially renamed Praethet Thai, "land of the free" • 3 Sep: Australia and New Zealand declared war on Germany	• Feb: Coronation of 5-year-old Dalai Lama in Tibet • Mar: Japanese puppet government established in Nanking (Chn) • 22 Sep: Start of Japanese occupation of Indochina	• 13 Apr: Japan signed a 5-year neutrality agreement with USSR • Jul: Joint protectorate announced (Jap, Vichy Fr) over Indochina • 7 Dec: Bombing (Jap) of Pearl Harbor, Hawaii • 8 Dec: Start of Japanese occupation of SE Asia	• Feb–Apr: Japanese planes bombed N and W Australia • 15 Feb: Fall of Singapore to Japanese • May: Japanese occupation of SE Asia completed • 4–5 Jun, Battle of Midway: US naval victory over Japan	• Feb (from 7 Aug 1942), Battles of Guadalcanal: US Marines defended strategic site from Japanese occupation	• Dec: Australian Liberal Party formally constituted, under Robert Menzies	• 15 Aug: Japanese surrender – US atom bombs on Hiroshima & Nagasaki (6 and 9 Aug) • Aug: USSR and US split Korea on 38th parallel • 17 Aug: Republic of Indonesia declared • Sep: Republic of Vietnam proclaimed
...Apr: Switzerland ...ested uncon-...al neutrality, ...ague of Nations			• 9–12 Aug, Atlantic Charter: After meeting between Churchill (UK) and Roosevelt (US), principles for postwar world published; endorsed by USSR and 14 other Allies	• 1 Jan, Declaration of the United Nations: Anti-Axis pledge of cooperation by 26 nations • Aug: Manhattan Project set up in US, to develop atomic bomb	• May: Formal dissolution of 3rd International (Comintern) • 18 May–3 Jun: UN Food Conference in US • 9 Nov: UN Relief and Rehabilitation Administration founded	• Jul, Bretton Woods Conference (US): re International Monetary Fund (IMF) and World Bank (27 Dec 1945) • Aug–Oct, Dumbarton Oaks Conference (US): re UN organization and Security Council	• 4–11 Feb, Yalta Conference: USSR, UK and US leaders. 16 Jul – 2 Aug, Potsdam Conference • 25 Apr–26 Jun, San Francisco Conference (US): re UN constitution

Datafile

The Great Depression was at once a product of the dislocation of the world economy caused by World War I and a major contribution to the destabilization of world politics which caused World War II. The Great War had broken networks of international trade, forced industrial economies down dangerous corners of change, and artificially altered the balance between victor and vanquished. Recovery was an unstable process, attended by hot-house growth and massive speculation, and by the late 1920s the entire international economy was in a state of volatile disequilibrium, which required only the collapse of the US stock market to push it into longterm depression. The Depression, attended by mass unemployment and material shortages, inevitably produced political change. As traditional forms of government grappled ineffectually with huge problems, electors turned increasingly to advocates of strong government and radical political solutions. By the time the world economy began to recover, preparations for war were already well underway.

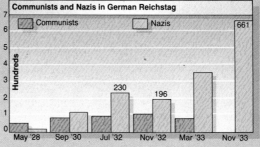

Communists and Nazis in German Reichstag

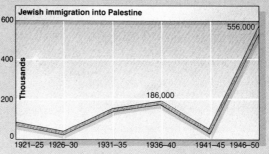

Jewish immigration into Palestine

◀ In Germany, the Communist and National Socialist (Nazi) parties presented rival solutions to the nation's problems. Although the Communists began with the political advantage, their rigid adherence to Moscow left them vulnerable to the popular nationalism that was being preached by Hitler.

▼ ▼ Between 1928 and 1940 the state-imposed policy of collectivization changed the face of Soviet agriculture, replacing small individual peasant holdings with large communal farms. The economic results were impressive but the human cost was high as a traditional way of life was destroyed and opposition ruthlessly suppressed.

▼ US domination of the world industrial scene was damaged by the Great Depression (which hit the American economy more heavily than many of its competitors) and by renewed competition. Particularly significant in the latter regard were Germany, reasserting its strength under new leadership, and the USSR.

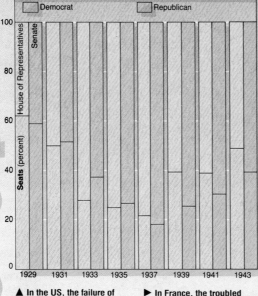

US representation

▲ Jewish immigration into Palestine rose dramatically in the 1930s as political persecution and economic difficulties drove many out of Europe in search of a fresh start in a new national homeland. The war rudely interrupted the migration, but with the return of peace those fortunate enough to survive genocide flooded towards Palestine.

Soviet collectives

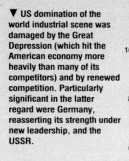

Manufacturing output

1928

1938

USA
Germany
UK
France
USSR
Italy
Others

▲ In the US, the failure of Hoover's Republicans to provide solutions to economic crisis, the Democrats under the banner of Roosevelt's "New Deal", produced a transformation of the political balance.

US Presidents
1929 H Hoover   R
1933 FD Roosevelt D
1937 FD Roosevelt D
1941 FD Roosevelt D

▶ In France, the troubled political climate of the 1920s produced heavy polarization, with the traditional radical, socialist and republican parties losing ground to Communist and rightwing extremists. The resulting governments were neither stable nor effective and France entered World War II in a state of political division and low morale.

French elections

1932 seats

1936 seats

Radical Socialist
Socialist
Republican
Left Republican
Radical independent
Center party/Right Wing
Communist

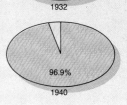

Soviet collectivization

1928

1932

1940

Households collectivized
Other farm households

POLITICS OF THE DEPRESSION

The Depression and the
New Deal

The fall of the Weimar
Republic and the rise of
Nazism

Collectivization in the
Soviet Union

The Popular Front in
France

At the beginning of 1929 the world seemed to
be dominated by democratic states with
political systems that were liberal in character.
The only major exceptions were Italy and the
Soviet Union. Among the democracies, the
United States was by far the most powerful and
the wealthiest. In March 1929 the new US president Herbert Hoover promised a "new day" that
would bring more progress towards prosperity.
Seven months later, on 24 October, the Wall
Street stock market collapsed and a catastrophic
slump led to widespread bankruptcy and unemployment both at home and abroad. Yet, despite
widespread impoverishment and insecurity, the
American people continued to support the traditional Republican and Democratic parties.

Franklin Delano Roosevelt, a Democrat who
succeeded Hoover as president in 1933, had been
an energetic governor of New York state,
introducing social reforms and state relief for
victims of the slump. Roosevelt demanded from
Congress the same powers to deal with the
economic emergency as would be granted to him
in a war against a foreign invader. Inaugurated
on 4 March, he at once closed all banks and sum-

moned an emergency sitting of Congress to enact
new banking legislation. In the following months, Roosevelt rushed through a mass of relief
measures for agriculture and the unemployed, including the establishment of a Civilian Conserva-
tion Corps for environmental protection and a
Federal Emergency Relief Administration. His
National Recovery Act, passed on 16 June 1933,
enabled federal agencies to regulate pricing arrangements and conditions of work in order to
halt the deflationary spiral and increase employment. By 1934 unemployment was falling, bank
reserves were rising and bankruptcies were in
decline.

However, despite Roosevelt's New Deal, as he
called it, the US economy remained depressed
compared with how it had been in 1928. In 1935
Roosevelt secured an Emergency Relief Approp-
riation of nearly five billion dollars, which was
channeled through a new agency, the Works Progress Administration, to create more work. The
Social Security Act of June 1935 provided federal
funds for the handicapped and the poor, and a
system for unemployment insurance.

In his foreign policy, Roosevelt was an isola-

▼ A world out of work.
The financial crisis of 1929
produced a massive business
slump, condemning millions
to unemployment. The
bewildered workforce
supported any leader who
promised to restore pride
and prosperity. In the United
States this produced
Roosevelt and the New Deal,
but in Germany it brought in
Hitler.

tionist. Although he recognized the threat to peace posed by Nazi Germany, he refused to allow the United States to become entangled in European affairs, preferring to concentrate on solving the domestic crisis. In August 1935 Congress passed the Neutrality Act, forbidding the United States to supply arms to belligerent countries. Roosevelt himself publicly boasted of American non-involvement in European conflicts.

The end of German democracy
By 1928, Adolf Hitler was the undisputed leader of racialist, intransigent anti-republicanism in Germany. However, in the elections to the Reichstag (German parliament) held in that year, his Nazi party gained only 12 seats. On 9 July 1929 the leader of the German National People's party, Hugenberg, set up a committee to oppose the Young Plan, a revised reparations payments scheme, by organizing a plebiscite to condemn as traitors politicians who accepted such a scheme. Hitler's participation in the campaign gave the Nazis good publicity through Hugenberg's syn-

dicated newspapers. Although the campaign failed, the Nazis benefited from it and lost none of their independence.

After the US stock-market crash had crippled the German economy, the republican coalition government faced a crisis over unemployment benefit, forcing socialist chancellor Hermann Müller to resign his office. His successor, Heinrich Brüning, invoked emergency powers to rule without a parliamentary majority, but was forced to dissolve the Reichstag and hold fresh elections. These gave Hitler's Nazis a gain of 107 seats, second only to the Social Democrats. The Nazi party appealed to nearly all sections of society, except for Roman Catholics and unionized industrial workers. In particular, the vote of smaller middle-class parties collapsed, as their supporters deserted to the Nazis.

To meet Germany's deepening economic crisis Brüning imposed austerity measures that forced many firms to close. As unemployment rose to five million in February 1931 and six million in February 1932, support for the Nazis grew. On 10 April 1932 Hitler stood as presidential candidate against Hindenburg, and though he was defeated, he gained over thirteen million votes. At the Reichstag elections held on 31 July of that year the Nazis received 37.4 per cent of the votes cast and became the largest party with 230 seats. Apart from the Communists and Social Democrats, most parties were willing to compromise with the Nazis if Hitler would accept a subordinate role. However, he refused, even after further elections in November showed a drop in Nazi support. By this time the official and propertied classes in Germany, who had hoped to use Hitler but contain him within a government of the right, were seriously alarmed. Franz von Papen, who had succeeded Brüning, was replaced by the army leader General Kurt von Schleicher, but he too failed to resolve the crisis and came under pressure from his military colleagues, who disliked the army becoming involved in politics.

► The pageantry of power. Hitler, like other rightwing dictators, made extensive use of paramilitary displays, uniforms and banners to underpin his grasp on power. To the dispirited people of Germany the Nazis promised the rebirth of a nation.

◄► The political parties of the 1930s made extensive use of the cartoon to attack their opponents and put across their own message. Some cartoons were grim and austere in their approach, others were flippant and amusing. To German Communists Hitler was an oppressor of the working class, enslaving it in the service of capitalism and militarism (left) – a view not always shared by the millions who regained employment, prosperity and a sense of national worth under the Nazi regime. European governments were too easily deluded by Hitler's love of display and histrionics, and even perceptive British cartoonists portrayed him as a bloated demagog with no firm grasp on his people's loyalties (right).

Conflict in Palestine

British colonialism faced intractable problems in Palestine, where tensions were growing between Arab inhabitants and an increasing number of Jewish settlers fleeing from persecution in Europe. In 1935 there were 65,000 new arrivals – double the figure for 1933. In December 1935 the British proposed a mixed legislative council for Palestine, but this was rejected by the Zionists because Jews would have considerably fewer representatives than Arabs. The Palestinian Arabs reacted strongly. Led by the Mufti of Jerusalem, Amin al-Husaini, they organized a strike which lasted from April to October 1936 and was accompanied by serious violence. With no prospect of a compromise settlement, the intensification of racialist pressure on Jewish communities in Europe and the ever-growing numbers of Jewish immigrants from Europe meant that the situation was bound to grow worse.

► A visionary Jewish settlement of the 1920s.

ALL BLOWN UP AND NOWHERE TO GO

SUPER-WINDBAG

TOTAL ABSENCE OF ANY CONSTRUCTIVE POLICY SO FAR

Hitler

end. On 2 May 1933 the Nazis abolished trade unions and on 14 July declared Germany a one-party state. They reduced the Reichstag to a rubber stamp and on 30 January 1934 abolished individual state (*Land*) parliaments.

Political opponents were held without trial, in concentration camps, tortured and sometimes murdered. The police were under Nazi control. The army was acquiescent, especially since Hitler promised large-scale rearmament. Ernst Röhm, the leader of the Nazi militia, the SA (*Sturm-Abteilung* or "stormtroops"), had himself hoped to take over the armed forces. However, the SA's unruly behavior had made them unpopular and on 30 June 1934 Hitler ordered Röhm's murder, a purge of the SA leadership and the liquidation of other political opponents. The SS (*Schutz Staffel*, or "defense squadron"), a Nazi elite force, carried out the killings on what became known as the "night of the long knives". To the German public, the eclipse of the SA seemed to herald a return to a more orderly method of government.

When President Hindenburg died on 2 August 1934 Hitler abolished the presidency and assumed dictatorial powers as Führer (leader). The army took an oath of allegiance to him on the same day. Hitler appointed Heinrich Himmler, who was head of the SS, to be in charge of the political police (Gestapo) in Germany and made the SS responsible for the concentration camps. The Hitler Youth movement and Dr Joseph Goebbels' Propaganda Ministry became increasingly important in preparing the German people for military struggle. In the autumn of 1936 a new four-year plan was announced under Hermann Göring's leadership, ostensibly to maximize economic self-sufficiency, but in reality to equip Germany for war by 1940.

Hitler's dictatorship was fascist and viciously antisemitic. It destroyed freedom of expression and denied parliamentary government and individual rights under the law. However, the Nazis did not threaten private property, except that belonging to Jews and political opponents,

Hitler's Third Reich

To fill the political vacuum, Hitler was called to office as chancellor on 30 January 1933. Hindenburg and his advisers still believed that Hitler could be controlled by experienced cabinet colleagues like von Papen and Hugenberg.

On 28 February 1933 Hitler accused the Communists of setting fire to the Reichstag building and obtained a presidential decree giving the government emergency powers to deal with subversion. This decree remained in force throughout the Third Reich, as the Nazi dictatorship was known, and enabled the Nazis to arrest or silence countless political opponents.

On 5 March, at a further Reichstag election, which was marked by officially sanctioned intimidation, Hitler gained less than forty–four percent of the vote. However, thanks to his nationalist allies and the arrest of Communist deputies before parliament assembled, on 24 March he succeeded in passing an enabling law giving the government the power to rule by decree. Germany's reign of democracy was at an

▲ The 1930s saw massive construction activity in the Soviet Union, as Stalin attempted to provide the country with the necessary economic infrastructure for a modern power. The Ferghana canal, in the southeast of the country, was built after 1935 with no large earthmoving equipment.

The question is sometimes asked, whether it is not possible to reduce the tempo, to hold back the movement. No, it is not possible, comrades!... On the contrary, it is necessary to increase the tempo, our obligations to the workers and peasants of the USSR demand this of us.

JOSEPH STALIN 1929

and business profited under National Socialism (Nazism), especially since trade unions were abolished. Civil servants and army officers, too, welcomed the end of parliamentary democracy, some of them under the delusion that Germany was returning to the kind of authoritarian society it had been under the kaiser.

Stalin's "socialism in one country"

By 1928 the Comintern (Communist International) had become an instrument of Stalin's foreign policy rather than an organization to promote worldwide revolution. At its meeting in Moscow in the summer of that year, the Third Communist International decided that fascism was just a symptom of the last throes of capitalism, and that it was therefore not fascism that was now the main enemy, but the Western Social Democrats and Liberals who tried to prop up parliamentary regimes. However, by 1935, Stalin had changed the party line to call for anti-fascist coalitions of Communists, Socialists and Liberals.

Throughout this period Stalin's main preoccupation was his domestic policy—the building of "socialism in one country"—and, in particular, securing his own personal rule. Having already ousted Trotsky, he next isolated and eliminated his former rightwing allies, Bukharin, Rykov and Tomsky.

From 1928, Stalin began to press for radical measures to industrialize the Soviet Union, introducing strict, centralized controls and encouraging the development of grandiose invest-

ment schemes. His Five-Year Plan, which was presented to the 16th Communist party Conference in April 1929 but had already been in operation for six months, was designed to revolutionize the Russian economy.

By the end of 1932, when it was claimed that the plan had been fulfilled, industrial production had increased dramatically. Electricity output had more than doubled, coal production had risen from 34.5 million tons to 64.3 million, and pig iron from 3.3 million tons to 6.2 million. There were huge new industrial plants in the Urals, the Volga region and Soviet Central Asia. However, the rapid pace of industrialization led to much waste and confusion, and certain industries, such as textiles or craft industries, as well as the consumer, suffered badly. By 1933 there was a sharp decline in the growth of industrial production, which had officially been rising at 20 percent per annum since 1928, and it was clear that the original targets had been optimistic and counterproductive. The second Five-Year Plan, adopted in February 1934, was less ambitious, but it still envisaged more than doubling Soviet industrial production by 1937. Once again the greatest successes were in heavy industry and armaments and the biggest losers were the consumers.

The shortage of consumer goods discouraged the peasants from delivering grain to the towns, since the money they received for it could buy little of value. Often they preferred to hoard their grain or feed it to their animals, so that confiscation and forced deliveries became the main ways of obtaining food for the urban

The Popular Front in France

Until 1933, the Comintern had denounced socialists (after then Communist party members) everywhere as "social fascists", but by 1934 the French socialists had overcome their deep resentment of the Communists and joined them in a "popular front" against "fascism and war". After the Franco-Soviet pact of 1935 the "radical" middle-class party in France, led by Herriot and Daladier, offered their support to the front and agreed on a joint program with the socialists and Communists. The seventh Comintern congress, held in the summer of 1935, praised this union of left-wing parties as a model for antifascist action everywhere.

In 1936 the front won a majority in parliament. The socialist leader Léon Blum formed a new government, which the Communists supported but did not join. Indeed they continued to organize strikes against the government and attacked it for not intervening in the Spanish Civil War. Blum banned fascist organizations and introduced important reforms. These included a 40-hour working week, paid annual vacations and the nationalization of the armaments industries and the Bank of France. Measures such as devaluing the franc made little impression on unemployment, however, and the Popular Front government fell in April 1938, unable to win the parliamentary support needed to pay for its social reforms.

▶ Socialist leader Léon Blum in the 1930s.

population. The government accused the *kulaks* (literally "fists"), the richer peasants, of deliberately creating shortages by speculating and hoarding. In fact, the number of *kulaks* was much smaller than the propaganda suggested.

To overcome the problem of food shortages the government decided to rationalize production by collectivizing agriculture. In 1928 only 2.7 percent of arable land in the Soviet Union was controlled by collective or state farms. The other 97.3 per cent was tilled by individual peasants. On 5 January 1930 the Politburo decreed a program for the collectivization of most of the Soviet Union by 1933. Party cadres were sent into the countryside to implement the plan, which included the collectivization even of peasants' tools and domestic animals.

Many party activists believed in the Leninist concept of class war between the richer and poorer peasantry and that the latter would support collectivization. In fact, only the use of brutal repression could induce the peasantry to collectivize. The collectives themselves were chaotically organized. Peasants resisted by destroying their livestock. Between 1928 and 1932, the number of cattle in the Soviet Union fell by nearly 45 percent, and sheep, goats and pigs by about 60 percent. Even grain production, at which collectivization had been primarily aimed, fell sharply and did not regain the already poor levels of 1928 until 1935.

Collectivization, however, succeeded in its objective of bringing grain production under government control. In 1933 agricultural produce was exported to finance the five-year plans despite widespread famine at home. By 1934 over 70 percent of peasant households had been collectivized, and 87 percent of the crop area was in collective farms. But this had been achieved only by the use of brutality and repression.

To consolidate his own position after the fiasco of collectivization, Stalin used the murder of S. M. Kirov, a Communist-party leader in Leningrad, on 1 December 1934, as the pretext for a massive purge of his former rivals, together with any other functionaries whose loyalty was questionable. (In fact, Stalin himself probably engineered the killing of Kirov.) Terror, once only a weapon used against "class enemies", became commonplace. The purges unleashed a wave of denunciations, mass arrests and forced "confessions" which spread fear and mistrust throughout the country. By December 1936, with the worst of the purges still to come, some five million people had been seized by the security police and many were never seen again.

Outside the Soviet Union, the horrors of collectivization and the purges attracted less attention than they might otherwise have done, because of the world economic depression. To those in the West who were disillusioned with capitalism, the five-year plans seemed a great achievement, and a major step forward at a time when Communism had seemed to be in retreat. To some leftwing intellectuals the Soviet Union presented the only alternative to fascism.

▼ First among equals. Stalin (left) in amicable discussion with associates at the sixth Communist party Congress of 1931. While Stalin was consolidating his grip on power, he paid lip service to the tradition of consultative government, cooperating with old comrades from the days of the revolution. Three years later, Stalin began a ruthless purge of the party leadership in pursuit of one-man dictatorship. Of 139 members and candidates of the Central Committee, 98 were arrested and shot along with 1,108 of the 1,966 delegates: and over one-fifth of the Red Army's officer corps was executed.

THE CULT OF THE DICTATORS

It was generally assumed in 19th-century Europe that all forms of despotism would gradually be replaced by representative government, but the 20th century proved to be as much the age of dictatorship as the age of democracy. The hallmarks of modern dictatorship is that it avails itself of the fruits of the technological revolution, especially where instruments of terror are concerned, and involves the exercise of autocratic powers for an indefinite period. In this latter respect it is the antithesis of dictatorship as it was known to Republican Rome, where it was considered an exceptional and strictly temporary expedient for the preservation of the state in a time of state crisis. Instead, it resembles more closely the type of rule instituted by Julius Caesar, who was granted autocratic powers for life, though modern tyrannies can just as well be associated with the relatively impersonal despotism of a political party or a military junta as with charismatic leadership.

Most dictatorships of the ultra-right are at least reminiscent of the Republican model in that they justify themselves as necessary to crush the enemies of law and order to resolve a state crisis. In the interwar period Admiral Horthy in Hungary, Miguel Primo de Rivera in Spain, Pilsudski in Poland, King Alexander in Yugoslavia and General Antonescu in Romania all claimed to have rescued the nation from risk of anarchy or a Bolshevik takeover. Military governments throughout the world since 1960 can be said to perpetuate this form of dictatorship in the sense that they took over power in *coups* against democratically elected governments.

Other forms of modern autocracy attached greater importance to mobilizing the masses in their support through elaborate structural transformation and propaganda, as was the case of Salazar in Portugal, Franco in Spain, Perón in Argentina, and Qaddhafi in contemporary Libya. The most sophisticated forms of dictatorship in this respect were those instituted by Mussolini and Hitler, in which the systematic eradication of liberal freedoms was accompanied by extensive structural change and propaganda designed to present the leader as the incarnation of the national will, so that the single-party state was allegedly more democratic than the liberal party-political system.

Dictatorships have also been instituted in all countries whose regimes are based on Marxist-Leninist theory. Though Lenin envisaged a transitional phase of the "dictatorship of the proletariat" before the state would "wither away", the result in practice was an extraordinary concentration of power within the hands either of a single leader (Mao Zedong in China, Fidel Castro in Cuba, Enver Hoxha in Albania, Tito in Yugoslavia, Ceaușescu in Romania) or small ruling factions. The potential for abuse of such concentrations of power whatever their theoretical democratic function was realized most gruesomely in the mass atrocities committed by the orders of Stalin in the Soviet Union and Pol Pot in Cambodia.

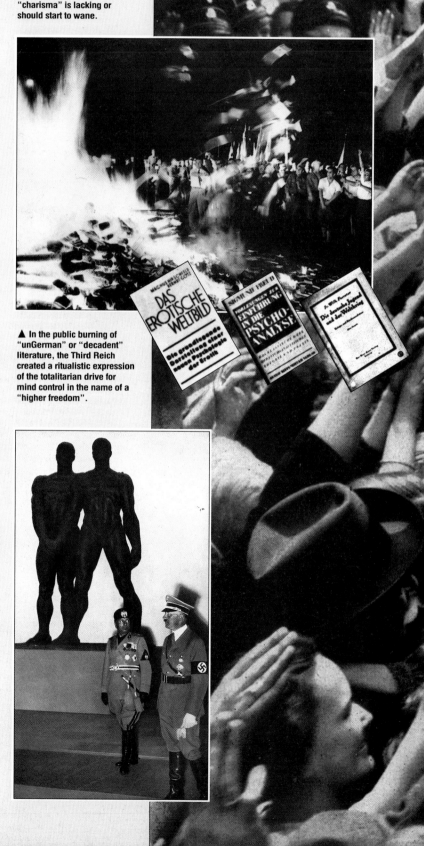

▶ The crowd's adulation of Hitler whenever he appeared in public constitutes an outstanding expression of the force of "plebiscitary" democracy on which modern dictatorships depend for their legitimacy and survival. Autocratic power needed to call on popular consensus, cynically manufactured if "charisma" is lacking or should start to wane.

▲ In the public burning of "unGerman" or "decadent" literature, the Third Reich created a ritualistic expression of the totalitarian drive for mind control in the name of a "higher freedom".

◄ In ancient Rome the emperor was considered divine. A personality cult is no less central to the power of the new Caesars, as can be seen from this portrait of Franco. In it symbols of medieval chivalry, monasticism, and modern militarism are interwoven into a composition in the baroque style associated with Spain's 16th century Golden Age. The result is an iconic representation of the *Caudillo* as a contemporary incarnation of Charles VI synthesizing past and present, tradition and modernity, the religious and the secular, monarch and savior.

▲ Iranian women in purdah display their enthusiasm (or conformism) at a political rally. When the Ayatollah ousted the Shah in Iran in 1979 a new permutation of charismatic dictatorship had arrived, one based on fundamentalist religion.

◄ Mass rallies, ritual and propaganda are not sufficient to ensure the survival of modern dictatorships. They must be reinforced by a climate of fear maintained by the ruthless use of paramilitary violence and torture. These two victims of El Salvador's government death squads stand for untold thousands who have "disappeared" for resisting autocratic law in the 20th century.

◄◄ Hitler and Mussolini, the archetypical new Caesars, celebrated the imminent appearance of a heroic race of "new men" born out of the ashes of the old order.

Datafile

In Western Europe democratic governments remained wedded to doctrines of appeasement and disarmament: internationally they were prepared to make concessions to avoid embroilment in another costly continental war; domestically they were largely concerned with economic retrenchment and hesitant to authorize increased public expenditure on armaments. Elsewhere, however, the escape from economic stagnation went hand in hand with an expansionist foreign policy and a reallocation of resources to arms production. The drift to war was accelerated by great-power involvement in local war: the League of Nations proved incapable of stopping the Italian conquest of Ethiopia; the USSR on one side and Germany and Italy on the other became heavily involved in the bloody civil war in Spain; and in the Far East the Japanese occupation of Manchuria in 1931 led directly to the invasion of China itself six year later. As the expansionist ambitions of the military dictatorships became clearer, so the democrats turned to rearmament themselves.

Spanish elections

1931 seats

- Socialist
- Radical
- Radical Socialist
- Right parties
- Catalan Esquerra
- ARAP
- Progressive
- CQGN

1933 seats

- Right parties
- Radical
- Socialist
- Others pro-government
- Acción Republicana

1936 seats

- Left
- Right
- Center

Aircraft production

- Germany
- UK
- Italy
- USA
- France
- Japan
- USSR

▶ Worldwide aircraft production increased from 5,000 to 40,000 per annum between 1932 and 1939. Early expansion was largely accounted for by German and Russian production, but as rearmament became more general and widspread, so other powers, notably Britain and Japan, contributed more to the growth of air power.

Defense spending 1937

▲ In 1937, Germany, the USSR and Japan were all spending approximately a quarter of their national income on their armed services, while the Western democracies, committed to appeasement, were allocating less than half of that proportion. Only in the last two years of peace did the balance begin to change.

◀ The outbreak of the Spanish Civil War was proceded by the collapse of broad-based coalition government and the defection of votes from the center parties to extreme left and right. In 1936, the leftwing coalition held an impressive majority, its rightwing opponents looked to military action to reverse the situation.

German military costs

Growth of German army

▲ Between 1930 and 1938 Germany transformed the small professional army it had been allowed under the Versailles peace settlement into a large force capable of offensive action. Using just over 100,000 trained professionals as a core, Germany built up a front line force eight times that size, backed up by even larger reserves.

The diplomatic counterpart of the national and democratically organized parliamentary regimes that dominated the world by the late 1920s was the League of Nations at Geneva. After a shaky start, it had established itself, with leading statesmen from all over the world playing a role. Economically, the world had also become more liberal. Commercial restraints imposed during and after World War I were relaxed, and currencies had become more stable.

On 24 October 1929 this stability was shattered by the US stock-market crash, producing the worst world depression in modern history. In the ten years that followed, the concept of collective security embodied in the Paris peace treaties of 1919 and the League of Nations Covenant gave way to national egoism as governments tried desperately to protect themselves from the effects of the slump.

Armaments and reparations

The first casualty of the new international environment was an agreement over German reparations payments for World War I, which had been imposed under the Paris peace treaty of 1918. On 7 June 1929, a new reparations scheme, the Young Plan, was announced to supersede the earlier Dawes Plan. It restored financial sovereignty to Germany but forced the country to pay larger annuities than before. The plan came into effect on 17 May 1930 but by that time the world's economic situation had deteriorated. The German chancellor, Heinrich Brüning, instead of seeking to reschedule the payments, or raise a loan, decided to force the issue by imposing harsh economic measures at home in the hope that the contraction in world trade would force Germany's creditors to seek a mutually acceptable solution. A credit crisis in Europe followed, and President Hoover announced a moratorium on war debts from France and Britain if they would suspend reparations demands from Germany. This arrangement, intended as a temporary measure, became permanent at the Lausanne Conference in June 1932.

Another aim of German foreign policy was to achieve equality of armaments and, above all, the right to restore conscription, or some form of short-term service, without which there would be no prospect of creating a powerful field army. The French, who feared a resurgence of German militarism, opposed any such move, especially after Hitler's Nazis became a political force. The British government, however, headed by the Labour leader Ramsay MacDonald, sought a general agreement on disarmament and was prepared to override French concerns. MacDonald's National Government, which was formed on 24 August 1931 and included Conser-

THE DRIFT TO WAR

vatives, wanted to keep Britain out of continental entanglements. The Treasury even refused requests by British army chiefs in March 1932 to increase resources to meet Britain's obligations under the League Covenant and the Locarno treaties.

The international disarmament conference at Geneva, which lasted from 2 February 1932 until October 1933, ended inconclusively. The British and Americans were eager for an agreement, but the French refused to reduce their land forces by as much as Britain requested, and the Germans looked for excuses to expand their own. Eventually, Hitler, acting under pressure from his generals, and backed by a plebiscite, left the disarmament conference and on 14 October 1933 announced Germany's withdrawal from the League of Nations.

Japanese aggression in China

After 1929 Japan was crippled by the world de-

▼ A Popular Front demonstration in Paris against the Nationalist uprising in Spain. The Spanish Civil War became a focus for left-wing opposition to the rise of fascism.

pression and morale was low. Its silk trade suffered a catastrophic decline and pressures for tariff protection against Japanese imports were mounting in the United States and the British Empire. At the same time, the military in Japan were alarmed at the prospect of an increasingly confident nationalist China, headed by Jiang Jieshi's Guomindang forces. In 1931, tension grew in Manchuria, an area where the Japanese controlled and policed parts of the railroad system, after the Chinese warlord Marshal Chang Hsueh-liang, aligned himself with the nationalists to initiate a railroad-building program that would reduce the province's dependence on the Japanese.

On 18 September 1931 the Japanese forces in Manchuria suddenly seized Mukden and captured other major cities. The Japanese cabinet had not sanctioned the action, but was too weak to countermand it. By the end of 1931 most of Manchuria had fallen to the Japanese army. The

▲ Cartoon attacking Japanese aggression in China.

◄ Chinese nationalist soldiers holding out against the Japanese.

▼ In 1931–32 the Japanese occupied Manchuria and installed the former Qing emperor Pu Yi (seated next to the emperor Hirohito) as a Japanese puppet.

following February the Japanese created a puppet republic of Manzhouguo, an action that they justified by claiming to restore order in a region torn by anarchy. After the Chinese had appealed to the League of Nations, a commission of inquiry was set up under Lord Lytton to investigate the events in Manchuria. The commission reported its findings on 2 October 1932 and on 24 February 1933 the League's assembly condemned Japan's aggression and called on the Japanese to withdraw. They refused, pressed farther into northern China and announced their withdrawal from the League. The Sino-Japanese conflict continued to smoulder, interspersed with periods of truce, until it burst forth again in 1937, with greater ferocity.

The Polish-German treaty

Although the European powers were concerned at the danger presented by a resurgent Germany, and by Japanese aggression, they could not agree on how best to deal with the situation. On 18 March 1933 Mussolini proposed to the British a four-Power pact between Britain, Italy, France and Germany to revise the terms of the Paris peace treaty of 1918, which had so offended Germany. However, the proposal was abandoned after protests from the Little Entente (Romania, Czechoslovakia and Yugoslavia), who feared its consequences, and by France. The Poles also became suspicious that their western border might be regarded as negotiable by the other powers and decided to look after their own interests by making a nonaggression pact with Germany. This agreement, which was signed on 26 January 1934, turned out to be worthless to the Poles, but greatly benefited Hitler by removing the danger of a Polish preemptive strike while Germany was rearming.

The pact also weakened the French security system in Europe. Louis Barthou, the French foreign minister, tried to rally former Entente countries, and the assassination of the Austrian Chancellor, Engelbert Dolfuss, by German-

backed Nazis, on 25 July 1934, drew Mussolini once more towards France. However, Italy was on bad terms with Yugoslavia, and once again splits appeared in the allied camp. On 9 October 1934, Barthou met King Alexander of Yugoslavia in Marseilles to discuss the situation in Central Europe, but both were murdered by a Croatian dissident.

Franco-Soviet treaty

During 1931 and 1932 the Soviet Union, increasingly worried about Japan's power in the Far East, signed nonaggression pacts with many of its neighbors, including Poland, Finland and Latvia, and with France. In September 1934 the Soviet Union was admitted to the League of Nations, sponsored by Britain, France and Italy.

Hitler's fierce anti-Bolshevism and his rapprochement with Poland further encouraged Stalin to mend fences with the West. On 2 May 1935 the Soviet Union and France signed a treaty of mutual assistance, which later that month was extended to include Czechoslovakia.

The change in Stalin's foreign policy was reflected in the Comintern, which now urged Communist parties everywhere to form a "popular front" with democratic forces against fascism, as the French had done. In his determination to create a European security system against Hitler, Stalin was pursuing Soviet interests, but at the time these coincided with the needs of the Western European democracies.

Britain, however, was most concerned about the Franco-Soviet alignment, both because it regarded the Soviet Union as an enemy of the British Empire, and because many Britons deplored the division of Europe into armed camps.

French attempts to buttress the security of Europe gave Hitler excuses for further breaches of Germany's treaty obligations. On 9 March 1935 the Germans announced that they had created an air force, and on 16 March Hitler reintroduced conscription, which was in clear breach of the Treaty of Versailles.

One month before, Britain and France had agreed not to release Germany from its obligations under the Versailles treaty without the consent of the other. Yet, on 18 June 1935 Britain, without referring to France, concluded a naval treaty with Germany allowing the Germans to build up to just over one third of the British naval strength. The British also tried—unsuccessfully—to make an air pact with the Germans to guarantee the security of their island by limiting offensive aerial forces.

German reoccupation of the Rhineland

Using as a pretext the ratification of the Franco-Soviet treaty that was in process in Paris, Hitler marched his troops into the demilitarized zone of the German Rhineland on 7 March 1936. This action violated not only the Versailles treaty but also the Locarno pact. The British, consistent in their policy of noncommitment, refused to mobilize forces against Germany in response to this provocation, and the French government under Pierre-Étienne Flandin was too weak to take action unilaterally. Hitler's bold action, having gone

The Chinese Civil War

Torn by warlordism since the collapse of the Qing dynasty in 1912, China was pushed into full-scale civil war when in 1927 Jiang Jieshi, leader of the nationalist Guomindang party, purged the Communists from the ranks of his army. After a series of abortive urban uprisings, the Communists finally established themselves in the countryside, using peasant guerrilla forces to neutralize superior Guomindang military strength. There followed a hard-fought three-year siege, with Jiang finally destroying the Communist mini-state in the east of the country, the Jiangxi soviet. However, Mao Zedong successfully led survivors on the Long March of 1934–35 to establish a secure base in Yunan province in the north. The Japanese invasion of 1937 led to an uneasy truce between the two sides. Guomindang forces recovered from early defeats, while the Communists fought an increasingly well-supported guerrilla war. In 1945 hostilities flared up again, developing into full-scale warfare a year later, after the failure of a US-sponsored compromise settlement. By the end of 1947 a massive Communist counteroffensive was in full swing and in 1949 the Communists emerged as victors. The People's Republic of China was proclaimed and Jiang fled to Taiwan.

▲ Mao Zedong leads his followers on the Long March of 1934–35, rescuing Chinese Communism from military defeat and securing his own position as party leader. Arguably the most influential political figure of the 20th century, he developed the ideological and political systems that welded millions of Chinese together as a Communist nation. He was also one of the major theorists of guerrilla warfare.

▼ Jiang Jieshi with the Indian leader Gandhi. Jiang was a curious blend of military dictator and populist leader. He rid China of its warlords and kept his forces together for years in the face of a fierce battering from the Japanese. But his administration was corrupt and inefficient and his failure to develop a coherent ideology led to his defeat by Mao's Communists.

unchallenged, further undermined the collective security of Europe.

Already on 6 March 1936 the threatening state of Franco-German relations and a distaste for the Franco-Soviet alliance had led the Belgians to renounce a military agreement with France that had existed since 1920. The Nazi reoccupation of the Rhineland increased their nervousness, and on 14 October 1936 King Leopold publicly stated that Belgian foreign policy would concern itself solely with Belgian interests. Strategically, this decision left the French with a vulnerable open flank that was not covered by their sophisticated defensive system, the Maginot Line, which had been under construction since 1929. At the same

time, Germany had created a "western wall" to prevent French incursions into Germany while Hitler's rearmament program, which surged into top gear in 1936, could continue unchecked.

Italian aggression in Ethiopia

Abyssinia (or Ethiopia as it is today) was one of the few remaining independent African states, having resisted colonization and repulsed an Italian invasion in 1896. In 1934 Mussolini, to enhance his own and Italian prestige, began preparing to attack the country, whose temperate highlands were long regarded as suitable for European settlement. From his colonies in Eritrea and Somaliland, on 5 December 1934 he provoked a clash between Italian and Ethiopian troops at Wal Wal in Somaliland, causing the Ethiopian government to appeal to the League of Nations to make peace. Determined on conquest, Mussolini rejected the League's peace proposal, and on 3 October 1935 Italian forces invaded Ethiopia. The Ethiopian army was defeated by aerial bombardment, using poison gas, banned by an international convention that had been signed by Italy.

Public opinion in democratic countries was outraged by Mussolini's aggression and supported the economic sanctions imposed by the League on Italy, on 11 October 1935. However, the governments of France and Britain, themselves colonial powers, were not wholly unsympathetic to Mussolini's aims in Africa. Furthermore, Italy was a former ally whose power might be needed to check Hitler in the future.

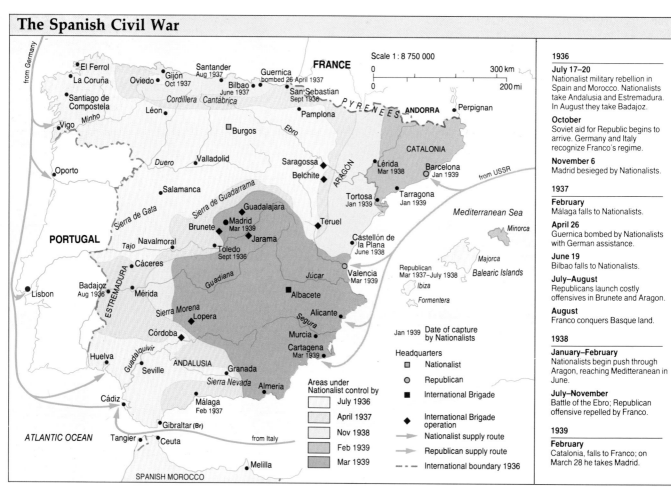

The Spanish Civil War

Scale 1 : 8 750 000

0 — 300 km
0 — 200 mi

FRANCE

from Germany

El Ferrol
La Coruña
Oviedo
Gijón Oct 1937
Santander Aug 1937
Guernica bombed 26 April 1937
Bilbao June 1937
San Sebastian Sept 1936
Pamplona
ANDORRA
Perpignan

Santiago de Compostela
Cordillera Cantábrica
Léon
Vigo
Minho
Burgos
Ebro

CATALONIA
Lérida Mar 1938
Barcelona Jan 1939
from USSR

Oporto
Duero
Valladolid
Saragossa
Belchite
ARAGON
Tortosa Jan 1939
Tarragona Jan 1939

Salamanca
Sierra de Gata
Sierra de Guadarrama
Guadalajara
Brunete
Madrid Mar 1939
Teruel
Mediterranean Sea
Minorca

PORTUGAL
Navalmoral
Tajo
Jarama
Toledo Sept 1936
Castellón de la Plana June 1938
Cáceres
Guadiana
Júcar
Valencia Mar 1939
Republican Mar 1937–July 1938
Majorca
Balearic Islands
Ibiza

Lisbon
Badajoz Aug 1936
Mérida
Albacete
Formentera

Sierra Morena
Lopera
Alicante
Segura
Córdoba
Murcia
Cartagena Mar 1939

Huelva
Guadalquivir
ANDALUSIA
Seville
Granada
Sierra Nevada
Almeria

Jan 1939 Date of capture by Nationalists

Headquarters

Cádiz
Málaga Feb 1937
Gibraltar (Br)
from Italy

ATLANTIC OCEAN
Tangier
Ceuta

Melilla

SPANISH MOROCCO

Areas under Nationalist control by
- July 1936
- April 1937
- Nov 1938
- Feb 1939
- Mar 1939

☐ Nationalist
○ Republican
■ International Brigade

◆ International Brigade operation
→ Nationalist supply route
→ Republican supply route
--- International boundary 1936

1936

July 17–20
Nationalist military rebellion in Spain and Morocco. Nationalists take Andalusia and Estremadura. In August they take Badajoz.

October
Soviet aid for Republic begins to arrive. Germany and Italy recognize Franco's regime.

November 6
Madrid besieged by Nationalists.

1937

February
Málaga falls to Nationalists.

April 26
Guernica bombed by Nationalists with German assistance.

June 19
Bilbao falls to Nationalists.

July–August
Republicans launch costly offensives in Brunete and Aragon.

August
Franco conquers Basque land.

1938

January–February
Nationalists begin push through Aragon, reaching Mediterranean in June.

July–November
Battle of the Ebro; Republican offensive repelled by Franco.

1939

February
Catalonia, falls to Franco; on March 28 he takes Madrid.

▲ A Spanish Civil War poster satirizing the Nationalists. Republican forces counterattack against advancing Nationalists. The disunited leftist forces of the Spanish republic fought with great spirit, but Italian and German military assistance decided the issue in Franco's favor.

◀ The image of Mussolini in Ethiopia. The refusal of Western democracies to use force to oppose military aggression gave the fascist dictators a free hand in the imperial adventures.

Together, the French foreign minister, Pierre Laval, and his British colleague, Sir Samuel Hoare, secretly drew up a compromise arrangement to give Mussolini important trade routes and frontier areas, while formally preserving Ethiopian independence. When this scheme leaked out in Britain in December 1935, Hoare was forced to resign in a storm of public indignation. His successor, Anthony Eden, fully supported sanctions and loathed Mussolini. However, the League's sanctions proved useless, not least because they did not apply to oil traffic. Mussolini was angry with the democracies for trying to thwart him, and contemptuous of their failure. He pressed on with his invasion and by spring 1936 Ethiopia was overrun. On 2 May 1936 the Emperor, Haile Selassie, left his country and did not return until 1941. In July 1936 sanctions against Mussolini were lifted, having proved a failure.

The Spanish Civil War

On 17 July 1936 a group of disaffected army officers staged a coup to replace the democratic, if somewhat chaotic, Spanish republic with an authoritarian, nationalistic regime. The coup failed, in that only part of the country fell to the rebels, while the Republican government in Madrid rallied and appealed for help from abroad.

The rising, which sparked off a civil war, was led by Generals Sanjurjo and Mola, and—most importantly—Francisco Franco, who commanded the elite Spanish Foreign Legion in Morocco. From early on, Franco was aided by Hitler and Mussolini, who airlifted his crack military unit

from North Africa to Spain, and who continued to support the Nationalists throughout the three-year conflict. The Republicans, who were aided by volunteers of the International Brigade, eventually succumbed to Franco's military might when Barcelona, and Madrid in 1939.

Franco, having seized power, took the title of *Caudillo* (leader), rejecting parliamentary democracy in favor of a fascist corporate state. Unlike Hitler or Mussolini, who had a mass party behind them, from which they built up paramilitary forces, Franco had the backing of the regular army from the outset.

Hitler and Mussolini had political and strategic, as well as ideological, reasons for becoming involved in the Spanish Civil War. The Italians had hoped to extend their influence in the western Mediterranean. The Germans benefited from valuable battle experience, especially the deployment of the German air force's Condor legion. The Germans also secured a supply of strategic minerals such as iron ore from Spain. At first, the German foreign office had been concerned about Germany's involvement in Spain, but Hitler realized that the war would serve as a distraction to other powers while Germany was busy rearming. The war also helped to cement the relationship between Hitler and Mussolini. In the early 1930s Mussolini had regarded Hitler with contempt, deriding his antisemitism and rejecting any increase in German power in the Danube basin. By the end of 1936 his own commitments in Ethiopia and Spain had made him Hitler's natural ally.

▲ A child tries to shelter from the Nationalist bombs during the Spanish Civil War.

◀ The war began in the west and spread to the north and the east. As the war entered its second year, Franco's grip on the war tightened, with massive German and Italian military assistance. The Republicans, supported by the Soviet Union and European volunteers finally succumbed to superior military might.

Datafile

The economic and human impact of World War II dwarfed that of all previous conflicts, even the Great War of 1914–18. The greatly increased use of advanced military technology required far higher levels of industrial mobilization. A vast network of factories working flat out was needed to produce and sustain this technology to make it effective. The intensive load of operations all over the globe, on land, by sea and in the air, produced heavy wastage, while the continued importance of superior numbers produced a need for constant expansion. The widely exposed doctrine of strategic bombing placed noncombatants in the front line, and air raids on major cities resulted in terms of thousands of noncombatant casualties. Economic warfare placed the food supply of the civilian population under direct threat, exposing millions to undernutrition. Finally, the racist ideologies of the Axis Powers found expression in policies of genocide, which led to the murder of whole communities, most notoriously the Jewish population of Europe.

Tank production 1944

◀ As the war developed, the tank emerged as the most important weapon on the land battlefield. When production peaked in 1944, the annual output of the four largest producers was in the vicinity of 70,000 tanks, with the armored forces of the USSR receiving some 40 percent more machines than those of its poorest competitors.

▶ In Nazi Germany, one solution to the problem of maintaining a workforce in essential industries was mass conscription from captured territories to serve in German factories. At the beginning of the conflict, nonGermans had made up an insignificant part of the workforce; by 1944 they were filling almost 20 percent of all jobs.

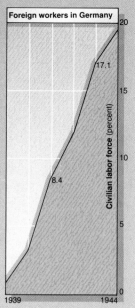
Foreign workers in Germany

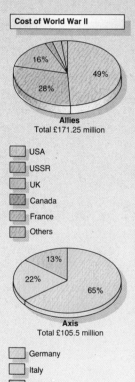
Cost of World War II

Allies
Total £171.25 million

- USA
- USSR
- UK
- Canada
- France
- Others

Axis
Total £105.5 million

- Germany
- Italy
- Japan

◀ In purely financial terms (as well as human terms), the cost of the war was astronomical. On the Axis side, Germany's share exceeded that of Italy and Japan combined. The US contributed almost half to the Allied war effort as well as paying for its own, while the USSR and the UK accounted for all but a tiny proportion of the remainder.

▶ European Jewry was ruthlessly sought out by the Germans across the entire continent. Polish Jews comprised half of the victims and occupied Russia yielded a third of the remainder, and the smaller communities of other countries, including Germany itself, were treated just as savagely in a program of genocide which left more than four million dead.

Jewish victims

2,900,000

Aircraft production

- USSR
- UK
- USA
- British Empire
- Germany
- Japan
- Italy

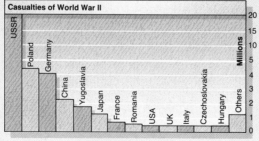
Casualties of World War II

◀ The dramatic increase in the proportion of civilian deaths pushed total war casualties to the appalling figure of 37.6 million. The USSR, fighting on a larger scale in terms of manpower than any other nation, lost more people than all the other nations combined, and five times as many as either of the other heavy sufferers, Poland and Germany.

▲ Aircraft production, already expanding rapidly, rose sharply after. Some nations, like Britain, had reached the limits of their productive capacity by 1941–42, but others, notably the USA, continued to expand their output until 1944. Even Germany achieved its highest level of production in the last full year of hostilities.

THE WORLD AT WAR

From the mid-1930s the world situation deteriorated rapidly, as fascist and militaristic regimes in Japan, Germany and Italy became more ambitious in their designs and more determined to use force to achieve them. The Western democracies were irresolute and ill-equipped to contain the threat to peace, and in the case of the United States, seemingly indifferent to the fate of Europe. Meanwhile, the Soviet Union, in theory the sworn enemy of fascism, was preoccupied with its own totalitarian violence undertaken in the name of rapid industrialization, the collectivization of agriculture and the sweeping purges of party officials.

The Sino-Japanese war

On 7 July 1937 an armed incident at the Marco Polo Bridge southeast of Beijing sparked off an undeclared war between China and Japan. Beijing, Shanghai and the capital Nanjing quickly fell to the Japanese and by 1940 they had taken all major Chinese cities along the eastern and southern coasts. They now controlled much of eastern China, including major trade centers and railroads, and exerted an economic stranglehold over the country as a whole.

In October 1937 the League of Nations had condemned Japanese aggression, with the US President Roosevelt, in his "quarantine speech" in Chicago calling for the isolation of Japan and economic support for China. However, Britain and France were too weak militarily and too preoccupied in Europe to help to check Japanese expansion, and so the Japanese "New Order" in the Far East went unchallenged.

For Japan territorial expansion represented a way out of pressing domestic problems including an increase in population from 44 million in 1900 to 69 million in 1935. As in many parts of Europe, the effects of the depression heightened social and political tensions and brought to power strong authoritarian and nationalist forces. In Japan's case these forces were sharply divided on how to improve the country's economic prospects, suppress reformist forces and meet working-class aspirations. Many people, however, favored expansion. The military looked to the seizure of Manchuria as a launching-pad for capturing Soviet-controlled territories to the north. The navy, the business community and the imperial court preferred to expand to the south, even at the risk of a confrontation with the Western Powers.

For all their military superiority and uncompromising methods of warfare, the Japanese failed to force China to surrender. Of the Chinese forces opposing the Japanese, only about 1.5 million, a fraction of the total, were properly trained and equipped. Yet despite suffering heavy losses,

they managed, under the command of Jiang Jieshi, to avert a military defeat and China survived. The seat of government was moved to Hankou and eventually to Chongqing. Many schools and factories were relocated to the interior. A puppet government set up by the Japanese in Nanjing under Wang Ching-Wei failed to win much support. However, civil unrest and repression kept China weak and divided. A manifesto for cooperation after the Japanese attack in 1937 brought about a precarious alliance between Jiang's Guomindang nationalists and Mao Zedong's Communists which lasted until 1945.

German war preparations

Germany's rearmament and military preparations, its foreign policy as well as its domestic programs, all pointed in the direction of war. To

▼ World War II began in Asia when Japan invaded China in 1937; the war continued there for eight years.

Hitler, war was an inevitable part of the struggle between racially "valuable" and "worthless" nations. Germany needed to expand, he believed, to gain *Lebensraum*, to secure agricultural land and manpower in the east, and to wipe out Jewish power and influence whenever it stood in the way. Western Russia would provide the necessary resources that would ultimately enable Germany to compete with the United States for world domination. Britain, he hoped, could be won over as a junior partner in his endeavors.

The annexation of Austria

On 12 February 1938 the Austrian chancellor Kurt von Schuschnigg was told by Hitler to make political concessions to Austrian Nazis. Schuschnigg agreed, but hoped to curb Hitler's influence by holding a referendum on a free and independent Austria on 9 March. Hitler responded by invading Austria on 12 March.

The Germans encountered no resistance. Indeed, after two decades of economic troubles, political uncertainty and bouts of civil war, most Austrians welcomed them as saviors. In Vienna, Hitler proclaimed *Anschluss* – full German-Austrian union – which received the almost total support of the Austrian people in a referendum held on 10 April.

Hitler's original aim had been a Nazi Austria rather than a complete union with Germany, but he was encouraged in his ambitions by the enthusiastic welcome he received from the Austrians and by the passivity of the British and French governments in not opposing him.

The fall of Czechoslovakia

Hitler's claims on Czechoslovakia were based on the pretext of "bringing home to the Reich" the ethnic German minorities of the Sudetenland. Yet by early 1938, he had ordered military preparations for a full-scale invasion of the country rather than confine himself to the fate of 3.5 million ethnic Germans who made up 28 percent of the population of Czechoslovakia. The Sudeten Germans held equal citizens' rights with the Czechs, who accounted for 46 percent of the population, but like other ethnic groups (including Slovaks and Hungarians) felt that they were disadvantaged. By 1937 the Sudeten-German party under Konrad Henlein was pro-Nazi and received two thirds of the Sudeten vote. Hitler ordered him to demand reforms that would be unacceptable to the Czech government and would throw them on the defensive.

As the tension mounted, the Soviet Union and France, who had treaties with the Czechs, offered their assistance. However, neither had a common frontier with Czechoslovakia and a more general conflict might have involved a reluctant Britain. To avert this possibility, the British prime minister, Neville Chamberlain, met Hitler in his Alpine retreat at Obersalzburg on 15 September to seek a peaceful solution. Britain and France were prepared to allow the Sudetenland to be annexed, provided that the remainder of Czechoslovakia received an international guarantee of its independence. The Prague government was reluctant to accept these terms, especially since

▲ The last months of old-world diplomacy – Britain's ambassador meets Hitler. Appeasement of Hitler was a complex phenomenon. Western statesmen, haunted by memories of the 1914–18 war and struggling to rebuild economies ravaged by depression, were desperate to avoid war and, in Britain at least, not unsympathetic to Germany's claims for a renegotiation of the Versailles settlement. Moreover, until the true nature of Hitler's territorial ambitions became clear in 1939, war against Germany was unlikely to command popular support. Even so, in their attempts to deal with a dictator by traditional diplomatic means, Western leaders displayed great naïvety.

Poland and Hungary made similar claims for their ethnic minorities. Hitler, however, would not be dissuaded and threatened to invade unless the Czechs would concede. The Czechs mobilized their armed forces, while – halfheartedly – France called up some of its reserves and Britain alerted its fleet.

On 28 September, a few hours before Hitler's ultimatum was due to expire, Chamberlain persuaded Mussolini to act as intermediary. Together with French premier Edouard Daladier they met Hitler in Munich on 29 September. Mussolini's compromise proposals, which had actually been drafted by the German foreign office, permitted Hitler to send in his troops on 1 October to take the Sudetenland. On the same day Poland claimed a piece of northern Czechoslovakia and the Hungarian and the Slovak provinces were given autonomous governments.

Czechoslovakia lost one-third of its territory including valuable lignite mines and manufacturing plants. At Munich, Germany signed an agreement with Britain to hold consultations on any future grievances and to never again wage war against each other. On his return to Britain, Prime Minister Chamberlain was greeted as a hero, having secured what he believed was "peace in our time".

Czechoslovakia's continuing ethnic problems and Slovak demands for national independence provided Hitler with the excuse to seize the rest of the country. On 15 March 1939 the Wehrmacht entered Prague unopposed, after Hitler had threatened to bomb the capital if the Czechs resisted. On the following day Germany established a "Protectorate of Bohemia and Moravia". Some southern areas were annexed by Hungary, and Czechoslovakia disappeared from the map.

Germany signed a trade agreement with Romania to gain access to the economic resources such as grain and oil.

Britain and France reacted angrily to Hitler's broken promise that the Sudeten area was to be his last territorial claim. Chamberlain guaranteed to protect the integrity of Poland and Romania against Hitler and to defend Greece and Turkey against a possible Italian invasion.

The end of "collective security"

At the beginning of 1939 Hitler ordered a rapid buildup of the German fleet to threaten the sea lanes to Britain in the event of a conflict arising between the two countries. As yet, he had no plans to attack Poland, whose rightwing government might be a potentially useful partner against the Soviet Union.

In fact, just a few days before the Germans took

▲ Abandoned by their allies, the citizens of Prague watch the German army arrive in March 1939. Czechoslovakia, a liberal democracy with much in common with Britain and France, was the real victim of appeasement. After acceding to Hitler's initial demands for territorial concessions in the German-populated border areas, the Western Powers were unable to prevent the occupation of Czechoslovakia. Paradoxically, having failed to defend democracy in Czechoslovakia, Britain and France finally went to war on behalf of Poland's rightwing military dictatorship.

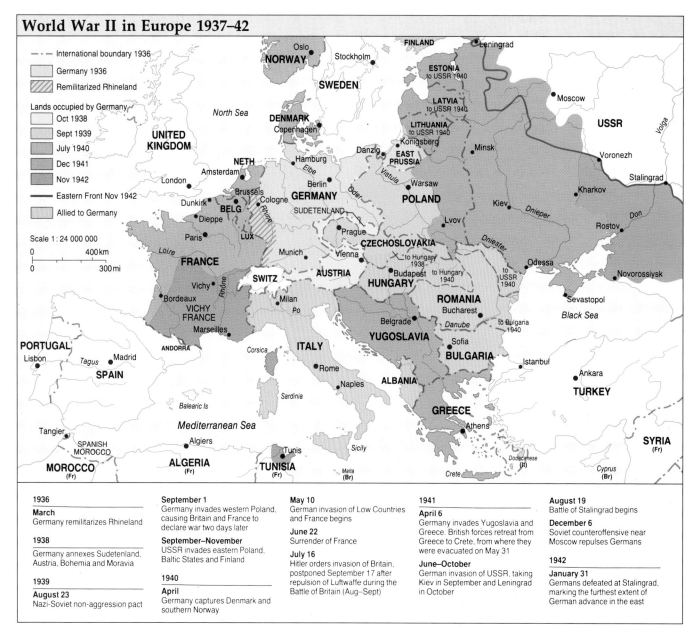

World War II in Europe 1937–42

- - - International boundary 1936

Germany 1936

Remilitarized Rhineland

Lands occupied by Germany
- Oct 1938
- Sept 1939
- July 1940
- Dec 1941
- Nov 1942

Eastern Front Nov 1942

Allied to Germany

Scale 1 : 24 000 000

0   400km

0   300mi

1936	**September 1**	**May 10**	**1941**	**August 19**
March	Germany invades western Poland, causing Britain and France to declare war two days later	German invasion of Low Countries and France begins	**April 6**	Battle of Stalingrad begins
Germany remilitarizes Rhineland		**June 22**	Germany invades Yugoslavia and Greece. British forces retreat from Greece to Crete, from where they were evacuated on May 31	**December 6**
1938	**September–November**	Surrender of France		Soviet counteroffensive near Moscow repulses Germans
Germany annexes Sudetenland, Austria, Bohemia and Moravia	USSR invades eastern Poland, Baltic States and Finland	**July 16**	**June–October**	**1942**
		Hitler orders invasion of Britain, postponed September 17 after repulse of Luftwaffe during the Battle of Britain (Aug–Sept)	German invasion of USSR, taking Kiev in September and Leningrad in October	**January 31**
1939	**1940**			Germans defeated at Stalingrad, marking the furthest extent of German advance in the east
August 23	**April**			
Nazi-Soviet non-aggression pact	Germany captures Denmark and southern Norway			

Prague, Stalin had accused the Western Powers of collaborating with Hitler against the Soviet Union. Fearing such a conspiracy, Stalin abandoned the notion of "collective security", dismissed his foreign secretary, Maxim Litvinov, who had advocated such a policy, and made contacts with the Germans. Stalin became the focus of diplomatic activity on the part of both Hitler and the Western Powers. The British urged the Russians to follow their example and to extend a guarantee of security to Poland. Stalin responded by demanding a wider guarantee that would include the Baltic states and Finland. Poland, however, fearful of Stalin's territorial ambitions, refused to allow the Red Army to cross its territory, which presented a major stumbling block in the negotiations. By August 1939 Britain and France were prepared to override the Poles' objections, but by then Stalin was on the verge of a deal with Hitler.

The Nazi-Soviet pact
On 14 August the Germans told the Russians that "between the Baltic and the Black Sea" there was no issue that "could not be settled to the full satisfaction of both sides". Nine days later, in Moscow, the German foreign secretary Joachim von Ribbentrop signed a nonaggression pact with his Soviet counterpart, Vyacheslav Molotov. Publicly, it bound each party to neutrality in the event of the other being involved in a war or attacked by another country. In secret, the two parties also divided up the area that lay between them. The Baltic states, Finland, eastern Poland and large parts of southeastern Europe east of an agreed dividing line were to go to the Russians while Germany claimed the lands to the west of the line. Hitler was now ready to attack Poland, having canceled the German-Polish nonaggression pact of 1934 and the 1935 naval treaty made with Britain.

For a long time, Germany had complained about the city of Danzig. Situated between Germany and Poland, and placed under the League of Nations in 1920, it was a symbol of the strained national feelings between Germans and Poles.

▲ The summer of 1942 saw Axis fortunes at their peak. The *Blitzkrieg* campaigns of 1939–41 had swept German forces across Poland, western Scandinavia, France, the Low Countries, the Balkans and deep into the Soviet Union. There and in the western desert, their progress had been halted, however, but in both theaters the Germans were again moving forward. By then, however, the Axis war effort had reached the limits of its strength – Italy was exhausted and Germany did not have the reserves to match Allied buildups in Egypt and the southern Soviet Union. Within months, a German army was being ground down in the ruins of Stalingrad and another was reeling from defeat at El Alamein.

▲ The German and Soviet foreign ministers sign the nonaggression pact that led to the partition of conquered Poland and kept their two countries at peace until June 1941. The pact served the Germans very well, allowing them to concentrate on Western Europe without fear of a two-front war. If the motive of the Soviets was to avoid an invasion by Germany, they succeeded only in postponing it.

Since June 1933, Danzig had had a Nazi government, but the Polish government had consistently refused to allow the city to tie itself more closely to the German Reich. Hitler's ambitions in Poland, however, extended far beyond resolving the Danzig question. Britain tried to defuse the situation by limiting its guarantee to cover Poland's borders as they stood, and Mussolini announced that he would not support Hitler. However, Hitler rejected compromise solutions, and decided to strike.

On 31 August German SS men in Polish uniforms staged several border incidents. The next day Hitler announced that the Wehrmacht were now "returning fire". Britain and France declared war on Germany on 3 September but despite their obligations to defend Poland they could not and would not provide substantial military aid. The French Communists' slogan *"Mourir pour Danzig? – Non!"* (Die for Danzig? – No!) symbolized the attitude in Western Europe.

The rape of Poland

The German forces that invaded Poland achieved a swift victory. The Luftwaffe destroyed much of the Polish air force while it was still on the ground. On 17 September the Soviet Red Army invaded eastern Poland and took over the city of Lvov from the Germans, who withdrew behind the agreed demarcation line. On 27 September Poland's capital Warsaw surrendered to the Germans after heavy aerial bombardment, and a week later the Polish army was defeated by the German *Blitzkrieg* campaign.

After Poland's defeat, Germany formally annexed nearly half of the country, although many provinces contained very few ethnic Germans. A Nazi lawyer, Hans Frank, was appointed governor general over the rest of the Nazi-controlled areas. Some 12 million Poles formally lost their citizenship and were subjected to slave labor. Poles were forbidden to receive higher education and members of the Polish elite were imprisoned or killed.

Although Britain and France were formally at war with Germany, their forces remained securely behind the heavily fortified French Maginot line, a vast system of underground shelters that extended along the German frontier from Switzerland to Luxembourg. Britain did impose a blockade, but Stalin supplied Hitler with essential raw materials (which later aided Germany's military buildup against the Soviet Union) to reduce its effect. Having missed an opportunity to attack when Germany's defenses in the west were left exposed by the invasion of Poland, Britain and France had little incentive to fight once Poland had fallen.

Meanwhile, in the east, the Russians, after holding some bogus plebiscites, joined their conquered territory of the former Polish state with the Ukrainian Soviet Republic. Many Poles were deprived of their property and deported to Siberia. Like the Nazis, the Soviets dealt ruthlessly with the Polish intelligentsia and political leadership. In one of the worst atrocities, allegedly committed by the Russians, some 4,100 Polish officers, who had been made prisoners of war in the east, were killed and buried in Katyn forest near the town of Smolensk.

The Soviet–Finnish war

Stalin demanded that Finland and the three Baltic states, Latvia, Lithuania and Estonia, accept Soviet military bases on their soil. When Finland, alone, refused to comply, the Soviet Red Army attacked on 30 November. With little more than 10 divisions and 150 airplanes, Finland faced the might of 4 Soviet armies and 800 airplanes. The Western Powers sent arms to aid the Finns, and some 8,000 Swedish volunteers fought on the Finns' side, but this did little to redress the balance of forces. The League of Nations responded by condemning the attack and expelling the Soviet Union for its aggression.

Yet, despite its vast superiority, the Red Army was initially held up at the Mannerheim line (named after the Finnish commander-in-chief). In February 1940, the Russians launched a massive attack, but refrained from seeking total victory after Britain threatened to enter the war. On 12 March the Finns signed a peace treaty in Moscow, yielding large parts of eastern Karelia to the Soviet Union and leasing Hanko on the southern tip as a Soviet military base. The Red Army's unimpressive performance led Hitler to believe he could eventually defeat the Soviet Union, a conclusion shared by British and American military experts.

The occupation of Norway

In January 1940 the French prime minister Daladier, fearing a German strike against France, proposed sending an Anglo-French expeditionary force to aid Finland and cut off Germany from her Swedish iron ore which was shipped from northern Norway, and on 28 March 1940, the Allied War Council approved plans to mine Norwegian waters and to establish several bases along the coast.

The British fleet sailed for Norway from Scapa Flow on 7 April, confident that Germany's much

▼ German infantry advance through a burning Norwegian village in April 1940, in a scheme that was repeated all across Europe for the next two years. The German tactic of *Blitzkrieg* depended on surprise, rapid movement and the coordination of all fighting arms to break through enemy positions, causing so much disruption as to render an effective counterattack impossible.

weaker fleet would not challenge them. However, rather than seek a naval engagement, the Germans landed troops in several major ports and quickly secured their positions. In Narvik and near Oslo Allied troops clashed with the Germans, but by 8 June they had been driven from Norwegian soil. Two days later, the brave but ill-equipped Norwegian army surrendered. The king of Norway and his government fled to London and established a government-in-exile, an example that was later followed by others.

On 9 April German forces also overran Denmark, which offered no resistance. The Danish government was not deposed but continued for the next three years under German supervision. Sweden was spared invasion on condition that it continued to sell iron ore to the Germans and acceded to their demands for transit and the use of Swedish territorial waters.

The fall of Holland and Belgium

Hitler's attack on France began on 10 May 1940 with the invasion of Holland. The Germans landed parachutists and bombed Rotterdam, forcing the Netherlands to surrender on 15 May. Two weeks later Hitler also defeated Belgium. His false excuse for these invasions was that Holland and Belgium had violated their status of neutrality by giving support to Britain and France.

On 21 May German tank units reached the Channel and turned north to pursue the British expeditionary forces who were retreating towards Dunkirk. Three days later, Hitler – surprisingly – ordered his tanks to halt, allowing some 338,000 British and French soldiers to escape to Britain. Hitler was apparently acting on the army's wishes to save the German tank forces for the decisive defeat of the French and on Marshal Hermann Göring's desire to let his prestigious Luftwaffe finish off the encircled Allied troops. In the event, bad weather spoiled Göring's plans.

The defeat of France

After attacking the Maginot defense line from the rear, the Germans encircled Paris. The French capital yielded on 14 June without a fight and French political leaders escaped westward and made arrangements to seek an armistice. Churchill urged them to continue the fight, using guerrilla warfare at home, and carrying on the war from colonial bases abroad. Churchill further suggested a political union between Britain and France, but many in the French cabinet expected Britain soon to be defeated and preferred to surrender to Germany to save France from further disaster.

When France was about to succumb to Germany, Italy declared war and launched an attack across France's southeastern border. Although Mussolini's poorly equipped forces suffered a quick defeat at the hands of the French, Hitler was concerned at his attempts to tamper with the fruits of the German victory and decided to make peace with France. On 22 June the French signed a humiliating armistice in the same saloon railway car, parked in Compiègne forest, where 22 years earlier Germany had surrendered at the end of World War I. Under this agreement, Germany would administer northern France and the western coastal regions direct, while the rest of the country, about one-third, would nominally remain under French rule, with an army of some 100,000 men, and be governed from the spa town of Vichy.

Vichy symbolized a crisis in French public life

◀ Hitler and his staff walk in the shadow of the Eiffel Tower in recently conquered Paris. The defeat of France, accomplished in a matter of weeks, was the greatest triumph of the *Blitzkrieg* years. The French had held out for four years in World War I and in 1940 mustered a force that was in some ways better equipped than Germany's. However, the French military system could not react to the ambitious thrusts of Hitler's Panzer divisions, and French national morale, weakened by the problems of the past three decades, did not survive the initial shock of defeat.

▼ A German Heinkel 111 bomber flies over London. The aerial assault was launched against Britain in the late summer of 1940. The German airforce was ill-equipped for its task. Lightly armed bombers had neither the payload nor the defensive armament to operate decisively and short-range fighters protection against Britain's modern air-defense system.

Propaganda in World War II

The scale of mobilization, duration and geographical extent of World War II multiplied propaganda functions. New media extended the possibilities – newspapers, leaflets and posters were joined by cinema and radio – but it was by no means clear how to exploit them, especially in the Allied countries.

The German Nazi government invested the greatest resources in propaganda, having established government control over the media before the war. Although the effectiveness of propaganda is hard to measure, German propaganda did not alter the course of events: success or defeat in the field sustained or undermined home morale.

In the long run the Allies were more successful. The UK and USA regulated the publication of information but allowed broadcasting companies and newspapers to remain independent. The British Broadcasting Corporation in particular was able to remain a credible source of information: British morale was sustained, resistance organizations on the continent were encouraged and Germany had an alternative source of information about the war. Perhaps the USSR was most successful: its call for massive sacrifice on behalf of "Mother Russia" helped the Red Army to victory.

▲◀ **The dignified SS soldier: a German recruiting poster.**

◀ **A US poster exploits the infamy of Pearl Harbor.**

▶ **Churchill suffers defeats: a German poster for France.**

that went beyond military defeat. It represented the erosion of French democracy from within. On 10 July 1940 the French parliament voted to abolish the constitution of the Third Republic and transfer all state powers to Philippe Pétain, who became both president and prime minister.

The Battle of Britain

With much of Europe in Germany's control, Hitler decided the time was ripe to strike against Britain. In July 1940 he began to prepare an invasion. To launch a successful landing operation, however, the Germans believed it was necessary first to establish superiority in the air. But while the Wehrmacht and German naval forces made preparations for an amphibious attack, the Luftwaffe failed to knock out the Royal Air Force. Indeed, the heavy losses sustained by the Germans during the Battle of Britain and the failure to break down British morale by large-scale aerial bombardment sufficed to persuade them to postpone the invasion indefinitely.

New theaters of war

Hitler believed that Britain first had to be defeated before he could attack the Soviet Union and sought further allies in his cause. On 27 September 1940 Japan joined the Axis powers in signing a treaty aimed at deterring the United States by the threat of war on two fronts in Europe and in Asia. Hitler and Mussolini also hoped to bring Vichy France and fascist Spain into an alliance with them, but Franco refused to involve Spain in the war.

On 28 October Mussolini attacked Greece, dealing Hitler's diplomatic efforts a telling blow, by involving his German ally in the Mediterranean campaign. Mussolini's ambitious assaults on the British in North Africa opened yet another theater of war in which Germany became engaged. As British forces advanced on the Italian colonies in Ethiopia and Libya, Hitler was forced to come to the rescue of his Italian ally in order to protect the southern flank of his planned campaign against the Soviet Union. General Erwin Rommel's Afrika-Korps landed in Tripoli in February 1941 and succeeded in pushing back the British to the Egyptian border.

Germany launched other successful campaigns against Greece and Yugoslavia, with Hungary, Romania, Bulgaria and Slovakia, who had become allied with the Axis powers, sharing the spoils. Although these Balkan campaigns seemed to strengthen the strategic position of the Axis, they also absorbed a large share of human resources in suppressing guerrilla activities, and further delayed the attack on the Soviet Union. Originally, this had been scheduled for May 1941 with a view to completing operations in three months before the onset of the harsh Russian autumn and winter.

Hitler's Soviet campaign

The German invasion of the Soviet Union finally began on 22 June 1941 and took Stalin by surprise. Earlier, he had dismissed warnings of his intelligence sources, believing that the Germans would continue to honor the Nazi-Soviet pact.

▲ Poster marking the defense of Moscow in the winter of 1941. This event was a significant turning point in the war because it both checked the German war machine, and served as a potent symbol for the Soviet people to rally behind what came to be known as the Great Patriotic War.

▼ Modern airpower made World War II a true people's war, the devastating air raids on centers of population bringing civilians directly into the front line. Prewar fears of mass panic and the collapse of morale proved largely unfounded, and wartime leaders like Churchill (seen here inspecting bomb damage in London) used the enemy threat to innocent life in his speeches to rally popular support for the war effort.

On the very first day of the invasion, the Luftwaffe knocked out some 1,200 Soviet war planes. With over three million men in 152 divisions the Germans advanced rapidly, taking over three million prisoners by the end of the year. By November the Germans had advanced to a line roughly from Leningrad to the northeastern corner of the Black Sea; their gunfire could be heard from the outskirts of Moscow. Yet victory eluded them, as they became bogged down by the worsening weather conditions. The *Blitzkrieg* tactics had not proved decisive and the Germans' preparations for the harsh Russian winter were inadequate.

The Soviet forces had suffered their initial heavy defeats because they were unprepared and badly led. Many of the more experienced officers had been liquidated in Stalin's purges a few years earlier. Based on the lessons of the Finnish campaign, a restructuring of forces had begun but was not yet complete. The Soviet air force lacked trained pilots and took nearly two years to become a match for the German. When it became clear that Japan would honor its neutrality pact made with the Soviet Union in April 1940, Stalin withdrew most of his 2.2 million troops from the Far East to assist the 2.5 millions originally stationed at the western border. Later, a further 10 million reserves were mobilized.

At the start of the invasion the Germans were hailed by some of the conquered Soviet national minorities as liberators from tyranny. Hitler, however, had no intention of treating the conquered races of eastern Europe as allies. To him they were inferior and could not become part of his own Aryan "master race". German soldiers were instructed not to treat Soviet soldiers according to the agreed international rules of warfare. Crimes and acts of brutality committed by German soldiers against Soviet civilians were not punishable. Soviet commissars (political officers) were killed on the spot. German *Einsatzgruppen*,

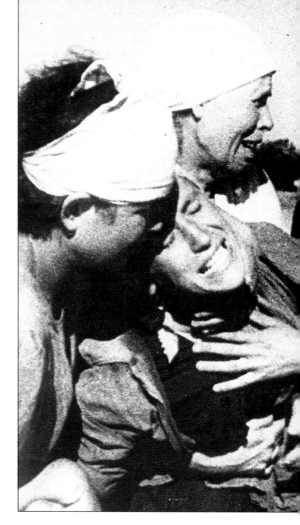

special security forces, rounded up and killed thousands of people, particularly the "eastern Jews", whom Hitler held to be responsible for Bolshevism.

US-Anglo-Soviet cooperation

The German invasion of the Soviet Union gave Britain a much needed breathing space. Equally important to the British was the growing support of the United States. Under the Lend-Lease Act of March 1941, Britain bought American arms which could be paid for later. In an undeclared war the US navy also helped to protect the shipping lanes across the Atlantic. Soon, the lend-lease program was expanded to include the Soviet Union. On 25 August British and Soviet forces occupied Iran to secure the southern Soviet flank and to bar the Axis troops from the Iranian oil wells.

Isolationist feelings in the United States, however, were still much too strong for Roosevelt to enter the war formally. In part, these went back to the World War I experience; also many Americans saw little to choose between Hitler and Stalin. Why not let them first fight each other to a standstill, they argued, before America comes in at the end to pick up the pieces?

The bombing of Pearl Harbor

These debates ended abruptly on 7 December, when Japanese naval forces attacked the US fleet stationed in Pearl Harbor, Hawaii. Relations with Japan were already bad on account of a clash of

possibly extending his power to Africa and the Middle East. The Anglo-American alliance gave rise to a complex network of programs, boards and committees to handle everything from economic issues to the most sensitive intelligence operations and the supervision of the construction of the atomic bomb.

The United States dominated the Pacific war after Britain's warships and bases in Singapore, Hong Kong, Malaya and Burma fell to the Japanese within a few months of their declaring war. The British Empire in the Pacific area was seriously overextended. Britain's naval forces were weak, had hardly any air cover, and proved to be no match for the well-equipped and highly trained Japanese. Australia and New Zealand, as British Commonwealth states, were advised to seek American protection. Britain maintained its influence in India even if it failed to reach a political solution with the nationalist movement against British rule. Friction arose between the British and the Americans, who bore the brunt of the Pacific war and who did not wish to see the colonial empires restored.

The turning of the tide

By January 1942 the German forces had withdrawn from the Moscow area and on the southern front were pushed back significantly by Soviet advances. The Germans found themselves unable to move during the harsh Russian winter but when the thaw came it transformed the snow and ice into one huge mudhole.

The Germans attacked Stalingrad, an important

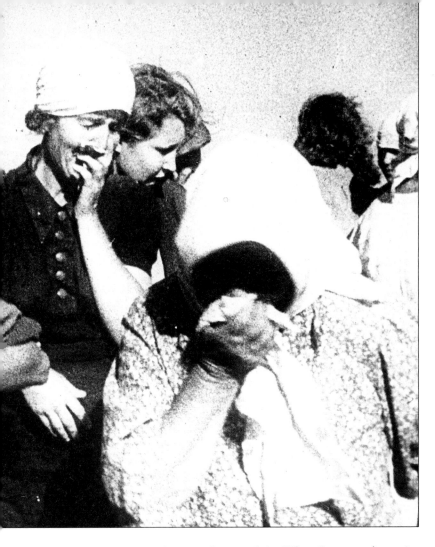

▲ On the Eastern Front, where the Germans soon resorted to systematic atrocities against the Soviet population, scenes like this one became commonplace. German policies of genocide and racial supremacy resulted in millions of deaths but made the achievement of victory all but impossible. The sheer level of suffering inflicted on the Soviet people transformed the war from the defense of a harsh Stalinist state into a national crusade for survival in which every hand was turned against a monstrous invader.

interests in east Asia. When Japanese forces invaded southern Indochina in July 1941, the Americans froze Japan's assets and imposed a crippling oil embargo on the country, backed by Britain and the Netherlands. After a series of secret negotiations between the rival powers, the Japanese government decided to go to war by 10 October unless its demands were met, but Japan's Emperor Hirohito reversed this decision and had the talks continue. On 25 November Roosevelt himself broke off negotiations and sent a 10-point diplomatic note to the Japanese which they found unacceptable. The Japanese decided to gamble on war.

On 11 December Hitler too declared war on the United States though he was not bound to do so by his pact with Japan, which had been made originally with the intention of keeping the United States out of the war. However, Hitler hoped that Japan would tie down both Britain and the United States in the Far East. This decision stunned German military leaders who did not share the Führer's optimism that the United States would expend most of its war effort in the Pacific.

The Allies' "Germany first" strategy

Two weeks after the attack on Pearl Harbor, Churchill and some 80 staff went to Washington for their first war conference with the Americans. They planned to defeat Germany first in order to prevent Hitler from gaining control of the European continent and the Soviet Union, and

War Production

▲ Checking aircraft tires.

The scale of hostilities, and their dependence on huge quantities of armaments and equipment produced the need for mass mobilization of economic and human resources. All combatants put women to work in the factories for the duration of the war.

Arguably, the outcome of the war was determined as much by economic planning and industrial mobilization as by the operations of the armed services. In this vast struggle of attrition, the Axis powers proved unable to match the output and organization of their opponents, and when the stream of quick victories ended in 1942, not even heavily industrialized Germany could avoid a slow drift toward collapse.

center of Soviet war industries, in August. By November, the city appeared to be about to fall, yet the Soviet troops deployed in that area did not yield but became part of a large-scale Soviet counterattack. At the end of November the Soviet troops encircled the German 6th Army and defeated it after a fierce battle. The battle of Stalingrad indicated a turning of the tide, largely perhaps because of Hitler's orders to his troops to hold out at all costs. Out of a force of 250,000 Germans, less than 100,000 survived to surrender on 2 February 1943 and of these a mere 6,000 eventually returned home. Strategically, the Germans' failure to capture Moscow may also have been decisive, but after Stalingrad many Germans began to doubt that another victory was possible.

The Germans suffered further serious reverses in North Africa. By June 1942 Rommel's Afrika Korps had advanced well into Egypt, but in October General Bernard Montgomery launched his counterattack and defeated Rommel at El Alamein. The Axis troops were driven west again and eventually forced to withdraw across the sea. On 13 May 1943 the remaining German and Italian forces surrendered in Tunisia and North Africa was finally lost to the Axis powers.

An American-led invasion of Algeria and Morocco had earlier secured a base for General Charles de Gaulle's Free French movement from where they could significantly aid the Allied cause. In retaliation the Germans occupied Vichy France, except for the southeastern Provence region which was taken by Italy. However, this move by the Germans was strategically counterproductive, as it widened their occupation commitments over an increasingly hostile French population.

Further US and Soviet successes

Soon after its entry into the war, the United States developed into a gigantic arsenal for the Allies. In 1944 alone the Americans produced 96,000 airplanes, and the total US output was twice that of the Axis nations combined. Using assembly-line methods that had been perfected by the shipbuilding tycoon Henry J. Kaiser, building time for a freightship was reduced from 105 days to less than five. The enormous American war production effort did not even require the austerity measures experienced in Germany, Britain or Japan, though it did lead to steep inflation and, with some 15 million Americans serving in the armed forces, to acute labor shortages.

Unable to match US war production, the Germans sought to disrupt the supply lines across the Atlantic. At first, their submarines achieved some success, but later the British and Americans perfected the World War I convoy system, bunching together large numbers of transport vessels guarded by warships. Technological advances in radar and sonar (sound-tracking) and, above all, the secret weapon, code-named ULTRA, that deciphered German radio communication, enabled the Allies to steer the convoys around the German U-boats and to attack them in their hiding places. By mid-1942 the Allies could build more vessels than the Germans could sink and in the following year the Germans virtually abandoned their large-scale submarine operations in the Atlantic.

In the Pacific war the Americans had a similar decoding capability – named MAGIC – which played a crucial role in locating Japanese naval forces. After Pearl Harbor the Japanese scored a series of notable victories, but in May 1942, at the battle of Coral Sea – the first in history to be fought with seaborne aircraft – they were stopped

▶ The war in the Pacific was essentially two separate campaigns – a situation produced by a Japanese strategy which had the army building a land-based empire on the Asian continent and the navy defending a sprawling island perimeter in the Pacific. After huge early gains in north and east China, the Japanese army failed to make further progress against fierce resistance and the campaign degenerated into a series of inconclusive local offensives. In Southeast Asia, the Japanese swept to the frontiers of India in 1942, but after a final offensive in early 1944 were forced steadily back by combined Allied attacks. In the huge arena of the Pacific, rapid Japanese expansion ended with a series of reverses in mid-1942, when the buildup of US resources made a sustained offensive possible. From then on Allied forces systematically dismantled Japan's defensive island barriers, destroying its naval and aerial fighting ability, before reaching the enemy's home islands in mid-1945.

◀ A US destroyer is hit during the surprise Japanese attack on Pearl Harbor in December 1941. Only lightly opposed by the surprised defenders, Japanese carrier aircraft were able to inflict heavy damage on the US fleet at negligible cost to themselves. But the US aircraft carriers, which were to prove decisive in the naval war that followed, were not in port at the time so escaped destruction. US resources were in any case too great to be crippled by a single blow, and the Japanese could not prevent a massive rearmament effort, providing US sailors and airmen with the equipment to sweep away early Japanese gains.

The War in the Pacific 1937–45

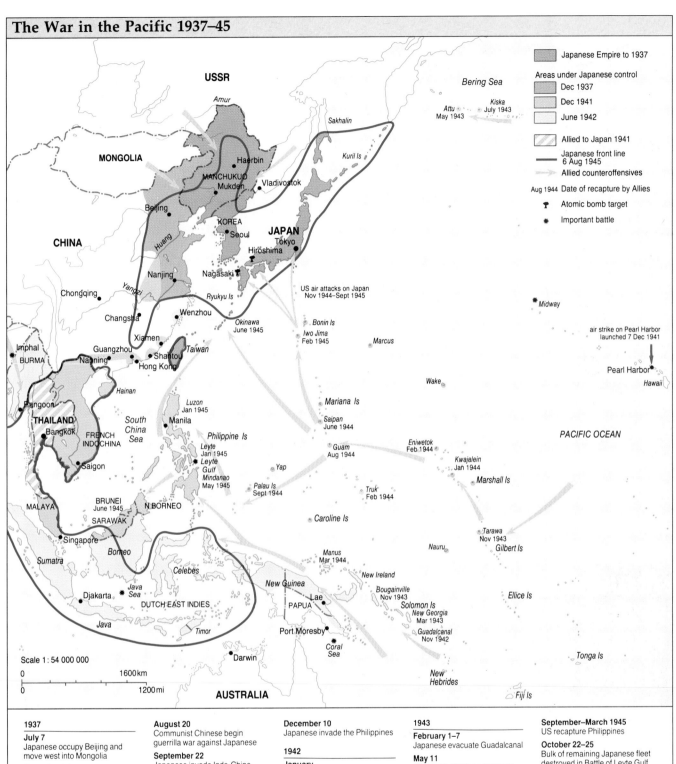

USSR

Amur

Bering Sea

Kiska
July 1943

Attu
May 1943

MONGOLIA

Haerbin

MANCHUKUO
Mukden   Vladivostok

Sakhalin

Kuril Is

Beijing

KOREA
Seoul

JAPAN
Tokyo
Hiroshima

CHINA

Huang

Nanjing   Nagasaki

Chongqing

Yangzi

Changsha   Wenzhou

Ryukyu Is

Okinawa
June 1945

US air attacks on Japan
Nov 1944–Sept 1945

Bonin Is
Iwo Jima
Feb 1945

Marcus

Midway

air strike on Pearl Harbor
launched 7 Dec 1941

Imphal
BURMA

Guangzhou
Nanning   Shantou   *Taiwan*
Hong Kong

Xiamen

Hainan

Rangoon

THAILAND
Bangkok   FRENCH
INDOCHINA

Saigon

Luzon
Jan 1945

Manila

South
China
Sea

Philippine Is

Leyte
Jan 1945
*Leyte
Gulf*
Mindanao
May 1945

Yap

Wake

Pearl Harbor
Hawaii

Mariana Is

Saipan
June 1944

Guam
Aug 1944

Eniwetok
Feb 1944

Kwajalein
Jan 1944

Marshall Is

PACIFIC OCEAN

MALAYA

Singapore

BRUNEI
June 1945
SARAWAK

N BORNEO

Palau Is
Sept 1944

Truk
Feb 1944

Caroline Is

Borneo

Sumatra

Djakarta   *Java
Sea*

DUTCH EAST INDIES

Celebes

Manus
Mar 1944

New Ireland

Nauru

Tarawa
Nov 1943

Gilbert Is

Ellice Is

Java

Timor

New Guinea
Lae
PAPUA

Port Moresby

Bougainville
Nov 1943
Solomon Is
New Georgia
Mar 1943
Guadalcanal
Nov 1942

Coral
Sea

Tonga Is

Scale 1 : 54 000 000

0   1600km

0   1200mi

AUSTRALIA

Darwin

New
Hebrides

Fiji Is

Legend

	Japanese Empire to 1937
	Areas under Japanese control
	Dec 1937
	Dec 1941
	June 1942
	Allied to Japan 1941
	Japanese front line 6 Aug 1945
	Allied counteroffensives
Aug 1944	Date of recapture by Allies
	Atomic bomb target
	Important battle

1937

July 7
Japanese occupy Beijing and move west into Mongolia

December 13
Nanjing falls to Japanese

1938

Japanese reach limit of their expansion in November

1939

May
Japanese and Red Army clash on Mongolian border

September
Nanning falls to Japanese

1940

March 30
Japanese puppet regime installed in Beijing

August 20
Communist Chinese begin guerrilla war against Japanese

September 22
Japanese invade Indo-China

1941

January
Bulk of US fleet ordered to Pearl Harbor

July 25
Japan declares Franco-Japanese protectorate over Indo-China

October 15
Martial rule declared in Japan

November 25
Japanese carrier fleet sails for Central Pacific, and Japanese attack US fleet at Pearl Harbor on December 7 without warning

December 10
Japanese invade the Philippines

1942

January
Japanese invade Burma

February–April
Japanese capture Singapore, Java, Burma, forcing British retreat to India

June 4–5
Japanese carrier fleet destroyed at Battle of Midway

August–November
US landing at Guadalcanal. Heavy mutual losses result in US supremacy

December
British offensive in Burma

1943

February 1–7
Japanese evacuate Guadalcanal

May 11
US launch attack on Japanese positions in Aleutian Islands

July–November
US penetrate Solomon Islands, eventually forcing Japanese withdrawal from New Guinea

1944

February 17
US airstrike inflicts heavy Japanese losses at Truk

March 6–June 22
Japanese offensive in Burma forces back British, but the former are eventually repulsed

June 15
Japanese carrier force crippled in Battle of Philippines Sea

September–March 1945
US recapture Philippines

October 22–25
Bulk of remaining Japanese fleet destroyed in Battle of Leyte Gulf

October–November
Allied offensive in Burma

1945

February 19–March 16
US recaptures Iwo Jima

March 9–10
Major US bombing raid on Tokyo

March 14–June 22
US invade Okinawa

May 2
Allies capture Rangoon

August 6–9
US drop A-bomb on Hiroshima and Nagasaki. Japanese surrender on August 15

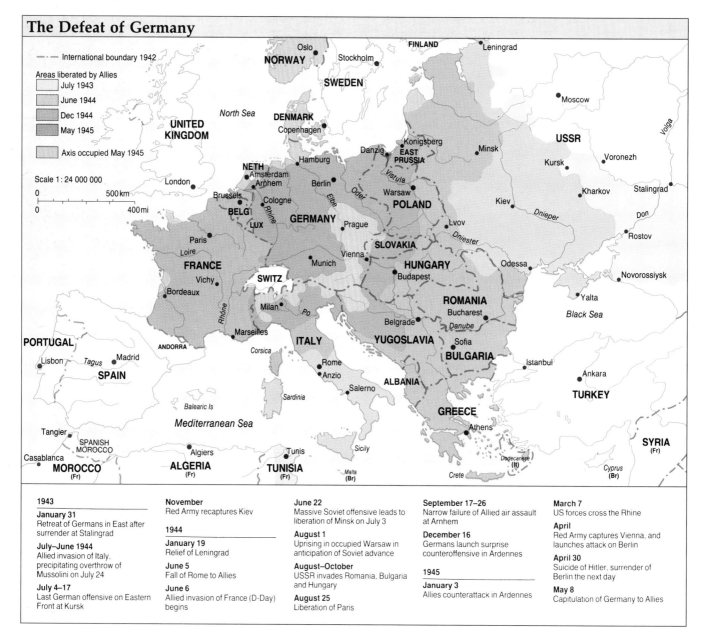

The Defeat of Germany

- — · — International boundary 1942

Areas liberated by Allies
- July 1943
- June 1944
- Dec 1944
- May 1945

- Axis occupied May 1945

Scale 1 : 24 000 000

| 0 | 500km |
| 0 | 400mi |

1943

January 31
Retreat of Germans in East after surrender at Stalingrad

July–June 1944
Allied invasion of Italy, precipitating overthrow of Mussolini on July 24

July 4–17
Last German offensive on Eastern Front at Kursk

November
Red Army recaptures Kiev

1944

January 19
Relief of Leningrad

June 5
Fall of Rome to Allies

June 6
Allied invasion of France (D-Day) begins

June 22
Massive Soviet offensive leads to liberation of Minsk on July 3

August 1
Uprising in occupied Warsaw in anticipation of Soviet advance

August–October
USSR invades Romania, Bulgaria and Hungary

August 25
Liberation of Paris

September 17–26
Narrow failure of Allied air assault at Arnhem

December 16
Germans launch surprise counteroffensive in Ardennes

1945

January 3
Allies counterattack in Ardennes

March 7
US forces cross the Rhine

April
Red Army captures Vienna, and launches attack on Berlin

April 30
Suicide of Hitler, surrender of Berlin the next day

May 8
Capitulation of Germany to Allies

▲ After 1942, Germany was in the impossible position of fighting defensive campaigns on multiple fronts while its industrial heartland was being devastated by strategic air attack. In the east, an attempt to reverse the defeat of Stalingrad ended in failure at Kursk, where the outnumbered Axis forces were pushed steadily back. In the south, North Africa was lost and the Germans were left alone to defend the Italian peninsula after the overthrow of Mussolini's government. A second front in Western Europe was decisively opened up with the Normandy landings of June 1944. After containing the invaders for several months, German forces were again forced back, and in early 1945 Germany was invaded from both east and west.

by the US Navy from approaching Australia. A month later, at the Battle of Midway, they lost all four of their aircraft carriers to a weaker American fleet, suffering a first and decisive defeat. From February 1943, after six months of fighting for Guadalcanal, the largest of the Solomon Islands, the Americans did not lose another naval battle.

While the Japanese were beginning to lose the war in the Pacific, the Germans were also suffering more reverses at the hands of the Soviet Red Army. The day of 17 July 1943 marked the beginning of a general offensive by Soviet forces in which they swiftly regained vast amounts of territory on the central and southern fronts. On 6 November they liberated Kiev and in early January 1944 they reached the former Polish border. By now the Red Army was a much better fighting force, commanded by a new generation of dynamic generals, mostly under 40 years of age, who had been chosen for their military, rather than for their political, credentials. Eventually, the Red Army greatly outnumbered the Germans everywhere.

In early 1944 the Soviets finally brought relief to the city of Leningrad, the victim of a terrible 900-day blockade. By April, the Red Army had retaken much of the western part of the Soviet Union and even reached as far as Romania, and in May they liberated the Crimea. By December, Romania and Hungary, both former allies of Germany, had been overrun by the Red Army and dropped out of the war.

The Italian campaign
Hitler's earliest ally, Fascist Italy, abandoned the Axis effort in September 1943 when the southern tip of the country was captured by the Allies. Earlier, on 10 July, 250,000 British and American troops, in what was the largest amphibious operation of the war, landed in Sicily and within five weeks had seized control of the island. A major bombing attack launched from Sicily on 19 July finally forced the Italians to surrender. King Victor Emmanuel III, who remained Italy's titular head of state through 21 years of Fascist rule, dismissed Mussolini and placed him under arrest. A

new government was formed, under Marshal Pietro Badoglio, which banned Mussolini's party and signed an armistice on 3 September.

The Germans responded immediately. They occupied Rome, and disarmed Italian troops in Italy and in occupation territories, including southeastern France, Yugoslavia, Albania and Greece. The king and Badoglio's government sought protection from the Allies. Meanwhile Mussolini was freed by German parachutists and installed at the head of a "Social Italian Republic" at Saló in the northern mountains, supported by four divisions of Italian volunteers.

Although the Germans still held much of northern Italy, the Allies' capture of airfields in the south brought their bombers within range of industrial centers and cities in southern and eastern Germany as well as oil installations in Vienna, Budapest and Ploesti, in Romania. However, the Alps presented a considerable obstacle to attacking Germany from the south. Churchill's idea of a thrust through the Balkans was perhaps more politically than strategically motivated. He was worried about the Red Army's achieving a quick breakthrough and occupying eastern and southeastern Europe. Eventually, the Anglo-American alliance decided to concentrate its forces, under the US General Dwight Eisenhower, on a large-scale invasion of France.

The Normandy invasion

To prepare for the landing on the beaches of Normandy, in northern France, some 2.8 million troops assembled in the south of England. However, the French coastline was defended by the "Atlantic Wall", massive fortifications with heavy artillery hidden in huge concrete shelters, and sown with tank traps and minefields. In addition, the Germans had 58 divisions in the west, including 10 tank divisions. General Rommel, the German commander, wanted to throw the Allied forces back into the sea before they could establish any major footholds, but Hitler and other generals favored a battle on land.

To clear the way for the landing, the Allies' superior air forces strafed and bombed both the coastal fortifications and German troops further inland. Up to the last moment the Germans were fooled about the timing and exact place of landing. Then, with complete control of the air and barely disturbed by German naval forces, the Allies invaded Normandy on 6 June 1944 with 600 warships, 4,000 supporting aircraft and 176,000 men. Within the week the number of troops put ashore had doubled, bringing with them 50,000 vehicles and over 100,000 tons of supplies. Beachheads were built up, before the British, American and Canadian divisions passed on further inland. By the end of July they had almost driven the Germans out of northwestern France. On 15 August another allied force landed on the Mediterranean coast between Cannes and Toulon, and pushed up the Rhône valley.

Eisenhower wanted to bypass Paris in pursuit of the German troops. But for de Gaulle, who had long awaited his return to France at the head of his Free French movement, Paris was of great importance symbolically. President Roosevelt feared the possibility of a civil war in France, impeding the Allied advance, and did not believe that de Gaulle would be able to unite the country. Nevertheless, Eisenhower let de Gaulle and a Free French division under General Leclerc enter Paris to liberate the city on 25 August.

Allied victory in Europe

On 3 September the Allies liberated Brussels, and two weeks later they reached the German border. As Hitler mounted a desperate effort to halt them, Eisenhower's chief commander of land forces, General Montgomery, sought a swift advance to the north German plains by the end of 1944. He ordered a large parachute force to land at Arnhem behind the German lines to secure a bridgehead over the Rhine. The attempt failed badly. In November the Allied advance came to a halt well west of the Rhine, and on 16 December the Germans launched their last major attack in the Ardennes. At first the surprise counterattack succeeded, as poor weather conditions prevented the Allies from making use of their superiority in the air. However, within a week, they had defeated the Germans, in a battle known as the "Battle of the Bulge".

Hitler, however, ordered a fanatical fight against the Western troops, and refused to regard the Eastern Front as his main priority. He further forbade the evacuation of Germans in the east who were trying to flee from the advancing Red Army. On 19 March he ordered all transport lines and industrial plants to be blown up rather than

▲ After Allied troops were ashore in Normandy, it was only a matter of time before their superior firepower would break through the enemy defences and drive them back towards the Rhine.

▼ By the beginning of 1945, the Germans could no longer prevent the closing Allied pincers, and despite desperate resistance, the Soviet flag was flying over Berlin by early May.

surrendered to the Allies – instructions that were largely ignored even by Nazi officials.

Eisenhower's forces finally crossed the Rhine in March. They swiftly advanced to the Elbe river, where a symbolic meeting took place with Red Army units near Torgau on 25 April 1945. Five days later Hitler committed suicide in his shelter in Berlin shortly before the arrival of the Soviet army. The German surrender on all fronts became effective on 8 May.

The defeat of Japan

In the Pacific war, Japan still refused to surrender. The US troops took the island of Iwo Jima in February 1945 and Okinawa in June. From there, B-29 bombers carried out raids on Tokyo and on other major Japanese cities, setting them ablaze with fire bombs. At sea Japan was also facing defeat, having lost its last big warships in April. However, there were still over a million Japanese soldiers in northern China and a much larger contingent in the home islands.

In fact, Japan capitulated in August, victim of the most terrible weapon to be unleashed in World War II or since then. On 16 July 1945, after years of intensive research and development, the Americans detonated the first atomic bomb in the New Mexican desert. Some people, including the great physicist Albert Einstein, believed that a mere demonstration of its powers would suffice to persuade the Japanese to make peace. However, the politicians rejected this suggestion and decided instead to bomb an industrial city. In late July, without being told about the atomic bomb, the Japanese government secretly offered in principle to surrender provided that the institution of emperor was preserved. But they found that they could not accept the terms of surrender laid down in the Allies' ultimatum. On 6 August an atomic bomb was exploded over the

city of Hiroshima, destroying 80 percent of it. Two days later the Soviet Union declared war on Japan and quickly advanced into Korea, Manchuria and the Kurile islands. On 9 August a second atomic weapon fell on Nagasaki. Altogether, in both attacks, 340,000 people were either killed instantly or died within five years. Many more were afflicted by hitherto unknown radiation diseases and died a lingering death much later. Japan's surrender was formally accepted on board the battleship *Missouri* in Tokyo bay on 2 September. Six days later the Americans under General MacArthur arrived in Japan and installed a US military government.

Postwar occupation and reparations

The "Big Three" – the United States, Britain and the Soviet Union – met for the first time in Tehran in November–December 1943, to discuss the postwar future of Germany. They tentatively fixed the western Polish border at the Oder river, which meant Germany would lose about a quarter of its prewar territory (before the *Anschluss* of Austria). In January 1944 Britain proposed that Germany be split into three occupation zones, each one to be run by one of the Big Three, and that Berlin would be divided up and ad-

▲ Hiroshima, the end of the war and the dawn of a new era. By July 1945, Japan was prostrate, its industry destroyed, its navy at the bottom of the sea, its air force virtually annihilated and its people preparing for a last-ditch defense of the homeland. Faced with a regime unlikely to chose surrender before conquest, the Allies resorted to the newly-invented atomic bomb to avoid a bloody conventional invasion. Two devastating strikes on Hiroshima and Nagasaki produced the desired surrender. By adopting such a terrible new weapon, however, the victors introduced the possibility of total annihilation into postwar strategic calculations.

◄ The end of the war brought Allied military occupation to Japan, exposing a war-weary and devastated country to control by foreign powers intent on dismantling a system of government and code of behavior that had exposed Asia and the Pacific to cruel, imperialist aggression.

extracted promises from the beneficiaries of lend-lease aid to cooperate in these schemes.

The Big Three met for a second time, in February 1945, at Yalta on the Crimea. In a secret agreement the Soviets were promised their former holdings in Manchuria, which Russia had lost in 1904-05, in return for entering the war against Japan two or three months after the German surrender. The conference granted France the status of fourth occupying power in Germany and Austria, and made a "declaration of liberated Europe" pledging that all democratic political forces – including the Communists but excluding fascists – would share in its political reconstruction.

At Potsdam, near Berlin, the Big Three met for a third time, in July/August 1945. They agreed that each occupying power would take reparations from their own zone, and that the Soviets would receive 10 percent of the dismantled industries of the western zones, and a further 15 percent in exchange for goods. The German economy would be run jointly on an economic program tied to a standard of living similar to that of 1936. Large businesses and cartels were to be broken up, all Nazi and military organizations banned, and democratic government rebuilt from the local level upward. It was further agreed that millions of ethnic Germans living to the east of the four occupation zones be moved to Germany. The Big Three decided to prosecute a few of the leading Nazis and to try them as war criminals before a four-power court (the Nuremberg trials).

The founding of the United Nations (UN) organization dates back to 1 January 1942, when 26 states signed the "Declaration of the United Nations", in which they agreed to continue the war effort jointly and not to make peace separately. At the Dumbarton Oaks Conference (Washington DC) in September-October 1944, the United States, Britain, the Soviet Union and China drafted what became the UN Charter, setting out the basis for future international cooperation and international security. Later, at Yalta, it was agreed that the UN Security Council could act only with the unanimous support of the five permanent members (France was added to the four original members). At its founding conference in San Francisco in April-June 1945 the United Nations consisted of 51 members, all of whom were countries who had declared war on Germany.

I was 13 years old; I was ordered into the center of the city to clean up the streets. I looked up at the sky – the plane had a pretty white tail, it was a sunny day, the sky was blue. This had happened many times before, so I didn't feel scared. Then I saw something drop – and pow! – a big explosion knocked me down.

HIROSHIMA SURVIVOR

▼ The three great Allied warlords, Churchill, Roosevelt and Stalin met for the last time at Yalta in February 1945. Within months, Churchill was voted from power and Roosevelt was dead. Long before this, the wartime alliance had begun to show signs of strain as the need to agree on postwar settlements became more urgent. In fact, it was only the presence of common enemies that had bound the great Allied powers together, and even in their strategic arrangements for the defeat of the Axis differences in national interests had often caused disagreement between them and mutual suspicion. With Britain's decline accelerated by the war, the lines of superpower conflict between the United States and the Soviet Union were already being drawn before the last shots were fired.

ministered jointly and serve as the seat of an Allied Control Council. However, the division of Germany was never finally agreed because of the three Powers' conflicting interests. Britain and the United States did not wish to rekindle an angry German nationalism crying for ethnic Germans to "come home", which had been exploited by Hitler and might equally be used by the Russians to extend Soviet power in Germany and in Europe as a whole. For their part, the Soviets opposed any division that would give the Western Powers exclusive control of Germany's industrial heartland, in particular the Rhine-Ruhr area.

The US leaders also sought a new international trade system that was free of the kind of trade barriers which, they believed, had led to the Depression of the 1930s and the consequent rise of dictatorships in Europe and Asia. At an international conference held at Bretton Woods, New Hampshire, in 1944, the International Monetary Fund (IMF) was set up to stabilize currencies on the basis of fixed exchange rates pegged to the US dollar, and proposals accepted for an International Bank of Reconstruction and Development, or World Bank, to offer credit loans for postwar economic recovery. The United States assumed the leading role in the new world economy and

GENOCIDE: THE FINAL SOLUTION

Widespread violence against cultural and racial groups is nothing new, but the idea of destroying an entire people, and the use of technology to put the idea into action, has been one of the particular horrors of 20th-century history. First invoked in 1915 in Armenia, when the Turks sought to deport almost two million people and some 600,000 lost their lives, it reached its most appalling form in the holocaust or Nazi persecution of the Jews in the 1940s.

Antisemitism had been endemic to much of Europe, particularly eastern Europe, for many years; and in the years following World War I those seeking scapegoats, whether for national decline, for international capitalist conspiracy, or, paradoxically, for the threat of Bolshevism found the vulnerable Jewish community an easy target. The antisemitism of the Nazis in the 1930s, though virulent, was not always seen as the most dangerous aspect of their rise.

Nevertheless, by 1939 about half the Jewish population of Germany and Austria had fled, and those who had not lived under discriminatory laws banning them from public life. After the invasion of Poland, Jews were rounded up and put into ghettos; others, particularly in occupied Russia, were summarily shot. At Babyi Yar, near Kiev, 34,000 Jews were massacred by the Germans in September 1941. For a time Hitler followed a plan to deport millions of east European Jews to Madagascar, but in January 1942 at the Wannsee conference, a group of government and SS officials proposed a "final solution" of the "Jewish question". Able-bodied Jews capable of hard labor would be forcibly conscripted to assist the German war production effort; others would be efficiently eliminated, using, in particular, pesticide gas Zyklon B.

Already since 1933 a vast system of nearly 200 concentration camps, which initially served to intern the Nazis' political opponents, had been under construction. To meet the needs of the "final solution", a number of huge new camps were set up in the east, including Auschwitz, Chelmno and Treblinka in Poland.

The "final solution" was kept secret from the bulk of the German people, but it was supported by thousands of willing SS personnel and Nazi guards who unquestioningly obeyed orders, as well as by police and militia forces in Vichy France and parts of eastern Europe who organized cattle rail cars to assemble Jewish population groups from every corner of occupied Europe. Towards the end of the war, efforts were made to destroy the evidence of the killings – which had amounted to an estimated six million Jews, plus hundreds of thousands of gypsies, mentally handicapped people and others; but the proof was too terrible and too widespread to be hidden.

In 1946 the United Nations defined genocide as a crime involving the deliberate and systematical destruction of a racial, national, religious or ethnic group, in response to these revelations, and in 1951 a Convention against genocide went into effect.

▶ Even before the decision to exterminate the Jews, the Nazis excluded them from public life, and forced people of Jewish descent to wear yellow stars.

▼ The crematoria in Auschwitz, where the bodies of more than one million victims of the gas chambers were destroyed. The task of stoking the ovens was given to Jewish prisoners.

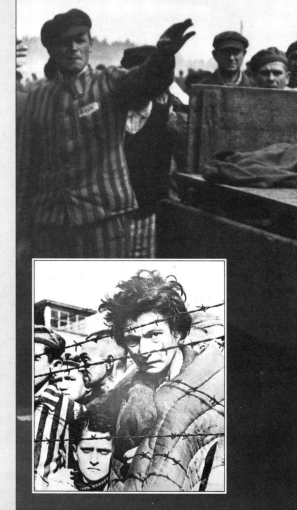

▶ After the Allied forces liberated the death camps they ensured that the evidence of almost unimaginable horror was preserved, with a full photographic record to complement such documentation as had not been destroyed by the Nazis. In this photograph surviving inmates at Dachau in southern Germany are seen helping to clear away the bodies of the dead. The Allies also showed German civilians first-hand evidence to ensure that the facts of the secret Nazi policy could be appreciated.

▶ After being taken to the death camps, inmates were selected either for hard labor, or for immediate death if they were too sick or old to work. In some camps such as Dachau, callous medical experiments were conducted on inmates, without concern for the survival of the patients. Despite the harsh conditions of life and the continual arrival of ever more inmates to camps such as Auschwitz, many prisoners (other than those charged with the disposal of the corpses) were unaware of their likely fate until the last minute; they were told the gas chambers themselves were mass showers.

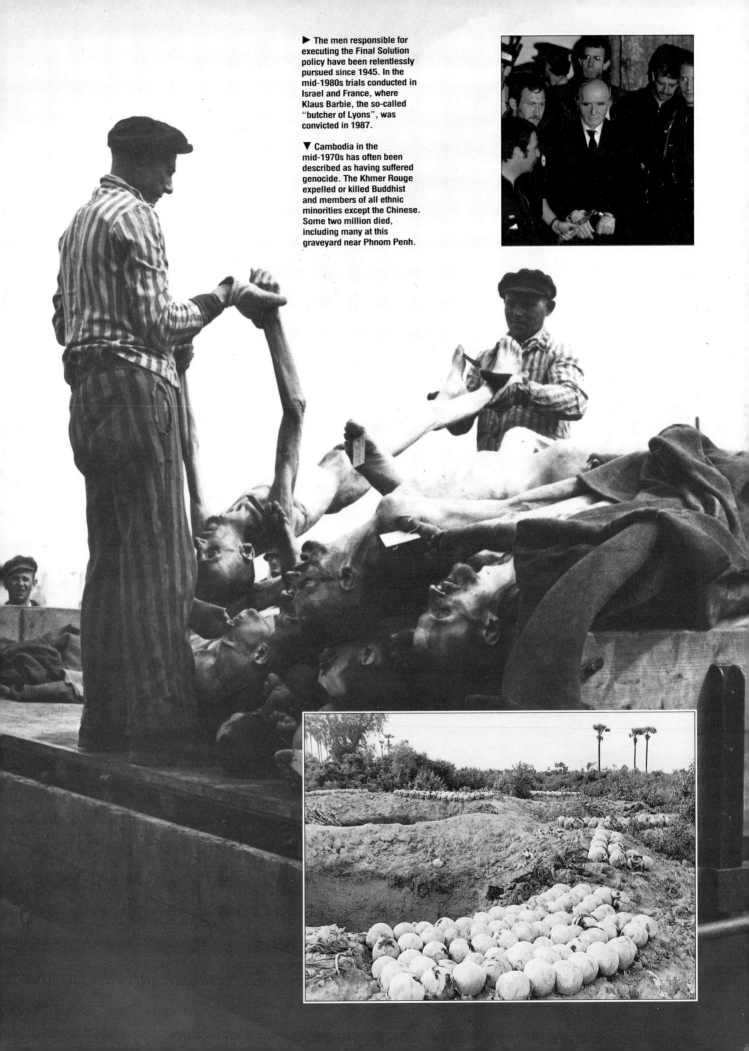

▶ The men responsible for executing the Final Solution policy have been relentlessly pursued since 1945. In the mid-1980s trials conducted in Israel and France, where Klaus Barbie, the so-called "butcher of Lyons", was convicted in 1987.

▼ Cambodia in the mid-1970s has often been described as having suffered genocide. The Khmer Rouge expelled or killed Buddhist and members of all ethnic minorities except the Chinese. Some two million died, including many at this graveyard near Phnom Penh.

1945 · 1960

THE
SUPERPOWER
SYSTEM

Time Chart

	1946	1947	1948	1949	1950	1951	1952	1953
Europe/Mediterranean	• Start of UK nationalization program • Republics declared in Hungary (Feb), Italy (Jun), Bulgaria (Sep) • Jul–Oct: Peace conference, Paris (Fr) • Sep: Restoration of Greek king; civil war (to Oct 1949) • Oct: 4th Republic (Fr)	• Benelux customs union formed by Belgium, Netherlands and Luxemburg • Federation of trades unions founded in W Germany • 10 Feb: Signature of Paris Peace treaties • 30 Dec: Romanian king forced to abdicate	• 17 Mar, Brussels Treaty: (UK, Fr and Benelux countries) • Apr–Jun: Berlin airlift • Jun: Yugoslavia expelled from Cominform • 9 Jun: Czechoslovak People's Democracy • 5 Jul: UK National Health Service opened	• Jan: Communist COMECON set up • 4 Apr: NATO formed • 18 Apr: Eire became Republic of Ireland • May: Berlin blockade lifted by USSR as E and W German nations formally set up • May: Council of Europe established	• May, Schuman Plan: Union of Franco–German coal, iron and steel industries proposed; led to establishment of ECSC (European Coal and Steel Community) in 1951 by Fr, W Ger, Ita, Benelux nations • 25 Dec: Scottish nationalists stole UK coronation Stone of Scone	• Apr: 1st health service charges imposed in UK; 1 shilling on every prescription	• Feb: Greece and Turkey joined NATO • 6 Feb: Death of UK monarch, George VI; succeeded by daughter Elizabeth II • Nov, Slansky Trial: Anti-Zionist purge in Czech Communist Party	• 14 Jan: Marshal Tito elected president of Yugoslavia • Mar: Death of Josef Stalin, president of USSR; Georgi Malenkov became premier; Nikita Khrushchev elected Communist Party 1st secretary (Sep)
The Middle East	• UK and USSR troops withdrawn from Iran • May: Transjordan became an independent kingdom under Emir Abdullah Ibn Hussein • 22 Jul: In Palestine, bombing of Jerusalem's King David Hotel (headquarters of UK administration) by Irgun Zvai Leumi, Zionist terrorists	• 15 Aug, midnight: Indian independence from UK; partitioned into India, under Nehru, and Pakistan, under Gov-Gen Jinnah; outbreak of Hindu–Muslim violence • Oct: Kashmir joined Indian Union; fighting between Indian and Pakistani forces on border (until Jan 1949) • Nov: UN resolution on partition followed by civil war in Palestine	• 30 Jan: Mahatma Gandhi assassinated • Feb: Ceylon became an independent dominion within Commonwealth • 14 May: Jewish State of Israel proclaimed; Dr Chaim Weizmann, president; David Ben-Gurion, prime minister • 15 May: Invasion of Israel by Arab League nations	• French imprisoned Tunisian nationalist leader Habib ibn Ali Bourguiba for 3rd time • Feb–Jul: Armistice agreed between Israel and Arab League • Jun: Transjordan renamed Hashemite Kingdom of Jordan • Dec: Israeli capital moved from Tel Aviv to Jerusalem, despite UN approval of latter's international status	• 26 Jan: India proclaimed a sovereign democratic republic • 8 Apr: Delhi Pact signed by India and Pakistan; bill of rights for minorities • May: President Inönü's government ousted by Adnan Menderes' Democratic Party, in Turkish Republic's 1st free elections	• May: Iranian oil industry nationalized; formerly run by Anglo–Iranian Oil Co. • 20 Jul: King Abdullah of Jordan murdered; succeeded by grand-son Hussein (in 1952) • Dec: Under King Idris I, leader of Senussi people, Libya became 1st state to become independent under UN resolution	• Formation of Ba'ath Socialist Party (Pan-Arab but primarily Syrian) • 23–6 Jul: Free Officers' Movement headed coup in Egypt; abdication and exile of King Farouk • Dec: Leaders of Moroccan nationalist party, Istiqlal, arrested by French authorities	• Libya joined Arab League • Jun: Egyptian Republic proclaimed under Brigadier Mohammed Neguib • 15–22 Aug: Power struggle in Iran led to exile of shah, then reassertion of control • Nov: Death of King Ibn Saud (Saudi Arabia); succeeded by son, Saud IV
Africa		• Jun: Jomo Kenyatta became president of the Kenya Africa National Union (KANU)	• Mau Mau secret society founded in Kenya, to expel white settlers from traditional lands of Kikuyu people • Jun: Dr Daniel Malan became S African prime minister; responsible for strict imposition of apartheid	• Jun: Convention People's Party founded by Kwame Nkrumah, to seek independence for UK Gold Coast colony (W Afr). Nkrumah became 1st prime minister, 1952			• 20 Mar: Supreme Court (S Afr) found Malan's apartheid laws unconstitutional • Sep: Eritrea made autonomous federal region within Ethiopia • Oct: State of emergency declared in Kenya because of Mau Mau uprising; Jomo Kenyatta arrested	• May: Founding of antiapartheid Liberal Party by Alan Paton in S Africa • Sep: Federation of Rhodesia and Nyasaland created, incorporating former UK colony of S Rhodesia and protectorates of Nyasaland and N Rhodesia (to 1963)
The Americas	• 24 Feb: Juan Perón elected president of Argentina	• US CIA set up • Anti-unionist Taft–Hartley Act (US) • 12 Mar, Truman Doctrine: US pledge to up overseas aid to oppose communism • 15 Aug – 2 Sep, Rio Treaty: Defense accord at Inter-American Conference	• 30 Mar – 2 May: Charter of Organization of American States (OAS) drawn up at 9th Pan-American Conference • 15 Nov: Resignation of Canada's long-serving Liberal prime minister, W. Mackenzie King; succeeded by Louis St Laurent	• 31 Mar: Newfoundland (including Labrador) became Canada's 10th province • Jul: US Congress ratified North Atlantic Treaty	• Jan: US hydrogen bomb development announced • Feb: Senator McCarthy claimed the existence of 57 Communist Party Members in US State Department • 16 Dec: US national emergency declared over Korean War	• Juan Perón (Arg) re-elected president • Jan: President Getúlio Vargas reinstated (Bra) • 26 Feb: 22nd Amendment limited US presidential term • Oct: Charter fixed for Organization of Central American States	• Vincent Massey was 1st native governor-general in Canada • Mar: Return to Cuba of exiled General Batista as dictator • 26 Jul: Death of Eva Perón in Argentina • 4 Nov: Dwight D. Eisenhower elected US president	• Jan: In US McCarthy became chairman of Senate Subcommittee on Investigations • 19 Jun: Ethel and Julius Rosenberg executed in US for treason • 6 Oct: UK troops sent to British Guiana to counter feared Communist uprising
Asia and Pacific	• 1 Jan: In Japan, Hirohito renounced his divinity as emperor • Mar: Democratic Republic of Vietnam, free within Indochina and French Union • 4 Jul: Independent republic of Philippines established • Aug: Start of civil war in China	• 1st Dutch "police action" against Indonesian nationalists • South Pacific Commission formed (Aus, Fr, NZ, UK, US), with headquarters in New Caledonia • Dec: Start of 7-year civil war in Vietnam, with Viet-Minh attack on Hanoi	• Federation of Malaya set up: Communist guerrilla war (Jun) • Jan: Provisional rule of all Vietnam set up • Aug–Sep: Republics declared in North and South Korea • Dec: City in Formosa named Nationalist capital of China	• 1 Oct: Chinese People's Republic proclaimed • Nov: End of 14 years of Labour rule (NZ); National Party elected • Dec: Election of Prime Minister Menzies (to 1966) • 27 Dec: Independent Republic of Indonesia formally proclaimed	• Feb, Alliance: People's Republic of China and USSR • 25 Jun: Korean War began; Soviet-backed N Korean troops crossed 38th parallel; UN intervention in S Korea authorized by Security Council • Oct: Start of Chinese occupation of Tibet (to May 1951)	• 10 Jul, Korean War: Cease-fire talks began • Sep: Bilateral security agreement for stationing US troops in Japan • 1 Sep, ANZUS Pact: Tripartite security treaty (US, NZ, Aus) • 8 Sep: Peace treaty: Japan and 49 nations (less USSR)		• 27 Jul: Korean War ended, with signature of armistice by N Korea and UN officials
World	• Jan: Trygve Lie (Nor) elected 1st UN secretary-general • Jun: 1st meeting of UN Atomic Energy Commission • Nov: Foundation of UNESCO and UNICEF	• Eleanor Roosevelt chaired UN Human Rights Commission • 5 Jun, Marshall Plan: US aid for European economic recovery • Sep: Cominform established	• WHO and GATT set up as UN agencies • UN adopted Universal Declaration of Human Rights • Apr: OEEC established	• International Confederation of Free Trade Unions established, with representatives from 51 nations • May: Israel admitted to UN	• Jan, Colombo Plan: Commonwealth foreign ministers met to plan economic aid for S and SE Asia	• Jul: Socialist International reconstituted, at conference in W Germany	• UN Disarmament Commission founded • Nov: 1st hydrogen bomb tested by US, on Eniwetok Atoll in mid-Pacific	• Dag Hammarskjöld (Swe) elected UN secretary-general • Jan: Asian Socialist founded, in Rangoon, Burma

1954	1955	1956	1957	1958	1959	1960
Apr: Bomb attacks in [Cyp]rus began 4 years of [ter]rorism by pro-Enosis [(un]ion with Greece) EOKA [gu]errillas, led by George [...]vas (Dighenis)	• May: W Germany and Austria regained sovereignty; former joined NATO • May: USSR and Tito's Yugoslavia reconciled • 14 May: Warsaw Pact signed (Communist bloc) • Oct: Constantine Karamanlis elected Greek prime minister	• Feb: Stalin repudiated at 20th Soviet Communist Party Congress • 9 Mar: Archbishop Makarios arrested in Cyprus and deported as terrorist suspect • 28 Jun: Anti-Soviet riots in Poznań (Pol) • 23 Oct–4 Nov: Hungarian National Rising suppressed by Soviet tanks	• Jan: Harold Macmillan succeeded Anthony Eden as UK prime minister • 1 Jan: W Germany regained Saar region • 25 Mar, Treaties of Rome: Creation of EEC and Euratom (Fr, W Ger, Ita, Benelux) • 16–19 Dec: 1st NATO heads-of-government conference, Paris (Fr)	• 17 Feb: CND (Campaign for Nuclear Disarmament) launched in UK • Mar: Return to 1-man rule in USSR, as Khrushchev assumed full control of government • May–Sep: Threat of civil war in France over Algerian crisis led to de Gaulle's return to government and proclamation of 5th Republic (Oct)	• 20 Nov: EFTA (European Free Trade Association) established (Aut, UK, Den, Nor, Port, Swe, Sui)	• 16 Aug: Cyprus became an independent republic within Commonwealth, under Archbishop Makarios' presidency • Oct: UK supplied US with Holy Loch naval base for its polaris submarines
[Ap]r: Gamal Abdel Nasser [ele]cted Egyptian prime [mi]nister [1]9 Oct: Anglo–Egyptian [Sue]z Canal treaty signed, [ple]dging withdrawal of UK [troo]ps within 20 months [...] Nov: Start of guerrilla [war] (to 1962) by Algerian [nat]ionalist FLN movement [(Fro]nt de Libération [Na]tionale) under its leader [Mo]hammed Ahmed Ben [Bel]la, seeking inde[pen]dence from France	• Armed uprising against French in Morocco • Baghdad Pact signed by Turkey and Iraq (Feb), UK (Apr), Pakistan (Sep), Iran (Oct); US as participant nation	• Independence gained by Sudan and Tunisia • Mar–Apr: French and Spanish Morocco united under Sultan Mohammad V • 23 Mar: Pakistan became world's 1st Islamic republic • 26 Jul: Anglo–French Suez Canal Co. nationalized by Nasser (Egypt) • Nov: 1st UN Emergency Force (UNEF) sent to Egypt after Israeli and Anglo–French invasions	• Mar: Israeli troops evacuated Sinai • Apr: King Hussein survived coup attempt in Jordan	• Tunisia and Morocco joined Arab League • 1 Feb: UAR united Egypt, Syria; and Yemen (Mar) • Feb–Jul: Jordan and Iraq united, as Arab Union • 14 Jul: Arab nationalist coup in Iraq • Oct: Martial law proclaimed in Pakistan • 23 Oct: USSR pledged $100 million loan to Egypt, for Aswan Dam	• Iraq withdrew from Baghdad Pact (Mar); organization renamed CENTO (Central Treaty Organization) in Oct • Feb: S Arabian Federation of Arab Emirates set up; mutual assistance treaty with UK • Jul: US troops sent to Lebanon at request of Lebanese government • Sep: Assassination of Ceylonese prime minister, Solomon Bandaranaike	• 27 May: Military coup led by General Jemal Gürsel ousted Turkish prime minister Adnan Menderes (executed Sep 1961) • 21 Jul: Sirimavo Bandaranaike elected world's 1st female prime minister (Cey)
[De]c: Malan retired as [S Af]rican prime minister; [su]cceeded by Johannes [Str]ijdom	• 31 Jan–9 Feb: 60,000 black Africans took part in peaceful protest against removal from Johannesburg to new township (S Afr); forcefully evicted by police		• 1st elections took place in Belgian Congo, for municipal governments • 6–8 Mar: Ghana (former UK mandate of Togoland and Gold Coast colony) gained dominion status within Commonwealth • Aug: Tafawa Balewa became 1st federal prime minister of Nigeria	• *Mouvement National Congolais* founded by Patrice Lumumba, in Belgian Congo • French W African colony of Guinea achieved independence	• In Kenya, Jomo Kenyatta released from prison (since 1953) • State of emergency declared in UK protectorate of Nyasaland (C Afr); arrest of Hastings Banda • Aug: Anti-apartheid Progressive Party set up in S Africa	• Independence for W African and French Equatorial African states • Jul: Independent Somali Republic created (E Afr) • 1 Oct: Nigeria became dominion in Commonwealth • 5 Oct: White referendum approved creation of S African republic
[1]7 May: Racial [seg]regation in US state [sch]ool system ruled [un]constitutional [Ju]n: Military coup over [so]cialist government (Gua) [A]ug: US Communist [Par]ty outlawed [2]4 Aug: Pres. Getúlio [Var]gas (Bra) resigned and [com]mitted suicide	• Sep: Argentinian dictator Juan Perón deposed and exiled by military coup • Oct: Juscelino Kubitschek elected president of Brazil, introducing program of economic reform	• Martin Luther King convicted of organizing anti-segregationalist bus boycotts in Montgomery, Alabama (US) • Sep: Nicaraguan president, Anastazio Somoza, assassinated; succeeded by son, Luis • 2 Dec, 26 July Movement: Fidel Castro returned to Cuba at head of small guerrilla band	• CACOM (Central American Common Market) set up (Sal, Gua, Hon, Nic, CRC) • 5 Jan, Eisenhower Doctrine: US aid for Middle East, against Communism • Jun: 22 years of Liberal rule ended (Can) with election of Conservatives • 22 Sep: François Duvalier (Papa Doc) elected president of Haiti	• NASA (National Aeronautics and Space Administration) founded (US) • 3 Jan: West Indies Federation formed within Commonwealth (to 1962, Bar, Jam, Tri, Leeward Is less Virgin Is, Windward Is) • Dec: Rómulo Betancourt elected president of Venezuela (to 1964)	• Jan: Batistá dictatorship overthrown in Cuba; Castro became prime minister (Feb) • Alaska became 49th US state (Jan), and Hawaii the 50th (Mar) • Jul: 500,000 US steelworkers began strike (116 days)	• US property in Cuba nationalized • 26 Sep: In Chicago, 1st of 4 televised debates between US presidential candidates Richard Nixon and John F Kennedy • Nov: Kennedy elected 35th president of US
[Ap]r: Diplomat exposed [So]viet spy ring (Aus); USSR [bro]ke diplomatic ties [2]1 Jul, Geneva Agree[me]nts: End to French [ca]reer in Indochina. [Ce]ase-fire marked on 17th [par]allel between N and [S V]ietnam; not signed by [S V]ietnam or US [8] Sep: SEATO (SE Asia [Tre]aty Organization) [est]ablished	• Cambodian independence from French Union proclaimed • 26 Oct: Emperor Bao Dai deposed and S Vietnam declared a republic, with Ngo Dinh Diem as 1st president		• 31 Aug: Malaya gained sovereign independence within Commonwealth, with Tunku Abdul Rahman as 1st prime minister	• Great Leap Forward: Period of radical change began in China, including establishment of huge agricultural communes (to 1961)	• Mar–Apr: Failure of nationalist uprising by Tibetans against Chinese rule; Dalai Lama fled to India • Jun: Singapore became autonomous state within Commonwealth; with Lee Kuan Yu as 1st prime minister	• 27 Apr: S Korean president, Syngman Rhee, resigned and fled to exile; 2nd Korean republic established (15 Jun)
[1]st nuclear-powered [sub]marine launched, by [...] [...]May–Jul: UN conference [on] Indochina and Korea [hel]d in Geneva (Sui)	• Start of UN talks on nuclear and conventional weapons (to 1957) • 17–24 Apr, Bandung Conference: 1st meeting of African and Asian nations • 18–23 Jul: Geneva "Cold War" summit conference	• Apr: Dissolution of Cominform	• Intercontinental ballistic missiles tested by USSR and US • 4 Oct: World's 1st artificial satellite, *Sputnik I* (USSR) • 26 Dec: Afro–Asian Peoples' Solidarity Conference opened		• 1 Dec: 12 nations signed Antarctic Treaty, reserving region for peaceful development and pledging international scientific cooperation	

Datafile

The end of World War II left the world in an uncertain and potentially unstable situation. The victorious powers were in occupation of large areas of conquered territories, nervous of each other's intentions and often tied to loosely-established client regimes. Two of the most important world economic powers – Germany and Japan – had been devastated and were in need of massive aid before they could take their place in a stable global economy.

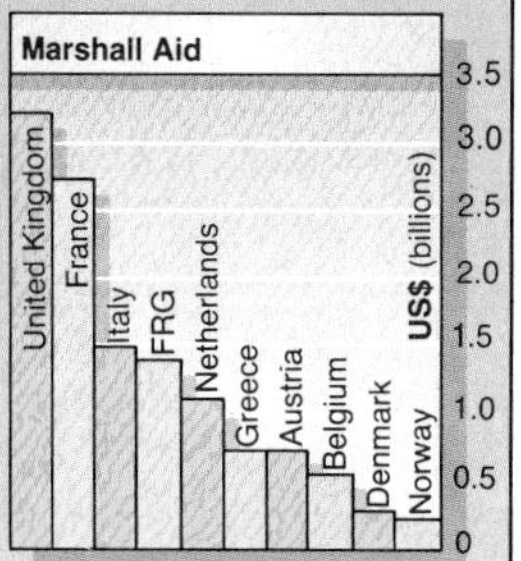

Marshall Aid
United Kingdom
France
Italy
FRG
Netherlands
Greece
Austria
Belgium
Denmark
Norway
US$ (billions)
3.5
3.0
2.5
2.0
1.5
1.0
0.5
0

▼▲ **US aid, allocated under the Marshall Plan, was initially committed heavily towards the rejuvenation of Allied Powers. Until the European economy as a whole had been restored, the world economy could not be expected to function normally and aid to other areas remained of secondary importance.**

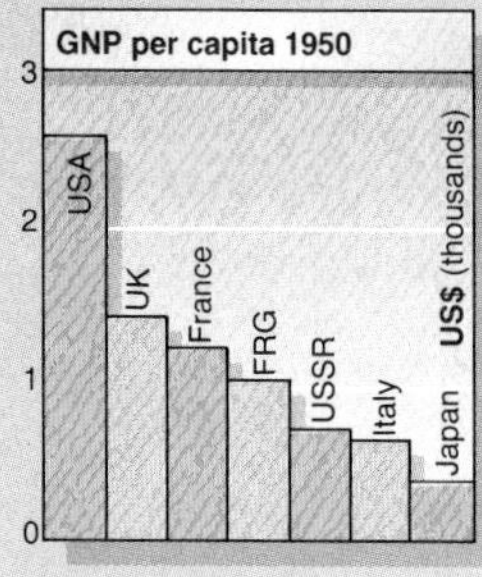

GNP per capita 1950
USA
UK
France
FRG
USSR
Italy
Japan
US$ (thousands)
3
2
1
0

▲ **The postwar US economy was in a position of great, but artificial strength. The Soviet Union had suffered heavy loss during the war and had a long way to go to gain a position in keeping with its size and economic potential. The defeated Axis powers were just beginning to move from devastation and dislocation.**

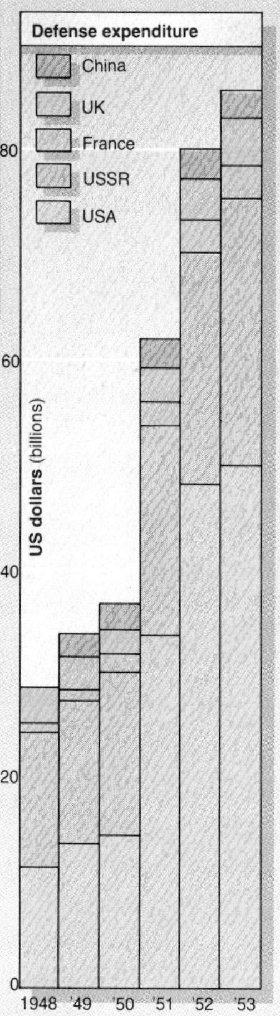

Defense expenditure
China
UK
France
USSR
USA
US dollars (billions)
80
60
40
20
0
1948
'49
'50
'51
'52
'53

▶ **Defense expenditure had been seriously cut back at the end of World War II, but by 1950 spending on arms procurement was again rising. The major causes were the deterioration in relations between the superpowers, the beginning of the nuclear arms race and the need to replenish national arsenals with more advanced weaponry.**

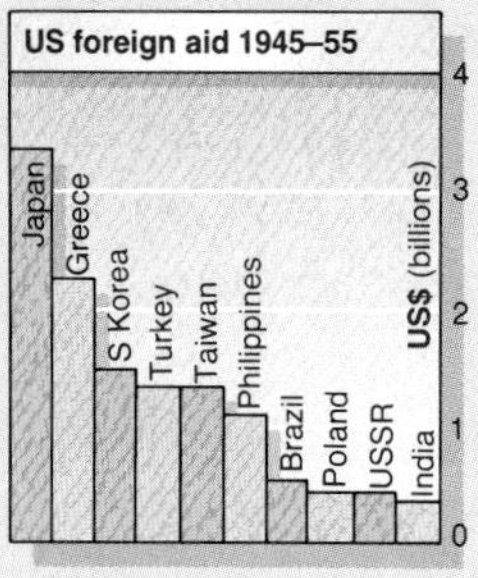

US foreign aid 1945–55
Japan
Greece
S Korea
Turkey
Taiwan
Philippines
Brazil
Poland
USSR
India
US$ (billions)
4
3
2
1
0

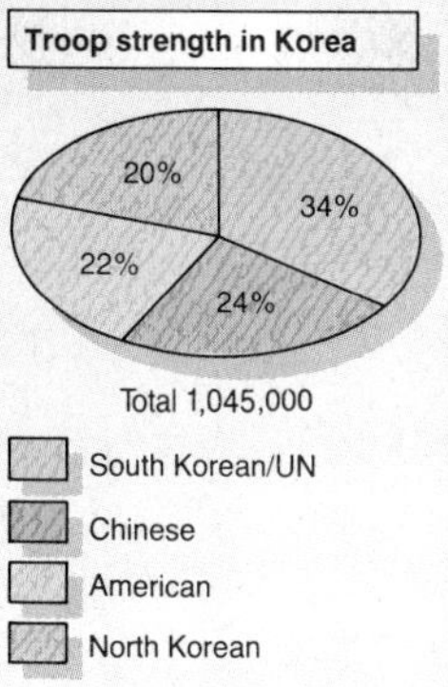

Troop strength in Korea
20%
34%
22%
24%
Total 1,045,000
South Korean/UN
Chinese
American
North Korean

◀ **The Korean War was as much a trial of strength between the United States and Communist China as a national struggle between North and South Korea. By the time the war entered its second year, almost half of the combatants were American or Chinese, and the Korean forces were in receipt of massive logistical support.**

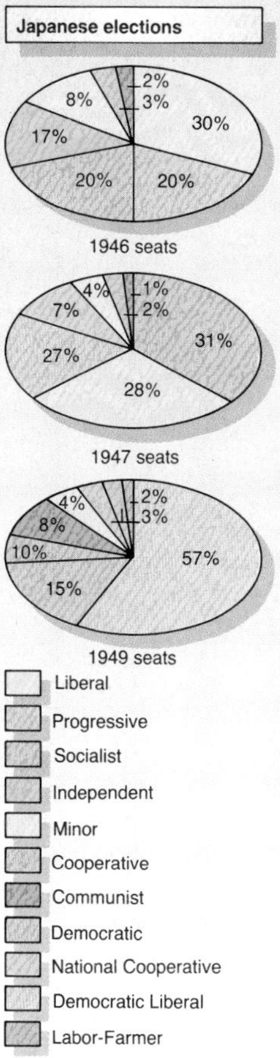

Japanese elections
2%
3%
8%
30%
17%
20%
20%
1946 seats
4%
1%
2%
7%
31%
27%
28%
1947 seats
4%
2%
3%
8%
10%
57%
15%
1949 seats
Liberal
Progressive
Socialist
Independent
Minor
Cooperative
Communist
Democratic
National Cooperative
Democratic Liberal
Labor-Farmer

▶ **Japan's first postwar elections, carried out under the shadow of occupation, saw the brief flowering and dramatic extinction of the socialist challenge, and the emergence of a strong US-orientated Liberal Democratic party – committed to economic recovery – which would dominate domestic politics for decades to come.**

World War II redefined relations both between nations and continents and between citizens and the state. The political consequences of the war further reflected its ideological quality. All the major combatants had fought to impose or protect their own way of life, presented during the war as unique, natural, and essential for the existence of their nations.

The war diminished the place of Europe in the world. Britain, France and the Soviet Union were ready to play a key role in the postwar reconstruction of an international order, but–unlike the United States – none of them had the political scope to reorder the world. The United States was not just another actor in politics; it emerged as the organizing center for global affairs.

Forty years of political turmoil had further exhausted Europe intellectually. Nationalism, socialism, and liberalism – the grand political schemas of the 19th century – had now been discredited by the triple calamity of the 1930s: the world economic crisis debunked classical notions of liberalism; Stalin's tyranny and the Nazi–Soviet pact of 1939 tarnished socialism; and the genocidal policies of Nazi Germany struck at the heart of nationalism.

Nationalism, however, still thrived among independence movements in the old colonial world and in the new Latin American populism, while Communism inspired the mobilization of Asian peasant societies, such as China. Although heir to European traditions of liberalism and republicanism, the United States developed its own militant, domineering republicanism, a mixture of grass-roots mobilization, anti-Communism and consumerism. The postwar period saw the emergence of the United States and the Soviet Union as superpowers, while economic, political, and military penetration of Europe divided the continent.

The limitations of the United Nations

In June 1945, the United Nations charter was drawn up in San Francisco, under the leadership of the United States, the Soviet Union, China, Britain and France. Its aim was to solve global and regional problems, on the basis of the representation of all independent nation states in a General Assembly and the creation of a Security Council with wide-ranging powers to keep peace and to enforce the settlement of disputes.

The limits of a global concert had been apparent at Yalta in February 1945 on the disagreement between the Soviet leader Stalin and US president Roosevelt over the future of Poland. Other conflicts followed, in which political intent and the practice of foreign policy were clearly at odds. Neither Britain nor the United States would allow the Soviet Union to participate in the

THE ORIGINS OF THE COLD WAR

organization of governments in "their" liberated areas – Italy, Greece, North Africa or, eventually, Japan, while in its own zone of influence the Soviet Union would not permit elections without having first assured the sociopolitical and institutional bases of power. The tug-of-war in Europe undermined attempts to preserve cooperation in global affairs.

The division of Germany

At the Potsdam conference of July–August 1945, the United States, Britain and the Soviet Union had reached an agreement over the occupation and administration of Germany, but left unresolved the question of reparations and the character of a unified administration for Germany. Germany was divided into four occupation zones under the control of Britain, France, the United States and the Soviet Union, and an Allied Control Council supervised local administrations. However, American and Soviet representatives were suspicious of each other's motives and could not reconcile Soviet reparation demands with the American interest in reconstructing the German economy. Separate economic, political and social practices evolved in the Western and in the Eastern zones, and in 1947, a foreign ministers' conference in Moscow finally abandoned negotiations toward a peace treaty with Germany.

The growing discord reached a head with the failure of the disarmament negotiations conducted between the superpowers by the United Nations. Against massive domestic opposition, the US administration under President Truman proposed sharing management and ownership of atomic energy, but in return demanded the right to inspect and licence any nuclear development projects. The Soviet Union responded by calling for the immediate destruction of all atomic devices and the prohibition of their production and use, but rejected any inspection procedures.

After two years of unsuccessful negotiations and with the global concert in jeopardy, Stalin became convinced of the essentially hostile intent of the capitalist camp and the intrinsically imperialist nature of US foreign policy. For their part, the Americans believed that their previous policies had been misguided and that the Soviet Union was an expansionist state, determined either to follow czarist goals of imperial aggression or Bolshevik goals of world revolution.

The Cold War that followed produced politics of escalating tensions, backed by huge propaganda machines, as neither the Americans nor the Russians could be sure of the loyalty of the countries in their own camps. The slow Western European recovery and an acute shortage of dollars precipitated a serious economic crisis in

The United Nations Organization

The world after the World War

The birth of NATO

The superpowers – the United States and the Soviet Union

Germany and Europe divided and rebuilding

Occupied Japan

▼ Douglas MacArthur receives the UN flag in 1950 as the Korean War turns the Cold War into military confrontation.

1946–47, leading to waves of strikes and popular unrest across the continent. In Eastern Europe, Soviet reparations policies undercut the postwar regimes and further weakened their legitimacy in the eyes of the people. On both sides, measures to alleviate and stabilize the situation combined economic initiatives with overt attempts to impose political control.

The birth of NATO

The dissolution of Western postwar ties with the Soviet Union and the incipient revival of Germany led, in 1947, to moves to strengthen Western European military ties. These were formalized in the Brussels treaty, a long-term alliance of Britain, France, and the Benelux countries (Belgium, Netherlands, Luxembourg). However, the inclusion of the United States placed

▲ Much of the UN's best work has been carried out by its subordinate agencies. Between them, the International Court of Justice, the International Monetary Fund and the UN Conference on Trade and Development handle international legal, financial and trade problems, while the World Health Organization, UNESCO and UNICEF have made important contributions to the struggle against poverty and sickness.

European military considerations squarely in the context of East-West conflict. The assurance of a US presence in Europe allowed France and Britain to pursue multiple goals: controlling a revived Germany, reducing their military burden in Europe to concentrate on their empires, and detering the Soviet Union. For the United States, peacetime participation in a military alliance in Europe represented a drastic break with past US foreign policy. Its sole purpose was to contain the Soviet Union.

American opinion in support of participation in a regional European alliance increased after an incident in Berlin. In 1948 the former German capital, which lay within the Soviet zone of occupation, became a source of conflict. Unlike the rest of Germany, it was jointly administered by the four Powers, Britain, France, the United States and the Soviet Union. At a conference held in London in 1948 the Western Powers decided to integrate the three Western zones of Germany into the Atlantic economy and to establish a political basis for West German political recovery. This move angered the Russians, who, in June 1948, blocked access to Berlin and sought to cut the city off. In May 1949 the Soviet Union abandoned its blockade, which had proved ineffective after food and supplies were airlifted to the beleaguered city.

One month earlier, on 4 April, 1949, 11 nations signed the North Atlantic Pact, and soon afterwards the US Congress passed a 1.3 billion dollar aid program for Europe. The North Atlantic Treaty Organization (NATO), which had its headquarters in Paris, was established to coordinate the military, political, strategic and organizational goals of the alliance.

To begin with NATO was nothing more than a European regional alliance, supported by American military aid and the Anglo-American atomic monopoly. However, the explosion of a Soviet atomic device in 1949 and the European panic over the implications of the Korean War turned this alliance into a fully integrated organization that militarized the division between East and West from Norway to Turkey. The remilitarization of West Germany and its admission to NATO in 1955 completed the process. It also ended any dreams about the unification of Germany, though this remained an official policy objective of the Anglo-Saxon powers and the West German government.

The United States – the world's leader
As the most powerful nation to emerge into the postwar world, the United States expected to take the lead in shaping international order. However, its entry into the international arena had produced a deep split in US foreign policy, between internationalism and isolationism, between elitist politics that favored an international role and popular resistance against any foreign involvement.

The liberal internationalism of men like Cordell Hull, who had served under President Roosevelt, gave way to tougher newcomers who included bankers, financiers and investment lawyers from Wall Street. They placed their faith in a revival of

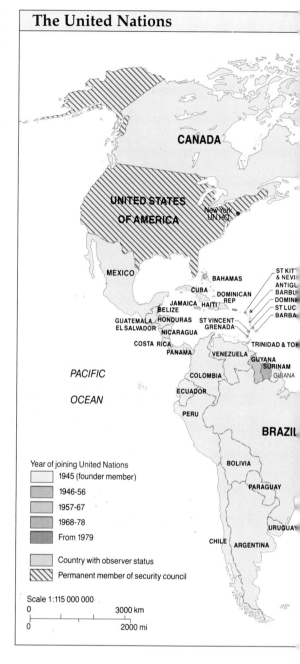

The United Nations

Year of joining United Nations
- 1945 (founder member)
- 1946-56
- 1957-67
- 1968-78
- From 1979

Country with observer status

Permanent member of security council

Scale 1:115 000 000
0   3000 km
0   2000 mi

an international economic order under American leadership and saw the reconstruction of the world, and particularly of Europe as their primary challenge.

Isolationism was reborn after 1945 as a Republican ideology with strong nationalist leanings, founded on faith in American economic might and military power and preoccupied with the traditional American spheres of interest in Latin America and the Pacific. The old-style isolationism based on idealistic opposition to involvement in foreign affairs and concern for welfare at home was largely a thing of the past. The new isolationism quickly became an "America first" movement, scornful of social and economic intervention and opposed to the centralization of power whether in the federal administration or in a highly concentrated, corporate economy. These alternative perceptions of American power reflected deeprooted conflicts over who would control the destiny of the nation.

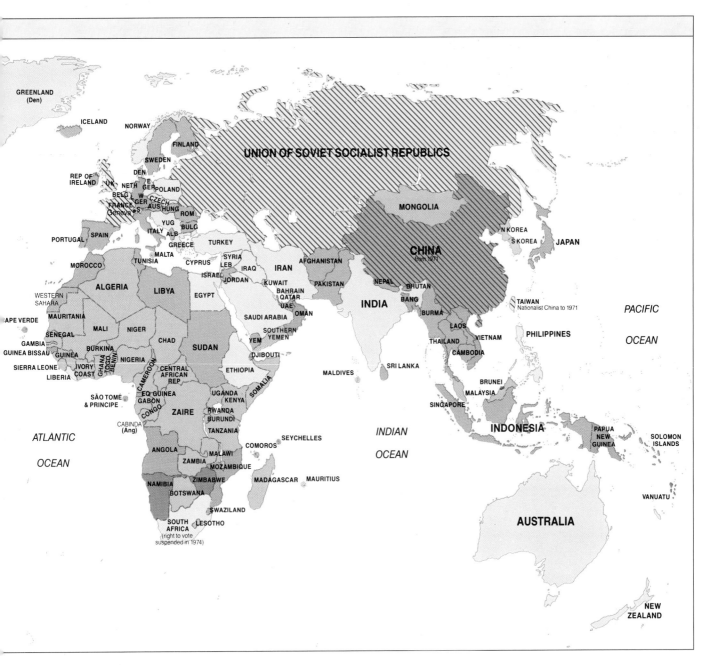

Truman's "Fair Deal"

President Harry S. Truman, who succeeded Roosevelt in 1945, decisively tipped the balance within the Democratic party in favor of the managerial internationalists. Cutting ties with the radical fringes of the electorate, his administration aimed for a domestic consensus between organized labor, management, farmers and "responsible" black leaders. Abroad, Truman pursued a *pax Americana* dominated by economic concerns, but this policy lacked the broad domestic support which Roosevelt had enjoyed during the war. The populist New Deal, Roosevelt's program of economic and social reform, became the Fair Deal between corporate interest groups.

Truman's consensus politics faced problems from the outset, both internationally and at home, where the Republicans regained a majority in the 1946 elections for Congress. The margin of victory suggested success in the 1948 presidential elections, followed by a full-scale reversal of Truman's policies. These considerations lent a sense of urgency to US foreign policy, and American frustrations over European stubbornness and Soviet intransigence produced a crisis in managerial politics.

During the war the status of professionals in the State Department had declined. Now such expertise again became valuable. In particular, Truman sought the advice of George F. Kennan, counselor at the US embassy in Moscow, and expert on Soviet affairs. According to Kennan, the Soviet Union, as a historical and ideological opponent of the Western world, was set on expansion wherever the West would yield. His analysis provided an explanation for past American failures and prepared the ground for a major departure in policy. Active intervention overseas would replace the previous power brokerage in international affairs. The Truman doctrine and the Marshall Plan developed from this new, more decisive mood.

131

The Truman doctrine and Marshall Plan

When, in February 1947, Britain announced that it could no longer shoulder the responsibility of the defence of Greece, Truman, on 17 March, requested 400 million dollars from Congress for immediate assistance to Greece and Turkey, to prevent more European states from being brought under Soviet control. This was all in accordance with the new doctrine.

The Truman doctrine also afforded political advantages at home. Not only did the assertion of American leadership allow the executive to drive a wedge through the Republican opposition, but its strident anti-Communism provided the basis for bipartisan support to stabilize the international situation. The simultaneous approval by Congress, in 1948, of aid to Europe under the Marshall Plan and of the expansion of the US air force and nuclear program emphasized a new consensus of US foreign policy based on Kennan's notion of "containment" of Soviet expansionism by military means.

The new consensus mobilized society in a massive campaign of moral persuasion – for the Marshall Plan, for the goal of an international economic order, for the Fair Deal, and for the Truman presidency as the epitome of the rule of the honest "common man". This combination gained Truman the Democratic nomination for the 1948 presidential elections and returned him to the White House. Most importantly, it closed the gap, albeit temporarily, between the foreign policy establishment, Congress, and a restless American public, who came to identify its own future with an international order under US leadership.

The right wing in the United States

The submerging of domestic problems, however, only disguised the deep internal social and economic splits that existed within American society. Rightwing militant nationalism, pushed out of the political mainstream, reemerged on the political fringes. There, it combined with forces that rejected corporate domination of the economy, big-machine politics, labor bosses, "welfare loafers" and blacks, and accused the government of conspiracy against all righteous people in America. From 1949, Senator Joseph McCarthy of Wisconsin and others, repeatedly attacked the federal government with allegations of subversion and corruption. According to McCarthy, the Department of State and other government offices in Washington were riddled with Communist spies.

At first, these charges and the witchhunts initiated by McCarthy against liberal politicians, writers and artists had little effect. This situation changed, however, after the Chinese revolution of 1949. East Asia had traditionally been a cause of concern for many right wing groups and for American nationalists generally. To the McCarthyites the revolution was an example of Soviet expansionism, of the failure of containment, and of the treachery of State Department officials. The "conspiracy" of the US government, they alleged, was part of a global conspiracy centered in Moscow. Such a threat required

Americans to ferret out all reds, "pinkos", fellow travelers, New Dealers, and liberals in the government – to purge the executive and renounce the political and economic compromises which kept it in office.

Senator McCarthy and his supporters ultimately failed to achieve their goal of transforming the US government. Yet their impact on domestic and international affairs was profound and lasting. McCarthyism exemplified the tensions in American society in an age of mass politics and corporate organization.

The "Asia first" campaign of the right after the "fall of China" left Truman little choice but to intervene with US military forces, when, in 1950, North Korea invaded its southern counterpart. American involvement also ended all attempts to come to terms with the new Chinese regime. However, attempts by the right to use the war to "roll back" Communism in mainland Asia failed. When the commander of troops in Korea, General MacArthur, tried to carry the limited war in Korea into China, Truman dismissed him. Although MacArthur, on his return to the United States, was feted in city after city, Washington held firm in its decision to fight a limited war.

▲ In Soviet eyes the early UN was a US puppet, but even the widening of membership did not solve the problem of superpower-led block-voting.

▼ The Berlin airlift. In June 1948 a threat by the Allies to unite their zones of occupation in Germany caused the Soviets to close all surface routes into West Berlin. The city was kept alive by an 11-month-long airlift with all supplies flown in by Allied aircraft.

Postwar Japan

After Japan's unconditional surrender on 2
September 1945, the country was taken over by
Allied forces of occupation under *de facto* US
control. Economically prostrate, devastated by
conventional air attack and reeling from the twin
atomic strikes on Hiroshima and Nagasaki, Japan
was at the mercy of its conquerors. The US
Supreme Commander of Allied Powers, General
Douglas MacArthur, was intent first and foremost
on dismantling the militarist socio-political
system and replacing it with Western-style
democracy. It was also important to repair the
physical damage done to the economy by the war
and and rebuild a viable industrial system from
the ruins of devastated cities, factories and
communications networks.

To accomplish the first task, MacArthur
demobilized the army and navy and imposed a
new constitution (1947) that included a
renunciation of war though permitting
self-defense. High-ranking wartime officials were
brought to court but worries about the possible
breakdown of order and public confidence saved
Emperor Hirohito from being brought to trial.
The emperor's role in the new system of
government was, however, largely ceremonial.
The new system comprised two democratically
elected legislative institutions – a bicameral Diet
(composed of a lower House of Representatives,
elected every four years, and an upper House of
Councillors, serving for six years, but elected half
at a time at three-year intervals) and an executive
cabinet headed by a prime minister. It took effect
long before the occupation was formally ended in
1952.

The Japan–US Security Treaty (1951), which
established the United States as the effective
arbiter of Japanese defense policy, also caused
longterm political difficulties. Japan's economic
recovery, however, was far more straightforward.
Once the physical damage had been repaired and
peacetime trading conditions had returned, the
country's industry reasserted its natural strength
and by the 1960s had far surpassed the
international position it had held before 1941.

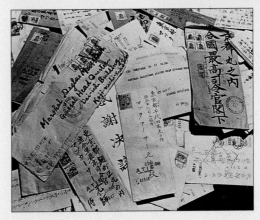

▲ ◀ Although Emperor
Hirohito remained on the
Japanese throne after 1945,
his position as constitutional
monarch was purely formal,
and he adopted a Western
style of clothes and behavior
to emphasize the new
direction for this country. The
true rulers of postwar Japan
were the US-dominated forces
of occupation under General
MacArthur. As the piles of
letters of supplication written
to MacArthur make clear, the
Japanese people were under
no illusions as to where real
power lay.

As a result of the anti-Communist furore,
Truman was unable to preserve the Democratic
electoral alliance. The presidential election of 1952
ushered in eight years of Republican rule.
However, Truman had, during his term, established the postwar domestic and international
foundations for a militarized *pax Americana*.

Reconstruction in the Soviet Union

Unlike the United States, the Soviet Union had
struggled to survive the war. Its place among the
global powers after 1945 was due to the heroism
of its armed forces and the sacrifices of the Soviet
people. World War II had cost the Soviet Union
between 20 and 25 million lives. The scorched-
earth tactics of the German army during its three
years of retreat had destroyed much of the country's infrastructure, industry, agricultural production and livestock. The Soviet Union entered the
postwar world as a weak and exhausted power
whose main concern was to assure the postwar
security of the homeland. This meant retaining a
defensive perimeter through the control of the
local power structures in Eastern Europe. The

Soviets insisted on autonomy and the right to
conduct its Eastern Europe affairs free of foreign
interference. Unfortunately, these objectives were
at odds with the American vision of "one world".
The Russians were faced with a choice: abandon
their aims in the hope of attracting American investment capital; or pursue them and expect no
outside help.

By autumn 1945, it was clear to the Russians
that American loans were not forthcoming and
that they would have to extract reparations from
their own zone of influence. The capital necessary
for reconstruction would have to be generated internally, as had happened in the 1930s. Not all the
Soviet leaders agreed, but this was the policy that
was adopted in 1945 with the Five Year Plan for
economic reconstruction. However, the Soviet
Union could not simply continue with its former
domestic policies, because wartime mobilization
had considerably weakened the state.

The fusion of nationalism and Bolshevism during the war had created a wide range of of
opinion, especially among the intelligentsia, and
the Soviet administration and the party had had

▶ **The geography of confrontation.** A map of the international political situation in 1960 showing how far regional power blocs had developed in the Cold War years since 1945. Europe remained the major area of US-Soviet confrontation, with the rival military alliances of NATO and the Warsaw Pact maintaining massive opposing military forces. However, the spread of US bases around the world and the creation of the anti-Soviet alliances SEATO (1954) in the Pacific and CENTO (1955) in the Middle East demonstrates that the superpower antagonism was truly a global phenomenon.

▼ **A show of anti-Soviet unity** – NATO delegates at a meeting in France in 1959. NATO was in many ways a natural extension of US participation in the liberation of Europe during World War II, but it was held together as much by fears of Communist expansion as by a deeper community of interests. The United States was afraid of isolation in a Communist-dominated world, while the European nations did not feel strong enough to deter a possible Soviet invasion by themselves.

to relax their grip on both the peasantry and the industrial proletariat. Often the party had retreated behind experts, notably military professionals, while management had become more independent-minded. The war had shown that Soviet society was prone to disaffection.

The hard-line Stalinists entrusted with the task of reconstructing Soviet society were led by Andrey Zhdanov. The measures he used to re-impose state control and ideological purity throughout society included a crackdown in the arts and sciences. Ideological rectification led to purges and mass arrests and to the expansion of the prison-camp system, where up to 13 million people were detained. Zhdanov's close associate, Nikolay Vossnesenky, supervised the administration of the new Five Year Plan and brought professional experts to heel under party rule.

Meanwhile, fierce debates continued between supporters of a confrontational course with the West, led by Zhdanov, and those who, like Foreign Minister Vyacheslav Molotov, favored the "containment" of American influence and "damage control" measures. These arguments took place against the background of the slow start of the Five Year Plan, and the dubious loyalties of the Eastern European countries, where national Communists battled with Stalinists over how social change was to be achieved.

Sovietization of Eastern Europe

The hardening of attitudes in the United States favored the supporters of confrontation in the ongoing debate in the Soviet Union. At the end of February 1947 in Sklarska Poreba, Czechoslovakia, a meeting took place between Eastern European, Soviet, Italian, and French Communist leaders to draw up an agenda for the Sovietization of Eastern Europe.

From July 1947 the local multiparty regimes were forcibly replaced with Stalinist ones, culminating in the coup in Czechoslovakia in February 1948. The Eastern European Communist parties were purged of "nationalists", "cosmopolitans" and, after 1951, "Zionists" to ensure a strictly pro-Soviet party leadership. At the same

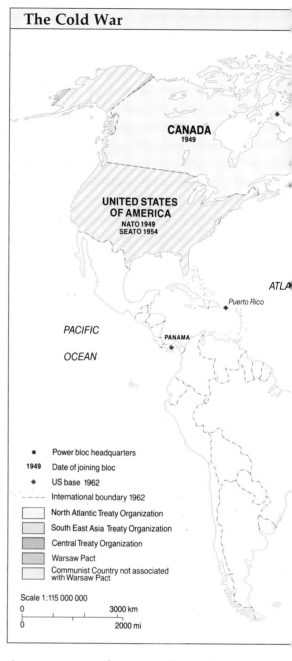

The Cold War

CANADA
1949

UNITED STATES
OF AMERICA
NATO 1949
SEATO 1954

ATLA

Puerto Rico

PACIFIC

PANAMA

OCEAN

• Power bloc headquarters
1949 Date of joining bloc
◆ US base 1962
---- International boundary 1962
North Atlantic Treaty Organization
South East Asia Treaty Organization
Central Treaty Organization
Warsaw Pact
Communist Country not associated with Warsaw Pact

Scale 1:115 000 000
0   3000 km
0   2000 mi

time, an array of propagandist and coercive measures were introduced to enforce the control of all aspects of society by Stalinist cadres. National economies were modeled after the Soviet example, duplicating centralized planning, intense industrialization and the collectivization of agriculture (except in Poland, where the tight control of the Catholic church over the countryside prevented it), and with an emphasis on self-sufficiency. The Soviet Union imposed bilateral economic, political and ideological relations between itself and the Eastern European client states. A hierarchy emerged, in which Eastern European states and their ruling Communist parties related to each other through the Soviet leadership, a system of exchange in which the Soviet Union remained separate and superior.

The only country in Eastern Europe to escape Soviet domination was Yugoslavia. In 1948 Yugoslavia was expelled from the Socialist bloc, economic ties were cut, and ideological protection

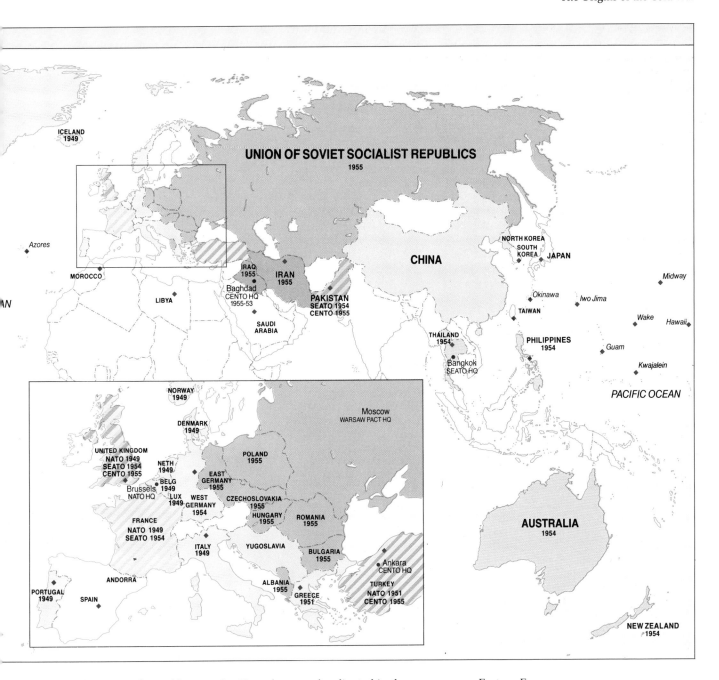

was withdrawn – a bitter blow to the Yugoslav Communists, who wished to maintain close ties with Soviet Union in order to escape the grasp of Western "containment". However, Yugoslavia survived pressures from both East and West because it could rely on the popular appeal of the Yugoslav Communists, who had led the resistance against Nazi Germany, and especially of their leader, Josip Broz (Tito).

Soviet retrenchment
Yugoslav resistance, the failure of the Berlin blockade, and in 1949 tensions within the Soviet Union between control by the party and economic efficiency showed to the Russians that they had overreached themselves in following Zhdanov's confrontational course. The success of the Chinese revolution in 1949, however welcome for ideological reasons, stretched them still further. China was a drain on Soviet resources and too independent – and too large – to be easily

subordinated in the same way as Eastern Europe.

Even before Stalin's death in 1953, there were some indications that the Soviet leadership was moving toward retrenchment and change. Amid growing fears of a new purge, the Soviet leadership engaged in intense debates over the best domestic and international course for the country to follow and criticized cadre rule. The calls for "scientific" and regular social and economic developments signaled that the Soviet Union wished to consolidate its position at home and abroad and alleviate the Cold War atmosphere.

This change of attitude reflected the fact that the Soviet Union, like the United States, was now a superpower. Since 1949 the Soviets had an atomic bomb and had established autonomy within their own sphere of influence. The Soviet Union controlled only a small part of the world compared to the United States, but had achieved its superpower status by a ruthless self-transformation between 1945 and 1953.

European democracies sought speedy reconstruction by means of corporate policies uniting disparate interest groups

Political parties in Europe

The immediate task facing the nations of Europe after World War II, which affected the defeated and occupied, liberated, and victorious countries alike, was that of social and political reform. Initially, antifascist mobilizations, developing out of resistance movements, took the lead through a new kind of grass-roots politics, but these radically democratic groups were quickly demobilized. Attempts to eliminate radical movements sometimes met with fierce resistance, as in the civil war in Greece, where the National Liberation Front held out against the US-backed royalists until 1949. The Front was supported by Yugoslavia and Albania, the only countries in which the resistance movements against Nazi occupation took power after the war and held on to it despite opposition from both within the country and outside.

Political and grass-roots radicalism quickly settled down into party politics and the party-based competition for control over an expanding state. Parliamentary politics relied much more than it had done before on party-based governments and on negotiations between the state bureaucracies, industry and the trade unions.

European socialist parties maintained the closest ties with the past both politically and in terms of leadership and membership. The Communist parties of Western Europe were newer, having lost some of the old cadres and rank-and-file membership in the turbulent 1940s but gaining new recruits from the resistance movements. In Italy and France, Communists captured between a quarter and a third of the national vote, thanks to their wartime resistance record and the tightly organized sociopolitical networks that they had developed, especially in rural areas. Overall, however, the most successful party formations in postwar Europe were the new Christian parties, who solved the political problem of the interwar years of how to unite the urban and rural bourgeoisie.

Reform in Europe

The various programs of reforms carried out by parliaments across Europe shaped the postwar political and economic structure of the continent. The socialist parties in Scandinavia concentrated on welfare and full-employment, but stopped short of large-scale programs of public ownership. In Britain, the newly-elected Labour government limited nationalization largely to the ailing coal and steel industries and to basic services such as health and transport. In East Germany, Czechoslovakia, Austria, Italy and France, mixed economies emerged on the basis of large-scale nationalization in all sectors of production. In Italy state involvement in industry and public welfare was at its highest, while France pioneered national planning under the direction of Jean Monnet.

In Eastern Europe the most pressing problem was land reform. From Poland to Bulgaria, the combined pressures of peasant parties and national Communists forced a wholesale redistribution of land to smallholders. For a while, it appeared that Eastern Europe could establish itself

as the vanguard of peasant production. Land reform also offered resettlement opportunities to minority populations displaced by the war.

Although important nationally, these reform programs were never coordinated on a European-wide basis. A European movement did exist but failed to gain political significance, while national governments were reluctant to engage in large-scale cooperation with other European states. The internal divisiveness of Europe came into the open when tensions between the two superpowers increased their doubts about the loyalties of their respective European allies. While the Americans worried about the growth of Communism in Italy and France, and feared an impending collapse of continental Europe, the Soviet Union was alarmed by the weakness of the Communist parties in Eastern Europe and the spread of peasant nationalism.

The division of Europe

After the announcement of the Marshall Plan and the failure to achieve agreement on the future of Germany, the Soviet Union saw itself as potentially under threat from a "revanchist" West Germany with US backing. The Sovietization of Eastern Europe aimed to consolidate the Soviet hold on the area and established new

▲ Delegates at the Yugoslav Communist party congress of 1948 express approval for Marshal Tito's stand against the Warsaw Pact. The Communist regime in Yugoslavia owed its position to a successful guerrilla resistance against German invasion rather than a conquering Soviet army, and it staunchly defended its independence from outside control. Nevertheless its control over the country remained circumscribed by differences between the various nationalities that make up the country.

supranational conformities where there had been deep divisions. However, in its emphasis on national autarky, Stalinization also preserved many national peculiarities, reinforcing social and cultural differences. Soviet practices thoroughly alienated Eastern Europeans from their former liberators, creating tensions which later came to the fore after Stalin's death in 1953.

In the Western camp, the Marshall Plan had encouraged an alliance between European technocrats and American multilateralists, and consolidated the power of the new European Christian parties, providing a powerful, conservative rallying point for a bourgeois Europe. By 1951, much of Europe was governed by centrist and conservative parties headed by men such as Konrad Adenauer (West Germany), Alcide de Gasperi (Italy), and Winston Churchill (Britain),

who had shed their nationalist leanings in favor of a strong Atlanticism. The Marshall Plan deepened the split between the Communists and socialists. One by one, the socialist parties moved towards an Atlantic and technocratic agenda to reinforce the primacy of the Atlantic economy. Slowly, a new Atlanticist consensus emerged in Europe, supported by both the left and right and underwritten by the rapid economic growth of the 1950s.

The deepening division of Europe manifested itself in the permanent presence of the Soviet Union and the United States, and in their respective emphases on a politics of production and a state-centered rule. Western Europe and, more gradually, Eastern Europe regained their stature as economic powerhouses and developed robust political structures. Europe did not develop its

The Marshall Plan

Believing that the social, political and economic chaos of postwar Europe would benefit only the Communists, in 1947 US President Truman and his Secretary of State for foreign affairs, General George Marshall, proposed a plan for European economic recovery, pledging help to the whole of Europe to fight "hunger, poverty, desperation and chaos". President Truman made it plain that the intention was partly political. "We must assist free people to work out their own destinies in their own free way." One of its main objectives was to achieve a coordinated European economy. In due course an Organization for European Economic Cooperation (OECD) was set up to administer the scheme, which distributed $6 billion over its first 15 months. It also regulated the various devices which prevented the US dollar from causing financial problems for the various economies, thus promoting European integration and industrial renewal at the same time.

Marshall Aid was offered to all European states prepared to support liberal democracy, in the hope that even those already run by Communist-led governments would be able to free themselves from Moscow's influence. Indeed, the Czech government (still not wholly dominated by the Communists) joined Britain and France in accepting the offer and both Poland and Hungary expressed their enthusiasm

for the scheme. Stalin, however, very quickly ordered all the countries under Russian "protection" to reject the Marshall Plan. In this way, Marshall Aid cemented the division of Europe rather than preventing it, though it did succeed in tying Western Europe together and promoting political liberalism.

Marshall Aid was used by the 16 Western European states who received it in a variety of ways; continental Europeans used it first for food and then for modernizing their industrial base and building homes. By 1950 industrial output was a quarter higher than in 1938. In the case of Britain, whose economy was strained by overseas commitments, Marshall Aid went toward the construction of a welfare state and the Labour party's program of nationalization.

▲ US money played a central role in European reconstruction.

◀ Rebuilding Berlin with American support.

own distinct identity, but it did achieve stability, albeit at a price, after nearly a century of internal and extraterritorial conflict.

Unrest in East Asia

Before World War II, East Asia was an integrated political and economic unit with Japan at its center. Japan controlled and developed Korea, Manchuria, and Formosa (now Taiwan) and its military industrial expansion radiated outward into Southeast Asia to compete with British-Indian, Dutch, French and American interests. Japan's defeat in the war, and the dispossession of its colonies, necessitated the reconstruction of a political and economic order in East Asia.

Many of the East Asian countries were agricultural societies which were engaged in a civil war that had been fueled by peasant rebellions. As part of its colonization strategy Japan had sponsored strong states led by national elites made up of the powerful local gentry or landed classes. Thus, the civil wars often took the form of pro- and anti-Japanese mobilizations. In Korea a Japanese-installed state and security apparatus in the South, headed by a pro-Western nationalist, Syngman Rhee, opposed Kim Il Sung, an anti-Japanese guerrilla leader who had been installed in power by the Soviet Union in the North. Similar, but less clear cut, divisions ran through all of the Southeast Asia as far as Burma.

Outside influences affected developments in East Asia. The Soviet Union had gained some

influence in Manchuria and helped to install Kim Il Sung in North Korea, but by 1949 it had all but withdrawn its troops from both areas.

After Japan's defeat in the Far East, China was left to the two great rivals to struggle for control of the country—the Communists, well organized but far fewer in numbers, and the nationalist Guomindang. The United States channeled aid to the Nationalists, and the Russians appeared briefly in Manchuria to support the Communists. But otherwise the civil war developed free of outside interference.

Initially, the Nationalists held the upper hand, but corruption within the government and the military lost them support, and the hostility they faced in the countryside made their position untenable. By the end of 1948 Mao Zedong's Communist forces had cleared all of Manchuria of the Nationalists and was pushing their disorganized troops south, from where many fled in 1949 to the former Japanese colony of Taiwan.

The People's Republic of China was proclaimed in Beijing in October 1949, shortly after the first Communist state, the Soviet Union, had exploded its atomic bomb. At the end of 1949, Premier Mao Zedong and Foreign Minister Zhou En Lai went to Moscow to sign a Treaty of Friendship, Alliance and Mutual Assistance, which placed China in the socialist camp.

However, among the victors there were a number who wanted to maintain relations with the West, even at the cost of leaving the revolution

▶ The power of propaganda. North Korean posters showing the South Korean leader Syngman Rhee as a weak puppet given teeth by the US impressed a largely illiterate population. This was not altogether unfair since the portrayal of US support for a corrupt regime played a crucial role in bringing about the Korean War.

▶▶ The Korean War was a brutal seesaw contest in which neither side displayed much military or logistic skill. After an initial series of sweeping advances and counterattacks it degenerated into a stalemate.

▼ Civil war broke out again in China soon after the Japanese surrender. After initial setbacks at the hands of Nationalist forces, the superior organization of Mao's Communist movement, and the popular support it received, turned the tide in dramatic fashion. Nationalist forces were driven back to the sea and in 1949 were forced to flee to Taiwan.

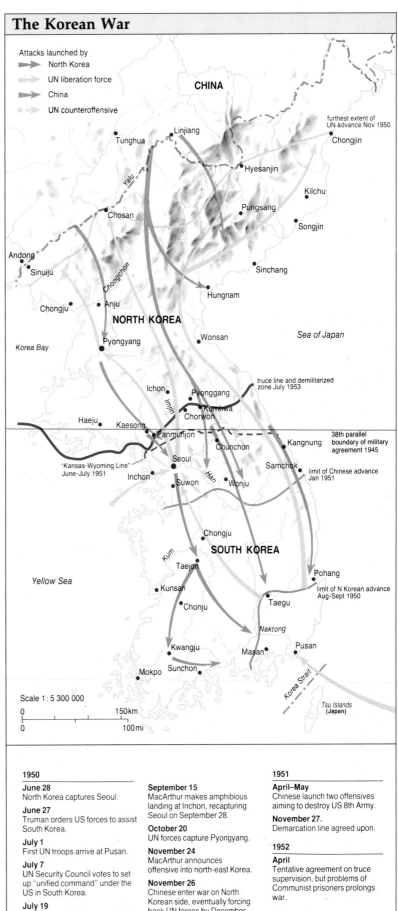

The Korean War

unfinished and failing to eradicate the rival Guomindang regime in Taiwan. Fears of an American-led counterrevolution conducted by Chinese proxy-forces motivated much of Chinese foreign policy at this time. In the United States, some people wondered about the possibility of an autonomous course for the new People's Republic, if America withdrew support for the nationalists, but confrontation with China during the war in Korea ruled out the possibility.

The Korean War

In June 1950 North Korean forces, encouraged by social unrest in South Korea, overran the South. The US entry into the war came under the auspices of the United Nations, but in fact the Korean War was the first American war fought on the Asian mainland. When General MacArthur launched an offensive deep into the North to end the war before Christmas 1950 he was thrown back by Chinese forces. The ensuing war of movement ended in 1951 in a stalemate near where it had begun, the 38th parallel, dividing the North from the South. Peace eventually came in 1953 but the international repercussions were evident long before.

The Korean War established China as the foremost champion of peasant-based national liberation movements in Asia, much in contrast to a cautious Soviet Union. To hold China in restraint, the United States extended its defense perimeter onto the Asian rim of the Pacific with the deployment of the Seventh Fleet between Taiwan and the China mainland, and the stationing of troops in South Korea.

After signing a peace treaty with the United States in 1951 Japan became the staging ground for the Korean War. The United States used the treaty to secure military bases in Japan, and later to expand its treaty network to cover the whole of Asia. A military line of containment stretched from Europe to East Asia, but already in 1951 this line intersected with a north–south axis of conflict, pitting Third World nationalists and nonaligned nations against the military might of the United States.

1950

June 28
North Korea captures Seoul.

June 27
Truman orders US forces to assist South Korea.

July 1
First UN troops arrive at Pusan.

July 7
UN Security Council votes to set up "unified command" under the US in South Korea.

July 19
North Korean tanks penetrate US defenses at Taejon.

September 15
MacArthur makes amphibious landing at Inchon, recapturing Seoul on September 28.

October 20
UN forces capture Pyongyang.

November 24
MacArthur announces offensive into north-east Korea.

November 26
Chinese enter war on North Korean side, eventually forcing back UN forces by December, when Communist troops begin second invasion of South Korea.

1951

April–May
Chinese launch two offensives aiming to destroy US 8th Army.

November 27.
Demarcation line agreed upon.

1952

April
Tentative agreement on truce supervision, but problems of Communist prisoners prolongs war.

1953

July 27
Armistice concluded.

NUCLEAR WEAPONS AND THE COLD WAR

As early as the 1930s, long before the Manhattan Project team tested the first atomic bomb, the Danish physicist Niels Bohr warned of the arms race that would follow from the development of nuclear weapons. Indeed, when the US air force B-29s dropped the atom bombs Little Boy and Fat Man on the Japanese cities of Hiroshima and Nagasaki on 6 and 9 August 1945, it not only brought an end to World War II; it was the parting shot between the United States and the Soviet Union for a longer, more insidious – and potentially far more dangerous – war: the Cold War.

To the Soviet Union, excluded by its wartime allies from the operation against Japan and the scientific research that preceded it, such a show of devastating power signaled the United States' bid for world supremacy in the postwar period. Moreover, the timing of the attack was rightly perceived in Moscow as an attempt to preempt the Soviet invasion of Japan, which had been scheduled for late August, so as to reap the spoils of victory for Western capitalism.

When, in June 1948, with the Cold War at its bleakest, the Soviets sealed off Berlin, the Americans immediately dispatched B-29 bombers, designated as "atomic capable", to Germany and Britain to warn off the Communists. The announcement in September of the following year that the Russians had exploded an atomic bomb stunned American politicians – President Truman at first refused to believe it – though not American scientists, who had regarded a Soviet breakthrough as imminent. However, the anti-Communist paranoia of the times required that the Soviet success was subsequently attributed to the treachery of the "atom spy" Klaus Fuchs, who was arrested on 2 February 1950 in Britain. Most worrying of all to the Americans, the Soviet Union's possession of an atomic device undermined US postwar military strategy (which has informed NATO policy since its inception) that the greater numbers of Soviet troops and conventional arms should be counterbalanced by the United States' nuclear superiority.

Faced with the choice of building up its conventional arms to match those of the Soviets or increasing its nuclear firepower, the United States chose to develop the hydrogen bomb, which gave a "bigger bang for a buck", though experts regarded its extra destructive power as more of a symbolic than strategic advantage. On 1 November 1952 an American H-bomb exploded on Eniwetok Atoll in the Pacific with a force equivalent to 10.4 million tonnes of TNT – a thousand times greater than Little Boy's. Within nine months, the Soviet leader Grigoriy Malenkov announced that the United States no longer had an H-bomb monopoly, a claim that American scientists confirmed by testing air samples. The arms race predicted by Bohr was under way. The world had entered a phase described by Winston Churchill as "a delicate balance of terror" – it as to last until the mid-1980s.

► (main image) The spectacular "mushroom cloud" produced by the detonation of a hydrogen bomb, the world's first thermonuclear device. Codenamed "Ivy Mike", it took almost a decade to develop amid growing controversy and Cold War intrigue. The test took place on the surface of a barge at Eniwetok Atoll in the Marshall Islands on 1 November 1952. The mushroom cloud spread across 150km or more and attained a height of 15km.

►► J Robert Oppenheimer (left), who headed the team of scientists at Los Alamos, and (right) General Leslie Groves, the director of the Manhattan Project, were responsible for developing the atomic bomb. The underlying theoretical principle, however, that of the conversion of matter to energy, had been established many years earlier by Albert Einstein (far right). Horrified at what had ensued from it, Einstein in 1955, shortly before his death, made an impassioned appeal on the radio for a halt to the arms race. It "beckons annihilation", he said.

▼ NATO observers witness the detonation of an atom bomb at Yucca Flats, Nevada, in May 1957. This was the first occasion that NATO was invited to attend a US nuclear test. Despite an agreement between Roosevelt and Churchill during World War II to cooperate in the development of nuclear power, the Americans were very reluctant to share their nuclear secrets. Britain tested its first atomic bomb at Monte Bello island, near Australia, on 3 October 1952, after failing to obtain permission to use an American test site in the Pacific.

► The caption to this figure from a 1950s British civil defense pamphlet reads: "A slit trench with earth covering protects against blast and radiation." As a nuclear power in its own right, and with many US military bases on its soil, Britain was a prime target in the event of a nuclear war. The public therefore had to be convinced that, by taking sensible precautions, it was possible to survive a nuclear attack, as many had survived aerial bombardments during World War II.

▼ Titan II strategic missile in its underground silo at a US air force base near Wichita, Kansas in 1963. It carried a 3,500-kg thermonuclear warhead with an explosive power of 9 megatons. Retractable platforms on the silo walls allow the missile to be serviced while on alert.

Datafile

The 1950s saw domestic stability and economic growth return to many parts of the world. In the United States, Britain and West Germany, consecutive political groupings consolidated their grip on power, whereas in France, domestic problems, complicated by divisions on colonial policy, delayed the emergence of stable political alignments. China began to flex its economic muscles as the Communist regime strove to create a sound industrial base.

German elections 1957

9%
35%
56%

☐ CDU/CSU
☐ SPD
☐ FDP

Production in China

1952   1957

Grain
Coal
Electricity*
Oil
Iron and steel
Cotton

Tonnes/*kWh (billions)
200
150
100
50
40
30
20
10
0

▲ West German politics returned to stability soon after the war ended. In 1949 the Christian-Democrat-dominated moderate rightwing coalition won a majority over the leftwing Social-Democrat party. The Christian Democrats were able to consolidate their position with triumphs of similar magnitude in the 1953 and 1957 elections.

French elections

☐ Christian Democrat
☐ Socialist
☐ Communist/Progressive
☐ Moderate
☐ Radical
☐ Gaullist

Seats (percent)
100
75
50
25
0
1945 '46 '46 '51 '56 '58

▲ Ravaged by decades of war and political upheaval, China faced a slow and difficult climb to economic well-being. State-dominated economic planning was able to improve the production of staple products, though starting from a very low base, the total supply remained very poor over the whole country.

▶ Britain's Conservative party had lost power in 1945 to a Labour party widely seen to be more in line with the requirements of peacetime government. Labour narrowly held onto power in 1950, but lost it one year later, and the Conservative share of the vote rose steadily, surviving even the fiasco of the invasion of Suez in 1956.

UK elections

☐ Liberal/others
☐ Conservative
☐ Labour

Seats (percent)
100
80
60
40
20
0
1945 1950 1951 1955 1959

▲ France, divided by the bitter legacy of wartime occupation and embroiled in wars of decolonization, faced a difficult path to political stability. Immediate postwar political groupings proved ineffectual and was only the arrival of the Gaullist phenomenon which finally imposed a new order and to stability.

▶ While the US presidency passed from the Democrats to the Republicans, with Eisenhower in 1953 this change was balanced by stable Democratic majority in Congress.

US Presidents

1945	F D Roosevelt	D
1945	H S Truman	D
1949	H S Truman	D
1953	D D Eisenhower	R
1957	D D Eisenhower	R

US representation

☐ Democrat   ☐ Republican

House of Representatives
Senate
Seats (percent)
100
80
60
40
20
0
1945 1947 1949 1951 1953 1955 1957 1959

The administration of US President Eisenhower, who took office in January 1953, had been elected on a platform of "rolling back Communism", as opposed to Truman's more restrained policy of "containment". By 1954, when Stalin's successors were beginning to soften their line on Soviet foreign policy, John Foster Dulles, Eisenhower's Secretary of State, raised the stakes in the Cold War propaganda debate. The globe, according to Dulles, was divided between the Western "free world" and the "world of Communist dictatorships", and nations had to choose between them. Accordingly, the Western alliance pressed ahead with its plan to anchor the Federal Republic of Germany to the West by rearming the country and allowing it to take its place as a member of NATO. The United States and its allies had earlier rejected Soviet proposals that free elections be held throughout Germany to reunify the country, provided that the new Germany was forbidden to join any alliance, East or West.

In the autumn of 1954 the crucial decision to rearm West Germany as a member of NATO was confirmed. The Federal Republic, together with Germany's wartime ally Italy, would be invited to join NATO by becoming members of the Brussels Treaty Organization, a body that Britain, France and the Benelux countries had set up in 1948 as a safeguard against Germany.

The Warsaw Pact and Comecon

In the same month as the Federal Republic of Germany's entry into NATO, the Soviet Union set up the Warsaw Pact, an alliance of Soviet-dominated eastern European states (later joined by the German Democratic Republic), which together with Comecon (Council for Mutual Economic Assistance) marked a further consolidation of the two Cold War power blocs.

Through Comecon which was set up in January 1949, the Soviet Union ensured that the economic development plans of its East European allies were geared to the central requirements of the bloc, and that their foreign trade was reduced in favor of a trade with the Soviet Union and other Comecon members. The Soviet Union also set up joint companies for industrial production in some of these countries and forced East Germany, together with Romania and Hungary (former allies of Hitler) to make extensive reparation payments for war damage.

Negotiations and rapprochement

A change of attitude on the part of the Soviet government toward Austria was an encouraging sign for the future of East-West relations. Austria, like Germany, was divided into zones of occupation, the Russians refusing to consider giving the country full independence. In 1955, however, the

CONFRONTATION AND DÉTENTE

Soviet government finally allowed Austria to become a sovereign state (and, by tacit agreement, nonaligned) through the State Treaty signed on 15 May.

In July 1955, arms control negotiating between the superpowers began in Geneva, with President Eisenhower proposing an "open skies" concept, under which East and West should have the right to fly over each others' territory to check on military preparations and arms levels. The British prime minister, Anthony Eden, further suggested reduction of conventional forces in Central Europe. On the Soviet side the Polish foreign minister, Adam Rapacki, made a plan in October 1957 for a nuclear-free zone, a test-ban treaty, and a nonaggression pact between the Warsaw Pact and NATO.

The new Soviet leadership under Khrushchev also made attempts to repair relations with Stalin's old enemy Marshal Tito, whom Stalin had expelled from the Cominform (the new Communist International) in 1948. In June 1956, Khruschev and Tito signed a joint statement renouncing the Soviet Union's claim to infallibility in Communist doctrine.

Crises in Poland and Hungary
Despite the "spirit of Geneva", in Eastern Europe unrest continued to grow. In June 1956, workers rose up in Poznan, western Poland. The situation was saved by bringing back Wladyslaw Gomulka, a popular national figure who had been forced out of the Communist party's leadership by Stalinist pressure. Gomulka was trusted by Moscow not to let "revisionism" get out of hand, and in any case Poland would always need to depend on Soviet protection in the event of any revival of German aggression.

Events in neighboring Hungary took a more tragic turn. In the autumn of 1956 the Hungarians staged an all-out revolt against Soviet rule, demanding an end to the one-party state and the recognition of Hungary's neutrality, independent of both blocs, like their neighbor Austria. Khrushchev, fearful that if Hungary achieved its objectives, other Warsaw Pact countries would want to follow, sent in the Red Army to crush the rebellion. The Russians appointed as Hungary's new leader Janos Kadar, and in the years ahead he moved very slowly and cautiously toward winning a degree of freedom for Hungary to run its own affairs.

Berlin and the U-2 crisis
In 1958, Berlin, the scene of the spectacular airlift of 1948–49, again came to the fore. Suddenly, in November 1958, the Soviet leader Khrushchev declared that four-power control of the city under the Potsdam agreement of 1945 was no longer

effective and should be considered null and void. A summit conference was scheduled to take place in May 1960 in Paris to discuss Berlin, the future of Germany and other matters such as arms control. However, an angry Khrushchev called off the conference after revealing that the Soviet Union had shot down an American U-2 spy aircraft in the act of photographing military sites in the Soviet Union.

Eisenhower and the end of McCarthyism
The year 1954 marked the end of the era of McCarthyism. McCarthy had accused the Department of State and other government agencies in Washington of being full of Communist infiltrators. In fact, only one former diplomat, Alger Hiss, had been convicted, in 1950, of perjury in connection with charges of having worked for the

▼ Revolution in Hungary – jubilant Hungarians burn the works of Lenin in the streets of Budapest in 1956.

Russians and his guilt remains in doubt to this day. In December 1954, the United States Senate overwhelmingly passed a resolution condemning McCarthy. Three years later, McCarthy died, defeated and discredited.

In 1956, President Eisenhower was re-elected for a second term. Americans were now enjoying stability and prosperity and respected Eisenhower as a statesman. He had honorably ended the Korean War and helped to promote the "spirit of Geneva" in 1955. He had also taken steps to reduce taxation, root out corruption in government and introduce the Federal Department of Health, Education and Welfare. Eisenhower's second term as president was markedly less successful, however, both in the international arena, where he faced crises such as the U-2 incident, and at home, where racial discrimination had sowed the seeds of civil unrest.

American Civil Rights movement

From the 1950s the American political system came under growing pressure from blacks demanding racial equality. Demands for civil rights were fueled by the participation of many blacks in the war, and by massive shifts in population which made inequality a national issue, even though conditions remained worse for the blacks of the South, who made up one-quarter of the total population.

On 17 May 1954, after continued pressure by campaigning organizations such as the NAACP (National Association for the Advancement of Colonial People) the Supreme Court ruled that schools should be desegregated "with all deliberate speed". In 1956, a campaign led by the Reverend Martin Luther King ended segregated seating on buses in Montgomery, Alabama.

However, when the school board in the Southern town of Little Rock, Arkansas, tried to admit 17 black pupils to the formerly all-white Central High School, the state Governor Faubus posted the National Guardsmen outside the school to bar their way. The crisis prompted President Eisenhower to intervene personally. He placed the National Guard of Arkansas under Federal command, and despatched 1,000 paratroopers to Little Rock to maintain order during the whole school year 1957-58.

De-Stalinization and the rise of Khrushchev

Inside the Soviet Union, Stalin's death, on 6 March 1953, prompted a swift reaction against the excesses of Stalinism. Denouncing Stalin's "cult of the personality", his heirs divided power among themselves to form a collective leadership. Nikita Khrushchev, a leading party activist of Ukrainian peasant stock, became First Secretary of the Communist party, while Stalin's other post, that of chairman of the Council of Ministers, or prime minister, went to Georgiy Malenkov, a middle-class intellectual. Vyacheslav Molotov continued as foreign minister. Stalin's head of the secret police, Lavrentiy Beria, was arrested in July 1953 for planning to seize power in a coup, and executed without a trial. Beria's fall reduced the power of the police and enhanced that of the military under Bulganin.

Malenkov, at the head of the Soviet state apparatus, and the party boss Khrushchev, realizing that Stalin's death might have opened the way for popular unrest at home, agreed that the new regime should give higher priority to consumer goods at the expense of industrial investment. However, they disagreed over defence. Malenkov wanted to spend less on conventional defence, particularly as the Soviet Union had conducted its first hydrogen bomb test in August 1953. Bulganin, fearing that his power would be reduced if Malenkov had his way, formed an alliance with Khrushchev to oust Malenkov and take over as prime minister in 1955. It was a sign of changing times that the demoted Malenkov was not killed, as Beria had been, and was even allowed to keep his place in the party presidium.

The hallmark of Khrushchev's de-Stalinization policies was his "secret speech" delivered in February 1956 to the 20th Congress of the Communist party, in which he denounced Stalin's excesses, the Stalinist "cult of personality" and the crimes that had been carried out against its victims. The overall message – that the new leadership was set on a new course – was underlined in a public speech to the Congress by Anastas Mikoyan, another veteran of the Stalin years.

In February 1957 Khrushchev launched his economic and political reform program. He put forward a plan to decentralize decision-making and to devolve economic management onto new local authorities. New regional economic councils took over many of the duties of national ministries, some of which were abolished. In 1961 the Soviet Communist party boasted that its new economic program would soon allow the Soviet Union to catch up with the United States in industrial production and to complete the transition from socialism to communism, bringing with it a much higher standard of living for everyone.

To combat the backward state of agriculture, Khrushchev launched a campaign to bring larger areas of virgin land into cultivation, and began a program of decentralization. Individual collective farms were given much greater autonomy in managing their affairs and in marketing their own produce, and farm deliveries to the state were no longer compulsory, but could be arranged through a marketing system.

In 1958, the Khrushchev administration also introduced a number of important legal reforms.

The Secret Services

During the Cold War the intelligence and security services had vital tasks to fulfill, respectively to protect their domestic political systems from subversion or infiltration and to gain reliable intelligence about the other side.

The political context of this battle between the intelligence and security systems had been created by World War II. From 1941 to 1945 the Soviet and Western intelligence services collaborated against Nazi Germany. However, by 1946, fears that Stalin had developed plans for bringing as much of the European continent as possible under Soviet control prompted the need for further Western intelligence, security and counterintelligence agencies. The Americans, in particular, made full use of ex-Nazi intelligence officers who had been involved in spying in the Soviet Union before 1945.

The chief source of intelligence, however, derived from monitoring the wireless traffic between governments and their embassies and, more important still, between armed units in the air, at sea (and under it) and on the land and their bases and headquarters. The successes scored by Allied intelligence in decoding German and Japanese ciphers in 1940 and 1941 established the basis for postwar work against the Soviet Union. Soviet atom spies such as Julius and Ethel Rosenberg and Klaus Fuchs, as well as "moles" in the British secret services such as Kim Philby and George Blake, were all uncovered by this means.

▲ Espionage in the 1950s took many forms. Despite the notoriety won by the double-agents within the security services, governments probably acquired more useful information from surveillance techniques. The US pilot Gary Powers was shot down while on a reconaissance mission in the USSR in 1960. He was sentenced to ten years in prison, but exchanged in 1962.

Vague charges such as "counter-revolutionary activities" were removed from the penal code and defendants could no longer be found guilty on the evidence of their confessions alone (which in Stalin's time were often extracted under torture) and sentences could only be imposed by properly-constituted courts.

By May 1957, Khrushchev had closed two-thirds of the Siberian prison camps, which had the worst conditions and the harshest regimes. There was a general improvement in conditions in the "labor colonies", already removed from the charge of the security services and transferred to the Ministry of the Interior. The security services also lost control of the network of economic enterprises which used prison labor.

In 1957 Malenkov joined with Molotov to oppose Khrushchev's economic reforms, a challenge that Khrushchev defeated by making an alliance with old party officials and with the armed forces under Marshal Grigori Zhukov. After further maneuvering Khrushchev dismissed Zhukov and in March 1958 took over the post of prime minister from his former ally Bulganin to become both party boss and head of the state apparatus.

Political patterns in Western Europe

By the 1950s the Christian Democrats formed the central element of the coalition governments that characterized much of Western Europe. They stood for welfare services, for greater public accountability of economic power and, initially, for the nationalization of industry. The outstanding representative was Konrad Adenauer who, as chancellor of the German Federal Republic between 1949 and 1963, brought a sense of continuity and stability to the new German democracy. Adenauer was also committed to the cause of a united Europe.

The socialists and Communists, lost ground after their immediate postwar electoral successes. Indeed, by the 1950s, under the impact of the Cold War, the two groups were often deadly enemies, with Communists in France, Italy and Belgium removed from the ministerial offices they had once held.

Outside of the Christian Democrats, Socialists and Liberals who made up the European coalition governments only Gaullism, in France, was strong enough to challenge the political mainstream. General de Gaulle returned triumphantly to power in Paris in May 1958 during the colonial crisis in Algeria. He set up the Fifth Republic, in which he greatly enhanced the president's powers relative to parliament, and increased his authority still further by his right of appeal to the people in a referendum. Gaullism was highly patriotic in tone and bore the characteristics of a rightwing authoritarian regime.

Politics at the edge of Europe

Off the north-western shore of the continent, Britain represented a form of political life that did not conform to the European mainstream. In 1951 Churchill's Conservative party (which had no real equivalent on the continent) took over from Attlee's Labour party (which kept its distance from socialist comrades across the Channel).

Postwar European governments sought to avoid the mistakes of the 1930s

Postwar Liberalism

Whereas World War I had provoked a profound crisis in European liberalism, the sheer scale of calculated inhumanity which characterized the war of 1939–45 inspired its renewal. On the economic front, the peace treaties imposed by the Allies ensured that Italy, Germany and Japan were not burdened with the punitive reparations with which the Versailles treaty had unwittingly destabilized the Weimar Republic, while the Marshall Plan made a significant contribution to the economic recovery of Western Europe.

Furthermore, all countries emerging with systems of representative democracy intact or restored experienced a surge of popular support for a more egalitarian society. Before long even rightist parties (Conservative, Republican, Christian Democrat) identified liberalism with universal adult suffrage and with some measure of state intervention in the community services and support for the most vulnerable members of society. By the late 1950s it could be truly said that the majority of the citizens of the developed world had, as British prime minister Harold Macmillan claimed, "never had it so good".

In the sphere of international relations as well liberalism appeared to have emerged from the war with renewed idealism for internationalist goals and for pursuing ideas of self determination. This created the necessary climate for the formation of the United Nations Organization, the decolonization of former possessions and the move towards the economic and political integration of Europe with a "common market" which culminated in the Treaty of Rome of 1957.

LIBERALISM

Ideal society
Individual can enjoy right and freedom to satisfy material and emotional needs as far as possible without infringing similar rights of others

Affirmations
Dignity, freedom, rationality and happiness of individuals
Freedom of speech
Dynamism of society composed of free people with minimal constraints
Separation of powers
Active citizenship ideal

Rejections
Political systems inimical to individual freedom: traditional cultures; tyrannies; dictatorships, fascism; revolutionary and state socialism; anarchism
Inhumanity of any kind: including racism, torture, persecution and exploitation

Dilemmas
Optimism or pessimism on human nature and on the effects of capitalism; democracy or elites; centralization or evolution; nationalism or supranationalism

Historical blind spots
Patriotic nationalism; colonialism; equality of women; impact of poverty on equality of opportunity; ecological constraints to unlimited growth

Permutations and factions
Political liberalism can be antistatist and suspicious of democracy; radical liberalism is prodemocratic; social liberalism urges state intervention for equality of opportunity; liberal nationalism sees nation state as unique cultural entity
Economic liberalism reduces state activity to minimum to allow commerce to flourish
Ethical liberalism attacks all human factors that encroach principles of tolerance and human rights

Revolutionary organizations and tactics
Use of press and intellectual freedom
Demonstrations
Broadly based political parties; electoral activity
Use of legal processes to challenge abuses

State structures and official policies
Separation of powers between executive, legislature and judiciary
Representative government
Written constitutions and rule of law
Press freedom
Minimal state interference

However, both parties generally favored the maintenance of the welfare state, the development of a mixed economy, and decolonizing Britain's overseas empire.

To the north, Sweden had been governed by the Social Democrats since the early 1930s and had remained neutral during the war. This political continuity was preserved in the long tenure of power by the Social Democratic prime minister Tage Erlander (1946-69) and in Sweden's refusal to join NATO (unlike its neighbors Denmark and Norway).

Further south, Switzerland, like Sweden, remained a neutral state and continued its tradition of combining economic prosperity with a commitment to international order, having many UN agencies based in Geneva. Austria, after having been given its independence by the international State Treaty of 1955, also became a host to the UN and other international bodies, though its political culture was closer to those of mainstream Europe. Only in the southwest corner of Europe did the power of the prewar dictators, Franco in Spain and Salazar in Portugal, remained undisturbed.

Treaty of Rome
In March 1957, France, West Germany, Italy, Holland, Belgium and Luxembourg signed the Treaty of Rome to establish the European Economic Community (EEC, popularly known as the Common Market). The treaty, which proclaimed as its

long term goal "an ever closer union" of the peoples concerned, also set up Euratom (European Atomic Energy Community) at the same time. Earlier, in 1952, the six countries had founded the European Coal and Steel Community (ECSC).

The developing countries of the Third World, especially French and Belgian colonies, were linked to the Community's new range of trade and aid agreements, while the Soviet Union and the other members of Comecon increasingly found themselves dealing with a West European economic bloc rather than with individual countries. The United States was sometimes annoyed by the Community's protectionist policies, especially in agriculture.

The new European Community (or EC, including the EEC, ECSC and Euratom) in some ways resembled a budding "United States of Europe". This "supranational" (or almost federal) element was represented by the Commission, comprising a small team of full-time political leaders and administrators of the Community; by a Court of Justice, responsible for ensuring observance of the Treaty; and by the European Parliament, consisting of MPs who were at first delegated from their national parliaments, but later directly elected. The international, or intergovernmental, part of the system was the Council of Ministers, a standing conference of the national ministers responsible for agriculture, trade and energy, and each concerned to promote national interests.

◄ Visitors flock to see Sputnik at the Soviet exhibition hall during the Brussels World Fair of 1958. Under Khrushchev the Soviet Union paid more attention to its image in the non-Communist world, exploiting its progress in space exploration to project an image of dynamism and progress. No attempts were made, however, to dilute the ideological message of Communism. The inscription at the entrance quotes the Soviet constitution, describing the Soviet Union as a "socialist state for workers and peasants". Western leaders reacted suspiciously to what they saw as attempts to spread Communism by new, more insidious means.

Datafile

At the end of World War II much of the nonwhite world was under some form of white rule or administration. The following two decades would witness a complicated and often violent trend towards local independence. As the former colonial powers withdrew, new nations and political alliances slowly emerged. But such was the destabilizing effect of the colonial experience, that Africa, South Asia and the Middle East were all plunged into crisis.

Life expectancy in SA

Male
Female

Years

70
60
50
40
30
20
10
0

White   Asian   Colored

▶ In 1948 Israel faced the threat of immediate extinction at the hands of its hostile Arab neighbors. The immediate priority of Israeli leaders, therefore, was to obtain sufficient military equipment to allow their soldiers to fight off attack on all fronts. They succeeded in assembling a force which guaranteed the survival of the new Jewish state.

◀ Racial inequality in South Africa denied the majority Asian and black African populations the same access to economic opportunity and material well-being as the ruling white minority. Better fed, better housed and better cared for, white South Africans could expect to live 10–15 years longer than the remainder of the population.

▼ Political inequality in South Africa was mirrored by inequality in economic opportunity. Whites earned 75 per cent of the national income: blacks, who made up 68 percent of the population, earned only 19 per cent of the national income. Such an imbalance could only result in huge differences in health and the general quality of life.

▶ Health provisions in South Africa reflected both the inequality of treatment of racial groups and the imbalance in the population's health. The better nourished and long-living white population had access to uncrowded and well-equipped facilities, while the majority black population was forced to use inadequate facilities.

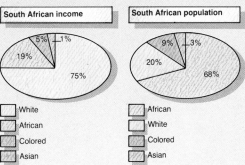

South African income

5% 1%
19%
75%

☐ White
☐ African
☐ Colored
☐ Asian

South African population

9% 3%
20%
68%

☐ African
☐ White
☐ Colored
☐ Asian

▶ The 1952 elections in India – the first to be held on the basis of universal adult franchise – cemented the primacy of the Congress party in the politics of the newly independent state. Drawing its strength from its leadership of the campaign for independence, the personality cults which had built around its senior figures, and its possession of the most extensive party organization. Congress, known after as a freedom movement rather than a party, was able to establish a firm grip on political power and to bring a semblance of unity to the country. This grip was only rarely shaken in the next 40 years. The Communist party had grown considerably during World War II but made an effective showing in only four states.

Indian elections 1948

1%
11% 2%
12%
16%
68%

Total seats 489

☐ Congress
☐ Other/Independent
☐ Socialist
☐ Communist
☐ KMPP
☐ Jan Sangh

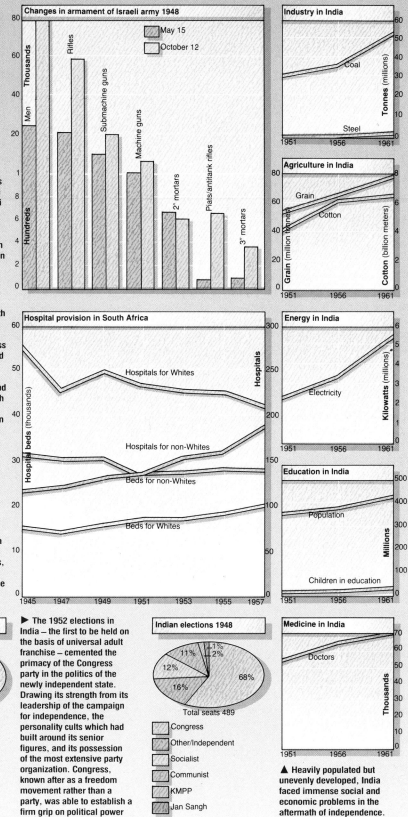

▲ Heavily populated but unevenly developed, India faced immense social and economic problems in the aftermath of independence. In both economic output and the provision of social services, the Indian government managed to achieve impressive improvements. Yet in 1961 India was still considered an undeveloped nation.

INDEPENDENCE AND NONALIGNMENT

The deepest division in the world after 1945 was between the rich industrial nations on the one hand and the much poorer, agricultural and raw-material producing countries of the non-Western world on the other. Despite different cultural and social traditions, unequal ties to metropolitan countries, and, not least, radically opposing political aims and methods, these poorer countries were at one in their desire for political and economic independence.

During the 1930s, those countries that relied on sale of raw materials and commodities had shouldered the heaviest burden of the Depression, as colonial powers passed on the costs of their recovery strategies to their colonial subjects. The stricter colonial controls that this entailed provoked nationalist agitation, which national elites hoped to exploit in their desire to eliminate colonial dependency and ultimately to take power themselves. However, the impact of the Depression on agriculture divided colonial societies along communal, ethnic, and class lines, which threatened the postcolonial ambitions of the national elites. All too often, the withdrawal of colonial administrations and, hence, of a unifying opponent, only brought to the fore the deep internal divisions within newly independent nations.

The future of colonial rule was circumscribed in the UN Charter. A new Trusteeship Council was formed for the former German and Italian colonies and the Charter also included a declaration on "nonself-governing territories" which bound imperial countries to expedite the process of self-government in their colonies. This declaration satisfied American sentiments that colonies belonged to the past as well as reformist sentiments in the European empires—in Britain more so than in France. It did not address the hopes and aspirations of the colonies themselves. When the question of their basic role as suppliers of raw materials was raised by Latin American countries, it was ignored. The transition to selfgovernment was envisaged as a slow and orderly process, controlled by the imperial governments and the UN. In fact, decolonization turned out to be as rapid, precipitate and violent a process as colonization itself. Few expected that the new nations would acquire their own very distinct voice in international affairs or that the emerging Third World would become the main source of postwar instability.

British and French decolonization

Decolonization proceeded unevenly according to the attitude of the colonial powers. Britain proved to be more flexible than France, having already created self-governing white dominions and introduced the Government of India Act in 1935. By later promising self-government to

India, Britain crossed the "color line" and encouraged all British colonies to aspire to independence. The pace of this development, however, took Britain by surprise, even though the principle was accepted.

The French colonial model, on the other hand, traditionally bred contempt for local practices and cultures but offered no promise of self-government or autonomy, or even of assimilation and equal rights in a Greater France. The situation was further complicated by disagreements over colonial policies within the multiparty French coalition governments. These uncertainties, coupled with mounting pressures from independence movements, saddled France with two protracted wars of succession, in Indochina (1945–54) and Algeria (1954–62), as well as a host of other smaller, but equally bitter conflicts as in Madagascar and in the Cameroons.

The partition of India

India, which had been the showpiece of colonization, became the foremost example of decolonization. Despite Britain's imperial interests and its worsening relations with the Indian Congress party, which in 1939 refused to join the war effort in the face of an "arrogant imperialism" that it likened to fascism, Clement Attlee's Labour government determined, in 1945, to transfer power as soon as possible.

▼ Dutch rule in Indonesia, weakened by the Japanese occupation of 1942–45, was confronted by a well-armed nationalist movement with massive popular support when it tried to reassert itself after the war. The resulting declaration of independence in 1949 (seen here celebrated by schoolchildren) and the British withdrawal from India marked the first significant steps in the postwar decolonization.

On the face of it, India possessed advantages that should have eased the transition to independence. It had a highly developed civil service as well as a tradition of nationalist organizations that were rooted in Indian society. However, India faced profound problems. The expansion of self-government in the midst of the agricultural crisis of the 1930s had split the country so deeply that independence was feared as much as it was fought for. The Muslim League, representing largely Islamic elites and the landlord classes embraced independence only reluctantly. They feared that their social and economic position would be challenged after independence and they insisted on the formation of a separate Muslim state.

British policy-makers had planned to hand over power to a single Indian government formed in a constitutional assembly, but the situation became so tense that the last British Viceroy, Lord Mountbatten, opted for an immediate transfer of power. Despite the opposition of the (predominantly Hindu) Congress party, the country was divided and, in August 1947, India and Pakistan gained independence before a constitutional assembly could meet.

Communal division and conflict had a long history on the Indian subcontinent, which the British had at one time sought to suppress and at other time exploited for their own ends. In both India and Pakistan, waves of mass-expulsions and mass-killings, burning and looting followed independence. Even Mahatma Gandhi, who, by passive resistance, had led the struggle to expel the British and now sought to reconcile Muslims and Hindus, became a victim of the violence. He was assassinated by a Hindu nationalist in 1948. Eventually, the government and the army re-

established control both in India and in the much weaker state of Pakistan, which was divided into East and West Pakistan with India in between. In both nations, the transition of power highlighted the deep gulf between the governing elites and their fractional societies.

Immediately after independence, India and Pakistan became embroiled in border conflicts over Kashmir and Junagadh and pursued increasingly antagonistic foreign policies. Whereas Pakistan moved into the pro-Western camp, India became one of the leading supporters of a policy of nonalignment for newly independent nations. Even before its independence, India objected to the division of Palestine, and later became an important mediator in ending the conflicts in Korea (1953) and Vietnam (1954), often finding itself in opposition to the United States.

War in Southeast Asia

In Southeast Asia the overthrow of the old colonial regimes by the Japanese during the war aided anticolonial movements. Japan's defeat left a power vacuum in these states that was quickly filled by local nationalists. This set in motion new conflicts and new struggles, in which the reentering of the old colonial powers and their strategies were only one, albeit important, factor.

In the Philippines, where the United States willingly relinquished control over its former colony, the newly established regime immediately became embroiled in a civil war against the Hukbalahab, a rebellious peasant movement which had begun as an anti-Japanese guerrilla force. Both the government and the rebels were staunch nationalists, but social and religious tensions drove them into a desperate conflict.

Unlike the Americans, the British (in Malaya), the Dutch (in Indonesia) and the French (in Indochina) opted for reoccupation. The British to some extent diffused resistance by separating Singapore and its Chinese merchant and entrepreneurial community, and by assisting the Malayan sultans to combat insurgencies on the mainland and on the island of Borneo. The Malayan guerrilla movement was inspired by the Chinese revolution, but motivated by the resistance of the Malayan Chinese to political encroachment by an Islamic majority backed by British colonialism.

▲ Independence celebrations at India's Red Fort. Independence was a triumph for the nationalist leaders of the long and largely nonviolent campaign for freedom. Celebrations, however, soon gave way to bloodshed.

▲ ◄ The Indian leader Nehru in conversation with the British viceroy Mountbatten. Colonial rule had brought economic development, literacy and an advanced administrative system, but it left behind political instability in the form of two antagonistic new countries.

◄ Civilians in Hanoi watch the arrival of Vietminh troops after the defeat of French colonial forces. Unlike the British in India, the French used force to try to maintain their rule in Indochina, but after a major defeat at Dien Bien Phu the French were forced to withdraw, leaving a country divided between a Communist North and a pro-US South – a situation that would soon bring war back to Vietnam.

The Dutch in Indonesia were supported in the outlying islands, but could not defeat the nationalists on Java or Sumatra, led by Achmed Sukarno and Mohammad Hatta, who had proclaimed the Republic of Indonesia in August 1945. However, their rule was by no means assured, as, in addition to fighting the Dutch, they were engaged in internal struggles against radicals in their own ranks, ethnic minorities and rebellious peasants. The weakest of the colonial powers were the Dutch, who came under pressure from the United States, India, Australia, and China to withdraw. Eventually, in 1949, Indonesia achieved independence and entered a new round of bitter ethnic and social conflict.

One of the worst trouble spots was the French colony of Indochina (Vietnam) where, from 1946, the French fought a tenacious war against the forces of Indochinese nationalism represented by the Vietminh. Yet, while the Vietminh had most of the local support in the north and the center of the country, as the elections in February 1946 showed, the main contingents on the French side, who supported emperor Bao Dai, were also Vietnamese, and they, together with Foreign Legionnaires and North African troops, carried the brunt of the war effort. After 1950, they came under increasing pressure when the Vietminh received the support of the new Chinese regime,

and suffered a humiliating military defeat at Dien Bien Phu in March 1954. A few weeks later, Indochina received its independence, though part of the area (South Vietnam) kept a national government that was Western-inclined, and was later to become an ally of the United States.

Although the French attempt to establish a collaborationist regime failed, the anticolonial war in Vietnam was, even from the outset, an expanding civil war in which outside forces intervened. Moreover, like other colonial crises, it threatened to escalate into a wider war. In 1954, the French, in desperation, asked the United States to intervene with nuclear weapons, a request that, wisely, Washington turned down.

In Vietnam, as distinct from Indonesia and Malaya, peasant mobilization and the assertion of nationalist independence came together in the Vietminh, much as had happened in China. The Vietnamese civil and anticolonial war thus reflected the leftwards tendencies of anticolonial nationalism.

Middle Eastern instability
After World War II, the French were virtually shut out of their former mandates, Lebanon and Syria, with British help. Britain acted out of fear of inflaming anti-Western sentiments among Arab nations, but also with the intent of creating

We are now terribly sick of this British government. They may go to hell but this government must get out of our country. There is a fire raging in our hearts. We must be free soon.

JAWAHARLAL NEHRU 1945

pro-British successor governments in the "fertile crescent" – Lebanon, Syria, and Transjordan – with the help of Transjordan's Emir Abdullah, whose army was British-trained.

In the Middle East, the struggle for control over Palestine overshadowed all other conflicts. There, Jewish immigration and Zionist aspirations to create a national state were pitted against the Palestinians' desire to have their own state. Palestinians and Jewish settlers had fought each other and the British throughout World War II, but in addition each side was engaged in its own internal conflicts. The Jewish-Palestinian struggle condensed all these squabbles into a major conflict, between religious, social, and ethnic groups, over the control of land and water in the whole "fertile crescent".

This conflict drew in the UN, which ultimately proved ineffective in the face of irreconcilable forces, and the United States, where pro-Zionist sentiments overwhelmed the cautious policy of the State Department and forced the British out under terrorist attacks from both sides.

British withdrawal led to the proclamation of the state of Israel, in May 1948, which was recognized by the United States but attacked by all of Israel's neighbors. After a brief ceasefire arranged by the UN, a furious 10-day war gave Israel victories on all fronts. The Israelis expanded their

territory beyond the initial UN proposal for a settlement, and expelled the Palestinians from the newly gained territory. In a countermove, Abdullah, the king of Transjordan, incorporated Arab Palestine into the new kingdom of Jordan.

The 1948-49 Arab-Israeli war settled, for the time being, the boundaries between Israel and its neighbors and established Israel as one of the powerful states in the region with a Western-style parliamentary democracy which, however, denied full citizenship to its Palestinian inhabitants. The defeat of Israel's neighbors and the influx of Palestinian refugees led to a new round of instability in the Middle East, in which domestic and interstate conflicts intertwined. Lebanon, Syria, Iraq and Jordan were in a state of turmoil in which, one by one, governments of pro-Western oriented notables were replaced by nationalist regimes.

Egypt and the Suez crisis

In Egypt in 1952 a military coup brought to power Colonel Gamal Abdel Nasser, whose secular, nationalist pan-Arabism became the new center of Middle East contention. He unified the front-line states on a common anti-Israeli course, which was matched by an implacable Zionism in Israel. Nasser was opposed not only by the British, who held on to the Suez Canal zone, but also by the

▼ After the aftermath of a bomb blast in Tel Aviv in 1946. The arrival of survivors from the holocaust of World War II increased pressure for the creation of a Jewish homeland. As Jew and Arab resorted more and more to violence, British forces were exposed to terrorist action by Zionist guerrilla groups. A wave of bombings and assassinations increased domestic pressure for a British withdrawal.

rising power of the oil-rich, but religiously orthodox, rulers of Saudi Arabia and by the British-backed sheikhdoms along the Persian Gulf.

In July 1956 Nasser outraged Britain by nationalizing the Suez Canal, and Britain together with France and Israel colluded in a plan to attack the Suez Canal zone. All three had their reasons for wanting to depose Colonel Nasser, a prominent spokesman for Third World nonalignment. France wished to stem the Egyptian flow of support for the national independence movement in Algeria (where an armed revolt had started late in 1954); Israel aimed to crush Egypt's ability to promote guerrilla raids across its frontiers; and Britain was alarmed at the seizure of the Suez Canal by a dictator whom the prime minister Anthony Eden compared to Hitler and Mussolini. However, the Suez invasion, launched early in November, ended in humiliation for the attackers. They were forced to withdraw (largely by American pressure) almost as soon as they had landed. One lesson of Suez was that Third World nationalism was a rising force, with which the Western powers would have to come to terms.

A second wave of tensions arose at the other fringe of the Near East, between Saudi Arabia and Iran, when Iran briefly came under control of a nationalist-populist front led by Mohammed Musaddiq. This confrontation receded when the Musaddiq government was toppled with American help in 1953.

"Wind of change" in Africa
In Africa, as in Asia, anticolonial mobilization was widespread and thrived on social and ethnic tensions. From Algeria to the Gold and Ivory Coasts, Nigeria and Cameroons, East Africa and the island of Madagascar, strikes and anticolonial mass movements exposed the weaknesses of colonial regimes. However, in the wake of postwar unrest, no nationalist leaders, not even the flamboyant Kwame Nkrumah in Ghana, or Nnamdi Azikiwe in Nigeria, succeeded in overthrowing the colonial regimes. Not only were conditions less favorable than in Southeast Asia and the

◄ An Israeli soldier relaxes with a captured Egyptian magazine during the Suez war. While European forces were attacking the Canal zone, the Israeli army inflicted a series of defeats on their Arab neighbors.

► Palestinian refugees leave the Al Faluja pocket for Gaza in 1949. The formation of the state of Israel led to an exodus of the Palestinian population and created a refugee problem that still afflicts the region today. The arrival of new waves of Jewish settlers and a series of Israeli military triumphs against their Arab neighbors exacerbated the problem and spawned a host of Palestinian guerrilla resistance movements.

▼ The Union Jack is lowered for the last time at Haifa, as British troops embark for their journey home. Britain's Palestine mandate ended on 14 May 1948 at midnight leaving Palestine without a British military presence for the first time since 1917. Britain's withdrawal allowed the creation of the state of Israel, which immediately provoked a war with Arab neighbors and led to lasting unrest in the Middle East. However Israel failed to solve the problem of the Palestinian refugees that its formation had created.

Middle East, but also the nationalists were more wary of the outcome of a seizure of power and sought to avoid civil war. Consequently, the colonial powers bore the brunt of postwar stabilization and "pacification", leaving Africa in a halfway house between colonial dependence and limited self-government. Often the key confrontations were not so much between the colonial administration and the independence movement as between the nationalists and the white settlers. These confrontations, where the issues were land and white rule, centered on Algeria, East Africa, and South Africa. In Algeria, the day of the German capitulation, 8 May 1945, marked the beginning of one of the bloodiest and ugliest wars of independence. It began with a minor fracas and ended only after seven years of bitter fighting, when in 1962 France finally granted independence. Algeria thus joined its neighbors Morocco and Tunisia, who had gained their independence from France a few years earlier.

In Southern and Northern Rhodesia and Nyasaland (which later became the independent states of Zimbabwe, Zambia and Malawi), hopes for a partnership between white farmers and entrepreneurs on the one hand, and black peasants and workers on the other, quickly evaporated and gave way to white rule, which was only marginally controlled by Britain. In postwar Kenya, the white minority faced a rebellion spearheaded by a violent nationalist group called the Mau Mau. Kenya eventually achieved its independence from Britain in 1964. Between them, France under de Gaulle and Britain under Harold Macmillan handed over power to a score or more of new African republics during the early 1960s (though the ex-British colonies remained members of the Commonwealth). As Macmillan

Apartheid in South Africa

South Africa is the last of many racially dominated societies created by European expansion between the 17th and 19th centuries. In the first half of the 20th century its particular variant of racial domination was known as segregation – a system beneficial to English-speaking big business and its associates, and to the English-speaking white working class. While large Afrikaner landowners – descendants of the original Dutch colonists of the region – also benefited, the numbers of Afrikaner poor whites increased considerably.

After World War II, with growing industrialization and increasing urbanization of black workers, the government of General Jan Smuts, veteran of the Boer War, was divided over the need for reform. This division allowed a narrow electoral victory to an Afrikaner nationalist coalition in 1948, elected by a minority of the virtually all-white electorate. This coalition became the National party in 1950. Its major objectives were fourfold; the consolidation of its own power, the maintenance of white power against rising African nationalism, increasing white prosperity, and rewards for the members of its own Afrikaner alliance. This combination of racism, nationalism and economic self-interest became known as apartheid.

These Afrikaner leaders achieved a virtual parliamentary coup, making it effectively impossible for the white opposition to regain power. They introduced legislation determining where blacks could live, with whom they might marry or cohabit, what jobs they might take and what schools and unions they might enter.

The National party increased the Afrikaner share of an expanding economy, transforming a small Afrikaner middle-class into a substantial business class. It protected white workers against competition and benefited Afrikaner farmers.

Yet a policy so blatantly self-serving could survive only if underpinned by moral justification. The policy of "Separate Development", evolved at the end of the 1950s, envisaged black rights as being achievable within independent "Bantu Homelands", and the Afrikaner intelligentsia justified the ensuing black suffering as a stage in a process of social engineering that would justly divide the country.

This "relocation" was begun in the 1960s and 1970s, but African resistance and the policy's high cost limited the extent of the restructuring. In the 1980s the National party was concerned merely with maintaining white power and its own leading role, despite a loss of part of its support to authoritarian Afrikaner groups.

◀ **The National party enforced apartheid in many ways of daily life, segregating buses, railroads, post offices and even park benches and staircases. Personal contact between the races – whether casual contact in the streets or more intimate relations – was systematically discouraged. Whereas this policy was sometimes presented as separate development rather than the institutionalization of privilege, it was underpinned by a sense of white superiority which derived from a Calvinist interpretation of the Bible.**

▼ **The Pan-African Congress organized a non-violent protest against the pass laws, which culminated in a demonstration of 20,000 people at Sharpeville, in Transvaal province, in March 1960. After demonstrators began throwing stones at police, they were met with submachine gun fire, which left 67 Africans dead, 48 of whom were women and children. The use of blatant violence to enforce apartheid brought international condemnation of National party policies.**

warned the white South African parliament in a speech in 1960, a "wind of change" was sweeping the whole continent of Africa.

South Africa had proceeded on its own separatist course, limiting the rights of black and "colored" South Africans that had been inherited from the days of British colonial rule. The victory of the National party in 1948 enshrined racial segregation, or apartheid, in the South African constitution. At the root of apartheid, a complex system of social discrimination on grounds of color, involving spatial segregation and economic exploitation, was the power to deny political representation to South Africa's majority population. Even at the time, South Africa represented an exception to the general, albeit embattled progress toward independence and political emancipation for Africans.

US involvement in Latin America

Since the 19th century US policy in central and South America had been governed by the Monroe Doctrine. Formulated in 1823 by President James Monroe, its ostensible purpose was to protect the area from exploitation by the European colonial powers. In effect, it gave the United States a free hand to interfere in the affairs of its southern neighbors. Governments in Central America and the Caribbean were made and unmade as a result of US policy with direct military intervention in Mexico, Cuba, Panama, Haiti, the Dominican Republic and Nicaragua.

Dictators such as Rafael Trujillo in the Dominican Republic and Anastasio Somoza in Nicaragua began as commanders of a US-created National Guard. Others, including Fulgencio Batista in Cuba and Hernandez Martinez in El Salvador, quickly allied themselves to the United States once they had seized power.

After World War II struggles within Latin America were assessed in terms of Cold War ideology, as the United States sought to extend its diplomatic and economic power across the southern mainland. Nationalistic governments that put social reform before US interests were denounced as Communists and pro-Soviet. In 1954 the democrat government of Jacobo Arbenz Guzmán in Guatemala, which had Communists among its ministers, was overthrown in a CIA-backed coup. Elsewhere in the region, the United States supported democratization movements to keep out the Communists as in Brazil in 1945, Bolivia in 1952, after a revolution, and Colombia and Venezuela in 1958.

The fall of America's ally Batista in 1959, and the revolution that brought Cuba within the Soviet orbit, served to justify a more aggressive policy of intervention in the years that followed. President Kennedy sponsored the overthrow of Juan Bosch in the Dominican Republic, while his successor Johnson backed a coup to unseat the government of João Goulart of Brazil and sent 20,000 US troops to the Dominican Republic.

New states and Third World nonalignment

The main focus of anticolonial fervor and national pride was often the individual new state. In the late 1950s and early 1960s several dozen new states emerged from under the rule of the former colonial powers: from Indochina (where North and South Vietnam, Laos and Cambodia achieved independence from France) through North, East and West Africa to the Caribbean (where the British and French colonial possessions became independent states). Although some, such as North Vietnam and Cuba, aligned themselves with the Communist movement, others, such as some of France's former colonies in Africa, remained closely linked, commercially, economically and politically, with the former colonial power.

Many new states declared themselves as "nonaligned". The nonaligned movement, which rejected both the Cold War blocs, came into formal existence at the conference held in Bandung, Indonesia in April 1955. It represented the "Third World", distinct from the capitalist West and the Soviet (or socialist) East, the "first" and "second worlds", respectively. The 29 countries attending the conference were mainly Asian—most of Africa was still under colonial rule—but they stood for principles that applied throughout the underdeveloped world. These included national independence, nonalignment in the Cold War, and the right of the poorer countries to a fairer share of the world's wealth (the concept later known as a New International Economic Order). Although the nonaligned movement aimed at neutrality with respect to the Soviet and Western blocs, its anticolonialism inevitably had an anti-Western character and, to that extent, it drew closer to the Soviet bloc. This was often reflected in the votes cast by the Bandung countries at the UN.

The nonaligned movement provoked different reactions among the Western powers. Britain, who had given diplomatic recognition to the Communist regime in China as early as 1949, and had with some success transformed its Asian imperial dominions into members of a new multiracial Commonwealth, regarded Asian nationalism as an irresistible force that should be guided into a better relationship with the West (though Britain later adopted a less enlightened attitude to nationalist stirrings in the Middle East). To the United States, Third World nationalism was little better than Soviet Communism. In particular, the new republic of China was seen as an intimate ally of the Soviet Union, and a spreader of Communism throughout Asia. John Foster Dulles, the US Secretary of State under President Eisenhower, responded to the rise of Third World nationalism by trying to "contain" it – in the same way as NATO was intended to contain Soviet power in Europe – by constructing a worldwide system of anti-Communist alliances. These included the ANZUS Pact (1951), made with Australia and New Zealand, the South-east Asia Treaty Organization (SEATO), set up at Manila in 1954 to include Pakistan, Thailand and the Philippines, and CENTO (1959), an alliance with Pakistan, Iran and Turkey, countries which the United States regarded as subject to direct Soviet pressure. However, none of these regional defense pacts ever developed the cohesiveness and permanence of NATO.

▼ An essential element in apartheid was the "pass laws", which from 1950 required blacks to carry identification and permitted them into white areas only at certain times. African opposition to apartheid often took the form of attacking this system, as here by burning the pass books. The laws were abolished in 1986.

▶ Decolonization gathered momentum in the late 1950s and early 1960s. In Africa the movement began with the independence of Ghana (formerly the British colony of the Gold Coast) in 1957, and by 1960 had brought national identity for most of West and Central Africa. The French withdrew from Algeria after a bitter war in 1962, and the British from their East African possessions in 1963–64. By 1970 Portugal maintained a colonial presence.

The emerging Third World quickly gained its voice under such leaders as Ahmed Sukarno (Indonesia), Jawaharlal Nehru (India) and Gamal Abdel Nasser (Egypt). Those who, like Ho Chi Minh (Vietnam) and Fidel Castro (Cuba), were indeed Communists as well as nationalists aroused even deeper fears and suspicions in the United States. The principles of nonalignment and coexistence were further elaborated at conferences in Cairo in December 1957 and Belgrade early in 1961. Hosting the 1961 conference, Marshal Tito of Yugoslavia stressed to delegates from Africa, Latin America, Asia and Europe the necessity to "take coordinated actions, primarily through the United Nations, in order to find a way out of the present situation". However, while the nonaligned states supported general principles of anti-imperialism, condemnation of the arms race, and the demand for more aid for economic development, they found it harder, as the movement expanded, to agree on what action to take. In addition to its Asian members the movement now included African ex-colonies of Britain and France, as well as the Belgian Congo, which gained independence and became the state of Zaire after a confused and bloody struggle in 1960. The nonaligned states continued to vote together against Western colonial countries at the United Nations, and to call for an end to the Cold War, but failed to mobilize their limited political and economic resources to coordinate their efforts. Regional organizations that were closer to the problems of individual states thus grew in importance at the expense of the worldwide nonaligned movement. These bodies included the Organization of African States, the Arab League (whose influence was reduced by conflicts between Egypt, Iraq and later Syria over the leadership of the Arab world), and corresponding bodies in Latin America and Southeast Asia.

Third World unrest
Decolonization, while settling the succession of empire, generally created a host of new confrontations. Independence and political emancipation, state power and political rights, government

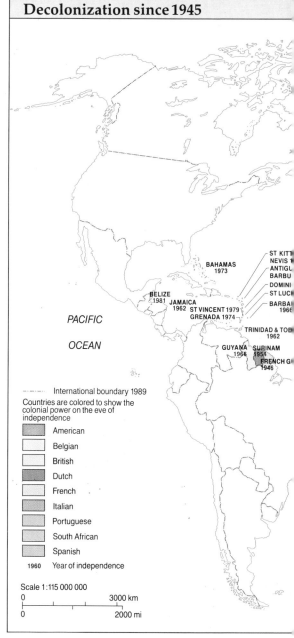

Decolonization since 1945

PACIFIC

OCEAN

BAHAMAS 1973

BELIZE 1981
JAMAICA 1962
ST VINCENT 1979
GRENADA 1974

ST KITT
NEVIS
ANTIGU
BARBU
DOMINI
ST LUC
BARBA
1966

TRINIDAD & TOB
1962

GUYANA 1966
SURINAM 1954
FRENCH G
1946

- - - - - International boundary 1989

Countries are colored to show the colonial power on the eve of independence

	American
	Belgian
	British
	Dutch
	French
	Italian
	Portuguese
	South African
	Spanish

1960 Year of independence

Scale 1:115 000 000

0 — 3000 km

0 — 2000 mi

▶ Third World leaders gathering at a conference of the nonaligned movement in Belgrade in 1961. Although it maintained a profoundly anti-Western stance, a product of the colonial past of most of the participant nations, the nonaligned movement represented a significant break from the polarization of the world into two superpower-dominated groupings. Prominent among the group photographed are Tito of Yugoslavia and Sukarno of Indonesia in the centre, Makarios of Cyprus, Nasser of Egypt, Haile Selassie of Ethiopia and Nehru of India.

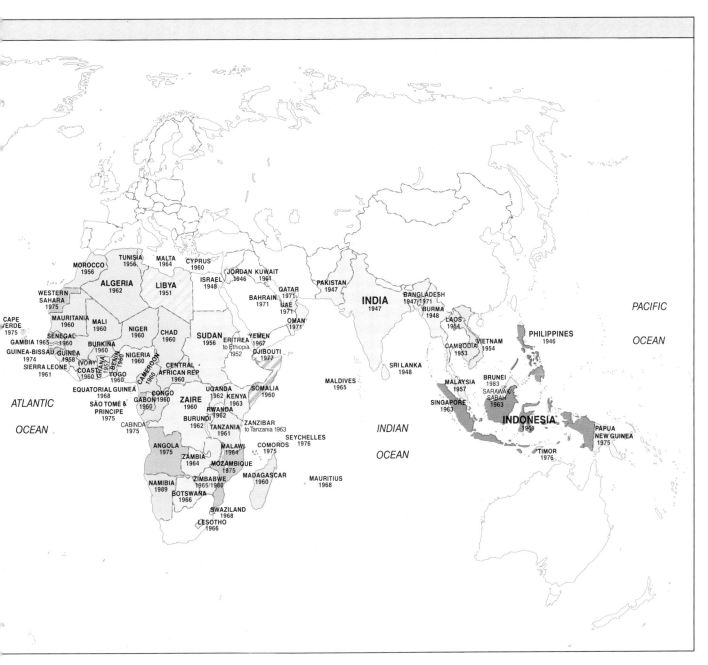

and mass-mobilization proved to be extremely difficult principles to reconcile with each other. Often this led to protracted conflict, ethnic and social tensions and even to war. The wave of Third World unrest threatened the idea, the ideals, and even the leaders of nationalist, anticolonial mobilization. Whereas the European and East Asian postwar settlements were frozen in the Cold War, the larger part of the world remained in turmoil.

The widespread conflicts of the Third World sometimes provided opportunities for the two superpowers to extend their Cold War into new areas, and to compete for the support of the new states. Similarly, some of the new states attempted to use this global rivalry for their own purposes, in particular to encourage competition between the superpowers to provide economic aid. However, neither the Soviet Union nor the West was prepared to become too deeply embroiled in the problems of the Third World.

REFUGEES: THE HUMAN FALLOUT

The profoundly disturbing experiences of refugees – alienation, persecution and forced migration – have been documented for a long time. What distinguishes this century is the volume and global scale of the problem. Refugees constitute a highly politicized challenge to the sovereignty of nation states, to the operation of international law and to the ethics of humanitarian assistance.

In the mid-1980s there were about 14 million refugees, defined by the 1951 UN Geneva Convention as people "who are outside their country because of the well founded fear of persecution". The apparently simple definition conceals complex root causes and consequences; it avoids the highly contentious issue of asylum and the millions who are undocumented or displaced.

Recognizing the growing international dilemmas of the refugee problem, in 1921 the League of Nations created the post of High Commissioner for refugees and the foundations of modern practice were institutionalized. During the interwar period the causes of refugeehood were reasonably clear cut – national wars (two million refugees from the Greco-Turkish war of 1922) and persecution in fascist Europe (800,000 refugees from Germany, Italy and Spain) in the 1930s. Group orientated and depersonalized solutions became inevitable.

The aftermath of World War II saw the creation of the UNHCR (United Nations High Commissioner for Refugees) in 1950 to afford protection and seek permanent solutions. It assisted in settling the remaining refugees from war-torn Europe – many were successfully repatriated – and then in handling the increasing flow of refugees from the Communist bloc in the 1950s.

Significantly, a Eurocentric perception of refugees was established. The refugees were white, European and were usually skilled or professional, seeking asylum in countries which, by and large, had sufficient resources to accommodate them. Additionally, it was useful political propaganda for Western countries to label people escaping from Communist Europe as refugees.

In modern times, however, over 90 percent of the world's refugees are in the developing world. Despite the new conditions of forced displacement and the extension of the 1951 Convention by the 1967 Protocol to cover this change, the preconceptions from the developed world still predominate.

Independence wars since 1960, the legacy of colonial insensitivity to racial origins, conflicts accentuated by extreme scarcity of basic provisions and the adoption of often inappropriate theories of economic development have combined to produce often catastrophic disruption that resulted in millions of refugees.

Modern mass movements tax the resources of host countries. "Donor fatigue" and donor dependency now challenge the humanitarian claims of the "north". Even more disturbing is a growing tendency in the developed countries to deny access to refugee asylum seekers.

◀ In the early years of the century, refugees – like this Catholic girl displaced from Belfast to Dublin in Ireland in 1922, posed relatively minor problems of resettlement.

▼▼ In the 1970s and 1980s many Vietnamese fled the Communist state, often enduring hardships at sea to reach Japan or Hong Kong. Many were said to be fleeing economic disruption rather than persecution, and their claim to refugee status was disputed.

◀▼ The Palestine people displaced by the establishment of Israel were forced into refugee camps in the late 1940s (main image). The harsh conditions of life, and the despair, in the camps fueled Palestinian terrorism for 40 years.

▼◀ Refugees were by no means always made welcome in their new countries. Here Central American refugees attempting to enter the United States have their papers scrutinized by border guards.

▼▼ Ethiopian refugees of the civil war of the 1980s. More than two million refugees in this area of Africa alone stretch scarce resources. Although news stories about the conditions endured by such refugees regularly arouse sympathy in the affluent West, aid is supplied patchily and is rarely sufficient to deal with the root cause of the problem. Additional problems arise in ensuring that aid reaches those most in need, and that recipients do not come to rely on aid.

THE
VIETNAM
YEARS

Time Chart

	1961	1962	1963	1964	1965	1966	1967
Europe/Mediterranean	• 22–26 Apr: Rightwing military rebellion in Algeria defeated. Later attempt by OAS (Secret Army Organization) to assassinate De Gaulle also failed • Aug: Border closed between E and W Berlin • 31 Oct: Stalin discredited (USSR)	• Mar: Conclusion of Evian agreements ended Algerian guerrilla conflict • 11 Oct: 21st Ecumenical Council (Vatican II) opened by Pope John XXIII – largest ever gathering of RC hierarchy with Protestant observers	• 14 Jan: De Gaulle (Fr) blocked UK entry to EEC • 22 Jan: French and W German treaty pledging cooperation in foreign policy, defense and cultural affairs • 30 Aug: Hotline telephone link opened between US and USSR presidents	• 15 Oct: Khrushchev replaced by Leonid I. Brezhnev as party leader and Aleksei N Kosygin as premier (USSR) • 15 Oct: In UK, Labour government elected under Harold Wilson after 13 years of Conservative rule	• 12 May: 10 Arab nations cut ties with W Germany after it established diplomatic relations with Israel	• 29 Mar: 23rd Soviet Union Communist Party congress marked by absence of Chinese • July: France withdrew military support from NATO: HQ moved to Brussels. 7 Sep, French announced their share of NATO military expenses to be halted from Dec 31	• 21 Apr: "Greek colonels'" regime imposed. 13 Dec, King Constantine exiled after failure to restore democracy. Col. George Papadopoulos became premier; "regent" appointed • 16 May: UK membership of EEC blocked by De Gaulle (Fr)
The Middle East	• 29 Sep: Declaration of Syrian independence after revolt of army officers against Egyptian domination of UAR under Nasser • 18–19 Dec: Portuguese colonies of Goa, Damoa and Diu invaded by Indian troops	• 3 Jul: Algerian independence won through referendum. Socialist Mohammed Ahmed Ben Bella elected first premier after 20 Sep elections following power struggle • 20 Oct: Mass Chinese invasion of India – withdrawn after 2 days	• 8 Feb: Premier Kassem killed in pro-Nasser military coup (Irq)	• April: UN peacekeeping force sent to Cyprus. 10 Aug, Turkey and Cyprus accepted UN cease-fire, ending threat of Mediterranean war • 27 May: Death of Nehru, prime minister for 17 years. Succeeded by Lal Bahadur Shastri	• 19 June: Algerian President Ben Bella deposed by army-supported socialist nationalists under Col. Houari Boumédienne	• 19 Jan: Indira Gandhi, daughter of Nehru, elected prime minister of India • Nov–Dec: Continuing Middle East conflict – border clashes between Israel and Jordan, backed by Arab League. Israel censured by UN Security Council	• 5–10 Jun, Six-Day War: Israeli air force destroyed almost entire Arab air forces on the ground. By the time of the UN cease-fire on 10 June, 4 times its own size had been captured by Israel in sweep toward Suez canal • mid-Nov: Pact signed by Greece, Turkey, Cyprus averted threatened Greco–Turkish war
Africa	• 31 May: S Africa declared an independent republic • 13 Sep: "Congo Problem": UN forces attacked the seat of the Katangan secessionist regime	• 17 Jun: African common market established (Mor, Gha, Gui, Mali and UAR) • 9 Oct: Uganda gained independence within British Commonwealth under Dr Milton Obote • 9 Dec: Tanganyika became republic within British commonwealth under Julius K. Nyerere	• 15 Jan: After UN campaign President Moise Tshombe agreed end of 30-month secession of Katanga from Congo • May: Organization for African Unity formed by 30 states, Addis Ababa, to maintain solidarity and abolish colonialism	• 26 Apr: Zanzibar merged with Tanganyika to form Tanzania • 12 Jun: Life sentence for Nelson Mandela for "sabotage" (S Afr) • 26 Jun: Moise Tshombe, ex-president of Katangan secessionist state called out of exile to help form new Congolese government	• 11 Nov: Rhodesia's illegal Unilateral Declaration of Independence (UDI) from Britain: sanctions imposed by Britain and UN	• 6 Sep: Prime Minister H.F. Verwoerd, originator of apartheid, assassinated (S Afr) • 27 Sep: End of S African mandate in Namibia (SW Afr) voted by UN General Assembly	• 13 Mar: Ex-Premier Moise Tshombe sentenced to death in absentia for treason by military court (Congo) • 30 May: Majority Christian Ibo Eastern region of Nigeria seceded as Biafra: civil war lasted in this region 2½ years
The Americas	• 3 Jan: US severed diplomatic and consular links following Cuban request to cut personnel in Havana • 20 Jan: John F Kennedy inaugurated as 35th and youngest President • 17 Apr: Failed invasion by CIA-backed anti-Castro Cuban exile force at Bay of Pigs. US internationally criticized for intervention	• 30 Sep: US race riots as 1st black student enrolled at southern university under military escort • 28 Oct: "Cuban missile crisis" ended as US agreed to lift trade embargo (imposed 3 Feb) in return for dismantling of USSR missile bases	• Continuing racial unrest focused in Alabama (US) • 22 Nov: Kennedy assassinated, Dallas, Texas. Lyndon B Johnson sworn in as next President	• 9–10 Jan: Panama crisis with clashes over disputed rights in Panama Canal. Relations briefly severed by Panama when US refused to renegotiate treaties • 2 Jul: Civil Rights Act signed by Johnson (US) • 7 Aug: Gulf of Tonkin Resolution passed by US Congress, enabled Pres. Johnson to commit large forces to Vietnam	• 21 Feb: Malcolm X, founder of proviolence Black Nationalist group, assassinated (US) • 28–29 Apr: US military aid sent to stall Communist takeover in Dominican Republic • 15–16 Oct: Mass antiwar demonstrations held (US) • 1 Dec: start of US airlift of Cuban refugee exodus	• International protest over US involvement in Vietnam war	• 12 Jul: Huge race riots, Newark, NJ. US Federal troops first used to quell riots, Detroit, 23–30 Jul • 23 Jul: Puerto Ricans voted to remain in US commonwealth rather than become federated or independent • 8 Oct: Death of Cuban guerrilla Che Guevara, shot after capture (Bol)
Asia and Pacific	• 19 May: S Korea – anticommunist military junta deposed government and arrested president • 11 Dec: After Kennedy's undertaking to massively increase number of US advisors, arrival in Saigon of 2 US Army helicopter companies with 400 troops (S Vnm)	• 8 Feb: US Defense Dept. created Military Assistance Command (MAC) in S Vietnam • May: Hong Kong erected barrier to deter illegal immigration from China • 12 May: US and other forces sent to Thailand to counter Communist threat in Laos	• 16 Sep: Malaysia created from federation of Malaya, Singapore, Sarawak and North Borneo • 1–2 Nov: President Diem killed in US-supported military coup (S Vnm)	• 30 Jan: S Vietnamese government ousted – 3 more changes within a year • 16 Oct: China, after 1st successful nuclear test, called for world summit to ban nuclear weapons and destroy stockpiles	• 2 Mar: US declared its combatant status (S Vnm) • 7 Aug: Singapore left Federation of Malaysia • 2 Sep: Start of Chinese cultural revolution • 5 Dec: China entered Vietnam conflict • 17 Dec: Ferdinand Marcos became President after coup (Phi)	• End of Robert Menzies' 17 years in government (Aus) • 1 May: 1st intentional shelling by US in Cambodia • 29 Jun: N Vietnamese capital, Hanoi, first bombed by US	• Jan: People's Liberation Army mobilized to support worker-peasants against Red Guard (Chn) • Mar: Thailand allowed US bomber bases for closer access to Communist targets (N Vnm) • 11–14 Sep: Border clashes between Chinese and Indian troops
World	• 7 April: UN voted unanimously to censure S Africa's apartheid policy • 18 Sep: UN Secretary-general Hammarskjöld's death in plane crash precipitated UN crisis; succeeded by U. Thant of Burma	• International nuclear weapons disarmament talks fail with main lack of agreement from USSR and France • 14 Dec: Signing by 5 states of San Salvador Charter to establish Organization of Central American States	• 19 Mar: Declaration of San José called for Central American Common Market • 5 Aug: Signing of nuclear test-ban treaty by UK, US and USSR: a permanent ban on nuclear testing in the atmosphere, outer space or under-water	• 21 Jan: 6th session of disarmament conference with participation of 17 nations, Geneva (till 17 Sep)	• 2 Mar: W Germany, France, Italy and Benelux nations agreed merger of EEC, Euratom and ECSC (effective 1 Jan 1966)	• 24–25 Oct: Manila Conference – Australia, New Zealand, Philippines, Thailand, South Korea, South Vietnam – pledged political self-determination and aid to S Vietnam also withdrawal of troops 6 months after N Vietnam's end of aggression	• 27 Jan: Treaty limiting use of outer space for military purposes signed by 62 nations • 12–14 Apr: 19 countries met to form economic program for the Americas • May: Bertrand Russell's "International Tribunal on War Crimes" condemned US for Vietnam. Australia, New Zealand and S Korea named accomplices

1968	1969	1970	1971	1972	1973
—9 Mar: Clashes between [stu]dents and police spread to [oth]er workers (Tch). 20–21 Aug: [inva]sion by Soviet forces to [res]tore strict communism [?] May: Student protest spread [to] civilian population and [thr]eatened stability of regime [.] De Gaulle announced [ref]orm program	• 28 Apr: De Gaulle replaced as president by Georges Pompidou following referendum defeat (Fr) • 23 Jul: Prince Juan Carlos was selected to succeed Generalissimo Franco as ruler of Spain on his retirement • 15 Aug: UK army given control of Ulster security • 21 Oct: Willy Brandt became Chancellor of W Germany	• 18 Jun: Conservative Edward Heath became UK prime minister • 12 Aug: Soviet and W German leaders signed nonaggression treaty • 7 Dec: W Germany and Poland signed pact renouncing force to settle disputes and agreeing border	• 3 Sep: 1st postwar Berlin accord signed by UK, France, US, USSR, E and W Germany: freedom of Western traffic to cross Eastern territory to West Berlin; Wall to remain; border to remain closed • 24 Sep: UK expelled 105 Russian officials on evidence from USSR defector	• 30 Jan, "Bloody Sunday", Belfast: 13 civilians were shot in army/Catholic clashes spurring further antiBritish attacks throughout Ireland and in London. 30 Mar, end of 51 years' semi-autonomous rule in Ulster. Direct government from UK imposed • 12 May: 1st treaty between E and W Germany	8 Mar: Referendum in N Ireland voted to remain part of UK. 21 Nov, compromise plan for coalition government of Protestants and Catholics • 19 May: USSR and W Germany signed 10-year pact for economic, industrial and technical cooperation
[2]8 Dec: Israelis took [rep]risals against Lebanese-[ba]sed attacks: start of conflict [thr]oughout 1969	• 27 Jan: Mid-east crisis as Iraq executed 25 "spies" despite international criticism • 17 Mar: Golda Meir became premier of Israel • 1 Sep: Capt. Muammar el-Qadhafi proclaimed Socialist Libyan Arab Republic after military coup	• 28 Sep: Death of President Nasser (Egy); succeeded by Anwar Sadat	• 12 Mar: Bloodless military coup to resolve civil disorder (Tur) • 1 Sep: New constitution for federal union of Egypt, Syria and Libya, supported in referendum, came into effect • 6 Dec: India recognized rebel government of Bangladesh	• 6 Apr: Egypt cut ties with Jordan over plans for Israeli territory on West Bank • 9 Apr: 15-year friendship pact signed (USSR, Irq) • 22 May: Ceylon became independent Sri Lanka • 28 Jul, Simla Pact: India and Pakistan renounced force in their dealings and resolved border conflict	• 1 Jun: Greece proclaimed a republic • 6 Oct: Start of Yom Kippur war: largest Arab–Israeli conflict in 25 years • 7 Nov: Resumption of diplomatic relations broken in 1967 between US and Egypt
[?] Aug: Nigeria rejected Red [Cr]oss plan to aid starving [Bia]frans [?] Nov: Britain withdrew troops [fro]m Aden	• 30 Oct: Nigerian nationalist party banned by Jomo Kenyatta	• 12 Jan: End of Biafran secession from Nigeria on flight of leader	• 25 Jan: Idi Amin ousted Milton Obote in military coup (Uga)	• 27 Mar: End of 17-year state of emergency when treaty was signed ending civil war between Arab Moslem north and Black Christian and pagan south (Sud) • 9 Aug: Asians expelled from Uganda by Idi Amin: many with British passports were accepted by UK • 27 Apr: Death of Kwame Nkrumah, leading statesman of Ghana from 1957 to 1967	• Serious famine in Ethiopia with failure of annual rains, causing unprecedented distress
[?]–7 Feb: Revision of Canadian [co]nstitution: gave French and [En]glish official language status [?] Apr: Assassination of Martin [Lu]ther King at Memphis, [Te]nnessee (US) [?] 20 Apr: Pierre Trudeau voted [pri]me minister (Can) [?] Assassination of Senator [R]obert F. Kennedy (US) [?] Nov: Richard M. Nixon [el]ected US president	• 24 Jun: Undeclared war started between El Salvador and Honduras • 15 Oct and 15 Nov: Mass national antiwar demonstrations (US)	• 6 Mar: Rise in terrorist bombings after explosion of Weather Underground bomb factory (US) • 4 Jun: Demilitarized zone policed by OAS advisory force along agreed border between El Salvador and Honduras	• 21 Apr: Death of François (Papa Doc) Duvalier; replaced by son Claude (Hai) • 8 Jun: President Allende imposed state of emergency following civilian unrest (Chi) • 13 Jun: Top-secret Pentagon Papers, study of US involvement in Vietnam 1945–67, published in *The New York Times*	• 29 Sep: Accord signed ending technical state of war between China and Japan since 1937. Japan severed relations with Taiwan	• 11 Sep: Death of Allende and 2,700 others in bloody coup under military junta led by General Pinochet (Chi) • 23 Sep: Perón elected president; wife, Isabel, vice-president (Arg) • 10 Oct: US Vice-President Spiro Agnew sentenced on tax evasion charges
[?] Jan: Communist Tet Offensive [ga]ined much ground but was [for]ced to retreat: the initial [su]ccess further lessened US [su]pport for war (Vnm) [?] 16 Mar: Massacre by US [tr]oops of hamlet of My Lai [(V]nm)	• Mar: Military clashes between Chinese and Soviet troops • Jul: Start of "Vietnamization" with gradual withdrawal of American troops from Vietnam, handing combat role to S Vietnamese	• 9 Oct: Cambodia became Khmer Republic under Lon Nol. Supported by US troops, 30 Apr – 29 Jun	• 17 Jun: Return of Okinawa to Japan after treaty with US • 18 Aug: Anzac troops to be withdrawn from Vietnam by Dec	• 25 Jan: US moved 8-point peace plan: US troops to be withdrawn in return for cease-fire and POW release. S Vietnam then to hold new elections: US to remain neutral. 30 Mar: US air force retaliated against strong N Vietnamese attack • 2 Dec: 1st Labor Party election win in 23 years (Aus)	• 27 Jan: USA, N and S Vietnam and the Viet Cong signed agreement to end Vietnam war. 2-party version was signed by N Vietnam and US (28 Jan) as S Vietnam refused to recognize Provisional Revolutionary Government of Viet Cong. Last US troops left 29 Mar; 8,500 civilian technicians remained • 27 Feb: Cease-fire between government and Pathet Lao announced ended 20 years' war (Laos)
[?] 20 Nov: Meeting of 10 leaders [of] noncommunist European [na]tions regarding currency crisis	• 17 Nov: Start of US and USSR SALT talks, Helsinki. 24 Nov: Nuclear Nonproliferation Treaty signed pledging nonpromotion of nuclear technology to non-nuclear nations	• 13 Oct: Canada opened diplomatic links with China; broke those with Taiwan	• 11 Feb: Treaty signed by 63 nations banning nuclear weapon installations on seabed in international waters • 21 Dec: Kurt Waldheim (Aut) appointed UN Secretary-general (to 1981)	• 5 Sep: Israeli Olympic team killed by Arab Black September terrorists, Munich • 3 Oct: USSR and USA signed last papers implementing SALT accords limiting submarine-carried and land-based missiles	• 1 Jan: UK, Ireland and Denmark entered EEC • 16–25 Jun: Antinuclear war accords (USSR, US) • 19–21 Oct: Energy crisis and severe recession in US and Europe after Arab oil cuts and (from 2 Mar) European monetary crisis • 25 Oct: US forces placed on alert for fear of USSR joining Middle East conflict

Datafile

In the early 1960s, the tension between the two superpowers mounted alarmingly in Europe and around Cuba. In Europe, problems centered on the divided nation of Germany. In Cuba, they were the product of Castro's successful Communist takeover and of subsequent US/USSR interference in domestic affairs. Expenditure on arms continued to increase, and the Western alliance prevailed simply because of its superior economic might.

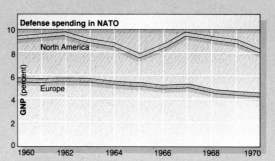

▲ The maintenance of NATO's military might depended on US willingness to spend money on a global defense policy. While the Western European defense budget was around 5 percent of GNP, the wealthy US still allocated 8 percent of GNP to military expenditure in 1970 after a decade in which, proportionately, defense spending had decreased.

▶ The defense expendure of the major Powers doubled in the 1960s as military technology became more complicated and costly. The USA and USSR continued to account for about 80 percent of the total, with Soviet expenditure rising steeply as they strove to close the gap opened by US progress in conventional and nuclear arms in the 1950s.

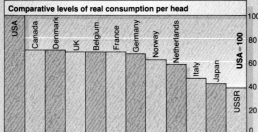

▲ Mid-1960s figures for comparative levels of real consumption highlight American, prosperity. Consumption even in advanced industrial nations like Canada, the UK and West Germany reached only 70 percent of US levels. With the USSR and Japan, the contrast was even sharper, neither nation reaching 50% of the US level.

▶ In the 1960s, the less developed industrial nations began to close the gap on the mature economics of the US and UK, where GNP per capita increased by less than 50 percent. The frontrunner was Japan, where rapid development of an export-driven manufacturing economy resulted in an increase in GNP per capita of almost 150 percent.

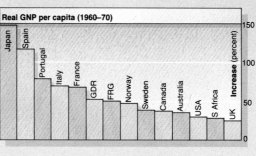

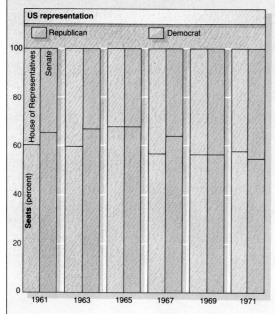

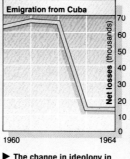

▼ In the early years of Castro's rule, Cuba lost large numbers of its best educated citizens in politically-motivated emigration to the USA. This phenomenon, damaging to both society and economy was, however, short-lived. But in 1962 and 1963, emigration fell by more than 75 percent and remained at a relatively low level.

▶ The US, while prosperous, remained an economically divided nation. Although family incomes rose steadily across the board, blacks continued to lag far behind whites and in many cases remained well below the poverty line – a major cause of the racial conflict which was to sweep the nation in the mid-1960s.

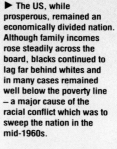

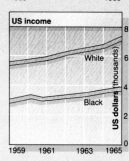

▲ The 1960s saw the political balance in the US swing heavily toward the Democrats. The advantage gained under Kennedy was held by Johnson, and the Democrats maintained a majority in both houses.

US presidents
1961   J Kennedy   D
1963   L Johnson   D
1965   L Johnson   D
1969   R Nixon   R

▶ The change in ideology in Cuba produced a dramatic change in trading partners, with the new regime looking abroad to Eastern bloc markets and suppliers, and trying to generate real domestic economic growth by centralizing and restructuring the production processes along established Soviet lines, concentrating on heavy industry.

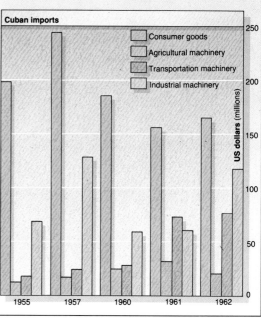

POWERS IN CONFLICT

The United States and the Soviet Union, wartime allies, had become postwar rivals for the place in the global power structure once enjoyed by imperial Britain. In what became known as the Cold War, this rivalry threatened a conflict more terrible than any in human history, as both the superpowers built up arsenals of nuclear weapons capable of destroying the world several times over. Most attempts from either side to break the deadlock were received with distrust and suspicion.

Kennedy and Khrushchev

Soviet leader Nikita Khrushchev, believing that the Soviets' nuclear strike capability freed them from the danger of a US attack, advocated a new policy also aimed to win the support of the growing number of nonaligned countries and to woo the American public.

The election of John F. Kennedy to the US presidency in 1960 enhanced Khrushchev's hopes of achieving a superpower rapprochement. Kennedy presented an image of idealism and commitment to the betterment of all mankind, which augured well for international cooperation. In

▼ The ideological barrier assumes concrete form – Berliners watch the construction of the wall dividing their city. Berlin, divided between Allied and Soviet zones of occupation but located in the heart of East Germany, was the focal point of European confrontation. The construction of the wall was an attempt to block the easiest route to the West.

1961, talks between the superpowers led to the McCloy–Zorin recommendations, laying down the ultimate goal of complete nuclear disarmament and the principles that would govern subsequent disarmament talks. Unfortunately, both sides lacked the political will to turn the recommendations into a binding agreement.

That same year, East–West tension rose again over the troubled city of Berlin. The East Germans were "voting with their feet" by crossing the still open frontier from Soviet-controlled East Berlin to West Berlin at the rate of several thousand a week. By July 1961 the figure had reached 1,000 a day, and on 12 August 4,000 crossed to West Berlin. On the next night, in the middle of the holiday season, the East German authorities erected a barrier, which became the Berlin Wall, permanently cutting off the east of the city from the west. The Western allies protested that the wall breached the agreement of 1945, under which all Berlin was to be governed as a single unit by the four Allied powers, but took no action for fear of escalating the crisis.

The Soviets and East Germans claimed that West Berlin was the center of a Western network

◀ Communism reaches the Americas – Fidel Castro's successful Marxist revolution in Cuba threatened nervous US policy-makers. Castro's populist style made him appear all the more dangerous, persuading Kennedy to embark on the disastrous Bay of Pigs invasion in an attempt to overthrow him.

▼ ▼ The Cuban missile crisis brought the superpowers closer to war than any other event in the modern era. It was the result of the competitive buildup of arms over the previous decade, the failure of the superpowers to find effective diplomatic channels and, in the short term, of the fiasco at the Bay of Pigs and the emergence in both the US and the USSR of leaders intent on ending the Cold War. Kennedy and Khrushchev (see below) were the central players in the dangerous game of brinkmanship over Cuba. The crisis marked a turning-point in East–West relations, with both sides adopting more flexible attitudes to key issues and moving toward negotiation on nuclear arms reduction.

Revolution in Cuba

In 1959 the focus of East-West relations switched to the Caribbean island of Cuba. At the beginning of the year Fidel Castro had replaced the discredited dictator Fulgencio Batista as leader. At first, Castro did not claim to be a Marxist, or a Communist, perhaps because he feared that his country would share the fate of Guatemala, where a leftwing government had been overthrown by the United States in 1954 in the name of the Monroe Doctrine. In April 1959 Castro had visited the United States to give assurances that foreign investments in Cuba (mainly American) were in no danger. Shortly afterward, however, Cuba started to increase its trade with the Soviet Union, and in the course of 1960 nationalized all US property on the island. During the US presidential election campaigns of that year, both Kennedy and his Republican opponent Richard Nixon had promised to act against Cuba. In April 1961, President Kennedy, on the advice of the CIA (US Central Intelligence Agency) backed an invasion of Cuba by anti-Castro emigrés, at the Bay of Pigs. It failed miserably as the small emigré force was easily overpowered by Castro's troops. Kennedy admitted to a serious error of judgment, which admission was not lost on Khrushchev, and resolved to be less dependent on the CIA.

▶ Che Guevara, guerrilla and student icon.

of spies and saboteurs operating against East Germany: and the wall was designed to keep them out. While this was partly true, the main purpose of the wall was rather to keep the East German population in. The East German regime was losing too many of its citizens to the West – including highly skilled people – and needed to seal its frontiers to preserve its stability.

The Cuban missile crisis
During 1962 the Soviet leadership, perhaps encouraged by Kennedy's humiliation at the Bay of Pigs and by the West's refusal to respond to the Berlin Wall with force, began to build sites for nuclear missiles in Cuba. This action posed a direct challenge to the strategic supremacy of the

United States in the Western Hemisphere. By mid-October the Kennedy administration, having rejected the options of a "surgical strike" against the Soviet bases, decided on a naval blockade to prevent further Soviet missiles reaching Cuba.

For a few days, an anxious world waited to see whether the Soviet missile-carrying ships would encounter the waiting ring of US warships. Kennedy insisted that no Soviet missiles would be tolerated in Cuba. Khrushchev demanded that, in return for withdrawing them, the United States remove its missiles from sites near the Soviet Union, particularly those in Turkey. On Sunday 28 October, after several critical incidents (including the boarding of a Soviet merchant ship by the US Navy, and the shooting down of an American U2 spy plane over Cuba), the superpowers reached a mutually face-saving compromise. Kennedy undertook not to invade Cuba, and Khrushchev withdrew his missiles from the island.

The Cuban crisis was a chastening experience for the Soviet Union, forcing it to back down before the eyes of European satellites and exposing its deteriorating relations with Communist China, who denounced Khrushchev's foolhardiness. Despite the illusion of Russian technological superiority over the Americans created by the successful firing of Russian intercontinental ballistic missiles (ICBMs) in August 1957 and launching of the *Sputnik* satellite three months later, the military balance between the superpowers clearly remained on the side of the United States. Following the Cuban missile crisis, the Soviet Union both resumed its diplomatic quest for peaceful coexistence, to avert the danger of

I want to be the white man's brother, not his brother-in-law.

MARTIN LUTHER KING 1962

▼ ▼ Racial discrimination in the US had backed systematic government attention since the emancipation of slaves. The racist attitudes of many whites caused politicians to shy away from action and produced ugly incidents of harassment (such as that pictured below) when the first steps were taken toward desegregation. Civil rights campaigners like Dr Martin Luther King fought the existing situation to the attention of the nation in a series of rallies. Kennedy's Civil Rights Act of 1963 dismantled the formal framework of racial discrimination but tension remained high and often broke out into violence and riot.

nuclear war, and embarked on a long-term military armaments program designed to give parity with US nuclear and naval power by the early 1970s. Politicians in the Kremlin had concluded that arms control must be achieved by energetic participation in the arms race, and that meaningful superpower negotiations were possible only between equals.

By October 1964, when Leonid Brezhnev came to power, having ousted Khrushchev, the Russians were well advanced towards their goal of military parity. They had increased their strategic rocket forces and the number of submarine-launched and intercontinental ballistic missiles, and expanded the Soviet navy, previously confined to coastal defense duties, to project its power into the Mediterranean and the Pacific and Indian Oceans.

US Civil Rights movement
While abroad the United States' interests were threatened by the Soviet Union, at home civil unrest was beginning to take its toll. A century after President Lincoln's proclamation of 1862 freeing them from slavery, black Americans were still a long way from achieving their constitutional rights and equality of status with whites. Many lived in poverty and squalor, were poorly housed, fed and educated, and had a life expectancy barely two-thirds that of white Americans. By the early 1960s, black leaders had become impatient for change, and some, like Martin Luther King, organized nonviolent mass demonstrations and used civil disobedience tactics to instill a greater awareness in the whites. Sympathetic white Americans, especially the young, lent their support to the movement, which began to have an effect. Slowly, lunch counters, rest rooms and hotels were desegregated, and racial discrimination in employment was reduced.

President Kennedy's Civil Rights Bill, which became law the year after his death, represented a major breakthrough in establishing the principle of racial equality, though it did not go as far as many blacks would have liked. The Act empowered the attorney-general to prosecute those

employers who discriminated against blacks, and made segregation in hotels, restaurants and other public places illegal. It also forbade discrimination in any project or program receiving federal funds, and permitted the attorney-general to file desegregation suits on behalf of individuals or organizations who found it too risky or expensive to do so themselves.

Despite the Act, in the South many blacks were still prevented from registering as voters through delaying tactics and intimidation, so that President Lyndon Johnson was forced, in March 1965, to secure additional legislation authorizing federal officers to enter names on the voters' lists. Desegregation, too, was ignored as late as 1966, with many examples of blacks being deprived of state medical care because hospitals refused to comply with the law.

Yet even the modest laws passed provoked the Ku Klux Klan into launching a campaign of terror and murder against the black population. Young blacks retaliated by looting and burning property owned by whites. By the late 1960s, race riots had become commonplace in many American cities, especially those with large black populations such as Chicago, Miami and Los Angeles. As blacks and whites increasingly saw their interests as incompatible, and American society became engulfed in race war, the hopes of the moderate civil rights movement that the black population could be accommodated in mainstream American life looked less and less realistic.

Johnson's "Great Society"
Earlier, in 1964, in an effort to bridge the growing gap between "haves" and "have-nots", and avert its potentially explosive social consequences, Lyndon Johnson had produced the concept of a "Great Society" dedicated to the eradication of poverty, unemployment and racial conflict, and to the establishment of equal opportunity for all.

Aided by the mid-1960s economic boom, Johnson introduced new health provisions and sickness insurance for the elderly and increased social security payments. He set aside substantial sums for improving education, especially in the deprived inner-city areas, devoting extra funds to the recruitment and training of teachers, and established new scholarship schemes. He funded the building of new libraries and community centers and made available federal grants for the promotion of the arts. To combat inner-city decay, a federal agency for housing and urban development was set up, with an allocation of $7 billion for slum eradication and rehousing schemes.

Already by 1966, however, much of the impetus of the "Great Society" reform initiative had been lost. The United States had become deeply involved in the Vietnam War. Congress decided that US prestige in Southeast Asia was more important than the eradication of poverty at home, and so Johnson's reform program was scaled back, putting paid to his hopes of ending American poverty. Nevertheless, Johnson's initiative made subsequent administrations recognize the need to address the issues of poverty, inequality and injustice as a prerequisite to making progress on human rights issues.

The Assassination of Kennedy

The assassination of President Kennedy on 22 November 1963 was an event whose emotional reverberations were felt around the world. A widely popular leader, with the successful solution of the Cuban missile crisis and the passage of the Civil Rights Act behind him, Kennedy had become the symbol of America's emergence as a dynamic and liberal world power, and his violent death, in full view of a huge television audience, threw the entire nation into a state of post-traumatic shock. Driving in a highly publicized motorcade through the streets of Dallas, Texas, Kennedy was felled by bullets from an unseen sniper's rifle.

The authorities quickly discovered and arrested the supposed assassin, Lee Harvey Oswald, but Oswald was himself murdered, again in front of television cameras, by a local nightclub-owner before he could be fully questioned or put on trial. In the aftermath of the affair a host of unanswered questions, contradictory evidence and sinister rumors began to cast doubt on the officially accepted view that the president had been shot by a single assassin acting on personal motives. The possibilities – that more than one gunman had been involved, that Oswald was simply a pawn in a wider conspiracy who had been deliberately silenced before he could implicate others, and that the real agents of Kennedy's death had been either foreign Communists, the Mafia or members of his own government and the CIA, alarmed by the directions his foreign and domestic policies were taking – were all widely canvassed. Among the more lurid rumors, it was claimed that Kennedy's body was surreptitiously tampered with en route from Dallas to Washington, to disguise the evidence of the gunshot wounds.

President Johnson eventually commissioned a fullscale inquiry (the Warren Commission) in 1964. This inquiry collected a mass of evidence before concluding that the official "single assassin" hypothesis was correct. The Warren verdict went along way towards allaying public concern and brought the incident to an end as a political issue. A number of informed observers, however, have never been convinced by the report and have uncovered sufficient evidence of a possible cover-up and dubious official practice to cast a shadow over the accepted verdict. While it is most unlikely that any counter-hypothesis will ever be conclusively proven, questions remain about what actually happened, and the full story of how one of America's best-loved leaders was murdered will probably never be uncovered.

▲ President Kennedy tours the streets of Dallas on 22 November 1963 with his wife Jackie and the Governor of Texas, seconds before his assassination.

▼ One man's revenge or sinister cover-up when nightclub-owner Jack Ruby fatally shot Lee Harvey Oswald, President Kennedy's suspected assassin, as Oswald was being transferred from the Dallas city jail to a more secure prison. Ruby was arrested and executed for murder.

Datafile

Confrontation between the USA and USSR exercised a profound effect on Third World countries. Both superpowers had expansionist aspirations and were able to coerce the economically weak and politically unstable nations of the Third World by making strategic offers of aid and military assistance, often resulting in the creation of regimes which were little more than clients of superpowers. The presence of large, politically motivated armed forces wreaked havoc on fragile societies and undermined attempts to establish effective civilian rule. This form of war by proxy reached its most advanced form in Southeast Asia where the US actually committed its own troops in resisting a Soviet-backed North Vietnamese attempt to bring the entire area under Communist control. Meanwhile, other nations were emerging as major economic forces; the most obvious case being Japan, which within 25 years of near annihilation had become one of the major industrial powers of the world, with a booming economy which rivaled that of the USA.

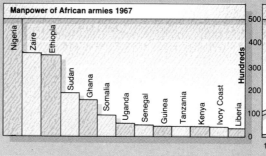

Manpower of African armies 1967

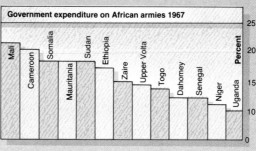

Government expenditure on African armies 1967

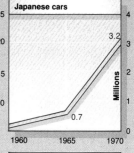

Japanese steel

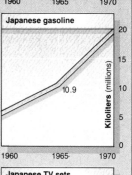

Japanese cars

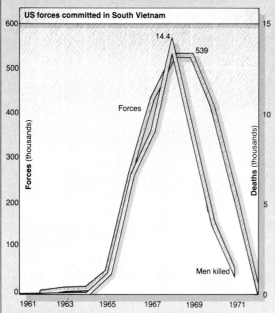

US forces committed in South Vietnam

◀ US presence in Vietnam, at first limited to a few advisors, had grown by 1968–69 to an entire army of half a million men. The failure to win a decisive victory and mounting public disapproval produced a dramatic reversal in policy and in the early 1970s US forces in Vietnam decreased as dramatically as they had risen five years before.

▲ By 1967 the new nations of Africa, helped by massive arms shipments from the developed world, had far larger armies than they could otherwise have sustained. The three largest forces, those of Nigeria, Zaire and Ethiopia, were all engaged in prolonged civil wars, while many others were active against dissenters or bordering nations.

Japanese gasoline

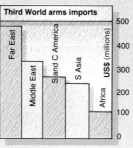

Third World arms imports

◀ Arms imports all over the Third World reached extraordinary levels. The wars fought in Vietnam and around Israel were heavily underwritten by US and Soviet arms shipments, and even in less sensitive areas, the stream of modern military equipment arriving from abroad produced potential conflict and instability.

Japanese TV sets

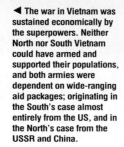

Aid to Vietnam 1967

North Vietnam
Total US $300 million

South Vietnam
Total US $456.70

- USA
- USSR
- China
- Others

▶ The US spread its hegemony across the non-Communist world by the expenditure of millions of dollars on foreign aid. Significantly, it was those nations (primarily, war-torn Vietnam) which were perceived to be of the greatest strategic importance or under threat from Soviet backed neighbors which received the most help.

◀ The war in Vietnam was sustained economically by the superpowers. Neither North nor South Vietnam could have armed and supported their populations, and both armies were dependent on wide-ranging aid packages; originating in the South's case almost entirely from the US, and in the North's case from the USSR and China.

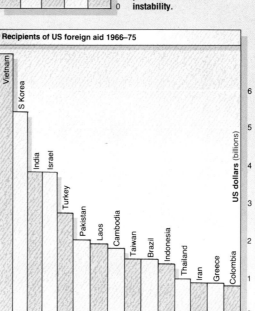

Recipients of US foreign aid 1966–75

▲ The growth of Japanese industrial production accelerated steeply in the mid-1960s. Japanese industry flourished not only at home but by penetrating Western markets. As economic growth became increasingly dependent on exports so the Japanese diversified into expensive, high-technology products such as cars and television sets designed specifically for the USA and Europe. Initially dependent on the products of Western industry for its development of a modern industrial economy, Japan had, by the 1970s, become the leading producer of many of the most sophisticated mass consumer goods and was subjecting the economies of its erstwhile benefactors to severe competitive pressures.

CHALLENGE TO THE SUPERPOWERS

Sino-Soviet relations plummet

Mao Zedong's Cultural Revolution fails

Sino-Indian conflict

Indo-Pakistan war

The emergence of Bangladesh

War in Vietnam

Struggle in the Congo

Nigerian civil war

Arab-Israeli conflict

▼ Political radicalization in China – posters proclaiming Mao's Cultural Revolution cover the walls of Guanzhou.

Differences between China and the Soviet Union dated back at least to 1935 when Mao Zedong broke with his Soviet advisors during the "Long March" and developed a version of Communist strategy and ideology more suited to China's needs. As long as Stalin remained alive, however, Mao paid lip service to the Soviet claim to leadership of the Communist bloc. But Mao despised Stalin's successor, Khrushchev, and disagreed with him profoundly over a whole range of issues, finding him too lenient.

Sino-Soviet differences became more critical in the early 1960s when Mao perceived that Soviet policies were actually detrimental to China's interests and even slighted its national honor. Moscow's refusal to share its nuclear secrets with China, its new policy of peaceful coexistence with the West, and its reluctance to give more than verbal support to China's bid to regain the off-shore islands of Taiwan, Quemoy and Matsui convinced Beijing of the fickleness of China's former ally.

The rift between the two great Communist powers deepened after the Cuban missile crisis of 1962, when the Chinese publicly accused the Soviets of foolhardiness. During its border conflict with India in 1962, China was further angered by the Soviet Union's maintaining a strict neutrality and even condoning India's appeal for intervention by the United States. Furthermore, domestically Mao was now fighting for his political life and enmity with Moscow gave him a pretext for purging some of his major opponents.

Beijing publicly rejoiced at the fall of Khrushchev in 1964. In 1967, at the height of the Cultural

▲▶ **Two faces of ideological upheaval – (above) female Red Guards march through the streets of Beijing; and (right) a party militant forces commuters to read aloud from the famous "little red book". China's Cultural Revolution arose from diputes within the Communist party about the political future of the country. The aging Mao found his ideologically based leadership threatened by pragmatic modernizers drawing their inspiration from the Soviet Union. He responded with a drive for ideological purity, rejecting all forms of compromise with doctrinaire Communism, and utilizing discontented young workers and students, as Red Guards, to launch attacks on the existing bureaucracy at both national and local levels. For ten years China turned its back on modernization as ideological warfare burnt a violent path through the country.**

Revolution, Red Guards sacked the Soviet embassy in Beijing, and in 1968 China condemned the Soviet invasion of Czechoslovakia. With relations between the countries at their lowest ebb, in 1969 a border dispute almost resulted in war, with the Soviets backing down at the last moment.

China's Cultural Revolution

By the early 1960s the fervor of the 1949 Chinese revolution had begun to wane. Mao Zedong feared the Chinese people's conversion to consumerism, which might lead to the reestablishment of capitalism in China. Opinion among China's leadership on how to cope with the country's problems was divided. Marshal Lin Biao, head of the influential Military Affairs Committee of the Chinese Communist party (CCP) Central Committee, emphasized morale and the need for recurring mass movements in order to prevent any dilution of revolutionary ideals. Liu Shao-chi, the president of the Republic, favored consolidation of the social and economic gains of the revolution by increasing reliance on bureaucratic and technocratic expertise. Beneath these ar-

guments was a power struggle between radicals and moderates.

In April 1966 Mao ended these debates by launching the Cultural Revolution. Its aim, as outlined in Mao's directive of May 1966, was to mobilize the masses and stimulate the growth of self-sufficient communes and rural industrialization. According to Mao, workers, peasants, students and artists were interchangeable. Urban professionals and students sent out to the communes to work under the direction of peasants would, he believed, develop a better understanding of the rural economy. He hoped to create a healthy and self-sufficient rural economy. The decentralization of economic control and the encouragement of mass participation was also intended to curb the spread of bureaucracy and check the trend towards capitalization of production and exchange.

As always, Mao tried to combine ideological aims with practical realities. By 1966, the Chinese higher education system was swamped by the huge rise in student numbers resulting from the post-1949 baby boom, so that all student entries

for that year had to be postponed. Mao decided to recruit these young people into the newly-established revolutionary Red Guards, the spearhead of the Cultural Revolution in the countryside. Mao also hoped that sending the Red Guards into the countryside would help to boost agricultural production.

From Beijing the Red Guards fanned out into the countryside, with an estimated twenty million having been mobilized at the height of the Cultural Revolution. They organized mass rallies, wrote wall posters attacking party officials, bourgeois intellectuals and "capitalist roaders", denounced their teachers and parents, and ransacked party offices. Many ordinary Chinese were killed or tortured by these young fanatics. Economically, culturally and socially, the years of the Cultural Revolution were a disaster for China. Agricultural production and industrial output actually fell, devastating the country.

With the fall of the ultraleftist faction in the Central Committee of the Chinese Communist party in September 1967, the Cultural Revolution began to ebb. Mao himself recognized the difficulties and grew increasingly disillusioned with faction fighting among the Red Guards and eventually ordered them to return to their studies. In October 1968, the party congress confirmed the swing away from revolutionary violence and the return to a semblance of normality.

The Sino-Indian conflict

In 1962 a longstanding border dispute between China and India erupted in conflict. Historically India had secured its northern frontiers by establishing its influence over a string of buffer states – Sikkim, Tibet, Bhutan and Nepal – situated high on the slopes of the Himalayas. However, when China invaded Tibet in 1950–51, Tibet's position as a buffer state was transformed, exposing India's northern frontiers to Chinese penetration. Initially India accepted the situation, but China's ruthless suppression of the uprising in the

Tibetan capital, Lhasa, in March 1959 and the later subjection of Tibet to direct Chinese rule alarmed the Indians, who now faced a massive Chinese military presence on their northern border.

When the Communists took power in China in 1949, they had inherited border problems with several of their neighbors dating back to the colonial period. However, by the early 1960s, Beijing had, by a process of negotiation, already resolved most of its outstanding boundary disputes with its South Asian neighbors. The boundary dispute with India was more difficult to settle and complicated by the Chinese occupation of Tibet. To secure their new territory, the Chinese had started to build a military road to link up with Sinkiang, but this passed through territory claimed by the Indians in the Aksai Chin area north of Kashmir. To make matters worse, on the Assam frontier in the east, the Chinese demanded a revision of the 1914 MacMahon line, which drew China's boundary along the spine of the Himalayas from Bhutan to Burma but had never been formally ratified by Beijing. They insisted that the line pass along the southern slopes of the Himalayas.

In 1962 China suggested to India that the *status quo* on the border be maintained while the two countries negotiated a settlement. However, Jawaharlal Nehru, the Indian prime minister, rejected the proposal and ordered the Indian army to expel the Chinese. The first skirmishes took place on 20 September 1962 and a month later the Chinese launched a decisive full-scale attack. On 21 November, the Chinese declared a unilateral ceasefire, by which time they had securely occupied almost all the territory they had claimed.

The defeat was a humiliation for India and a blow to the aspirations of the nonaligned movement, as Nehru, its chief spokesman, had been forced to appeal to the United States to consider direct military intervention. On the other side, the Soviet Union's neutrality in the face of an attack upon its Communist ally angered the Chinese and led to the Sino-Soviet split.

Indo-Pakistan conflict

At the time of the British departure from India, and its division into the sovereign states of India and Pakistan in 1947, the political status of the numerous states ruled by princes was left unresolved. It was hoped that they would seek accession to India or Pakistan in accordance with the broad principles of partition, the majority Muslim states acceding to Pakistan and the rest to India. In Kashmir, however, a state with a three-quarters Muslim population and sharing borders with both Pakistan and India, the local Hindu ruler demanded autonomy. The Muslim population rose in revolt, giving Pakistan the pretext to invade. Belatedly, the ruler opted for accession to India, and, against all the principles on which India was partitioned, the Delhi government accepted, dispatching troops to Kashmir to drive out the Pakistanis. Kashmir's incorporation into India, however, was never accepted by Pakistan.

Unable to deal with India on its own, Pakistan sought outside help and, in 1954, signed a mutual

defense agreement with the United States, which was looking for an ally to contain Communism in Asia. Early in 1965 rioting in Kashmir gave a newly fortified Pakistan the opportunity to reopen the Kashmir question by force. Politicians in Islamabad hoped that as the Pakistani armored columns punched deep into the Himalayan province, the Kashmiris would rise in support and drive the Indians out. The plan backfired, however, because India, believing Kashmir to be indefensible, launched a massive attack on Pakistan itself. Islamabad was forced to pull back its forces from Kashmir to protect its frontier with India and the war ended in stalemate on 17 September 1965. Under Soviet persuasion, both sides agreed to withdraw their troops and the *status quo ante bellum* was restored.

The emergence of Bangladesh

The Indo-Pakistan war of 1971, which led to the secession of East Pakistan as the new state of Bangladesh, was a sequel to the 1965 conflict. Many in the predominantly Bengali Muslim province of East Pakistan did not share the hostility toward India of the politicians in Islamabad. Before 1965 the two wings of Pakistan, East and West, had been held together by the threat of Indian expansion. Yet in 1947 and 1965 India had made no attempt to take advantage of East Pakistan's defenselessness.

Increasingly, after 1965, the Bengalis, convinced that India had no designs on them, began to demand greater autonomy in order to escape the economic exploitation of West Pakistan. Mass agitation eventually forced the military rulers in Islamabad to hold a general election in 1970, the first since Pakistan's formation in 1947. The result was a clearcut victory for the Awami League, the Bengali party, which had led the preelection agitation for autonomous status. The Pakistani junta, however, refused to hand over power to a civilian regime in East Pakistan, particularly one dominated by the despised Bengalis.

In March 1971, West Pakistan invaded, forcing millions of Bengalis to flee into neighboring India. At first, the Delhi government refrained from intervention, but provided weapons and supplies for the Bengalis to continue their fight for independence. However, on 3 December 1971, the Pakistani airforce rashly launched a preemptive strike on India, and the two countries found themselves at war for the third time. The outcome was never in doubt. East Pakistan, separated from West Pakistan by over 1,500 kilometers of hostile Indian territory, was virtually impossible to defend and Pakistan's international allies proved unreliable. On the Indian side, the Soviet Union, by contrast, used its veto in the UN Security Council to ensure that no hasty ceasefire would deprive Delhi of total victory. Unlike the previous wars, this conflict was decisive: Pakistan was truncated and Bangladesh emerged as an independent state.

The United States and the Vietnam War

At the Geneva conference of 1954 Vietnam, a former French colony, was handed over to the Vietnamese. The country was divided between

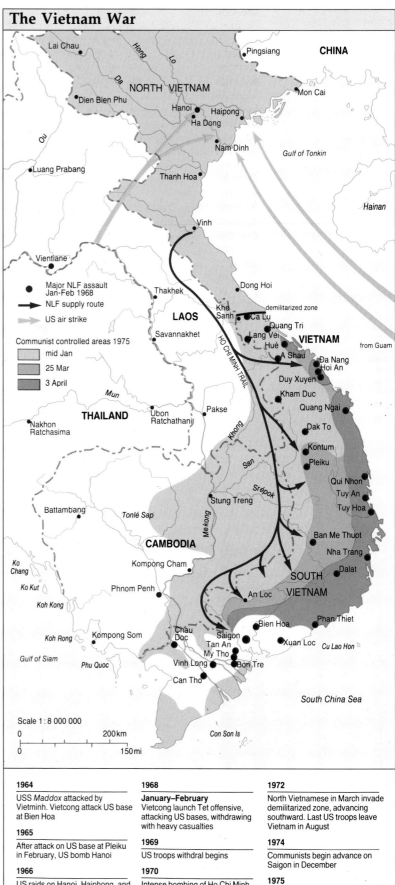

The Vietnam War

Major NLF assault Jan–Feb 1968
NLF supply route
US air strike

Communist controlled areas 1975
mid Jan
25 Mar
3 April

Scale 1 : 8 000 000

0   200km
0   150mi

1964
USS *Maddox* attacked by Vietminh. Vietcong attack US base at Bien Hoa

1965
After attack on US base at Pleiku in February, US bomb Hanoi

1966
US raids on Hanoi, Haiphong, and Communist strongholds in Saigon shelled

1967
North Vietnam attacks Laos

1968
January–February
Vietcong launch Tet offensive, attacking US bases, withdrawing with heavy casualties

1969
US troops withdral begins

1970
Intense bombing of Ho Chi Minh trail, to cut Vietcong supplies

1971
Southern offensive in Laos to cut Ho Chi Minh trail abandoned

1972
North Vietnamese in March invade demilitarized zone, advancing southward. Last US troops leave Vietnam in August

1974
Communists begin advance on Saigon in December

1975
Communists in March begin attack on Saigon, which falls on April 30

1976
Vietnam formally united

▶ The real victims of the Vietnam War were the Vietnamese civilians. In the south, the situation was particularly severe, with people like mother and her mutilated child being caught between ruthless bids for political control by Communist guerrilla forces and clumsy US attempts at counterinsurgency in which devastating firepower was employed indiscriminately. These horrors were brought direct to the US public by newspaper and television, causing widespread revulsion against the war.

▼ The limits of air power – North Vietnamese peasants move past bomb craters left in their rice fields by US air attack. American air raids on the north were largely ineffectual, the predominantly rural economy of the country providing few obvious strategic objectives and little scope for serious damage or disruption by anything short of nuclear attack.

the Communist Democratic Republic of Vietnam in the North and the pro-Western South Vietnam. The terms of the Geneva agreement required that elections be held in 1956 to unify the country, but the South Vietnamese government, fearing a Communist victory, reneged on its Geneva pledge. Meanwhile the United States saw South Vietnam as a bastion against Communism in Asia and began to pour aid into the capital, Saigon, to build up South Vietnamese defenses against the North.

However, the South Vietnamese regime, under President Ngo Dinh Diem, was corrupt, and the Communist National Liberation Front (NLF), or Vietcong, a guerrilla force supported by North Vietnam and China, formed in December 1960, enjoyed widespread local support. To prevent a Communist takeover, President Kennedy massively increased US military assistance. In November 1963, Diem was killed in a US-backed coup and replaced by a military junta, who also proved powerless to halt the Vietcong insurgency.

The conflict intensified after the so-called Gulf of Tonkin incident in August 1964, when the US government accused North Vietnamese leaders of ordering the torpedoing of two US destroyers in North Vietnamese waters. Between 1963 and 1968, the number of US combat troops in Vietnam rose from 16,000 to over half a million. The

North Vietnamese responded by deploying regular forces in the South to aid the Vietcong. The United States launched massive bombing raids against the North and employed napalm and defoliants, but in vain. At last, in the face of mounting domestic opposition to the war, President Johnson made an offer of unconditional peace negotiations in April 1965. This was rejected, because both the North Vietnamese and the Vietcong were determined to secure a united Vietnam. The devastating Tet offensive of 1968 eventually forced the Americans to the conference table to sue for peace.

War in the Congo

After achieving independence from Belgium, the Congo, scene of some of the worst excesses in the history of European colonialism in Africa, remained a byword for political exploitation and brutality. Even as late as the mid-1950s, few in Belgium had given any serious thought to the transfer of power. This complacency was rudely shaken at the end of the 1950s when the Congo, like other African colonies, was caught up in a wave of anticolonial nationalist agitation. British withdrawal from the Gold Coast (renamed Ghana) in 1957 and the rapid devolution of power in Nigeria raised political expectations in equatorial Africa. In 1959 riots broke out in Léopoldville, and soon spread to other Congolese towns. A hastily convened decolonization conference, meeting in Brussels in January 1960, fixed the transfer of power for the following June after Belgian business interests had been secured.

However, the Congo was unprepared for independence. A huge territory, it contained numerous ethnic groups and tribes each with different political aspirations. Patrice Lumumba's Mouvement National Congolais tried to secure a national following by cutting across ethnic affiliations, but its main support derived from the Oriental and Kivu provinces. The other main party, Abako, led by Joseph Kasavubu, was a mouthpiece of the dominant Bakongo tribe from Léopoldville province.

Within hours of the independence celebrations on 4 July 1960, the Armée Nationale Congolaise revolted. Moise Tshombe, Prime Minister of the copper-rich Katanga province, declared Katangan independence and received the backing of Brussels and the main Belgian mining conglomerate, the Union Minière du Haut, as well as the influential Katangan elite, who opposed

▲ UN forces arrive in Katanga at the height of the Congolese civil war. One of the most confused and bloody of Africa's decolonization conflicts, this war was complicated by Belgian interference and the use of white mercenaries by the rival Congolese factions. Its final resolution owed a great deal to one of the rare instances of effective UN intervention.

sharing wealth with the rest of the country. Within weeks of their withdrawal, the Belgians had rushed paratroops back to the Congo, ostensibly to protect the lives of Belgian citizens, but in reality to support Tshombe and to protect Belgium's mineral interests in Kitona and Kanina. The Congolese president, Kasavubu, and his prime minister, Lumumba, appealed to the UN for assistance. The UN responded by dispatching a 20,000-strong force to the Congo. But it confined its activities to expelling the Belgians and gave no help to Lumumba's attempts to crush the Katangan rebellion. Following Lumumba's murder by Tshombe in February 1961, the Congo split into three parts, each with its own government: Tshombe in Katanga, Kasavubu in Léopoldville (now Kinshasa), and Antoine Gizenga, Lumumba's successor, in Stanleyville (now Kisangani). The civil war dragged on for nearly two years, with the UN forces rendered largely ineffective by the divided counsel of the major powers who were aligned on different sides of the conflict. Only after heavy fighting did Katanga finally fall to the UN forces, and on 16 January 1963 Tshombe agreed to end his secessionist movement.

The Nigerian civil war

Like the Congo, Nigeria was an artificial creation. Boundaries drawn for imperial convenience in the 19th century bore little relationship to cultural and tribal demarcations. The 1961 census estimated its population at 55 million and listed eight ethnic groups with populations of over a million, and a further twenty-seven smaller ones. Nigerian politics were dominated by three groups: the Muslim Hausa-Fulani in the north, who occupied nearly four-fifths of the entire country, the Yoruba kingdom in the west, with a mixed Muslim and Christian population, and the mainly Christian Ibo in the east.

The Nigerian constitution of 1960 retained the old colonial administrative units under a new federal system. The powers of the federal government in the capital, Lagos, were kept in check by

◀ Belgium, one of the smallest of the European colonial powers, was also one of the most tenacious in its attempts to maintain power in Africa. Cynical political maneuvering, and the use of military force to defend longstanding economic interests were in a large measure responsible for the bloody civil war which attended the Congo's passage from colonial rule to a precarious independence.

▶ Congolese soldiers torment prisoners prior to execution. The civil war in the Congo was notorious for the atrocities carried out by the rival forces. The causes of this barbarity were a complicated mixture of tribal rivalries, the disruption of normal patterns of life by colonial exploitation, the intrusion of white mercenaries and the widespread use of badly trained and undisciplined soldiers. Responsibility lay mostly with the departing colonial power — which behaved with cynical brutality throughout.

placing the government under the joint control of the three major ethnic groups. However, in the early 1960s, this delicate balance was upset when the numerically superior Hausa-Fulani attempted to gain control by manipulating electoral procedures, particularly in the Yoruba west, which soon became a client region of the north. Lagos's blatant interference in regional affairs provoked widespread popular unrest, which prompted the army to seize power in January 1966.

General Ironsi, the army strongman, had little understanding of the strength of interethnic feelings or the abhorrence of outside control among the minorities. When, in May 1966, he abolished the regional governments and placed them under direct central authority, the regions reacted violently. Ironsi himself was killed in July 1966 in a military coup which brought Colonel Yakubu Gowon to power.

The failure of the constitution invited calls for change. The Ibos, in particular, demanded greater federal autonomy and limitation of the powers of the center. However Gowon, like his predecessor Ironsi, was an advocate of centralization, and his attitude reflected the interests of the ethnic groups from the "Middle Belt". Moreover, a strong central government, which was dominated by Gowon's fellow tribespeople, would be able to control the vital foreign exchange earnings from the Biafran oilfields in the east. In May 1967 Gowon divided Nigeria into 12 states answerable directly to a federal administration in Lagos.

On 30 May 1967 the Ibos revolted and Colonel Ojukwu proclaimed Biafra an independent state. In the ensuing civil war (1967–71), Gowon succeeded in preventing Biafran secession, but the costs in both economic and human terms were enormous.

The Arab–Israeli "Six-Day" war

The wars of 1948 and 1956 between Israel and its Arab neighbors had failed to resolve their differences. Israel, backed by her powerful Western allies, was able to defy the combined military strength of the Arabs and ignore international protests at the plight of Palestinian refugees. Tensions mounted in the early 1960s as the Palestinians began to launch guerrilla attacks on Israel from Arab sanctuaries. The immediate cause for renewed hostility, however, was Israel's irrigation and waterwork system, completed in 1964, which siphoned off scarce resources from the region between Lake Galilee and the Negev desert.

The crisis led to a rare moment of unity among the Arab states. In May 1967, the Egyptian president ordered the withdrawal of the UN emergency force which had policed Sinai since 1956 and threatened to close the vital straits of Sharm al-Sheikh at the head of the Red Sea, to Israeli vessels. In preparation for war, Egypt and Jordan placed their forces under joint command and were soon joined by Iraq. Israel, unnerved by the unprecedented Arab unity and chafing under the Al-Fatah guerrilla attacks, seized upon Nasser's threat to Sharm al-Sheikh as a pretext to strike. On 5 June 1967, Israel launched a devastating attack, destroying Egypt's air force on the ground. Deprived of air cover, the Egyptian armies were caught at the Gidi and Mitla passes in northern Sinai and annihilated. The war was over in six days. By the end, Israel had occupied Egyptian territory as far as the Suez Canal and the Straits of Tiran, had annexed all of Jordan west of the Jordan River, including Jerusalem, and had wrested control of the vital Golan Heights from Syria. These acquisitions made Israel far less vulnerable and far less amenable to a negotiated settlement on the Palestinian question.

▼ Starvation in Biafra – a young Biafran mother, aged by malnutrition, tries to feed her baby from an empty breast. The Biafran war (1967–70) was a small-scale military conflict, prolonged by the low fighting capabilities of both sides, which turned into a human disaster of major proportions due to the collapse of the marginal economy of the breakaway Biafran state. A devastating famine ensued, whose effects were mitigated only slightly by the launching of a worldwide relief operation.

We have pretended for too long that there are no differences between the peoples of this country. The hard fact which we must honestly accept is that we are different peoples brought together by recent accidents of history. To pretend otherwise would be folly.

NORTHERN NIGERIAN 1966

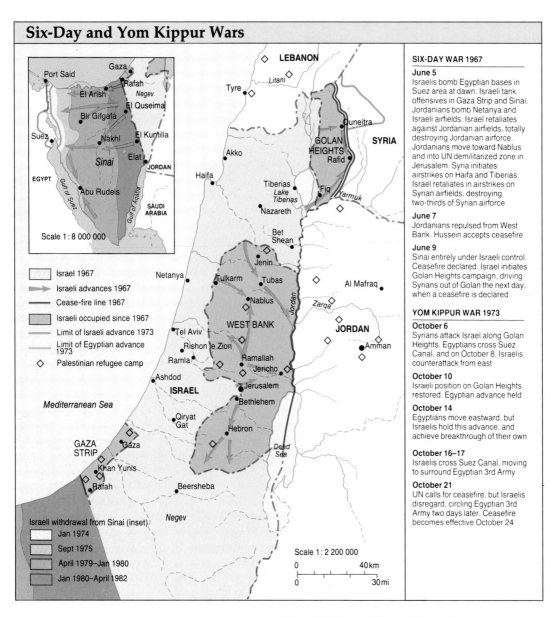

Six-Day and Yom Kippur Wars

LEBANON
SYRIA
GOLAN HEIGHTS
JORDAN
EGYPT
SAUDI ARABIA
ISRAEL
WEST BANK
GAZA STRIP

Port Said
Gaza
Rafah
Negev
El Arish
El Queseima
Bir Gifgafa
El Kuntilla
Suez
Nakhl
Elat
Sinai
Gulf of Suez
Gulf of Aqaba
Abu Rudeis
Scale 1 : 8 000 000

Tyre
Litani
Quneitra
Akko
Rafid
Haifa
Tiberias
Lake Tiberias
Fiq
Yarmuk
Nazareth
Bet Shean
Jenin
Netanya
Tulkarm
Tubas
Al Mafraq
Nablus
Zarqa
Jordan
JORDAN
Tel Aviv
Rishon le Zion
Amman
Ramla
Ramallah
Jericho
Ashdod
Jerusalem
Bethlehem
Qiryat Gat
Hebron
Dead Sea
Gaza
Khan Yunis
Rafah
Beersheba
Mediterranean Sea
Negev

Legend:
- Israel 1967
- Israeli advances 1967
- Cease-fire line 1967
- Israeli occupied since 1967
- Limit of Israeli advance 1973
- Limit of Egyptian advance 1973
- ◇ Palestinian refugee camp

Israeli withdrawal from Sinai (inset)
- Jan 1974
- Sept 1975
- April 1979–Jan 1980
- Jan 1980–April 1982

Scale 1 : 2 200 000
0   40km
0   30mi

SIX-DAY WAR 1967

June 5
Israelis bomb Egyptian bases in Suez area at dawn. Israeli tank offensives in Gaza Strip and Sinai. Jordanians bomb Netanya and Israeli airfields. Israel retaliates against Jordanian airfields, totally destroying Jordanian airforce. Jordanians move toward Nablus and into UN demilitarized zone in Jerusalem. Syria initiates airstrikes on Haifa and Tiberias. Israel retaliates in airstrikes on Syrian airfields, destroying two-thirds of Syrian airforce

June 7
Jordanians repulsed from West Bank. Hussein accepts ceasefire

June 9
Sinai entirely under Israeli control. Ceasefire declared. Israel initiates Golan Heights campaign, driving Syrians out of Golan the next day, when a ceasefire is declared

YOM KIPPUR WAR 1973

October 6
Syrians attack Israel along Golan Heights. Egyptians cross Suez Canal, and on October 8, Israelis counterattack from east

October 10
Israeli position on Golan Heights restored. Egyptian advance held

October 14
Egyptians move eastward, but Israelis hold this advance, and achieve breakthrough of their own

October 16–17
Israelis cross Suez Canal, moving to surround Egyptian 3rd Army

October 21
UN calls for ceasefire, but Israelis disregard, circling Egyptian 3rd Army two days later. Ceasefire becomes effective October 24

◀ In both 1967 and 1973 Israel successfully fought brief but decisive two-front wars against her Arab neighbors – in 1967 capturing the whole of Sinai, the West Bank and the Golan Heights in a daring pre-emptive attack, and in 1973 recovering from a surprise enemy offensive to cross the Suez Canal in the west and open the road to Damascus in the northeast.

▼ Jerusalem, August 1967: a young Israeli soldier makes his religious observances at the sacred "Wailing Wall", the Israeli capture of the city, had formed between the Israeli and another bloody episode in the bitter war with the Palestinians, for whom, also, this territory is home.

Kissinger and Shuttle Diplomacy

"Shuttle diplomacy" was the creation of Dr Henry Kissinger, US Secretary of State under President Nixon. His method was to travel to and fro between the capitals concerned, conveying the proposals and responses of each party to the other, but also injecting his own ideas and building up momentum in such a way as to give neither the chance to withdraw, until the point was reached where the parties were ready to sign an agreement which satisfied them both.

The first systematic use of this technique, and of the term "shuttle diplomacy" to describe it, can be dated to January 1974. In seven rounds of talks, four in Egypt and three in Israel, compressed into a single week, Dr Kissinger succeeded in drawing up an Egyptian-Israeli agreement for military disengagement in Sinai, which was signed on 18 January. In May of the same year, using the same method, he secured a parallel disengagement agreement between Israel and Syria on the Golan Heights: this time the shuttle lasted four weeks.

The Arab-Israeli "Yom Kippur" war

The death of the Egyptian leader Nasser in November 1970 led to a major shift in international alignments. Anwar Sadat, Egypt's pragmatic new President, responded to Washington's desire for improved relations by breaking with the Soviet Union. This new US-Egyptian rapprochement widened Washington's commitments in the Middle East beyond the preservation of Israel and enabled Sadat to forge a greater unity between Egypt, Saudi Arabia, Jordan and Syria in their opposition to Israel. Sadat also offered to negotiate bilaterally with the Israeli government.

The Palestinians were again central to the Arab-Israeli conflict. Following the Arab defeat of 1967, Palestinian guerrillas had decided that it was futile to depend on the Arab states for the recovery of their homeland. Instead, they determined to shock the world into an awareness of their plight by hijacking and blowing up passenger airplanes owned by Western countries, and by a spate of guerrilla attacks against Israel. But neither Sadat's sinuous diplomacy nor the terrorist tactics of the Palestinians could shake

▲ Israeli forces drive past Egyptian prisoners on their way to the Suez Canal during the Yom Kippur war of October 1973. The surprise Egyptian attack on the Israeli defensive line along the canal's west bank was a dramatic success, but failure to exploit the breakthrough and a rapid Israeli counteroffensive turned the situation into a disaster for the attackers. The Israelis threatened an advance on the Egyptian capital and a negotiated settlement was hurriedly reached under pressure from the USA and Soviet Union.

Israel's resolve. To break the deadlock, the Egyptian president, on 6 October 1973, ordered his forces to cross the Suez Canal, catching the Israelis unawares as they celebrated the Yom Kippur festival (day of atonement). The United States rushed to Israel's support, flying in massive military reinforcements,which helped Tel Aviv blunt the Egyptian attack, and soon put its own forces on the Cairo side of the canal.

The war ended in stalemate, exposing on the one hand Israel's vulnerability and on the other the continuing limitation of Arab arms. The conflict impressed on both sides the need for a political solution and gave the United States the opportunity to renew its role of mediator. The US Secretary of State, Henry Kissinger worked through shuttle diplomacy to bring about a reconciliation between Cairo and Tel Aviv. However, by concentrating on the Egyptian–Israeli border dispute, and failing to tackle the crucial Palestinian question, Kissinger and successive US administrations condemned the Middle East to continuing turmoil. Indeed, the unilateral peace between Egypt and Israel broke Arab unity, isolated Egypt and removed its moderating

influence in Arab affairs. The hope that similar agreements between Tel Aviv and other Arab states would follow was unfulfilleed.

The Yom Kippur War did nothing to resolve the Arab–Israeli conflict. However, the Arab states, in their newfound solidarity, emerged from it with a new economic weapon. Controlling the world's largest reserves of oil, they were in a position to disrupt supplies to the oil-dependent economies of the industrialized West. In December 1973, the Organization of Petroleum Exporting Countries (OPEC) announced a 70 percent increase in prices and threatened to lower production by five percent a month until Israel's Western backers forced them to evacuate the occupied territories. This did have some diplomatic impact. Britain stopped supplying arms to Israel, Japan reversed pro-Israeli policy, and the European Community (with the exception of the Netherlands) publicly censured Israel for obstructing the settlement of the Palestinian question. Even the United States was caught in the world recession touched off by the oil price increases. No longer could Israel's Western friends afford to ignore Arab demands.

PHOTOJOURNALISM

When American reporter John L. Spivak wrote an exposé of conditions in Florida chain gangs in 1931, he insisted on photographs to support his charges. Throughout the century photographs have been used as dramatic documents, not only illustrating historically significant events but influencing their reception.

In the 1930s the technology of small 35mm cameras and highspeed film made candid photography much easier, and created a new kind of news reporter, the photojournalist. Whether making single images for newspapers or for picture magazines such as *Life*, photojournalism was committed to the idea that the photograph was an impartial document.

And yet few forms of photography have shown themselves so open to distortion. Photographs rely on the words in their captions to supply and specify their meaning, a meaning which can be changed with the wording of the caption in perhaps the simplest and most obvious kind of manipulation. Among the most blatant instances of using photographs to re-order reality were Soviet pictures of the Politburo, in which discredited members had been removed by retouching. In the West the manipulation of the photographed image has more often been the result of a photographer's conflicting motivations. He or she has sought to present an "accurate record" of the event, yet also to provide a dramatic image.

After World War II the war photographer became an alternative hero to the soldier, shooting with a camera instead of a gun. In the wars since then, particularly in Vietnam, this heroic image was intensified by the unpopularity of the war. Every picture of the Vietnam war seemed to be an anti-war image, and photographers like Sean Flynn and Tim Page appeared as heroic figures who went into the hell of modern warfare.

But war photography required skills and a sense of detachment which seem frighteningly inhuman. On occasion, photojournalists become accomplices, however unwillingly, in the atrocities they photograph. The presence of news and television cameras guarantees publicity to those prepared to turn themselves or others into a spectacle for public consumption. Photographs of the atrocities of war or famine carry a powerful emotional charge for their viewers, but the effects of that charge may be questioned. British photographer Don McCullin's acutely painful images of the war in Cambodia appeared opposite advertisements for cars and perfume in the *Sunday Times Magazine*, and whatever their emotional effect upon the newspaper's readers, they did not lead its editors to change their policy of support for the American presence in Southeast Asia.

Many commentators, however, concluded that the cumulative press and media coverage of Vietnam had been an important factor in generating domestic opposition to the war, and military advisors voiced their reluctance to allows journalists free access to battlefields again.

▲ ▲ The Hungarian-born Robert Capa developed many of the techniques of modern photojournalism during the Spanish Civil War. His image of the decisive moment – such as this one of a Loyalist soldier being felled by a bullet in 1938, influenced much later photography.

▲ News photography of events such as famines in Africa in the late 1980s has proved a powerful means of turning the attention of the world to a crisis. Overfamiliarity with such images, however, may tend to soften the effect.

▶ The photograph of the naked girl in Vietnam, fleeing down the road and screaming from napalm burns, became world-famous as an indictment of the horrors of modern war. Yet other pictures taken at the same scene show the photographer as detached observer, seeking the most powerful image rather than helping the victims: journalists shot them with cameras while soldiers shot with rifles.

◀ When a Buddhist monk decided to burn himself to death in 1963 in protest at the Vietnam war, his sacrifice was consciously captured. His fellow monks recorded the event on film, ensuring that the protest would not be in vain, even if the world's press failed to arrive.

▼ While some photo-opportunities are carefully exploited, others are created. This image of the raising of the American flag on Iwo Jima in February 1945, was carefully posed and photographed by Joe Rosenthal hours after the actual event.

Datafile

The turmoil of the 1960s had far-reaching effects in the First World. Advances in levels of education had produced a large and politically radical student population. Demands for increased government spending on social services were leading to large increases in the public sector. Internationally, the antagonism between Israel and its Arab neighbors was reaching crisis point, exacerbated by increased superpower interest in the strategic assets of the Middle East.

▼ In addition to the rapid growth in overall student numbers in many countries, the proportion studying liberal subjects, sociology and politics also rose, contributing to student radicalism. Student unrest was felt all over Europe and Japan as well as in the USA.

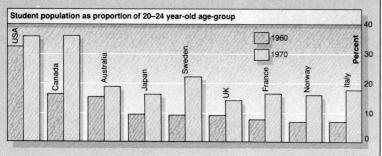

Student population as proportion of 20–24 year-old age-group

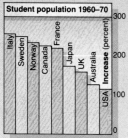

Student population 1960–70

► By 1967 the nations of the Middle East had built up large and well-equipped armed forces (supported by the USA). Although Israel's was the largest single force in the region, it was seriously outnumbered by those of its enemies combined. Only superior training, instruction and organization could guarantee Israel's survival.

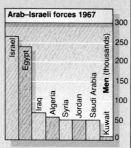

Arab–Israeli forces 1967

▲ Between 1960 and 1970 the student population of the Western world grew dramatically, both in absolute numbers and as a proportion of the under-20 age group. This resulted in a politically aware generation of generally progressive (and sometimes radical) views unlikely to accept established values.

▼ ► Israel's triumph in 1967 only made another war inevitable, and in a period of escalating tension, both Israel and her strongest enemy Egypt steadily increased military spending in an effort to re-equip their forces. Although Egypt made substantial progress, the surprise attack on Israel in 1973 turned into a disaster.

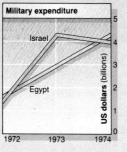

Military expenditure

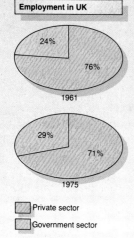

Employment in UK

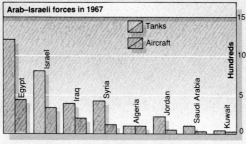

Arab–Israeli forces in 1967

◄ During the 1960s and early 1970s, Britain responded to public pressure for improved social services with increasingly heavy taxation. By 1975 well over a quarter of the UK workforce was employed in the public sector, and critics were beginning to see this as injurious to national well-being.

Since World War II the Eastern bloc states, held together largely by Soviet military might, have harbored the desire for greater autonomy. Beneath the Cold War rhetoric and outward displays of Communist unity nationalist aspirations have continued to burn strong, often flaring up as in Czechoslovakia in 1968.

Until then Czechoslovakia had been a most docile satellite, primarily because of the repressiveness of the regimes of Klement Gottwald and Antonin Novotny. In the mid-1960s, however, the worsening economic situation there provoked a movement toward political liberalization. Czechoslovakia's industrial decline was partly due to the Cold War and the consequent erection of economic barriers between East and West. Trade restrictions hit Czechoslovakia particularly hard because earlier it had been economically more allied with Western Europe than had its neighbors.

The Novotny regime cautiously accepted the need to decentralize economic planning, but found it difficult to implement reforms in a society dominated by the Czech Politburo's rigid adherence to Soviet-style Communism. By the late 1960s, with the Communist world in ferment, Czechoslovakia was ripe for change.

In January 1968, First Secretary Novotny was stripped of power and replaced by the reform-minded Alexander Dubček. Five months later, General Jan Svoboda, a nationalist and war hero, became President of the Republic. Dubček immediately relaxed press censorship, removed a number of hard-liners from the government and initiated a debate on the democratization of the Czech Communist party (CCP). In April, the Presidium of the CCP drafted an Action Program. This Program marked the beginning of the short-lived "Prague Spring". Its demands included the rehabilitation of victims of the 1940 Stalinist purge, the freedom of minor parties within the Communist-controlled National Front government, the democratization of the social and political system, equal rights for minorities, and, above all, more open government.

Whereas Dubček ensured that his personal relations with the Soviets remained cordial, he could not hide the fact that the reforms in Czechoslovakia implied a criticism of Soviet policies. Most alarming from the Soviet point of view was that the Czech reform program implicitly called into question the role of the Communist party and its relationship to government. The Soviets had learned from past experience that demands for political change in one Eastern bloc state would inevitably spread to others. Dubček had not only drawn closer to Tito and Ceauşescu, but, the Soviets feared, was also seeking closer ties with West Germany.

1968 AND AFTER

Failure of the "Prague Spring"

Uprising in France

The anti-Vietnam War movement

Germany and *Ostpolitik*

Arms control talks

Nuclear Nonproliferation Treaty

SALT I

Political extremism in West Germany

US withdrawal from Vietnam

Sino-US entente

The Watergate scandal

Britain and the EEC

Tensions mounted, and on 15 July the leaders of the USSR, East Germany, Hungary, Poland and Bulgaria met in Warsaw to send a joint communication to Dubček urging him to suppress his "antisocialist" program. Shortly afterwards, *Pravda* alleged that US arms had been discovered in Czechoslovakia, and a following Soviet note suggested that Soviet troops be posted on Czechoslovakia's western frontiers in order to guarantee its security. Dubček, sensing the danger of intervention, assured the Warsaw Pact allies at a meeting held on 3 August in Bratislava that Czechoslovakia would stand by its Warsaw Pact commitments.

On 10 August 1968, however, the CCP published new statutes aimed at ending "democratic centralism" (Communist orthodoxy) and granting substantial rights to the minor parties in the National Front. It seemed to the Soviets that Dubček could not, or would not, halt the reform movement and that their only option now was to remove him.

On 20 August Soviet troops, backed by other Warsaw Pact forces, crossed into Czechoslovakia.

They met with no resistance. The Soviet invasion met with worldwide condemnation, including criticism from many West European Communist parties. Moreover, as the Czechs remained firmly behind Dubček, the Soviets could not set up a collaborationist regime to replace him. Soon, he and other Czech leaders who had been arrested had to be reinstated.

However, this respite was only temporary, unlike the damage done to the Czech reform movement. In 1969, Dubček was dispatched to Turkey as Czechoslovakia's ambassador, before being recalled and expelled from the party. But the Czech people continued to see him as a hero. He was eventually replaced by Gustav Husak, a former member of Dubček's government.

The invasion of Czechoslovakia was one of several examples of the Soviet Union taking action against its allies; politicians in Moscow considered it their duty to prevent deviation. Under Leonid Brezhnev, this idea was developed into a doctrine named after him. This held that neither internal nor external forces would be permitted to change the socialist system into a capitalist one.

▼ **Men against tanks – Czech youths throw Molotov cocktails and stones in fruitless resistance as the Soviet army moves into Prague. Alarmed at the pace of liberalization under the new Dubček regime, the USSR sent in its army to reassert Communist orthodoxy and eliminate any chance of further reforms taking the country out of the Soviet bloc.**

▲▶ The state seen as the enemy of its people – this French portrayal of the police as armed, omnipresent (even on the radio) and unhuman typifies the attitudes of the student protesters of 1968. Here, protesters fill a Paris boulevard at the height of the 1968 uprising. In scenes reminiscent of the turbulent years of the previous century, barricades were thrown up, and cars and other property destroyed. Armed riot police were deployed, with tear gas and baton charges the order of the day. Although order was eventually restored without revolution, new forms of government were clearly necessary.

▼ Make love not war – an anti-Vietnam War demonstrator confronts a nervous National Guardsman. In the US, opposition to the stalemated war in Southeast Asia and to the military draft escalated in the late 1960s. Media coverage of the conflict transformed protest into a broad-based rejection of war and the sinister role of the state.

An extension of the "Brezhnev doctrine" was later invoked as justification for the Soviet invasion of Afghanistan in December 1979, and the threat of intervention hung over the Poles during the crisis with the Solidarity movement between 1980 and 1982.

Uprising in France

The Paris student uprising of May 1968, which was sparked off by problems within the French university system, formed part of a broader movement against governmental insensitivity, authoritarianism and patriarchalism everywhere. When, at the tailend of the "swinging sixties", inflation pushed up prices and wages could not keep pace, a niggling dissatisfaction peaked. To many of the young, in particular, modern society was cruel and unjust.

In the late 1960s student unrest was common, perhaps especially in France, where an inadequate system was strained to breaking point by an ever-increasing student influx. But, on 3 May 1968, a conflict that had started at Nanterre, an annex of Paris University, spread to the Sorbonne itself, and became a national movement. Moderate and radical students erected barricades on the left bank of the Seine. Police excesses were widely reported in the media, earning sympathy for the students from the French middle class. Workers in education and industry soon joined the students on the streets. By mid-May strikes in factories and mines resulted in some ten million workers being laid off.

President de Gaulle, encouraged by receiving pledges of support from the military, decided to see the crisis through and ignored calls on him to resign from members of his government.

By the end of May, the initial enthusiasm for the uprising had begun to wane, for although some students were political revolutionaries out to overthrow the state, most were concerned primarily with educational reforms. The French workers who had supported the movement were for the most part moderates whose grievances were economic.

De Gaulle's firm resolution and acute understanding of the crisis had enabled the government to weather the storm. When he sensed that the mood of the French people had become one of alarm, he called a snap general election. The result was a resounding victory for the Gaullists who mustered 291 seats, enough to form a government on their own for the first time.

With the elections over, the government began to address student grievances. Edgar Faure, the new Education Minister, drew up extensive reforms, whose effect, however, was limited. Paris continued to have the final say over the content of university curricula and examinations as well as the allocation of funds. Indeed, through lack of finance many reforms did not go beyond the planning stage. Instead, the government tried to reduce overcrowding by making university entry more selective – a risky policy which might have sparked off another revolt had it not been for the political caution exercised by the French government after May 1968 as well as the earnest desire of most middle-class French people to avoid further major upheavals.

The anti-Vietnam War movement

No conflict since the US Civil War (1861-65) has left deeper scars in the United States than Vietnam. The first war to receive extensive television coverage, it invaded the homes of millions of Americans, who nightly saw their young men dying in the jungles and on the battlefields. Many American liberals began to question the wisdom and morality of committing half a million GIs to the defense of a corrupt and incompetent regime in Saigon. Some even admired the courage and resourcefulness of the Vietcong, the liberation fighters in the South, and their North Vietnamese allies.

President Johnson saw his popularity plummet. Protesters who gathered in their thousands outside the White House taunted the President with their chants of "Hey! Hey! LBJ! How many kids did you kill today?", as mass antiwar demonstrations engulfed Washington. Across the country on university campuses students protested their opposition to the war and the drafting of young men to fight in it by actions of civil disobedience. Some of the demonstrations turned violent when police or National Guardsmen clashed with students, and thousands of arrests were made.

As the US casualty toll in the Vietnam War mounted, so the protests increased. By the end, the war had claimed some 44,000 American lives. The protests began overtly to flout the law, as many young Americans refused to be drafted and faced imprisonment. Some of the protesters were so appalled by the war, and by middle-class American values generally, that they simply "dropped out" of society or took to drugs. They included disillusioned Vietnam war veterans. The late 1960s were the high-water mark of the "counter-culture", represented by "hippy" communes, psychedelic drugs and free love.

With Johnson's dream of a "Great Society" shattered, and the morale of the US military devastated by the success of the North Vietnamese Tet offensive of January 1968, even members of Johnson's own party called for his removal.

Germany and *Ostpolitik*

For a long time, the question of Germany remained the main stumbling block to superpower détente. Despite the construction of the Berlin Wall, many of the older generation of Germans still clung to the hope that the country would be reunited. When Willy Brandt came to power in 1969, however, he announced that he would accept the political *status quo* in Europe and initiated a policy of détente between East and West. In August 1970, Brandt signed a nonaggression pact with the Soviet Union which recognized the existing frontiers in Eastern Europe. This move opened the way to the Soviet leader Brezhnev's agreement to a Mutual and Balanced Force Reduction (MBFR) conference, which met in Helsinki in January 1973.

Brandt's *Ostpolitik* (East European policy) also achieved some success in its own right. In 1971 East and West Germany signed an agreement which for the first time tacitly endorsed the separate status of the two states. The German settlement removed a vital impediment to the normalization of East-West relations.

Arms control talks

As the arms gap between the United States and the Soviet Union narrowed, it became clear that neither could hope to win a nuclear war. In these circumstances, the superpowers sought to resume the arms limitation talks that had stalled since 1963.

In 1969 President Nixon announced the start of a phased withdrawal of US troops from Vietnam. The West Europeans too looked for a new agreement on arms control to maintain the military balance between NATO and the forces of the Warsaw Pact.

Political Extremism in West Germany

Between 1966 and 1969, during the time of the so-called "big coalition", there was virtually no organized opposition in the West German federal parliament. The worldwide economic crisis increased the disillusion with government and once again facilitated the rise of rightwing extremism.

Founded in 1964, the rightwing National Democratic party (NPD) attracted considerable attention through its fierce antigovernment stance. It demanded the immediate expulsion of foreign workers and the end of war-crime trials for former Nazis. The party's call for the restoration of pride in the "Fatherland" also won the vote of sections of the German youth. By 1969, it had secured some 60 seats in seven state assemblies.

The successes of the NPD angered German students and leftwing groups. The student movement, at first focused on the reform of German universities, soon widened its demands to include social reform. On the far left, Rudi Dutschke's Socialist Students' Federation called for a revolution to overthrow liberal democracy in Germany. The protest movement soon spread to most German university campuses.

To the older generation these events awakened uneasy memories of the 1930s. The Soviet Union, fearing a revival of German fascism, even hinted at the possibility of military intervention to stamp it out. Such a threat coming so soon after the Soviet invasion of Czechoslovakia, the Germans decided, could not be taken lightly and so in the elections of September 1969 they voted heavily for the center-right and center-left parties. The NPD failed to capture even the 5 percent minimum vote needed for a seat. A subsequent upswing in the economy put paid to the resurgence of the right.

► In the Kurfürstendamm, West Berlin's main street, in April 1968, demonstrators are savagely assaulted by police as they make their way to a meeting in protest against the attempt on the life of Rudi Dutschke, a leading member of the Socialist Students' Union (SDS).

▼ The leftwing student movement gave rise to urban terrorist violence with the emergence of the Baader-Meinhof group, which was formed in 1968. After a campaign of violence against economic and political targets, most leading members were arrested in 1972.

Other factors also influenced superpower relations during these years. In 1964, the withdrawal of France – a nuclear power – from the NATO alliance and the economic success of the European Community had made Western Europe less dependent on the United States. The unity of the Soviet bloc was tested by the invasion of Czechoslovakia in 1968, while the improved relations between China and the United States aroused old fears in Moscow. Many newly independent states were nonaligned and their collective political weight represented a third major political force.

While there was little prospect of complete disarmament by the superpowers, the fear of nuclear weapons proliferating to other states eventually drove them toward serious arms limitation talks. When the superpowers' (and Britain's) nuclear monopoly was broken by France in 1964 and China in 1970, arms control suddenly became top of the agenda, with the superpowers united in their desire to prevent others developing a nuclear capability.

In July 1968 the United States, the Soviet Union and Britain signed a Nuclear Non-Proliferation Treaty (NPT), undertaking not to transfer nuclear technology or weapons to nonnuclear powers. The nonnuclear powers were invited to join the NPT by pledging never to develop or acquire nuclear weapons. By 1980, 114 countries had become signatories, although Israel, South Africa, India, Pakistan and Brazil, all of which had nuclear programs capable of weapon production, were significantly not among them.

First proposed by the Soviets, the Strategic Arms Limitation Talks (SALT) began in Geneva in 1969. The SALT I interim agreement, which was eventually ratified by Nixon and Brezhnev on 26 May 1972, stipulated that each side would have only two defensive systems, each with a maximum radius of 120 kilometers. One would protect the capital city and the other, at least 1200 kilometers away, would defend major provincial centers. The treaty was intended to last indefinitely, but was subject to review every five years.

◀Republican supporters celebrate Nixon's landslide victory in the presidential election of 1972. Defeated by Kennedy in his first bid for the presidency, Nixon had narrowly won the right to lead the nation in 1968. While benefiting from a relaxation of the domestic tension of the 1960s, he made his reputation in foreign affairs, successfully extracting the US from the Vietnam War and making milestone visits to the Soviet Union and the People's Republic of China which established him as the unlikely apostle of détente.

◀ US foreign policy continued to revolve around the maintenance of an overpowering nuclear deterrent – a policy which guaranteed US leaders domestic support from traditionalist voters but damaged America's reputation abroad. In both Europe and the Third World, the US came to be seen as the main stumbling-block to progress with arms control.

Although it was modest in scope and had little effect on offensive weapons, SALT I represented the first successful attempt by the superpowers to agree on arms limitations. SALT also provided the basis for future negotiations between Gerald Ford and Leonid Brezhnev, resulting on 24 November 1974 in an agreement on the guidelines for the SALT II treaty. This was eventually ratified by Jimmy Carter in 1978. Indeed, it was not until President Reagan's ambitious Strategic Defense Initiative (SDI) of the 1980s that the strategic parity principle, on which the SALT treaties had been based, was challenged.

US withdrawal from Vietnam
Following Johnson's withdrawal from the political scene, Republican candidate Richard Nixon, campaigning on the twin themes of Vietnam and national unification, defeated Hubert Humphrey in an election which many voters felt had denied them any real political choice. He immediately embarked cautiously on a policy of disengagement from Vietnam. When US forces intervened in Cambodia (Kampuchea) to support the new military government, more than a quarter of a million people marched on Washington and student strikes and sit-ins closed down university campuses right across the country.

US military involvement in Vietnam finally ended in January 1973 with the signing of the Paris Peace Accord. Both sides agreed to end their direct military intervention in the South. On 30 April 1975, North Vietnamese tanks entered Saigon, ending a war that had lasted for 15 years.

Sino-US relations
Ever since Mao Zedong's Communists came to power in 1949, China had been ostracized by the West. The government of the island of Taiwan – all that remained to the Guomindang nationalists after the Chinese civil war – was recognized by the United States and most of its allies as the only legitimate government of China, and accorded a permanent seat in the United Nations Security Council. However, once the Sino-Soviet split became public, Washington began to reassess its policy. A rapprochement with mainland China offered distinct advantages to the Americans. It would drive a deeper wedge into the Communist bloc, and at the same time enable the United States to force the pace in the arms negotiations with Moscow. There were other attractions, too. Despite Mao's quixotic leadership and the failure of the Great Leap Forward, and the Cultural Revolution, the billion-strong Chinese market offered a most tantalizing prospect for American

▲ ▼ By the end of the 1960s, US disillusionment with military involvement in Vietnam was extreme. Frustration at the failure to make any impact on Communist fighting capability was heightened by the high casualties and additional psychological distress of many soldiers.

businessmen. To the Chinese, the Americans offered an opportunity to escape from economic dependence on the Soviet Union.

In 1971, the United States revoked its trade embargo against China, and a visit in July by Henry Kissinger to Beijing paved the way for Nixon's historic tour of China in February 1972. Before his visit, Nixon jettisoned his "two Chinas" policy and did not exercise the US veto in the UN Security Council when China applied to replace Taiwan as a permanent member.

The improvement in Sino-US relations increased pressures on the Soviet Union to reach agreement with the United States on strategic arms limitation. However, speculation concerning the emergence of a tripolar international political system dominated by Beijing, Moscow and Washington was premature, as China, although a fully fledged nuclear power by 1970, remained technologically backward. Burdened by overpopulation and administrative inefficiency, China, even as late as 1960, experienced terrible famines. Internationally, China's alignment with the United States against the Soviet Union on a whole range of issues allayed Western fears of the solidarity within the Communist bloc.

The Watergate scandal

President Nixon's first term of office was marked by important achievements in foreign policy. When Nixon stood for reelection, a nation weary of the Vietnam War continued to see him as its best hope for peace and returned him to the White House for a second term with one of the largest majorities in American history. However, the administration was soon beset by a scandal which exposed corruption, deceit and perjury at the highest level, and led to the ignominious resignation of the president himself.

During the 1972 presidential election campaign, there had been a break-in and bungled attempt to bug the Democratic party offices in the Watergate Building in Washington D.C. Two investigative journalists of *The Washington Post* had reported a link between this burglary and the White House, but few had taken this seriously. The trial of the seven men charged with the Watergate break-in, including three connected with the White House and Nixon's re-election campaign, aroused no more than passing interest. But the presiding law officer decided to withhold judgment in the case pending further inquiries. On promise of a lighter sentence, James McCord, one of the Whitehouse aides, produced evidence which sparked off the Watergate scandal. McCord confirmed previous press speculation that attempts were being made by senior White House staff to block the investigation. The Senate decided to launch its own full-scale inquiry in February 1973.

It soon became clear that White House involvement was much greater than had been admitted. Until March 1973, President Nixon had maintained that he had no knowledge of any of his personal staff being implicated in the cover-up, but on 17 April he was forced to admit that they might have been and to agree to their testifying before the Senate Committee. By the end of the

month, the Attorney-General, Richard Kleindienst, and two senior presidential aides, John Ehrlichman and Robert Haldeman, had resigned, while a third, John Dean, a White House counsel, had been dismissed. Not even these drastic measures, however, could divert the growing suspicion away from the President himself.

When the Senate hearings resumed on 17 May, John Dean claimed that Nixon had not only offered executive clemency to the Watergate defendants, but had also tried to buy their silence. It was then revealed that, since 1971, Nixon had recorded all his own conversations and telephone calls and that it would therefore be possible to confirm Dean's testimony.

The president, however, now refused to hand over the recordings. But the Federal Court of Appeal refused to be browbeaten and ordered him to deliver the tapes. In October, after a Supreme Court ruling, Nixon finally surrendered them, after the House of Representatives had initiated impeachment proceedings.

To the American public Nixon's guilt looked still more certain when it was revealed that two of the tapes were missing, which included the vital meeting with Dean. Moreover, part of a recording of a meeting between the president, Ehrlichman and Haldeman had been clumsily erased from another tape. Despite the evidence against him, Nixon hung on until February 1974, when he finally resigned and handed over power to Gerald Ford. Ford promised Nixon executive clemency so that he would escape trial for perjury.

► ▲ Fallen hero. Just as it was basking in the glory of international achievement, the Nixon regime was brought crashing down. The Watergate affair began as a bungled burglary but spread to entangle the entire Republican hierarchy in a sordid web of corruption. Nixon was forced to resign.

The European Economic Community

When the European Community (EEC) came into existence in 1958, Britain refused to join it because of the difficulties of combining the EEC's common external tariff policy with its own existing trading obligations, the legacy of its imperial past, for Britain preserved its trade connections with the former colonies that made up the new Commonwealth.

To the countries engaged in building up the close-knit Community, Britain's attitude seemed inappropriate. So when in 1961 prime minister Macmillan, partly at the prompting of President Kennedy, began to explore the possibility of British membership, the French president de Gaulle gave a very cool response. At this time, Kennedy was urging Macmillan to seek a new role for Britain as part of the West European "pillar" of the Atlantic alliance.

President de Gaulle, however, was determined to develop the European Community as a "third force" independent of both the United States and the Soviet Union. He felt that admitting Britain would be letting in an undesirable bias toward US interests. During 1962 Edward Heath took part in intensive negotiations in Brussels covering all the technical details of Britain's application to join the EEC. By the end of the year, however, the application had fallen through, after a row over the politics of Western nuclear defense. Whereas the French nuclear force was being developed by and for France alone, Britain's had always been based on cooperation with the United States. In December 1962, President Kennedy met Macmillan in Nassau in the Bahamas and agreed to continue this arrangement. To de Gaulle this was further proof of Britain's non-European character and he used his veto to break off the EEC's entry negotiations with Britain.

By the mid-1960s Britain was regretting its isolation from Europe, for the importance of the European market had steadily grown. Encouraged by the other members of the EEC, apart from France, Harold Wilson's Labour government, in 1967, tried again to gain entry. De Gaulle still believed that Britain was too close to the United States, and too tied by obligations to the Commonwealth, but hoped for an Anglo-French alliance to balance West Germany's influence in the Community and help contain US dominance overseas. When the French president's motives were revealed by a British diplomatic leak, there was a public outcry in Europe and negotiations for Britain's entry once again collapsed.

In December 1969, after de Gaulle's resignation, the six heads of the member governments announced their willingness to let Britain join. On 1 January 1973, Britain was formally admitted to the EEC. However, public opinion in Britain was divided on whether to accept the new European commitments or pursue the older ties with the Commonwealth. The Labour leader Wilson, not wishing to jeopardize his party's electoral prospects, promised a national referendum, the first in modern British history. Wilson became prime minister in 1974 and held the referendum in 1975. The result was an overwhelming endorsement of Britain's EEC membership.

Northern Ireland

From the early 1920s the six counties of Northern Ireland have been a partially self-governing province within the United Kingdom. Throughout its existence the province has been dominated by what has been called a "double minority" problem. Within the island of Ireland the Protestant "unionist" population, who are opposed to the "nationalist" cause of independence and wish to remain a part of the United Kingdom, are in a minority position numbering about a quarter of the total. The Northern Ireland state was set up to protect their interests with its boundaries carefully drawn to ensure a unionist electoral majority. However, one effect was to create a disaffected nationalist minority of some 30 percent within the new state which was hostile to its very existence and sought unification with the "Free State" in the south.

◄▼ Ulster's political troubles are rooted in its religious past: evocations of the triumph of Protestant forces at the Battle of the Boyne in 1692 and the continuing strength of the Orange Order are products of the importation of a Protestant community into a traditionally Catholic society three centuries ago. The Catholic population justifiably claims that it has been discriminated against, while its Protestant counterpart defends rights which it fears would be swept away in a Catholic state.

The outbreak of civil strife in 1968 followed the demand by the nationalist minority, who felt themselves politically and economically discriminated against, for their full rights as United Kingdom citizens. This call for reform within Northern Ireland aroused the suspicion of many unionists who felt it was an attempt to undermine the very existence of that state and further the cause of a united Ireland. The failure of the regime to reform itself led to an escalation of the conflict and the decision in 1972 by the British government to suspend the northern parliament and rule directly from London.

Early attempts at a solution concentrated on tackling the minority's grievances and on efforts to promote some sort of power sharing between the nationalist and unionist communities within Northern Ireland. However, with the continued escalation of the conflict and the re-emergence of the Provisional Irish Republican Army (IRA), the military wing of radical nationalism, more fundamental questions about the constitutional status of Northern Ireland and the possibility of unification with the south forced themselves on to the agenda. These issues have provoked major disagreement between the southern Irish state, which claims *de jure* jurisdiction over the north, and the British government, which has pledged to maintain the constitutional position until a majority in the north demands change. In practice both sides made concessions. An agreement of 1985 indicated an unequivocal acceptance by both sides that the problem was a joint one: the southern state was given a consultative role regarding policy in Northern Ireland in return for which it recognized that Irish reunification could only follow from its acceptance by the majority in the north.

▼ Violence in an urban wasteland. While Ulster has always been troubled by politico-religious tensions, the upswing in violence and discontent after 1968 was strongly connected with the stagnation of the regional economy. Unemployment, poverty and urban decay produced a discontented young generation susceptible to the sectarian message and willing to look for escape either in the turmoil of riot and destruction of property, or, more dangerously, in enlistment in armed terrorist groups.

YOUTH POWER

A striking feature of the 20th century has been the major role played by youth in the many violent upheavals and revolutionary movements which have so dramatically affected traditional political structures all over the world. It was among the young that Lenin recruited the most enthusiastic supporters of his vanguard strategy for engineering the Marxist overthrow of czarist Russia and who went on to supply the new cadres of the Soviet state. It was squads of ex-combatants, many of them still in their teens, who made up the rank-and-file of Mussolini's infant *Fascismo* in 1919, and their ruthless use of terror tactics against the "reds" which culminated in the March on Rome in 1922. In Germany the Hitler Youth coordinated the disparate youth movements which had sprung up at the turn of the century into a highly politicized section of the NSDAP (Nazi party), while the membership not only of the paramilitary SA and the SS, but the entire Nazi movement, was predominantly under 30. In the 1960s the radical disaffection with consensus values experienced by the postwar generation erupted, and within a few years militant students were throwing down the gauntlet to governments in both East and West, accusing them of collusion with imperialist aggression or with suppressing "true" democracy.

The emergence of the young as a new constituency of political activism can be traced to the break-up of traditional power structures and the rise of populist and activistic politics. In the 19th century the most important ideologue of democratic nationalism, Mazzini, declared war against the old order in the name of a Young Italy, and the success of the *risorgimento* to unite Italy inspired "young" liberation movements in a number of European countries still under foreign domination.

But it was particularly in the wake of World War I that a small but vociferous section of the young became convinced that they had both the mission and the power to eradicate the evils of "old" Europe, whether absolutist or liberal, so as to create a new society. For a time the clashes between the ultra-left and the ultra-right which ensued threatened to eclipse liberalism for good. Though the defeat of fascism reestablished liberal norms in Europe and with them the rule of the older generation, the radicalism of youth continued to be the dynamo of political violence and mass militancy.

Since 1960 the fanaticism of youth has been the major component of the politics of violence which has erupted throughout the world. In China's Cultural Revolution and in many struggles against foreign domination or fight for a higher ideal of ethnic or human solidarity, young people have provided the bulk of the freedom fighters and terrorists. And in many instances, following the lead of the student radicals of the 1960s, their fight has been seen as a crusade against the "gerontocracies" (hierarchies dominated by the old) which seem to have lost sight of the true needs of society.

► In May 1968 a wave of hostility to proposals for changes in higher education in France quickly developed into a fullscale attack on the authority of the government. Its political and ideological foundations were questioned, and the students sought to combine their opposition movement with that of the leftwing trade unions. For several days the country approached civil war, as barricades were thrown up in the center of Paris and the riot police sought to re-establish government authority.

► A boy in Belfast, armed with petrol bomb and gas mask in the early 1970s, exemplified the trend towards the involvement of extreme youth in some of the world's most intractable political trouble-spots, such as Belfast and Beirut.

▼ The Khmer Rouge, who took over the government of Cambodia in 1975 and were responsible for the persecution of anyone with even the slightest contact with Western society or ideas, relied heavily on often undisciplined teenagers. Their fanatical xenophobia was inspired by a form of nationalist vision.

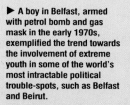

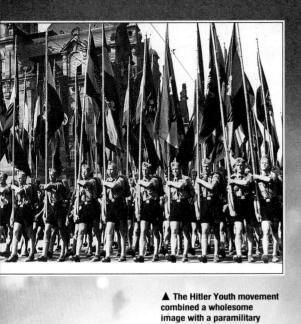

▲ The Hitler Youth movement combined a wholesome image with a paramilitary training that did much to make the rise of the Nazis acceptable to many Germans.

▲ Protests against US involvement in Vietnam resulted in the killing by the National Guard of two students at Kent State University, Ohio, in May 1970.

► ▼ Students protesting against corruption and the rule of old men in China in 1989 were seen as such a threat that the government killed more than a thousand.

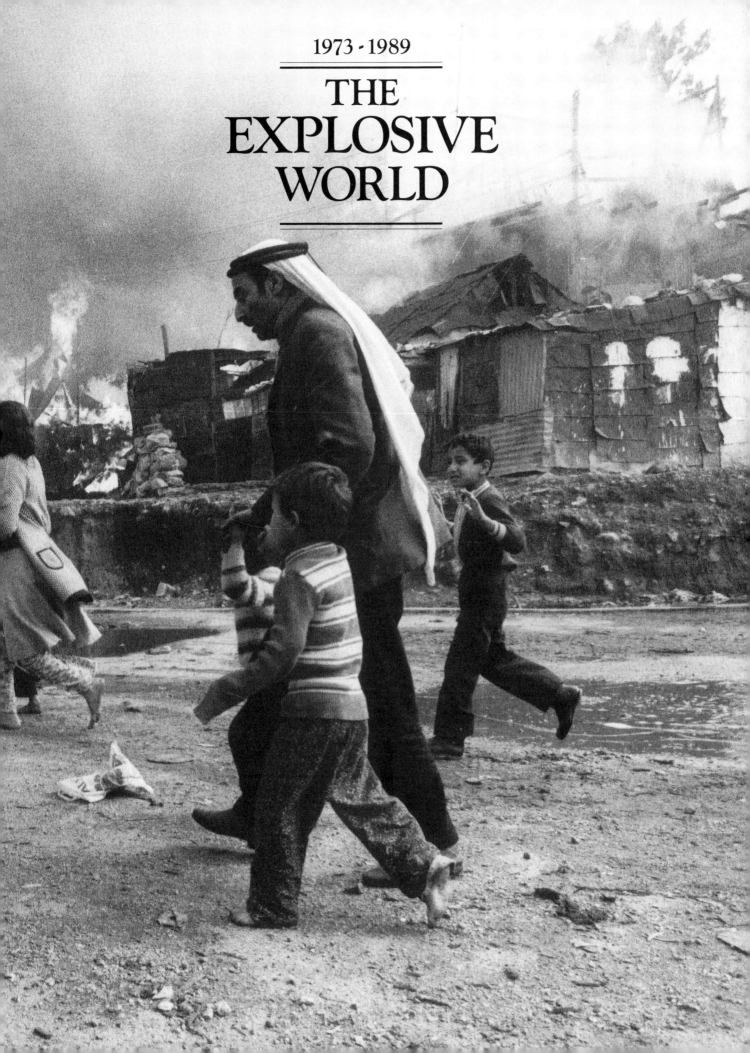

1973 - 1989

THE EXPLOSIVE WORLD

Time Chart

	1974	1975	1976	1977	1978	1979	1980	1981
Europe/Mediterranean	● 4 Mar: 1st UK minority cabinet since 1929 ● 2 Apr: Valéry Giscard D'Estaing elected Pres. (Fr) ● 6 May: Willi Brandt succeeded by Helmut Schmidt (W Ger) ● 29 May: UK resumed direct rule of Ulster ● 15 Jul: Coup in Cyprus; Turkish invasion, 20 Jul. UN cease-fire, 22 Jul	● 24 Apr: Siege of W German embassy, Stockholm, by terrorists demanding release of members of Baader–Meinhof group ● 20 Nov: Death of dictator Franco (Sp); succeeded by King Juan Carlos (22 Nov)	● 6 Jan: Resignation of Prime Minister Aldo Moro and cabinet after claims of CIA funding of noncommunists ● 16 Mar: Resignation of UK prime minister Harold Wilson (since 4 Mar 1974): succeeded by James Callaghan ● 23 Jul: In Portugal, Mario Soares was 1st constitutional prime minister since coup (25 Apr 1974)	● 23–24 Jan: Spanish constitutional rights suspended for 30 days after political violence and strikes in Barcelona and Madrid ● 15 Jun: Adolf Suarez elected in 1st free elections in Spain for 41 years ● 16 Jun: Brezhnev named USSR president as well as party chief – the 1st time in Soviet history	● 16 Mar: Kidnap of former Prime Minister Aldo Moro by Red Brigade – discovered dead, 9 May (Ita) ● 6 Aug: Death of Pope Paul VI. 28 Sept, death of John Paul I. 16 Oct, 1st non-Italian Pope elected since 1523: John Paul II of Poland	● 3 May: 1st UK woman prime minister, Margaret Thatcher, elected with large majority ● 27 Aug: UK Earl Mountbatten killed in IRA bomb explosion ● Dec: USSR invaded Afghanistan in support of Marxist regime following coup	● 4 May: Death of Tito (Yug): succeeded by collective rotating presidency ● 30 Aug: After labor unrest, workers at Gdansk Lenin Shipyard allowed to form independent trade unions: unprecedented in Soviet bloc	● Greece became a member of the EEC ● 2 Mar: Social Democrat Party formed (UK) ● 11–12 Apr: Nationwide racial riots, also in July (UK) ● 10 May: François Mitterrand elected President ● 13 Dec: Martial law declared (Pol) and Solidarity banned. Labor unrest continu
The Middle East	● 10 Apr: Resignation of Golda Meir; Itzhak Rabin replaced her ● 18 May: India became the 6th nation with a nuclear bomb ● 31 May: Agreement signed by Israel and Syria for armistice on Golan Heights ● 28 Oct: 20 Arab nations called for an independent Palestine state and recognized PLO leader Arafat	● 21 Feb: UN Human Rights Commission censured Israel for actions in occupied Arab territories ● 13 Apr: Fighting started between Moslems and Christians (Leb) ● 5 Jun: Suez Canal reopened after 8 years except to Israeli traffic ● 26 Jun: State of emergency declared in India	● 3 Jul: Entebbe hijack ended, Uganda, when plane held by pro-Palestinian terrorists was stormed by Israeli commandos	● 24 Mar: Morarji Desai replaced Indira Gandhi as prime minister (Ind) ● 21 Jun: Menachem Begin elected prime minister (Isr) ● 5 Jul: General Zia ousted Prime Minister Bhutto (Pak) ● 5 Dec: President Sadat (Egy) broke diplomatic ties with Syria, Iraq, Libya, Algeria and S Yemen	● 17 Sep: Camp David Accords between Sadat (Egy) and Begin (Isr) to fix schedule for peace negotiations: denounced by 20 Arab League nations at Baghdad summit (5 Nov) ● 19 Dec: Indira Gandhi expelled from Indian Parliament and imprisoned on charges of conspiracy, electoral misconduct and abuses during emergency rule	● 16 Jan: Exile of Shah. 11 Feb, Islamic law imposed on Iran by Ayatollah Khomeini ● 26 Mar: Peace treaty signed by Sadat (Egy) and Begin (Isr). Egypt censured by Arab League: diplomatic ties and economic boycott imposed ● 4 Nov: Iranian militants captured US embassy, Teheran. Most of 90 hostages freed 20 Jan 1981	● 6 Jan: Indira Gandhi reelected as prime minister of India ● 22 Sep: Start of Iran–Iraq war (cease-fire and start of UN-backed peace talks, Aug 1988)	● 5 Sep: Coptic Pope deposed and religious and other "dissidents" arrested through fear of religious factionalism (Egy) ● 6 Oct: President Sadat assassinated b extremist Moslem soldiers: succeeded by Hosni Mubarak (Egy) ● 18 Oct: 1st socialis government elected under Andreas Papandreou (Gre)
Africa	● 2 Sep: Emperor Haile Selassie deposed in bloodless coup by military leaders. 20 Dec, Ethiopia declared a socialist state	● 25 Jun: Mozambique gained independence from Portugal under Marxist President Samora Machel	● 16 Jun: Soweto racial riots started against legislation to force Afrikaans use in some teaching (S Afr) ● 4–5 Aug: Sudan broke relations with Libya and USSR after failed coup	● 4 Nov: UN voted embargo on military wares to S Africa in protest against racist policies	● 3 Mar: Pact for power to Rhodesian blacks by 31 Dec ● 22 Aug: Jomo Kenyatta succeeded by Daniel Arap Moi ● 28 Sep: PW Botha elected (S Afr)	● 11 Apr: Idi Amin deposed by Ugandan exile force and Tanzanian soldiers ● 21 Dec: Peace pacts signed in London to end conflict, Rhodesia	● 17 Apr: Rhodesia became independent Zimbabwe: end of 90 years of white rule. Robert Mugabe was 1st black prime minister	● Nov: Forays by S African troops into Angola to counter SWAPO guerrillas fighting for Namibian independence
The Americas	● 1 Jul: Death of Perón: widow Isabel succeeded him as 1st woman head of state in the Western Hemisphere ● 9 Aug: Resignation of Nixon following Watergate scandal. Gerald R Ford sworn in as next president, gave Nixon unconditional pardon (8 Sep)		24 Mar: Overthrow of Isabel Martinez de Perón (Arg) by General Jorge Rafael Videla ● 2 Nov: Jimmy Carter elected next US president	● 28 Apr: 1st formal negotiations between US and Cuba when fishing rights pact approved. Diplomats posted in each country (3 Jun) within foreign embassies without full restoration of relations ● 1–2 May: Arrest of Clamshell Alliance protestors in 1st mass civil disobedience against nuclear plant construction (US)	● 22 Aug: National Palace and 1,500 hostages seized by Sandinista guerillas. President Somoza refused to step down after strikes, and cutting of US military aid (Nic)	● 17 Jul: Sandinista rebels captured Nicaraguan capital: junta took power after resignation and flight of President Somoza ● 1 Oct: Panama took control of territory of American Canal Zone ● 21 Nov: US evacuated all non-essential personnel from embassies in 10 Islamic nations	● Jan: US trade embargo imposed after USSR invasion of Afghanistan ● 24 Mar: Assassination of RC Archbishop Oscar Romero (Sal) ● 4 Nov: Ronald Reagan elected as US President ● 13 Dec: José Napoleon Duarte was 1st civilian president in 49 years (Sal)	● 30 Mar: Failed assassination of President Reagan ● 6 Aug: Reagan decided on production of neutron weapons - 100 new MX missiles called for (2 Oct) ● 20 Sep: British Honduras became independent Belize with contingent of UK troops to guard against attack from Guatemala who claimed it
Asia and Pacific	● 9 Apr: India, Pakistan and Bangladesh restored diplomatic relations after agreement on dispute concerning Pakistani prisoners of war	● 16 Apr: Khmer Rouge took Cambodia ● 30 Apr: S Vietnamese surrender to the communists ● 23 Aug: Communist takeover of Laos completed	● 8 Jan: Death of Zhou Enlai. 9 Sept, death of Mao Zedong. Hua Gofeng succeeded Mao as chairman of Communist party ● 2 Jul: N and S Vietnam reunited as one nation	● 22 Jul: Gang of Four expelled from Communist Party and Deng Xiaoping "rehabilitated". 11th congress marked by creation of 26-member Politburo, new party constitution and arrest of Mao's widow	● 1 May: Ethnic Chinese "boat people" began to flee Vietnam ● 3 Jul: China cut all aid to Vietnam. 13 July, cut aid to Albania ● 3 Nov: Pact signed by US and Vietnam	● 1 Jan: Diplomatic relations established between China and US. US broke relations with Taiwan ● 26 Oct: President Park assassinated by director of Korean CIA after 18 years in power	● 23 Jun: Invasion of Thailand by Vietnam via Cambodia ● 7 Sep: Resignations as part of pro-modernization campaign against lifelong incumbency of official posts (Chn)	● 25 Jan: Sentences passed in trial of Gang of Four (Chn) ● 29 Jun: Hua Gofen replaced as head of Communist Party (Chn) by Hu Yaobang. Mao discredited for mistakes in leadershi
World	● 4 Sep: US and E Germany established diplomatic relations (US was the last major Western power to recognize E Germany since its emergence from international isolation in 1971)	● 1 Aug: Nonbinding security and cooperation pact signed in Helsinki by 33 European nations, Canada and US to freeze postwar borders, extend détente, renounce force and aid to terrorists and respect human rights	● 24 Feb – 5 Mar, 25th Soviet Communist Party Congress: Increased independence of Western Communist Parties ● 28 May: US and USSR signed 5-year treaty limiting size of underground nuclear test explosions and allowing US to inspect Soviet tests on-site	● 7 Sep: 2 Panama Canal treaties signed by US and Panama: canal to be under full control of Panama from 1999 and to be permanently neutral ● 21 Sep: USA, USSR and 13 nations signed nuclear non-proliferation pact to limit spread of nuclear weapons		● 18 Jun: US Senate refused SALT II treaty with USSR after Afghan invasion ● 17 Jul: 1st meeting of European Parliament ● 12 Dec: NATO agreed to install 572 medium-range missiles in Europe by 1983		● Mass European demonstrations for nuclear disarmament started in UK ● 1 Jan: Javier Perez de Cuellar (Per) became Secretary-General of UN

1982	1983	1984	1985	1986	1987	1988	1989
14 Dec: Garret ...zgerald replaced ...harles Haughey ...ected 9 Mar, Ire) • 1 Oct: Election ...Helmut Kohl (W Ger) • 8 Oct: Solidarity trade ...ion banned (Pol). 21 ...ec: martial law lifted • 28 Oct: Election of ...lipe Gonzalez (Sp) • 10–12 Nov: Brezhnev ...cceeded by Yuri ...ndropov (USSR)	• 5 May: France expelled 47 Soviet diplomats and nationals on charges of espionage: unprecedented in French–Soviet relations • 9 Jun: In UK, Conservative party under Margaret Thatcher reelected • 16 Jun: Yuri Andropov elected president of the Soviet Presidium	• 9 Feb: Death of Andropov; succeeded by Konstantin Chernenko as general secretary of the Communist Party (Feb) and president of the Supreme Soviet (Apr) • 17 Apr: UK cut diplomatic ties with Libya • 12 Oct: IRA bomb attack on UK Conservative Party at Annual Conference, Brighton	• 10 Mar: Death of Chernenko; succeeded by Andrei Gromyko as Soviet president (2 Jul) and Mikhail Gorbachev as general secretary of the Communist Party • 28 May: UK was found guilty of sex discrimination in immigration policy by European Parliament • 27 Nov: Anglo–Irish accord signed: Eire to be consulted in running of Ulster (UK)	• Kurt Waldheim elected President (Aut) • 16 Feb: Dr Mario Soares became 1st civilian president in 60 years (Por) • 28 Feb: Assassination of Prime Minister Olof Palme; succeeded by Ingvar Carlson (Swe) • 24 Oct: UK broke off diplomatic relations with Syria	• 10 Mar: Charles Haughey became prime minister of Eire • 17 Aug: Death of Rudolf Hess in Spandau Prison, Berlin (W Ger)	• Jan: Joint army brigade (Fr, W Ger) • 10 May: François Mitterrand reelected (Fr) • Jun: Poul Schlueter reelected (Den) • 30 Sep: Opponents to Soviet reforms voted out of office. Gorbachev appointed Soviet president (1 Oct) • 20 Oct: Abolition of criminal suspect's right of silence (UK)	• 1st democratic Soviet elections • 4 Jun: 1st partly democratic elections in Poland; Solidarity prime minister appointed (Aug) • 24 Jun: German–Soviet treaty • Jul: Southern Irish elections failed to find acceptable government • 10 Nov: Berlin Wall opened
24 Mar: Military coup ...d martial law (Bang) 6 Jun: Attack on ...aeli ambassador by ...alestinian terrorists ...untered with invasion ...southern Lebanon. ...ael agreed to PLO ...acuation plan under ...ultinational peace-...eeping force 28–30 Aug: Start ...war between Druse ...oslem militia and ...e Lebanese Army	• 11 Feb: Resignation of Israeli Defense Minister Ariel Sharon after inquiry into massacre of Palestinian refugees in West Beirut (16–18 Sep 1982) • 12 Sep: Resignation of Prime Minister Menachem Begin; succeeded by Yitzhak Shamir (Isr) • 15 Nov: Turkish Republic of Northern Cyprus declared	• 21 Feb: With deterioration of situation in the Lebanon, international peacekeeping forces withdrawn • 31 Oct: Indira Gandhi assassinated by 2 Sikh bodyguards; succeeded by her son, Rajiv Gandhi (Ind)		• 26 Feb: Corazon Aquino chose her cabinet after flight of ex-President Ferdinand Marcos (Phil)	• Peace accord signed with India to end bloodshed in Sri Lanka between separatist Tamil guerrillas and mainly Sinhalese government	• mid-Apr: (Pak) Afghan peace accord for Soviet pullout by Feb 1989 • Aug: Cease-fire agreed in Iran–Iraq war • 17 Aug: Death of General Zia (Pak); succeeded by 1st woman leader of Moslem country, Benazir Bhutto (1 Dec) • 14 Dec: Yasir Arafat (PLO) renounced terrorism, recognized Israel	• 4 Jun: Death of Ayatollah Khomeini after 10 years' power; succeeded by Hojatoleslam Ali Akbar Rafsanjani (29 Jul) as prime minister with extended powers under new constitution
17 Feb: Opposition ...ader Joshua Nkomo ...smissed by Robert ...ugabe (Zim). 16 Aug: ...retook his seat in ...overnment after exile ...Botswana and UK 7 June: Capital of ...had fell to rebel forces		• 20 May: Most serious black terrorist bomb attack against regime outside air force HQ, Pretoria (S Afr) • 3–4 Aug: US involvement in Chad crisis publicly angered French government	• 15 Apr: End to ban on mixed marriages announced: 1st ceremony took place 15 Jun (S Afr) • 27 Jul: President Milton Obote ousted in bloodless coup, Kampala (Uga)	• 19 May: S African forces carried out raids on Zambia, Zimbabwe and Botswana • 12 Jun: State of emergency declared with widespread unrest on 10th anniversary of Soweto uprising (S Afr)		• 8 Aug: Agreement between S Africa, Cuba and Angola over disengagement of troops from Angola • Oct: President Kenneth Kaunda reelected for 6th term in office (Zaire)	• 1 Jan: Namibia granted independence from S Africa • 11 Jan: Start of Cuban troop withdrawal from Angola
28 Mar: 1st free ...ections held in 50 ...ars (Sal) 2–3 Apr: Start of ...alkland Conflict with ...gentine invasion of ...K territory 17 Apr: British North ...merica Act of 1867 ...rminated (UK, Can) 8 Jun: Reagan ...ecame 1st US ...esident to address ...nt session of ...arliament	• 25 Oct: US troops landed on Grenada to "protect US citizens" after Marxist coup. Cuban and Soviet presence discovered	• 6 Nov: Ronald Reagan reelected as US President	• 30 Apr: Reagan planned total trade embargo on Sandinista regime in Nicaragua after request for aid for Contra rebels blocked by House of Representatives • 1 Aug: US House of Representatives voted to impose sanctions on S Africa			• Mar: US-backed coup to oust General Noriega failed (Pan) • May: Belize and Guatemala agreed a permanent commission to formulate treaty to end territorial dispute • 6 Oct: Gen. Augusto Pinochet refused to step down after election defeat (Chi) • 11 Nov: George Bush elected US President	• 2 Feb: Carlos Andres Perez reelected (Ven) • May: 1st free elections in Argentina
12–13 Sep: Hua ...uofeng lost his ...osition as successor ...Mao Zedong. Deng ...aoping was elected ...hairman of new ...entral Advisory ...ommission to the ...ommunist Party ...2 Nov 1987)	• 5 Mar: Election of Labour Party under Robert Hawke (Aus) • 9 Oct: Death of Korean government officials in bomb explosion during ceremony in Burma: N Korea was blamed			• 2 Mar: Australia Bill signed by the Queen severing constitutional ties with UK	• 14 May: Failed coup in Fiji against Indian political dominance: state of emergency declared. 1 Oct: Col. Rabuka declared himself head of state	• Feb: Cease-fire for Laos and Thailand • Feb: 1st democratically-elected president (S Kor) • 18 Sep: Military coup after civil unrest when 1st civilian elected (Bur)	• 7 Jan: Accession of Emperor Akihito (Jap) • 4 Jun: Student revolt quashed, Beijing (Chn) • 25 Jul: Liberal Democrats received first major electoral reverses for 30 years (Jap)
10 Dec: The Law of ...e Sea Convention ...gned after 10 years ...y 119 nations (refusal ...sign by UK, US and ...her industrialized ...ations): in favor of ...rofit-sharing and ...ooperation	• 14 Mar: OPEC group agreed to cut oil prices in view of world glut • 28–30 May: Economic summit (US, UK, Can, Fr, W Ger, Ita, Jap) • 22–23 Nov: Breakdown of US–USSR arms reductions talks as NATO and USSR announced increase in nuclear forces	• 30 Mar: US and several S American nations agreed to package of loans totaling $5 billion to aid Argentina with international debts • Aug: Equipment and experts sent by several countries to clear the Red Sea of mines placed by the Islamic Jihad	• 2 Jan: Official withdrawal of US from UNESCO	• 1 Jan: Juan Perez de Cuellar (Per) appointed for 2nd term as UN Secretary-General		• 14 Apr: Afghan accords, Geneva (Afg, Pak, USSR, US) • mid-Jun: Economic pact: EEC and Gulf Cooperation Council • Nov: Space technology cooperation agreement (Chn, Aus) • 7 Nov: UK and Iran restored diplomatic ties	• 12 Jan, Chemical weapons conference, Paris (Fr): 149 nations signed total ban on use of gas, toxins and bacteriological weapons • Salman Rushdie affair: UK/Iran relations broken after Moslem death threats to UK author. International controversy ensued

Datafile

The years since 1973 saw the arms race between the superpowers reach its most frenetic level since the 1950s and then begin to slacken as the long-obstructed channels of negotiation gradually opened to allow for real progress with arms reduction agreements. The intensification of competition in the late 1970s and early 1980s was caused by the arrival of new generations of nuclear and conventional weapons, while diplomatic positions became more rigid as the US reasserted itself after the trauma of Vietnam and the USSR intervened militarily in Afghanistan. The trend began to reverse as superpower allies in Europe began to question alliance arrangements which could turn their homelands into nuclear battlegrounds, as popular opposition to nuclear weapons began to grow, and as the staggering cost of modern military development began to do real damage to the flagging economies of the USA and USSR. In an era of economic retrenchment, the governments of both the US and USSR began to adopt less rigid stances towards each other.

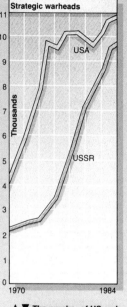

Strategic warheads

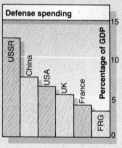

Defense spending

◀ By 1987, several Western powers had already reduced their defense spending, while even the US had brought its spending down. The USSR and China were still making relatively high allocations, and in the case of the former, the need to reduce military spending to allow for general economic recovery was urgent.

▲▼ The number of US and Soviet nuclear warheads, both land (ICBM, intercontinental ballistic missiles) and submarine (SLBM, sea-launched ballistic missiles) based, rose steeply in the 1970s, the US attaining a dramatic lead in the first half of the decade and the USSR making a huge effort to catch up thereafter.

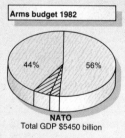

Arms budget 1982

44%   56%

NATO
Total GDP $5450 billion

☐ USA
☐ Other
▨ Defense spending

◀ While the massive nuclear arsenals of the US and USSR were relatively equal in aggregate, they depended on a different mix of bases and launch systems. Preparing for war in Europe, the USSR's strategic missile forces were overwhelmingly land-based. The US depended far less heavily on fixed sites.

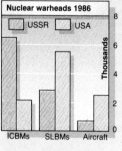

Nuclear warheads 1986

☐ USSR   ☐ USA

ICBMs   SLBMs   Aircraft

28%

75%

Warsaw Pact
Total GDP $1340 billion

☐ USSR
☐ Other
▨ Defense spending

◀ The USSR and its Warsaw Pact allies spent a far higher proportion of their GDP on defense than the US and its NATO allies. Both superpowers carried the greater proportional share of the total spending within their alliances, particularly in the Eastern bloc where the smaller countries were economically far weaker.

▼ Membership figures for the Campaign for Nuclear Disarmament (CND) in Britain typify changing public opinion to nuclear weapons. CND expanded rapidly between 1979 and 1984, driven by controversy on the basing of US Cruise missiles on British soil. With progress in arms reduction negotiations, membership fell.

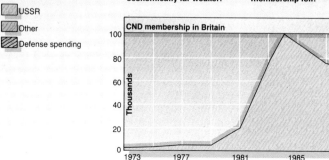

CND membership in Britain

From the late 1960s superpower relations had been complicated by the Soviet premier Brezhnev's "doctrine" that any attempt by an Eastern bloc country to abandon socialism would be resisted by all the other members of the "socialist commonwealth". At the same time, however, the hardline from Moscow seemed to be tempered by promises of détente. In March 1976 Brezhnev publicly endorsed "the principles of peaceful coexistence to reduce and eliminate the danger of world war" and spoke of "negotiation and not confrontation" as "the natural state of things".

The case for détente

Leading Western politicians believed that by accepting Soviet hegemony in Eastern and Central Europe (about which it could do very little), they could secure Soviet agreement on the urgent issue of arms limitation. Moreover, they reasoned that the greater contacts that would ensue from détente might even incite some of the satellite countries to press for greater independence from Moscow. By accepting that the Soviet Union would not abandon its military presence in Central Europe, which it regarded as the key to its security, the United States and its NATO allies hoped to defuse potential flashpoints of superpower confrontation such as the Cuban missile crisis of 1962.

Between 1970 and 1976 the superpowers held four summit meetings, of which three took place on American soil, and in 1972 Richard Nixon became the first US president to visit Moscow. Nixon's resignation on 9 August 1974, following a scandal over the bugging of Watergate building, the Democratic party headquarters, both weakened the Republican party and cast doubt on all of Nixon's actions, including his foreign policy, in which he had been so ably assisted by his secretary of state Henry Kissinger. However, Nixon's successor, Gerald Ford, remained undeterred in pursuing détente, fortified by Kissinger and by the belief that the development of better relations with the People's Republic of China would concentrate the mind of the Soviets enough to ensure further negotiations with them on arms limitation and a general reduction in East–West tension.

This approach led to a meeting between Ford and Brezhnev in Vladivostok on 23 November 1974 and the signing of the SALT (Strategic Arms Limitation Talks) II treaty. They also agreed to hold a general conference on security and cooperation in Europe (CSCE) in Helsinki in 1975. SALT II placed a ceiling on numbers of missile launchers and bombers and was designed to extend and complement SALT I (which had for five years frozen the numbers of ballistic missiles). However, this second treaty was never

SUPERPOWER RELATIONS

ratified, largely because of American disquiet over the Soviet invasion of Afghanistan at the end of 1979. The signing, in August 1975, of the Helsinki agreement, which was the culmination of the CSCE process, was attended by representatives from 33 European countries as well as the United States and Canada. Widely interpreted as legitimizing the Soviet hold on Central and Eastern Europe, the agreement actually did no more than guarantee the integrity of all European borders. Moreover, the regimes within those borders were committed to promote better East–West relations and uphold the primacy of "human rights". (Ultimately, the Soviet Union's failure to comply on human rights' issues was the ostensible – and certainly most emotive – reason why Helsinki did not succeed, though the most compelling reasons were certainly military.)

Further hope for better East–West relations in 1975 came with the ending of US support for the government of South Vietnam. Thus, when a Soviet *Soyuz* spacecraft docked in space with an *Apollo* from the United States, the union appeared to symbolize a new era in US–Soviet relations and fulfil Nixon's 1972 promise of the superpowers locked into "interdependence for survival". However, American optimism was short-lived, as intelligence reports suggested that the Soviets had begun to rearm.

► A US mobile Cruise missile launcher in the early 1980s. The introduction of Cruise threatened to upset the strategic balance. A mobile land-based nuclear weapon system did not fit into the idea of mutually assured deterrence, built around fixed missile sites.

▼ The dialogue of détente. US president Carter and the Soviet leader Brezhnev at arms limitation talks in 1979. Mutual suspicion and strategic intransigence ensured that the rate of change was slow.

With the election of Jimmy Carter as the 39th President of the United States in the autumn of 1976, a shift in US foreign policy took place. Whereas the Nixon–Ford–Kissinger line had been clearcut, Carter's was far less so. A former governor of Georgia, with little experience of foreign affairs, Carter relied on his secretary of state, Cyrus Vance, and his national security advisor, Zbigniew Brzezinski, for guidance on foreign policy. Vance, however, was a "dove" who supported détente, whereas Brzezinski, an expatriate Pole, was a "hawk" who distrusted the Russians. Meanwhile many experienced US politicians had begun to feel that Ford had conceded too much in the name of détente.

By the early 1970s the United States had stopped increasing the number of nuclear missiles, concentrating instead on developing multiple-warhead missiles (MIRVs) and Cruise missiles (an updated version of Hitler's V1 rockets). Meanwhile the Soviets had built a new bomber, launched the Kiev-class aircraft carrier and greatly expanded the Red Navy as well as developing SS20 and SS21 missiles. The SS20 was a powerful medium-range missile, highly mobile and impossible to monitor, and, like the short-range SS21, was deployed in Europe. By early 1983 the Soviets had 650 SS21s, compared with NATOs 100 equivalent weapons.

NATO rearmament

By the end of 1978 Carter was under pressure, both from inside the United States and in Europe, to act more firmly against the Soviets. On 1 July 1979 General Haig (who later became President Reagan's secretary of state) resigned as NATO supreme commander because of his differences with Carter. At about the same time, the West German chancellor, Helmuṭ Schmidt, and the British prime minister, James Callaghan, both urged Carter to begin the much-needed process of rearming NATO even at the risk of arousing Soviet hostility. They proposed a "twin track" approach, combining rearmament with talks on disarmament. This policy was formally ratified in Brussels on 12 December 1979. It stipulated that NATO would deploy 572 Cruise and Pershing missiles (intermediate-range nuclear forces, or INF) in Europe if negotiations failed to bring about reductions in armaments on the Soviet side.

In 1980 President Carter increased the US military budget by five per cent for the following year, introduced a grain embargo against the Soviet Union (alienating farmers of the American Midwest, whose anger cost him dear in the presidential elections) and urged the US Olympic team to boycott the 1980 Moscow games as a protest against the Soviet invasion of Afghanistan.

To many in the West it seemed that the Soviets had cynically used the decade of détente to massively reequip and rearm. Soviet armed forces in Europe now outnumbered those of NATO: 2.75 to 1 in artillery and 2.5 to 1 in tanks and tactical aircraft. The basis of détente had ultimately been the MAD (mutual assured destruction) doctrine: a strategic balance in nuclear weaponry whose intention was to deter an attack by either side since neither could hope to win an ensuing war. A strategic advantage, particularly, as in this case, in the European theater, was perceived as greatly increasing the vulnerability of Western Europe. NATO's answer was to threaten to deploy Cruise and Pershing missiles, and eventually to do so.

President Jimmy Carter's reputation for vacillation and his botched attempts to secure the release of American hostages seized from the US embassy in Iran highlighted American impotence under his stewardship and cost him the presidency in the 1980 elections. Indeed, his new, harsher policy towards the Soviet Union effectively endorsed the "new right" cause being advanced so eloquently by his Republican rival Ronald Reagan, who claimed that compromise had weakened the United States and disturbed the international equilibrium.

Reagan's election as 40th president of the United States on 4 November 1980 sounded the

► ▼ The Reagan presidency witnessed a perceptible shift in US policy towards the rival superpower. Early in his first term, Reagan reasserted the traditional anti-Soviet stance, describing the USSR as an "evil empire", but his attitude softened as dialog developed, and by the late 1980s he and Gorbachev exchanged visits.

▼ The British prime minister, Margaret Thatcher – nicknamed the "Iron Lady" by Moscow – emerged as a committed advocate of deterrence through strength – in terms of both nuclear and conventional military force. In the early 1980s, both NATO and the Warsaw Pact maintained huge forces in Central Europe.

Sino-Soviet Relations

A heavy Soviet military build-up in East Asia and along disputed border regions increased Chinese fears for their security in the mid-1970s, while the Soviet Union felt growing unease with China's developing strategic nuclear capability in the early 1980s. Tensions were heightened by Soviet support for Vietnam (a traditional Chinese enemy) when it invaded Cambodia in December 1978 and overthrew the Pol Pot regime (backed by China). China responded by launching a brief offensive against Vietnam in February 1979. Relations further worsened after the Soviet occupation of Afghanistan in December 1979 Pakistan, another Chinese friend, gave help to the Afghan rebels. Meanwhile Moscow looked with disfavor on Beijing's developing relationship with the United States.

By the late-1980s relations showed signs of improvement, with China and the new Soviet leadership keen to reduce the economic costs of confrontation and boost mutual trade. After Moscow's withdrawal from Afghanistan and reduction of its forces on the Chinese border, the first Sino-Soviet summit since the Khrushchev era was held in Beijing in 1989. Nevertheless, the long-standing border dispute and the conflict over Cambodia remained as serious obstacles.

◀ Chinese missile forces for deployment in the north.

death knell of détente, which he declared had been a "one way street that the Soviet Union had exploited to pursue its own aims". Reagan came to the White House firmly resolved to present an uncompromising face to the Soviet Union and to execute NATO's rearmament. In November 1983 the Soviets walked out of the INF talks at Geneva as a protest against the "twin-track decision" to deploy Cruise and Pershing missiles in Europe and refused to restart arms limitation talks unless the missiles were withdrawn.

Earlier in 1983 Reagan had proposed the "zero option": the total dismantling of all intermediate missiles in Europe. Yuriy Andropov, who succeeded Brezhnev as president in November 1982, dismissed this as "unrealistic", but in October 1983 made a counter offer for a mutual 25 percent reduction in intercontinental missiles and in return for no deployment of Cruise or Pershing, to reduce Soviet medium-range missiles to the number possessed by Britain and France. At that time, Reagan and his chief advisors, secretary of state Schulz and the hawkish Caspar Weinberger, showed no enthusiasm either for a summit to discuss these issues or for any compromise that might give the Russians the advantage. Instead they persisted in their attacks on the Soviet Union as the "evil empire", as Reagan called it. The shooting down, on 1 September 1983, of a South Korean Airline jumbo jet that had strayed over the Kamchatka peninsula, home of some of Russia's most sophisticated strategic technology, hardened American attitudes still further.

Perhaps the biggest sticking point following the rearmament of NATO was Reagan's "Star Wars" proposal, the Strategic Defense Initiative (SDI). Its purpose was to construct a laser shield around the American continent making it imper-

68

vious to attack from Soviet missiles. SDI alarmed the Soviets by undermining the principle of MAD, which depended upon both superpowers being equally vulnerable to attack by long-range strategic missiles. To the countries of Europe, it represented an isolationist, "fortress America" policy that potentially spelled danger for the European continent.

The appointment of Mikhail Gorbachev as head of the Soviet Communist party on 10 March 1985 began a new era in US–Soviet relations. On 19 and 20 November 1985 Reagan and Gorbachev met in Geneva, where the Americans proposed an interim agreement on INF missiles to limit their number, with the long-term intention of eliminating them totally. The leaders also agreed in principle to halve the number of offensive weapons.

In this new, optimistic political climate, Reagan and Gorbachev spoke to each other's nations on television in January 1986. Gorbachev in his address proposed to the American people a 15-year timetable for ridding the earth of all nuclear weapons. He also showed that he was not inflexible on human rights issues and the following month he freed the dissident Jew Anatoliy Shcharansky, exchanging him for a Soviet agent.

Following a visit by the French president Mitterrand to the Soviet Union in July 1986, Gorbachev proposed the immediate withdrawal of six Red Army regiments in Europe.

The US administration remained wary, however, and NATO's first response was to announce support for an American proposal to resume the manufacture of chemical weapons. Not surprisingly, the second Reagan–Gorbachev summit in Reykjavik, Iceland, in October was a disappointing failure. The Soviet leader felt himself snubbed while Reagan refused to be pressured into abandoning his prized Star Wars scheme.

Yet the Soviets did not stop trying: they agreed with 33 other European countries, the United States and Canada to a new system of prior

▶ "This way to the last peace – with dead certainty": German anti-nuclear demonstrators make their attitude to the missile buildup very clear. The intensification of the arms race and the deployment of short and medium-range nuclear missiles (like the US Pershing and Cruise, and the Soviet SS20) on European soil, brought the peace movement back to life in the early 1980s. Persistent mass protest at developments which could place European targets at direct, early risk in any superpower confrontation exposed the NATO and Warsaw Pact alliances to unprecedented strain. While other factors contributed to withdrawal of missiles in the late 1980s, popular protest also played a key role.

Women for Life on Earth

◀▼ The women's peace camp protests at Greenham Common, in Britain, presented the stark contrast between the values of life – represented here by images of dancing on a missile site during a mass-protest, or by family photographs attached to the fence of the airbase – and values of war implicit in the existence of Cruise.

In September 1981, a group of women set up a "peace camp" outside the US air base at Greenham Common in Berkshire, UK, as a protest against the NATO decision to site 96 ground-launched Cruise missiles there in December 1983. It was feared that these "theater" nuclear weapons made possible the concept of a "limited" nuclear war. It seemed to many women that the government, without parliamentary support or public debate, had taken a decision which endangered them and also, in their name, threatened the lives of Russian women and children.

For some of them the only way to deal with the fear, powerlessness and anger they felt, was to take action. Many came to Greenham to stay until the missiles were removed: they protested by demonstrating, by blockading construction work, by trespassing, by talking to anyone who would listen. They lived in primitive conditions

outside the gates of the base, where harassment and arrest were daily events.

Greenham Common women's peace camp became a focus for the peace movement. On 12 December 1982, 30,000 women from all over Britain, as well as groups from Sweden, Holland and West Germany, gathered at the base and encircled the 15km perimeter fence in a massive demonstration of collective and personal commitment. Many returned time and again over the next years so that a constant presence and vigil was maintained. Similar peace camps were set up at other missile sites in Europe and America: some were, like Greenham, women-only protests. All looked to Greenham as a model of a form of political activity in which ways of living and being – decentralized, non-hierarchical, supportive – were offered in opposition to the allegedly masculine, militaristic world view represented by the missile bases.

notification of any military activities, as one of a series of measures to promote confidence and security in Europe. They also reaffirmed their commitment to quit Afghanistan and undertook not to resume atmospheric nuclear testing unless the Americans did so first (which they did).

In February 1987 Gorbachev further proposed that US and Soviet INF missiles be removed from Europe over a five-year period and conceded that SDI need not be part of this package. This was a most warming introduction to the major Soviet-American arms talks that opened in Geneva in May and carried on throughout the summer. By August the West Germans had agreed to put their own Pershing rockets into any INF agreement thus removing one obstacle to a deal; and another fell when the Soviet Union accepted the principle of open inspection. When Gorbachev and Reagan met again, in December of the same year, in the United States, they agreed to eliminate all land-based INF weapons and to meet again in Moscow early in 1988 in order to finalize the details of the agreement.

In May the INF treaty was ratified by both American chambers and by the Supreme Soviet, so that when Reagan visited the Kremlin, he and Gorbachev became signatories in an historic first step toward the denuclearization of at least part of US and Soviet weaponry. Not only did the dismantling of INF weapons begin at once throughout Europe but television viewers in both the Eastern and Western blocs were treated to the

rare sight of inspections by the forces of the other side to verify that the nuclear warheads were truly being destroyed.

Among the political experts were those who argued that these agreements proved that the Cold War had been a fiction, created more by a distorted view of the intentions of the other side than by a realistic assessment. Others concluded that negotiations by the West had been successful only because they were conducted from a position of strength.

▼ Withdrawal of Cruise – a US missile launcher is loaded into an aircraft for transportation home from a European airbase. Mobile nuclear missile systems produced mass popular opposition, and threatened to upset the delicate balance of deterrence. Their withdrawal gave momentum to further arms reductions.

Datafile

The 1970s and 1980s saw an increase in conflicts around the world in which either the participants consciously challenged the authority of the superpowers in their regions, or from which the Soviet Union and the United States chose to remain aloof. New political movements such as Islamic fundamentalism challenged the old certainties of global geopolitics, and it became increasingly difficult to group the nations into the categories of East, West and nonaligned.

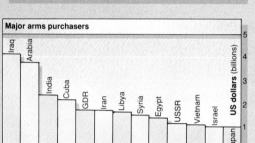

Armed forces personnel 1975–83

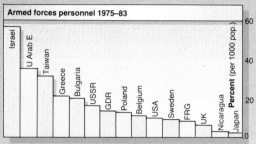

Major arms purchasers

► The international arms trade is dominated by the two superpowers, and the industrial countries of Western Europe. Governments may frequently use the negotiations for the sale of arms to further their diplomatic interests and to reinforce alliances. The need to supply technical backup commits the exporter and purchaser to close cooperation. It is sometimes suggested that arms manufacturing nations may welcome limited wars on distant continents to see their products tested on the battlefield.

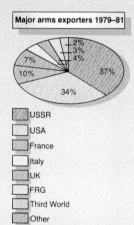

Major arms exporters 1979–81

- 2%
- 3%
- 4%
- 7%
- 10%
- 34%
- 37%

- ▨ USSR
- ☐ USA
- ▨ France
- ☐ Italy
- ▨ UK
- ☐ FRG
- ▨ Third World
- ▨ Other

► The large industrial powers are major consumers of oil, and while some rely on domestic production, others, notably Japan and the countries of Western Europe, need to import billions of barrels. When the oil producers of the Middle East cut production in 1973 the Western industrial world was forced into a severe energy crisis.

◄ The Western nations generally make less heavy military demands on their people than those of the Eastern bloc. Israel arms a large proportion of its relatively small population in defense against far more populous Arab enemies; Japan is restricted by treaty to maintaining only a small force for purely defensive purposes.

◄ The major importers of arms are concentrated heavily in the Middle East and the remainder of the Arab world where oil provides ready cash, while political instability offers a pretext for remaining heavily armed. There are few nations that do not receive a significant proportion of their military equipment from abroad.

▼ ► The stark division of the world into rich and poor is illustrated by figures for refugees and contributions to refugee assistance. Across much of Africa, South Asia and Central America, poverty and overpopulation produce misery which can easily turn into a demographic disaster. In Afghanistan and Palestine, the refugee problems are the direct result of war and foreign occupation; elsewhere disturbances of this nature help trigger off shortages of food, housing and the other necessities of life which drive millions away from their homes.

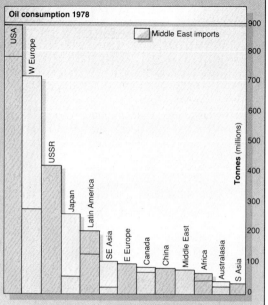

Oil consumption 1978

☐ Middle East imports

Tonnes (millions)

US foreign aid 1985

US dollars (billion)

◄ Statistics for US foreign aid in the 1980s provide an indication of American strategic interests. Massive aid is given to Israel and to pro-Western Egypt, while aid to Pakistan reflects US concern with Soviet aid to India and military activities in Afghanistan. Closer to home US aid goes to rightwing Central American governments.

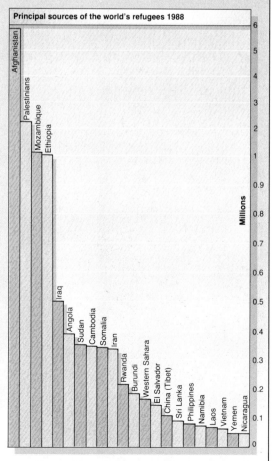

Principal sources of the world's refugees 1988

Millions

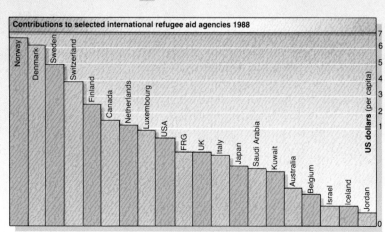

Contributions to selected international refugee aid agencies 1988

US dollars (per capita)

BEYOND THE SUPERPOWERS

The nonaligned countries of the Third World found it difficult to develop independently of superpower interests. The United States, having withdrawn its combatants from Southeast Asia, became increasingly involved in supporting pro-US groups in Central America, while stopping short of military intervention. At the same time the Americans punished those who, like Nicaragua and Libya, opposed US surrogates or challenged US supremacy. The Soviet Union became embroiled in a war in Afghanistan and, like the United States in Vietnam, was later ignominiously forced to withdraw.

In Vietnam and Afghanistan nationalism was an important weapon in the fight for independence and freedom from superpower interference. Likewise, the Islamic revolution in Iran won support because of its emphasis on religious nationalism and its rejection of both the US and Soviet systems. Equally, among ethnic minorities (or, in the case of South Africa, the black majority) nationalism represented a potent force for opposition and hope for change. The Palestinians on Israel's West Bank, the Sikhs of the Indian Punjab, the Iraqi Kurds and the Tamils of Sri Lanka all rebelled against the racial and cultural oppression of the countries within whose boundaries they resided and demanded the right to self-determination.

Southeast Asia after US withdrawal
Events in Southeast Asia were overshadowed by the collapse of the South Vietnamese government and the terrible massacres in Cambodia. Following the armistice agreement of 1973 and the withdrawal of US forces. South Vietnam fell to the invading North Vietnamese in April 1975. President Nguyen van Thieu resigned and fled to the United States. Saigon, the South Vietnamese capital, was renamed Ho Chi Minh City, after the late North Vietnamese leader. Meanwhile relations between the Communist regime of Vietnam, led by Ton Duc Thang (who enjoyed the full support of the Soviet Union) and the Chinese government deteriorated after disagreement over Cambodia.

In April 1975 the pro-US Cambodian leader Lon Nol was forced to flee in the face of the advancing Communist Khmer Rouge army. The erratic Prince Sihanouk, whom Lon Nol had deposed with US help, tried to take control of the country, but was removed by the Khmer Rouge

▼ Looting in Phnom Penh, 1975 – public order collapses as the US-backed regime crumbles before the advancing Khmer Rouge. The failure of the American war effort in Southeast Asia left former client regimes at the mercy of their Communist enemies. In Cambodia, where the Khmer Rouge had emerged as one of the most extreme Communist groups, the shift in power produced cataclysmic results.

The civil war in Lebanon in the 1970s and 1980s summed up the apparent hopelessness of Middle Eastern politics

◄ Life among the ruins – a Beirut woman collects water against a background of demolished building in the mid-1980s. Lebanon suffered the most severe consequences of destabilization in the Middle East. Israeli invasion, the Palestinian refugee problem, the emergence of rival forces of Islamic extremism and the interference by all the surrounding powers combined to reduce the small country to a battleground. A host of rival power groups fought out a confused and bloody civil war. Intervention by Israel and Syria, and interference by other powers ensured that no lasting settlement could emerge. The inhabitants continued to live under the threat of bombs and bullets.

► Ayatollah Khomeini, the Iranian Muslim avenging angel, tramples the devil of US capitalism underfoot. The Islamic revolution in Iran gave expression to the rising tide of religious fundamentalism – its identification of US interference as the villain of the piece transformed local rivalries into an explosive clash of values.

▼ Bound and blindfolded, the staff of the US embassy in Tehran are paraded before a hostile mob soon after their capture by revolutionary islamic students in November 1979. The hostages were held to ransom with the connivance of the new Iranian regime for 14 months. The plight provided a focus for the confrontation between the superpower that had once dominated the Middle East, and the new forces that had swept that domination aside. The dangers and difficulties of military intervention were highlighted by the failure of a rescue mission in 1980.

leader Pol Pot, who took over the government on 4 April 1976. Inspired by Chinese Communism, he emptied the towns and turned the whole country into a vast agricultural penal colony. Many hundreds of thousands died there or were killed in a regime of immense cruelty and savagery. Fighting between Vietnam and Cambodia (renamed Kampuchea) that began in 1975 culminated in a Vietnamese invasion in 1978. Pol Pot, who managed to escape, was sentenced to death in his absence for crimes against humanity but continued to lead the Khmer Rouge from Thailand. Almost one million people fled the upheavals in Vietnam and Cambodia. The new republic of Kampuchea (today, Cambodia; the name was changed back in 1989) became an increasingly troublesome source of contention between the Soviets and the Chinese, who resented Soviet support for the Vietnam-backed regime.

By 1989, the Vietnamese had begun to withdraw, under pressure from the United States, who had blocked economic aid to both Vietnam and Cambodia, and amid Cambodian fears that the Khmer Rouge would return.

Israel-Egypt peace agreement
Another traditional trouble-spot, the Middle East, remained a lasting source of conflict despite some optimism in the late 1970s. In May 1977, three and a half years after the Arab–Israeli Yom Kippur war, Menachem Begin, leader of the right-wing Likud party, became prime minister of Israel. Begin, himself a former terrorist and a hardline Israeli nationalist, was not, however, averse to seeking peace with his old enemy, Egypt.

In fact, as early as 1973, the Egyptian premier Anwar Sadat had proposed troop reductions with Israel and in November 1977 he amazed the world by traveling to Jerusalem to address the Knesset (Israeli parliament). Carter, the US president, invited both Sadat and Begin to Camp David, his presidential residence, where, in September 1978, the three leaders signed a historic "framework for peace in the Middle East". Egypt for the first time guaranteed Israel's right to exist while the Israelis agreed to return the Sinai desert to Egypt (completed on 25 April 1982). Both

Begin and Sadat received the Nobel Peace Prize for the work. However, the more extreme voices in the Arab world branded Sadat a traitor to the Arab cause. President Carter tried to encourage other moderate Arab states such as Jordan and Saudi Arabia to join in the peace process, but they met with no success. Egypt remained isolated and was expelled from the Arab League. On 6 October 1981 Sadat paid the ultimate price for breaking ranks when he was assassinated at a military review. Doubtless, had Begin been more flexible in his attitude toward Palestinian settlements and abandoned his call for a "greater Israel", Sadat's position in the Arab world would have been more tenable.

War in the Lebanon
At the root of the conflict in the Middle East was the Palestinian problem, which had attended the creation of the state of Israel in 1948 and had grown steadily worse since then. Many Palestinians lived precariously in refugee camps in the state of Lebanon, Israel's northern neighbor. From 1975 a Lebanese civil war raged between the Maronite Christians (a minority who wielded the power in Lebanese public life) and the Muslim Sunnis, Shiites and Druse. The presence of the Palestinians, who had made Beirut their operational base for guerrilla attacks on Israel and attracted Israeli reprisal raids, heightened the conflict.

In 1976 Syria, allegedly in the name of all Arab states, sent in its armed forces, prompting some, like Walid Jumblat, the left-wing Druse leader, to

The Gulf War

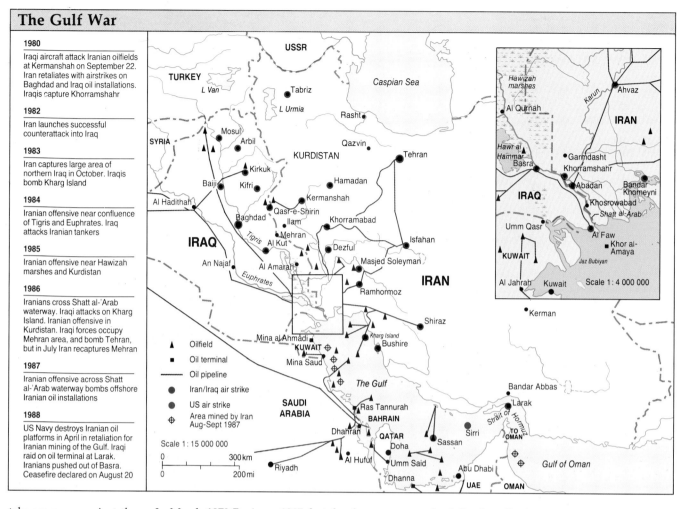

1980
Iraqi aircraft attack Iranian oilfields at Kermanshah on September 22. Iran retaliates with airstrikes on Baghdad and Iraq oil installations. Iraqis capture Khorramshahr

1982
Iran launches successful counterattack into Iraq

1983
Iran captures large area of northern Iraq in October. Iraqis bomb Kharg Island

1984
Iranian offensive near confluence of Tigris and Euphrates. Iraq attacks Iranian tankers

1985
Iranian offensive near Hawizah marshes and Kurdistan

1986
Iranians cross Shatt al-'Arab waterway. Iraqi attacks on Kharg Island. Iranian offensive in Kurdistan. Iraqi forces occupy Mehran area, and bomb Tehran, but in July Iran recaptures Mehran

1987
Iranian offensive across Shatt al-'Arab waterway bombs offshore Iranian oil installations

1988
US Navy destroys Iranian oil platforms in April in retaliation for Iranian mining of the Gulf. Iraqi raid on oil terminal at Larak. Iranians pushed out of Basra. Ceasefire declared on August 20

▲ Oilfield
■ Oil terminal
— Oil pipeline
● Iran/Iraq air strike
● US air strike
⊕ Area mined by Iran Aug–Sept 1987

Scale 1 : 15 000 000
0   300km
0   200mi

take up arms against them. In March 1978 Begin for the first time invaded the southern Lebanon to try to destroy the Palestinian bases but withdrew under UN pressure. Three years later, having rejected a Saudi peace plan, Begin annexed the Golan Heights on the Syrian border and, on 6 June 1982, invaded the Lebanon a second time. Israeli forces penetrated as far as West Beirut, but most of the Palestinian forces escaped, including Yasir Arafat, the leader of the Palestine Liberation Organization (PLO). Two days later a massacre of Palestinians by Christian forces took place in the Shattilla camp virtually in full view of the Israeli army.

The situation in Lebanon continued to grow worse. On 14 September the Christian Falangist leader, and president elect, Beshir Gemayel was assassinated. He was succeeded by his brother Amin. The next year 260 US Marines, part of a UN peace-keeping force, were killed trying to keep the warring factions apart from each other.

Israel was increasingly paying the price of its involvement, both in money and in reputation. The war cost more than one million US dollars a day, leading, in 1984, to 300 percent inflation. Israel also attracted growing hostility against actions that were seen as adventurist and expansionist. Begin had openly called for the annexation of the biblical lands of Judea and Samaria and continued to build Jewish settlements on the West Bank of the Jordan.

Israel began its withdrawal from Lebanon in

1985, but the deep scars remained. By then, Begin had retired through ill health and his successor, and leader of the Likud party, Yitzhak Shamir, had been forced in a coalition with the Labour party under Shimon Peres, who was keen to extricate Israel from the Lebanon.

Israel under pressure
The Israelis found it increasingly difficult to contain Palestinian nationalism within the occupied West Bank and Gaza Strip and retain the sympathy of the West.

In February 1988, television pictures showed

▲ The Gulf War began with a massive Iraqi offensive aimed at achieving territorial expansion while Iran was convulsed by revolution. Initially wavering, the Iranian forces managed to push back the Iraqis and a struggle of attrition set in along the original frontier.

▼ The success of the Tehran regime in mobilizing religious enthusiasm transformed the war into a religious crusade involving masses of fanatical revolutionary volunteers.

▲ The horrors of static warfare in the 1980s – bodies rot in foxholes and buildings burn as a soldier surveys the chaos of the war zone around Basra. The combat zone in front of the strategic Iraqi city of Basra soon resembled the Western Front of 1914–18, with tens of thousands of troops being fed into a confused and devastated battlefield where a decisive breakthrough remained impossible. Iran committed itself to the overthrow of the "heretic" government in Baghdad: Iraq, for all its anti-Khomeini rhetoric, was intent only on survival. In the end, mutual exhaustion would pave the way for a ceasefire in 1988.

Israeli soldiers forcing four Palestinians to lie down on a road while a bulldozer buried them with sand. The soldiers were also seen beating them and breaking someone's arm. The Israeli authorities promised to curb such excesses, but they remained as a solemn reminder of the bitterness of the conflict.

Consequently, the Western states decided to promote the fortunes of Yasir Arafat, the PLO leader. In September 1987 Arafat met left-wing Israeli parliamentarians in Geneva and in April 1988 he traveled to Moscow to meet Gorbachev (who told him to recognize Israel's right to exist). Further meetings in 1988 and 1989 with Western politicians and a declaration by the PLO that it no longer sought to destroy the state of Israel, encouraged both Britain and the United States to put pressure on the Israeli government to negotiate a settlement with the Palestinians.

The Iranian revolution

Elsewhere in the Middle East, US diplomatic endeavors received a savage rebuttal. Mohammed Reza Pahlavi, who had been Shah of Iran ever since 1941, was fully supported by the United States and the West. They saw in him a liberalizing and modernizing force in the Arab world, strongly pro-Western and anti-Soviet and a reliable supplier of oil. Even after the oil price hike in 1973, of which the Shah was one of the instigators, he was still regarded as an important ally. By 1978, however, opposition to his rule had

begun to destabilize his hold on power. The Shah's chief rival was the Muslim fundamentalist Ayatollah Khomeini, who had been exiled to Paris in 1946. There he recorded his denunciations of the Shah's "secularizing policies", which were smuggled into Iran on cassettes and widely broadcast. Despite forceful repression by the army and Savak, the notorious secret police, the Shah's situation rapidly became untenable.

On 16 January 1979 he handed over power to a regency council and left the country. On 1 February 1979 Khomeini returned to Tehran to a massive welcome to launch his Islamic revolution. Four days later, a provisional Islamic government was established with revolutionary tribunals, who condemned many thousands to death. On 31 March 1979 a referendum on whether Iran should become an Islamic republic returned a 99 percent vote in favor.

In November 1979 an international crisis inspired by Khomeini occurred when revolutionary students broke into the US embassy in Tehran and seized officials as hostages in a bid to force the United States to return the Shah to stand trial. Some blacks and women were released shortly afterward but 49 continued to be held. An attempted rescue mission by US marines in April 1980 failed miserably when their helicopter crashed in the Iranian desert. The crisis emphasized Carter's weakness and the hostages were not released until a settlement was negotiated the following year.

The "War of the Cities"

From 23 September 1980 Iran and neighboring Iraq were at war following a border dispute. Khomeini dismissed his president Bani-Sadr, who opposed the war, and replaced him first with Mohammed Rajai, who was later assassinated, and then by Ali Khamenei, a radical Islamic fundamentalist and supporter of the war.

It was a mark of the new caution governing superpower relationships that neither the United States nor the Soviet Union became deeply embroiled in the conflict through both stood to lose by it. The war threatened Western oil supplies, while to the Soviet Union it represented an in-

ternecine feud between two anti-American Muslim states. In fact, Iraq, despite violations of human rights in its treatment of its Kurdish minority, received arms from pro-Western Saudi Arabia and Egypt as well as France. The general dislike of the Ayatollah's regime may have been shared by the Soviet Union, which, with some 40 million Muslims of its own, viewed a victory for Islamic fundamentalism as a potential threat to its own internal order.

The Iran–Iraq war – often called the War of the Cities – rapidly led to an escalation of tension in the area. In May 1987 both Soviet and American ships came under fire in the Gulf, prompting the UN Security Council to call for a ceasefire, but the call was not heeded. The Iranians' claim that the Iraqis had used nerve gas and cynanide bombs added to the war a new and ugly dimension. By May 1988, when Iran seemed to have lost the war, Iraqi planes bombed the oil terminal of Hormuz and destroyed five tankers. On 18 July the Ayatollah Khomeini declared that he accepted the ceasefire, but the Iraqis, sensing victory, continued to fight on.

The presence of US warships in the Gulf to protect commercial interests led to an incident that brought Iran and the United States close to war. In August 1988 the USS *Vincennes*, a warship, shot down an Iranian airliner, killing everyone on board. The *Vincennes* had misread its radar and believed itself to be under attack. At the end of the year, an American civilian airliner was blown

▲ A civil war in Angola – Marxist UNITA forces parade beneath a poster of their leader. In Angola, as in many other new African nations, the withdrawal of the colonial power (Portugal) in 1975 transformed a war of independence into a civil war. The presence of well-armed guerrilla groups, some like the MPLA with Soviet and Cuban support, was seized on by powers such as South Africa to destabilize uncongenial new regimes.

◀ President (soon to be self-proclaimed Emperor) Bokassa of the Central African Republic (right) outshines his host President Amin on a state visit to Uganda in 1976. At their worst, the post-colonial conflicts in Africa allowed military strongmen like Amin (President of Uganda from 1971 to 1979) and Bokassa to use armed force and tribal rivalries to instal themselves as dictators. The comic-opera bombast of their rule could not compensate for widespread brutality, inefficiency and corruption. Although they were soon overthrown, the damage they caused made the tasks of their successors all the more difficult.

up over Lockerbie, Scotland, in what was thought to be a reprisal action.

Even after its war, Iran continued to show an uncompromising face to the world. In 1989 Khomeini put a price on the head of a British writer for publishing a blasphemous novel. The British government ordered full police protection for the author, Salman Rushdie, a former Muslim, and Britain's European partners also condemned such behaviour by a head of state. Khomeini's death in 1989 led to a power struggle in Iran between hardliners, including Khomeini's son, and comparative moderates such as Hashemi Rafsanjani.

War and famine in Africa

During the 1970s superpower relations, already uneasy over arms buildups, were further exacerbated by political and military conflict in Africa. Soviet support for the Angola liberation front led by Agosthino Neto enabled him and his Cuban troops to defeat both the pro-American FNLA and the UNITA forces led by Jonas Savimbi and backed by South Africa, who continued to fight a guerrilla war against the Marxist government. South Africa also supported antigovernment mercenaries in Mozambique.

Cuban troops also gave military support to General Mengistu's Marxist regime in Ethiopia during the war against neighboring Somalia (formerly Moscow's ally), which supported secessionist rebels in Ethiopia's Ogaden province, and Cubans assisted in the fight against Eritrean rebels on the Red Sea coastline. From 1977, the Soviets had poured arms into Ethiopia even

though the country faced terrible famine, which was worsened by government attempts to collectivize agriculture. In 1985, Ethiopia received aid in the form of money raised by the Irish rock-star Bob Geldof, in a concert staged in London and televised worldwide. The Ethiopian government, too, took measures, and by 1986 some 500,000 people had been resettled in the more fertile south of the country.

As in Angola, Mozambique and other African states, so in Rhodesia independence brought with it civil war. In 1965 Rhodesia had illegally declared its independence from Britain and maintained white-majority rule. However, by the late 1970s, under economic pressure and amid growing international condemnation and intensification of the civil war, the white minority government led by Ian Smith agreed to British proposals to end its rebel status. On 1 June 1979 Rhodesia became the Republic of Zimbabwe. In elections held the following February Robert Mugabe became prime minister and quickly established himself as one of Africa's most dynamic leaders. After independence differences emerged between Mugabe's ruling ZANU-PF (Zimbabwe African National Unity – Patriotic Front) party and that of his former guerilla ally, Joshua Nkomo, whose ZAPU (Zimbabwe African People's Union) party drew its strength from Matabeleland. In particular, ZAPU opposed Mugabe's plans for a one-party state. Some of Nkomo's followers were murdered, and he himself fled the country for a short time. However, in 1986 talks began with a view to merging the two parties. Internationally, Mugabe, as leader of a "front line state", has tried to muster support for economic and if necessary military measures against South Africa.

Crisis in South Africa

In South Africa, the only African state that was still ruled by whites, the situation deteriorated rapidly. In September 1978 Pieter Willem Botha succeeded Johannes Vorster as prime minister and also became the minister for national security. Announcing that South Africa was "multiethnic", he attempted to buy off the Asian and "colored" communities, who together represented 14 percent of the population, by offering them limited political consultative rights. The real power, however, still resided with the whites (19 percent of the population), while the two-thirds blacks majority remained disenfranchised. At the same time, Botha took apartheid – the policy of so-called "separate development" – a stage further by establishing *Bantustans* or "tribal homelands", which virtually made blacks aliens in their own country. In 1985, however, he repealed some apartheid laws, including the ban on marriage or cohabitation between blacks and whites.

From 1983, South Africa experienced a severe recession, made worse by foreign investors losing confidence in the South African economy. In succeeding years, political tensions heightened and in 1986 a state of emergency was declared and reporting restrictions were imposed on the Western media. Thousands of people were imprisoned without trial and many hundreds are

▲ Imprisoned by the South African authorities in 1963 for terrorism, the African National Congress leader Nelson Mandela proved as potent a threat to white minority rule behind bars as he did an inspirational leader of black resistance during his active political career. His isolation in prison had the effect of providing the black nationalist with a form of symbolic leadership, and the attention he attracted all over the world made it difficult for the South African government to execute or release him.

◄ One of the 23 victims of the Soweto riots of June 1976, when young blacks protesting about conditions in the black townships around Johannesburg were gunned down by police. Kept at boiling point by economic hardship, overcrowding and police interference, black opposition in the squalid townships of South Africa periodically erupted into widescale rioting. The beleaguered white regime never hesitated to use force to reimpose order, with the result that each outbreak has produced a new group of martyrs – killed by police bullets or beaten into prison – to keep the campaign against apartheid alive.

▲ Defiance on the rooftop of the world. Mujaheddin guerillas await the Russian invaders in Afghanistan in the 1980s. The Soviet intervention in Afghanistan in December 1979 was occasioned by concern at political developments in a country of critical strategic importance to the Soviet position in south Asia. Although a friendly regime was installed fairly easily, the presence of Russian troops stirred up a potent mixture of fierce tribal independence and Islamic fundamentalist feeling. Soviet and Afghan government forces soon found themselves embroiled in a savage guerrilla war in which even modern military technology and direct attacks on civilian life, property and morale could not win. The resistance movement was supplied with arms from the West. Once again, the cost of intervention by a superpower proved too high and after ten years of fighting the Soviets were forced to withdraw. Meanwhile several million refugees awaited the end of the war in camps in Pakistan.

believed to have been tortured and killed at the hands of the South African security forces. Botha now faced opposition not only from the blacks but increasingly from white neo-Nazi extremists. Outside the country, too, pressure was mounting to force South Africa to bring about changes. However, an attempt by the Commonwealth in 1986 to introduce economic sanctions against South Africa was blocked by the British prime minister, Margaret Thatcher. She argued that such measures would harm the black population, cause chaos in the "front line" states whose economies depended on South Africa, and encourage a siege mentality in South Africa itself. Britain had many business ties with South Africa, and indeed its economic importance for the West as a whole was considerable. South Africa supplied 97 percent of the West's platinum, 70 percent of its gold and manganese and 20 percent of its uranium.

To assuage world opinion after the introduction of emergency powers, Botha announced the abolition of the hated pass laws, which restricted the movement of blacks about the country, and promised new constitutional rights for both blacks and coloreds. In 1987 he even agreed to reform the group areas act, which was seen as the mainstay of apartheid. However, despite appeals from the European Community states and others, he refused to release the jailed African National Congress (ANC) leader Nelson Mandela. The United States extended its sanctions, begun in

1985, and banned airline flights to South Africa from American carriers. Several American, British and Canadian firms also closed down their South African operations.

Botha faced an invidious choice. Too much liberalization internally would promote a right-wing backlash and his National party (NP), which ruled the country since 1968, might be driven from power. Too little reform, on the other hand, would lose South Africa whatever little sympathy that remained in the West for it. In 1987 Botha suffered a stroke and with much reluctance gave way to F. W. de Klerk. Although he too promised reforms, his election and that of the NP, was marked by new levels of violence and police savagery in putting down protests against the limited franchise. However, he did permit an anti-apartheid march in Cape Town, which attracted tens of thousands of supporters.

South African aggression abroad
Despite P. W. Botha's pledge of South African neutrality in foreign affairs, in 1983 South Africa invaded Angola. Politicians in Pretoria refused to accept the independence of Southwest Africa (Namibia), and attempted to destroy the SWAPO (South West African Peoples' Organization) guerilla bases on Angolan territory. South Africa refused to bow to UN pressure to withdraw from Southwest Africa while Cuban troops remained in Angola. However, in 1984 an armistice was signed by the two states, leading to the weaken

Olympics and declining to attend official functions held in Moscow.

In fact, the Muslim insurgents, or Mujaheddin, received increasing support from Pakistan and, indirectly, the United States. Encouraged in their struggle by the outrage felt in the Western world at the Soviet invasion and the pressure on the Soviet Union to withdraw, they agreed to a ceasefire in January 1987 to give themselves time to regroup. In the autumn, Dr Najibullah succeeded Karmal as president and plans were made for the Soviets to withdraw. Karmal was arrested and taken to Moscow. Najibullah offered a program of national reconciliation, which the Mujaheddin, sensing that victory was close, rejected.

The withdrawal of Soviet troops continued in a worsening situation for both them and their Afghanistan comrades. The war had claimed the lives of thousands of Soviet troops, despite superior Soviet firepower, and the Mujaheddin pressed ever closer to the capital, Kabul. By August 1988 half the Soviet troops had withdrawn across the Friendship Bridge separating the two states, the rest following in December. However, Kabul did not fall, as was expected, and stiff resistance by government forces, coupled with dissent and faction-fighting among the rebels, led to stalemate.

Political turmoil in Southern Asia
In 1977 a military coup in Pakistan led by General Zia Ul-Haq ousted Zulfikar Ali Bhutto, the prime minister and leader of the Pakistan People's Party. Bhutto was hanged in 1979. Zia imposed harsh measures, banning political parties and waging a campaign of Islamification. However, he failed to eradicate corruption or the burgeoning opium poppy trade. Severe drought and poor harvests in 1983, and an inflation rate of 20 percent, as well as growing friction with India over the status of the border province of Kashmir, all added to his problems.

To improve relations with India, he visited the Indian prime minister Rajiv Gandhi in January 1986. However, he could not stifle political opposition at home from Bhutto's Oxford-educated

▼ Continuity and change in India – Rajiv Gandhi lighting the funeral pyre of his assassinated mother Indira in 1984. The death of Indira Gandhi at the hands of her Sikh bodyguard brought her politically inexperienced son Rajiv to power in an explosive but politically hopeful situation.

▼ The assassination of Pakistan's military leader general Zia ul-Haq left the way clear for the return of Benazir Bhutto, daughter of Zulfikar, former president and Zia's political opponent who was executed during the early years of his reign. Bhutto swept to power in the subsequent election, the first elected female leader of a strongly Islamic state.

ing of SWAPO, though it was recognized by the UN as the sole representative of the Namibian people. In 1989 Namibia became an independent state. South Africa also concluded a deal with Mozambique, another former Portuguese colony, promising to withdraw support from rebel mercenaries in exchange for Mozambique's denial of bases to the ANC.

The Soviet invasion of Afghanistan
If East and West were united in their condemnation of South Africa, they were deeply divided over events in Afghanistan. Since 1973 Afghanistan had been ruled by a left-wing regime, but a coup in April 1978 by Mur Taraki brought the country fully into the Soviet orbit. The Muslim population revolted, allegedly killing a thousand or so Soviet military "advisors". In September 1979 Taraki was overthrown by Hafizullah Amin who, according to the Soviets, asked for their help to "defend the revolution".

However, on 26 December Amin, his family and closest advisers were murdered and replaced by Babrak Karmal (whose assumed name means "workers' friend"), who had spent a period in exile in the Soviet Union. Aided by Soviet troops, he tried to crush Muslim resistance to the Soviet-backed regime. Outside Afghanistan, 35 Muslim states joined together in January 1980 to call for Soviet troops to withdraw. The West confined itself to a public condemnation of the Soviet action, including a boycott of the 1980 Moscow

daughter Benazir. Zia imprisoned her and then had her placed under house arrest in August 1986, but riots forced him to release her the following month. The tenth anniversary of his rule was marked by civil unrest and a bomb in Karachi that killed over seventy people. To make matters worse, in October, the Americans halted their aid program to Pakistan because they feared it had become a nuclear power.

In May 1988, under growing pressure, he announced new elections. Zia was assassinated shortly afterwards, together with the US ambassador to Pakistan, while flying to review troops. Benazir Bhutto swept to power in the elections as her nation's first woman leader.

India too, experience political crises beginning in the 1970s. In 1974 India carried out a successful nuclear test to become the sixth country to possess a nuclear bomb. However, the United States was concerned at the prospect of nuclear weapons falling into the hands of unstable states even if, like India and Israel, they were democracies. (The thought of Pakistan acquiring and sharing the secrets of its "Islamic bomb" with

Iran after 1979 filled them with horror.) In fact, American fears about India's instability were soon justified. In 1975, Indira Gandhi, India's prime minister, proclaimed a state of emergency to prevent opposition to her reforms, which included compulsory sterilization as a means of birth control. She suffered a humiliating defeat at the polls in 1977 but was re-elected and took office as prime minister once again in 1980. Five years later, however, she was assassinated by Sikh extremists who had penetrated her bodyguard and sought to avenge the storming of their shrine, the golden temple at Amritsar, which Gandhi had ordered to root out Sikh nationalist guerrillas. She was succeeded by her son, Rajiv.

Other South Asian states also experienced violent political upheaval. In December 1985 in the Philippines the chief of staff of the armed forces and several others were acquitted of the murder of Benigno Aquino, a respected democrat who had been shot on his return from exile to stand against President Ferdinand Marcos in the presidential elections. He was replaced as a candidate by his redoubtable wife, Corazon Aquino, who received massive popular support. When in the February elections Marcos claimed victory no one believed him. Indeed, television pictures had shown the intimidation and violence that attended his campaign and there were strong suspicions that the ballot had been rigged.

Both Aquino and Marcos were sworn in as presidents, but fighting around the presidential palace forced Marcos and his wife Imelda to seek safe conduct in a US helicopter to Hawaii. Investigations revealed that Marcos had embezzled millions of dollars and invested them in property and art. Aquino's murderers were tried and convicted. The new administration, however, though no longer corrupt, did not satisfy the Communists, who continued with guerrilla activities in their struggle to bring about a redistribution of resources in a country divided by extreme wealth and extreme poverty. When Marcos died in 1989 Mrs Aquino refused to allow his body to be returned home.

▶ In Argentina during the Falklands war the British prime minister became the focus of a propaganda campaign against the enemy; this magazine claims to expose Mrs Thatcher as "The Lady of Death – her husband hates her; her daughter is a drug addict; her grandfather was a thief…".

▼ US anti-Communist policy in Central America committed it to supporting rightwing militarist dictatorships, despite their corruption, inefficiency and disregard for human rights. In Nicaragua, the US threw its support behind the Somoza dynasty, but was ultimately unable to save it from the populist guerrilla forces of the Communist Sandinista movement (seen here). Following the Sandinista triumph. US support was transferred to a motley collection of resistance groups, collectively known as the Contras.

Human Rights

▲ Argentineans with photographs of dead children.

Classical liberalism asserted the universal rights of the individual for life, liberty and the pursuit of happiness, a position developed since 1945 actively to protect all people against oppression, even from the agents of their own state. The United Nations charter pledged all members to achieve "respect for, and observance of, human rights and freedoms without distinction as to race, sex, language or religion", a position endorsed in 1948. Concern for human rights was also expressed in a European Convention in 1950, and by the Organization of African Unity in 1981.

The public advocacy of human rights as part of national foreign policy by leading world statesman – particularly US president Jimmy Carter – and the growth in voluntary agencies aiming to protect human rights against the power of the state, brought the subject to wider public awareness in the 1970s. Protests against torture or judicial murder could lead to international action against the perpetrating government.

US intervention in the Third World

Because of his fervent anti-Communism President Marcos had received the support of the United States until he became a political embarrassment. Elsewhere in the Third World too the American criterion for support was based on to US interests rather than allegiance to democracy. In the Central American state of Nicaragua, where the pro-American dictator Somoza was overthrown by the Sandinista guerrillas in 1979, and El Salvador, where on 10 October 1982 rebels mounted a major offensive against the government, the CIA armed and trained anti-Communist forces. In 1985, US troops even invaded the West Indian island of Grenada, a member of the Commonwealth, to remove a Marxist regime. President Reagan's policy towards Central America, which he called "America's backyard", attracted criticism both in the United States and in Europe, if only because it made it harder to condemn Soviet actions in Afghanistan and risked escalating the Central American crisis into a new Vietnam.

The US bombing of Libya in 1986, following acts of terrorism by Palestinian guerrillas in Europe, was equally controversial. In December 1985, 17 people were murdered at Rome and Vienna airports, and in 1986 a bomb planted in a Berlin nightclub killed a US serviceman and injured many others. Further explosions caused havoc in Paris, and a bomb thrown at Israelis praying at the Wailing Wall in Jerusalem killed one person and injured 69 others. In Britain, a Palestinian terrorist, Nezar Hindawi, received a jail sentence of 46 years for having concealed a bomb in the suitcase of his pregnant girlfriend, who was booked on a flight to Israel.

The United States claimed that the Libyan leader Colonel Qadhafi was behind these attacks. It was well known that he supported terrorism with money derived from oil and that he also supplied arms and training to guerrilla groups (including the IRA). Britain, however, blamed the Syrian government, which had been strongly implicated in the Hindawi affair.

Matters came to a head when the US airforce bombed Libyan radar installations in retaliation for an alleged earlier Libyan transgression against the US Mediterranean fleet. Then, in April, US F111 aircraft attacked Libya itself, killing many civilians including Qadhafi's adopted baby daughter. The British prime minister Thatcher acquiesced in the bombing by permitting the F111s to fly from bases in Britain. The French and Spanish, by contrast, refused permission to overfly their airspace.

War in the South Atlantic

Ever the faithful ally of the United States, Britain itself was thrust to the front of the world stage when, in 1982, a crisis developed in the South Atlantic. For many years Argentina had tried to negotiate for the Malvinas (Falkland Islands), which Britain had taken as a colony 150 years earlier. On 3 April 1982, after a scaling down of the British military presence in the South Atlantic, Argentina invaded the Islands.

The move took Britain wholly by surprise and forced the resignation of the foreign secretary, Lord Carrington. The British prime minister Thatcher demanded an immediate Argentine withdrawal, at the same time preparing to send a massive task force to the South Atlantic. After some wavering, the Americans, whose anti-colonial stance made them naturally sympathetic to the Argentinean case, supported Britain, allowing Britain to use Ascension Island as a base. The European Community, including Italy who had close ties with Argentina, also gave Britain diplomatic support. After some very hard fighting in which 700 Argentineans and 255 Britons lost their lives, Britain retook the Falkland Islands in June 1982. Argentina's failure led to the fall of its military junta, and its replacement by a democratic government, while in Britain the war restored Mrs Thatcher's popularity.

▲ The Argentinean invasion of the remote Falkland Islands transformed an unwanted relic of the British imperial past into a symbol of national pride for which the Thatcher government and the majority of the British public were prepared to fight. The early sinking by the British of the elderly troopship *Belgrano*, with heavy loss of Argentine life (above) was condemned as an irresponsible act which destroyed any chance of a peaceful solution. Yet war was probably inevitable from the moment of invasion. While the Argentinean air force caused serious losses, superior British training and logistics allowed a relatively swift reconquest.

INTERNATIONAL TERRORISM

Terrorism is the systematic use of coercive intimidation to create a climate of fear among a wider target group. Perpetrators of terrorism include regimes and agencies of states as well as nationalist, ideological and religious extremist movements. Terrorism may be used to compel the target to comply with the perpretrators' demands, to "neutralize" particular sectors of the population, to publicize a cause, to demoralize and disorient perceived enemies, or to provoke a rival group of governmental authority into over-reaction. Terrorism since the 1960s has been ex-perienced in its "pure" form mainly in Western European and other industrialized states. In most Third World countries it has been intert-wined with far more extensive and lethal conf-licts as an accompaniment to civil and even in-ternational wars, as for example in Vietnam, the Lebanon, and Central America. A valuable dis-tinction can be made between domestic ter-rorism, confined within a single state, and inter-national terrorism, involving the citizens of more than one country.

Following World War II, major terrorist cam-paigns were waged in the course of anticolonial insurgencies in many countries, including Palestine, Cyprus, Algeria and Aden. Terrorism proved a very effective weapon of attrition in undermring the will of the colonial powers to sustain their colonial presence. Strategic political objectives were gained, mainly because of the enormous domestic support enjoyed by the insurgents and by the growing desire of the colonial authorities to withdraw from their heavy overseas commitments.

Far from ending terrorism, the process of decolonization paradoxically fueled international terrorism in the late 1960s and early 1970s, as numerous militant ethnic movements chose to challenge the new international order to gain self-determination. The best-known and most influential of these groups were the Palestinian PLO militants, who opted for terrorism as a weapon of last resort following the disastrous defeat of Arab conventional arms in the June 1967 war with Israel. Other factors conducive to the burgeoning of international terrorism in the late 1960s and early 1970s were the strategic nuclear balance between the superpowers which made low-cost, low-risk, potentially high-yield clandestine methods more attractive to both ter-rorist movements and their state sponsors; the shift of emphasis among revolutionary leaders in the Third World away from heavy reliance on rural guerrilla and towards greater use of urban terrorism; the emergence of the new-left student generation in the industrial countries such as West Germany, which created small residues of militants dedicated to the use of terrorism against Western capitalism in general and the United States in particular; modern technologies such as international jet travel, television satellite communications, and plastic explosives, which have greatly increased both the capability of the terrorist to cause terror and publicize the cause, and the vulnerability of society.

▼ Palestinian opponents of Israel have often resorted to terrorist attacks on Israeli civilian targets. This bus was hijacked on its way to Tel Aviv in November 1978.

▲ Aldo Moro, leader of the Italian Christian Democrat party, was kidnapped in 1978 by Red Brigades terrorists and killed after the government refused to negotiate.

◀ In the 1970s fears arose about the activities of "freelance" international terrorists. One of the most notorious was the Venezuelan Ilich Ramirez Sanchos, known as Carlos Martinez, who was implicated in actions involving Palestinian terrorist groups in Paris and London in the mid-1970s.

▶ The Provisional Wing of the Irish Republican Army (IRA) undertook paramilitary activity in their fight for a united Ireland in the 1970s and 1980s. As well as conducting a clandestine program of terror against civilian and military targets in Northern Ireland and mainland Britain, they openly patrolled areas of Northern Ireland and created "No-go" areas for British troops.

▼ Airlines – expensive, vulnerable and prestige targets – have often been terrorist targets. This aircraft was blown up in Amman in 1970, after the PLO had negotiated the release of a number of hostages.

▶ Terrorist tactics may be used by state organizations, as well as those seeking power. In 1985 the Greenpeace environmentalist ship Rainbow Warrior was sunk by French secret agents while conducting a campaign against French nuclear testing in the Pacific.

◀ In 1986 the United States, enraged by Libyan support for terrorism, tried to take revenge by bombing Tripoli. Some 16 adults and four children were killed. After this incident, both countries have been accused of fostering state terrorism.

Datafile

The end of the 1970s saw a widespread trend away from the centrist, welfare and consensus-based style of government that had prevailed, in many countries, since 1945. In much of Western Europe and the United States, center-right political parties began to win success in the early 1980s. As a result parties of the left tended to move towards the center ground to court the electorate once again – a tendency that was found in the Eastern bloc as well.

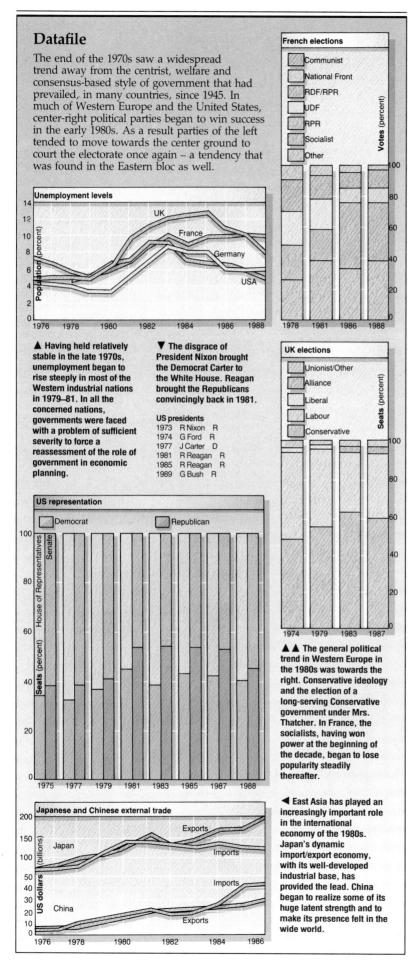

Unemployment levels

▲ Having held relatively stable in the late 1970s, unemployment began to rise steeply in most of the Western industrial nations in 1979–81. In all the concerned nations, governments were faced with a problem of sufficient severity to force a reassessment of the role of government in economic planning.

▼ The disgrace of President Nixon brought the Democrat Carter to the White House. Reagan brought the Republicans convincingly back in 1981.

US presidents
1973	R Nixon	R
1974	G Ford	R
1977	J Carter	D
1981	R Reagan	R
1985	R Reagan	R
1989	G Bush	R

French elections

UK elections

US representation

Japanese and Chinese external trade

▲▲ The general political trend in Western Europe in the 1980s was towards the right. Conservative ideology and the election of a long-serving Conservative government under Mrs. Thatcher. In France, the socialists, having won power at the beginning of the decade, began to lose popularity steadily thereafter.

◀ East Asia has played an increasingly important role in the international economy of the 1980s. Japan's dynamic import/export economy, with its well-developed industrial base, has provided the lead. China began to realize some of its huge latent strength and to make its presence felt in the wide world.

In the mid-1970s, it seemed that the future belonged to the left and to center-left. When the Democrat Jimmy Carter was elected to the White House on 2 November 1976, the United States followed Western Europe's leftwards tendency, with high welfare expenditure and defense cuts. In the face of an ever-worsening recession, however, federal expenditure increased dramatically along with unemployment and the plight of the US economy affected other capitalist economies. Carter's failures discredited left-of-center politics, and led to the victory of the Republican Ronald Reagan with an absolute majority in the presidential election of 1980.

Reagan promised to cut the budget deficit and government expenditure, control the money supply and reduce taxation. This entailed swingeing cuts in social welfare programs. At the same time, government expenditure on defense increased by US$1.5 billion. Budget deficits continued to rise and the value of the dollar remained high, though inflation was halved.

By 1983, amid worldwide decline in industrial production, the United States was producing little more than it had done in 1975. Thousands of businesses across the country went bankrupt. Drastic measures were called for to reverse the decline, and in 1983 the US Congress voted to raise taxes.

Despite such a traditionally unpopular move, Reagan was reelected in 1984. His tough-minded attitude to the Russians, his interventions in the affairs of sovereign states such as Grenada and Nicaragua, a growing right-wing trend within public opinion. His diplomatic successes in US-Soviet relations were likewise seen as the result of his firm stand against what he once called "the evil empire".

In February 1987 it was revealed that arms had been illegally sold to Iran in exchange for the release of hostages, and that the profits from the deal had been channeled to the Contra rebels in Nicaragua to whom Congress had denied military assistance. Although further inquiries implicated the then national security adviser, Admiral Poindexter, and Oliver North, doubts remained as to whether the President might not have given his tacit approval in aid of a cause so dear to his heart. Suspicion also fell onto Reagan's vice president, George Bush, but despite this he succeeded in winning the Republican nomination for the presidency, with the backing of Reagan. Bush, a former Central Intelligence Agency boss, went on to defeat the Democrat Michael Dukakis in the presidential election of November 1988. Bush emphasized the need for the death penalty, opposition to abortion, and the continuation of policies that had led to Reagan's successes at home and abroad.

REFORM AND RETRENCHMENT

The shift to the right in
the United States

Politics in Western
Europe

Gorbachev and
perestroika

Liberalization and
backlash in China

◀ Popular conservatism and
the return to US greatness –
Ronald Reagan and his wife
fly home from a summit
meeting with Gorbachev.

The move to the right in Britain
Britain's left-of-center Labour government took
office in 1974. By 1975 Harold Wilson's Labour
government faced inflation in double figures,
growing unemployment and the economic consequences of Britain's entry into the European
Community. In the first-ever referendum held in
Britain, however, the people voted to stay in
Europe.

James Callaghan, who took over as prime
minister in 1976, attempted to attack Britain's
economic problems and control inflation by
reducing public expenditure (including welfare
spending) and holding down wage levels. These
measures were very unpopular with the trade
unions and other traditional Labour supporters.

On 3 May 1979 Margaret Thatcher, a rightwing
Conservative, became Britain's first woman
prime minister, after an election campaign that

The New Right

Beginning in the late 1970s the domestic political
life of many Western states underwent a shift
towards new-style, rightwing conservatism,
represented by Ronald Reagan in the United
States and Margaret Thatcher in Britain.

The appeal of the new right lay above all in its
economic strategy. Socialist and social democratic
economic theories, its supporters claimed, had
proved incapable of dealing with the problems
of industrial stagnation, high inflation and
increasing unemployment. To combat these ills,
the new right proposed cuts in government
spending, high interest rates to bring down
inflation, and less government involvement in
industry (effectively a shakeout of "surplus
labor") as well as greater reliance on market
forces and individual enterprise. Forced to
concede that such measures would increase
unemployment in the shorter term, the new right
argued that in the longer term more jobs would
be created, even if full employment were a thing
of the past.

In matters of social policy, the new right
attacked government aid and instead stressed the
virtues of self-help and individual reliance. They
also advocated harsh "law and order" measures
(though more often than not these failed to
reduce the levels of crime). For many of society's
ills they blamed the "liberalism" of the 1960s – in
particular changes in the laws relating to murder,
sex offenses and abortion and called for the
restoration of the death penalty. In foreign
policy, they attacked détente which, they
claimed, had been promoted by the left and
center-left and had succeeded only in making the
world more dangerous. The apparent failure of
détente won increasing support for the strong
anti-Soviet line taken by the new right and
underlined their call for NATO to rearm. They
also called for tougher measures worldwide

▼ The hidden face of America
– urban poverty and lower
class despair. US
administrators in the 1980s
had to face difficult domestic
problems, notably inflation
and high unemployment rates,
particularly in the ethnic
minority groups in the inner
cities, which had endured
decades of neglect.

against "international terrorism", especially acts
that had an Arab connection.

Although the new right was electorally
successful, their economic policies were markedly
less so, except, in some cases, in reducing
inflation. The US debt continued to soar, as did
imports of high-technology and motor vehicles
from the Far East, along with, in most Western
countries, unemployment. The promised
"enterprise economy" offering a higher living
standard and jobs for all those who wanted
them, remained a very long way off.

Alternative Politics

Perhaps the most influential of the new political groupings was the Green movement whose major concern was the environment. The dangers of nuclear energy as shown by the disaster at Three Mile Island nuclear-power plant (1979), the accident of Chernobyl in 1986, as well as acid-rain pollution, pollution by oil slicks, the destruction of the rain forests, and the threat to endangered species were among their concerns.

In Western Europe, the "Greens" made their biggest impact in the Federal Republic of Germany, where they gained 2.2 million votes and 27 seats in the elections of 1983. In the 1984 European parliamentary elections they won 11 seats, and by 1986 most Western European states had Green parties.

Many Greens, as well as campaigning for the environment, also strongly opposed NATO's rearmament after 1979 and, in West Germany, they called the country's withdrawal from NATO as a first step towards the abolition of both military alliances. Having grown out of the protest movements of the 1960s, they often despised conventional politics, but were divided on whether to work towards or to object to anything other than total power. By focusing public awareness on environmental issues they forced other political parties to write policies for the protection of the environment into their manifestos.

Another movement that grew out of the 1960s was feminism. It was promoted largely by a well-educated female elite (itself the product of improved educational opportunities for women) aware of the social inequality that women faced and determined, through the availability of oral contraception and safer methods of abortion, to control their own fertility. The feminist movement gained impetus from the sharp increases in the number of single-parent families in the 1970s and numbers of working women. Across the Western world, feminist organizations sprang up to promote women's rights: the National Organization of Women in the United States, the National Women's Coordinating Committee and the 300 Group in Britain and the Dolle Mina in the Netherlands.

However, in most West European countries,

unemployment rates remained higher for women than for men, and women continued, despite equal-pay legislation, to receive 20–50 percent less than men for the same work. Moreover, women's work was overwhelmingly of the low-status or part-time variety. Between 1979 and 1986 the number of women in parliament in Britain and the United States declined (despite the election of a woman prime minister in Britain). However, elsewhere in the West (notably the Netherlands and Scandinavia) the number of women in politics considerably.

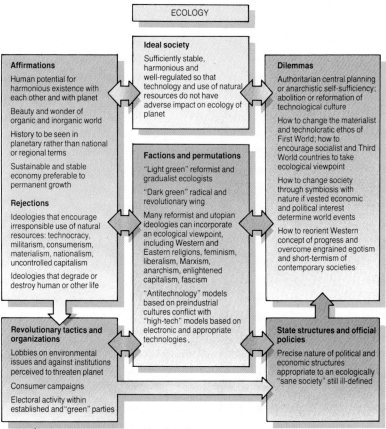

ECOLOGY

Ideal society
Sufficiently stable, harmonious and well-regulated so that technology and use of natural resources do not have adverse impact on ecology of planet

Affirmations
Human potential for harmonious existence with each other and with planet

Beauty and wonder of organic and inorganic world

History to be seen in planetary rather than national or regional terms

Sustainable and stable economy preferable to permanent growth

Rejections
Ideologies that encourage irresponsible use of natural resources: technocracy, militarism, consumerism, materialism, nationalism, uncontrolled capitalism

Ideologies that degrade or destroy human or other life

Dilemmas
Authoritarian central planning or anarchistic self-sufficiency; abolition or reformation of technological culture

How to change the materialist and technolcratic ethos of First World; how to encourage socialist and Third World countries to take ecological viewpoint

How to change society through symbiosis with nature if vested economic and political interest determine world events

How to reorient Western concept of progress and overcome engrained egotism and short-termism of contemporary societies

Factions and permutations
"Light green" reformist and gradualist ecologists

"Dark green" radical and revolutionary wing

Many reformist and utopian ideologies can incorporate an ecological viewpoint, including Western and Eastern religions, feminism, liberalism, Marxism, anarchism, enlightened capitalism, fascism

"Antitechnology" models based on preindustrial cultures conflict with "high-tech" models based on electronic and appropriate technologies.

Revolutionary tactics and organizations
Lobbies on environmental issues and against institutions perceived to threaten planet

Consumer campaigns

Electoral activity within established and "green" parties

State structures and official policies
Precise nature of political and economic structures appropriate to an ecologically "sane society" still ill-defined

▼ While the Greenpeace environmentalist group (left) successfully focused public attention by means of dramatic direct actions on issues such as the dumping of polluting waste at sea, the West German Green party used existing opposition to nuclear weapons and concern about pollution to transform itself into a successful political party (below).

focused strongly on the disruption caused by public services strikes. The early Thatcher years saw a steep rise in unemployment, urban rioting, and increased arms expenditure. Nevertheless, on 9 June 1983 she won her second election. By 1986, however, it was clear that, even though unemployment had reached 1930s levels in the great shake-out of surplus labor, industrial output was not higher than a decade earlier. In 1984–85 a costly miners' strike highlighted the disaster that could have faced British industry. A fall in oil prices in 1985 and 1986, and the consequent run on the pound sterling, added to Britain's economic and social problems though Thatcher won a third term of office in 1987.

The decline of the German center-left
West Germany, too, moved to the right in the later 1970s. In 1974, it was revealed that Willy Brandt, Social Democratic (SPD) chancellor since 1969 and one of the main architects of détente, had unknowingly used as one of his closest aides a Communist agent. Brandt resigned and devoted himself to studying world resource and wealth inequalities. The new SPD chancellor, Helmut Schmidt, who took over on 16 May 1974, was politically to the right of Brandt and in many ways closer to Helmut Kohl, the leader of the center-right Christian Democrats, who succeeded him as chancellor. Both believed in similar anti-inflationary measures, in the market economy and in the need for NATO's rearmament.

The SPD also faced a challenge from the Green party. The SPD decided to project a more leftist profile. Hans-Jochen Vögel replaced Schmidt as leader of the party, stressing its opposition to NATO's rearmament and its concern for ecological issues. However, in the parliamentary elections of 6 March 1983, which were won by the Christian Democrats (CDU), while the SPD booked its worst election result since 1961.

Under Helmut Kohl inflation fell, the value of the Deutschmark remained constant, and the economy experienced a boom in new businesses. However, cutbacks in social expenditure hit the poor and there was high unemployment. In its relations with East Germany, Kohl's government, somewhat surprisingly, continued to pursue Willy Brandt's *Ostpolitik*. In 1972, the two Germanies had signed a treaty in which each recognized the legitimacy of the other, though this was opposed at the time by the CDU. By 1984, however, the East German government was receiving payments of one billion Deutschmark (DM) per year from the West, in addition to payments for the release of political dissidents and credit loans. Increased trade between the two countries was particularly important to the East Germans, who lifted the ban on West German television broadcasting. Chancellor Kohl has since called for German reunification which, according to opinion polls, would be supported by the vast majority of West Germans.

Democracy in Western Europe
The Netherlands followed a similar pattern of political development. The socialist-led coalition government of Joop den Uyl that had held power

▲ British police face striking coal miners in a long and bitter dispute of 1985, which epitomized the conflict between new-right policies and traditional unionist concerns. The re-emergence of the political right in Britain showed its less pleasant face in the British government's handling of the strike. It was claimed the government deliberately turned an industrial dispute into a political one. It attempted to portray trade unions as enemies of economic growth and political stability in an effort to undermine a movement which had, at worst, only a fragmented minority interest in political issues.

the Communists, captured power. Mitterrand's government, which included Communists for the first time in 30 years, set about creating new jobs, increasing the basic national wage and nationalizing banks and insurance companies.

Mitterrand's domestic socialism, however, was offset by a strong commitment to the "Atlanticism" of Western Europe. At home, rising inflation and problems with industry persuaded Mitterrand to move away from socialist policies and introduce deflationary measures. Yet while Mitterrand's socialism appeared to be losing popularity, he himself was achieving greater respect among the French as a statesman. At the 1986 elections the socialists lost their majority, and Mitterrand found himself with a center-right prime minister, Jacques Chirac. In April 1988, Chirac stood against Mitterrand in the presidential elections, but lost badly. The rightwing extremist Jean-Marie Le Pen, though, polled 14 percent of the vote on the first ballot.

In European affairs, Mitterrand worked closely with the Germans in the cause of greater European unity. At an emotional meeting between Mitterrand and Kohl to mark the 25th anniversary of the Franco-German treaty of friendship in 1988 the leaders agreed on a joint political council and a joint troop brigade.

On Francisco Franco's death on 20 November 1975, Juan Carlos was proclaimed king and began to restore democracy to his country. He lifted the ban on political parties and at the end of 1978 promulgated a new constitution. After the elections held in October 1982, the Socialists were the largest single party in the Cortes (Spanish parliament), under the charismatic leader Felipe Gonzalez. Gonzalez was challenged within his own party in January 1986 over his support for Spain's continued membership of NATO. In fact, Spain voted in a referendum to remain in NATO, and in the 1986 elections the socialists lost 18 seats.

since 1973 fell to the Christian Democrats in 1982 in the wake of anxieties about inflation, a soaring deficit and Holland's role in NATO. The new prime minister Ruud Lubbers confirmed the swing to the right and consolidated his government in May 1986. Lubbers imposed austerity measures. His response to increased awareness over environmental issues, however, brought about a serious coalition crisis in 1989. A plan to end tax relief for commuters in a bid to reduce car exhaust pollution met with fierce opposition from the rightwing Liberals on whom his coalition government relied.

In 1975 the Italian Communists, who, under Enrico Berlinguer, had increased their support, resolved to lend support to any party promising reforms. This "historic compromise", as it was known, bore fruit after elections in 1976, with Communists occupying important positions in the senate and the chamber of deputies.

However in the 1983 elections, the vote of the center-right Christian Democrats fell by six percent, resulting in a socialist-led coalition, under the prime minister Bettino Craxi. Craxi's government, which included Christian Democrats but not Communists, gave Italian politics a new stability, until a deteriorating economy undermined his hold on power. In June 1986 his government fell and a series of governmental crises ensued.

Unlike some other countries, France did not veer significantly to the right until well into the 1980s. In 1974, Valéry Giscard d'Estaing, a center-right Independent Republican, became president after the death of the Gaullist Georges Pompidou, narrowly defeating the socialist François Mitterrand. However, the socialists rapidly increased their support and in 1980, Mitterrand, backed by

◄▲ **Lech Walesa, Polish leader of the Solidarity trade union, with a picture of Pope John Paul II. The emergence of Solidarity, a broad-based movement with strong connections with traditional Catholicism, presented the ruling Communist party with a protest challenge to liberalize the Polish state. In 1989 Solidarity was elected to form the government.**

◄ **The rise to power of Mikhail Gorbachev gave the Soviet Union a new leadership prepared to break down traditional political institutions to clear the way for economic reform. One aspect of the new policy was the opening of relations with the capitalist West. Here he is seen sealing a new trading agreement with West Germany in 1989.**

Soviet interregnum and the rise of Gorbachev

In November 1982 the 75-year old Soviet president Brezhnev died and was succeeded by Yuriy Andropov, a former KGB boss. However, Andropov himself died in February 1984, and was replaced by Konstantin Chernenko. Unfortunately, Chernenko himself was only in power for a year before he too died, in March 1985.

The new General Secretary, Mikhail Gorbachev, who in 1988 also became the Soviet president, was altogether different from his predecessors. He seized the initiative in improving diplomatic relations with the West and introduced radical changes at home. To remedy the seemingly severe economic problems of a planned socialist economy, he introduced *perestroika* (reconstruction) and a new policy of openness – *glasnost*. The main targets were bureaucratic inefficiency, corruption and shortages of food and other basics of life. In December 1985, the official newspaper *Pravda* attacked the rest of the Soviet press for boring and repetitive reporting, and in June 1987 a law was passed to promote nationwide discussion on important issues. Two months later, socialist and environmentalist (non-Communist) groups freely held a congress in

Moscow. In March 1989, for the first time since 1917, contested elections took place for a new Soviet parliament which was to meet annually, elect the state president for a five-year term, select his deputy and nominate a watchdog body of 15 deputies.

In the first round of elections in Moscow Boris Yeltsin – who had been sacked the previous May for taking Gorbachev's ideas too far – was elected to a Moscow constituency and the dissident nuclear physicist, Andrey Sakharov, also became a member of Congress. The Congress had over 2,000 members, of whom three-quarters were elected. A second chamber, the Supreme Soviet, would continue to be nominated initially but would represent the interests of the constituent republics and scrutinize the policies of the Politburo.

Unrest in the Eastern bloc

Conflict between reformers and conservatives within the Communist party was rife; while both inside the Soviet Union and within Eastern Europe, Gorbachev's policies had a dramatic effect on nationalist and democratic aspirations.

In Poland in 1980 a proposed massive increase

▲ Soviet Armenian demonstrators hold up pictures of recent victims of anti-government rioting in 1989. Gorbachev's campaign to open up Soviet society gave national minorities the opportunity to express their long-standing political grievances.

▼ Gorbachev allowed dissidents such as Andrey Sakharov a platform to criticize of Soviet society.

◄ The end of the aftermath of World War II – the Berlin Wall is breached by the East German authorities in November 1989 as one of the most dramatic moves in a year in which much of Eastern Europe witnessed an unprecedented rejection of traditional Communist rule. Days of mass demonstrations and a steady exodus of skilled workers to the West led Erich Honecker to resign and his successor Egon Krenz to initiate immediate reforms.

in food prices triggered a series of strikes in the dockyards along the Baltic. The Polish Communist party was so unnerved that it signed the Gdansk agreement, guaranteeing pay rises, less censorship, and, above all, free trade unions and the right to strike. For the first time in the Communist world an independent trade union, *Solidarnosč* (Solidarity), had the right to exist. Solidarity was particularly strong in Szczecin and Gdansk, the home of its leader, Lech Walesa, and had the backing of the powerful Roman Catholic Church. With a membership of 63 percent of Poland's 16 million workers, Solidarity escalated its economic demands to political demands, calling for free elections and backing this call with strike action.

Faced with a political crisis, the Polish leader, General Wojciech Jaruzelski, in December 1981, declared a state of martial law. Solidarity was banned but went underground. Ten thousand opponents of the regime were rounded up and Walesa himself was arrested. However, after two meetings between Jaruzelski and the Polish-born Pope John Paul II in 1983, a secret compromise was reached. On 22 July 1983 martial law was lifted. Later that year, Walesa was awarded the Nobel Peace Prize.

At the end of January 1988 further mass protests were once again triggered by sharp price rises. In May workers at the Lenin shipyards in Gdansk went on strike in support of steel workers at Nowa Huta. In August 1988, the Polish government, having announced the closure of the Lenin shipyards, but faced with the prospect of further strikes, agreed to new elections in which Solidarity would be free to play a part. These were held in May 1989 resulting in outright defeat for the Communist party, and a Solidarity prime minister, Tadeusz Mazowiecki, took up office.

Elsewhere in the Baltic region, the Soviet states

of Latvia, Lithuania and Estonia pressed for greater autonomy and challenged Soviet domination. In many Eastern European countries, popular pressure for reform became strong, though it was not always welcomed by the government. In November 1987 food riots broke out in Romania and, in June 1988, 5,000 Romanians protested in Hungary about the destruction of 8,000 Romanian villages that had been bulldozed in order to forcibly urbanize the peasantry. Nicolae Ceauşescu, the Communist dictator of Romania, was a bitter opponent of Gorbachev's *perestroika* plans.

In Czechoslovakia too there were few signs of *perestroika*. In December 1987, the aging Gustav Huşak resigned and was replaced by Milos Jakes, another traditional Communist. In Hungary, however, events took a different turn. In May 1988 Janos Kadar, its ruler since 1956, yielded to Karoly Grosz, seen as more moderate and liberalization of the Soviet system developed, with the opening of the border with Austria in 1989. Yugoslavia, meanwhile, experienced disputes between its various national groups. Within the borders of the Soviet Union itself, the authority of Moscow came under threat from extensive rioting in Armenia, Georgia and Azerbaijan, where once again *glasnost* had unleashed strong nationalist feelings.

The uncertain future of China

From the 1970s China faced increasing problems. Warring factions in the ruling Communist party moved the country towards a more open-door policy towards Western economic ideas. Change was in part due to the future of Hongkong which was due by treaty to be returned to China in 1997. An agreement between Britain and China in 1986 provided that the Hongkong Chinese would remain on the island and work for mainland China,

▲ Repudiating the post: China's "Gang of Four", including the widow of the country's patriarch Mao Zedong, were exposed to vilification and ridicule in effigy, soon after their overthrow in 1976.

The students were standing on top of cars, using microphones to cry out to the police: "The people's police love the people," "The people's police won't beat up people." A soldier rushed towards one of the students, kicked him in the stomach and scoffed: "Who loves you?".

CHAI LING
CHINESE STUDENT 1989

while retaining a special economic status to permit Hong Kong to compete internationally.

China stressed its commitment to liberalization and modernization to reassure the Hongkong Chinese of their future. However, the brutal repression of Tibetan nationalism after 1987 and a widespread unrest that swept through China after 1988 undermined this assurance.

After 40 years of austerity and the employment of some very ruthless methods, the Chinese economy was still very backward. Comparisons with the situation in the Soviet Union divided the leadership over whether they wished to pursue a similar course. Having called for better relations with the Soviets since 1982, in 1988 Deng Xiaoping, the Chinese leader, permitted an exchange of consulates. Some groups wished to emulate Gorbachev's achievement in the Soviet Union, and modernize the system.

The leadership sought to produce a coalition compromise. In January 1987 Hu Yaobang was ousted as general secretary of the Chinese Communist party and replaced by a modernizer, Zhao Ziyang. To counter his influence, however, Li Peng, a hardliner, was made prime minister. In November 1987 Deng Xiaoping was removed from the Central Committee of the party.

It was doubtful, however, whether the hardliners in the Communist party would be able to win popular support. Massive student demonstrations in 1989 showed the extent to which thinking Chinese wanted a new beginning but in June 1989 the Chinese army brutally carried out Li Peng's order to disperse them from the capital. Once liberty had been tasted, the Chinese people became unwilling to return to the old constraining diet of Marxist-Leninism. Yet in the months following the events of June the Communist orthodoxy was rigidly enforced and many of the liberals hounded out or executed. Whether China could maintain this policy of repression, yet continue its movement towards a Western economic system, remained unresolved.

◄▲ Tiananmen Square, 1989 – a dream destroyed. In the late 1980s, dissatisfaction with the progress of liberalization, began to find public expression among students and workers in China's cities. In 1989 peaceful mass demonstrations culminated in the occupation of Beijing's Tiananmen Square and the erection of a replica Statue of Liberty. The party leadership was briefly paralysed, but after a few weeks of hope, conservative elements reasserted control and sent in the army to crush the demonstration. Unable to resist, the protesters were bloodily scattered, although the photograph of a single student holding up a column of tanks will remain an inspiration and a poignant reminder of hope betrayed – all the more so following the execution of the lone hero.

POLITICIANS AND THE MEDIA

No political leader in the 1930s made more effective use of radio than Franklin D. Roosevelt, whose "fireside chats" to the American public projected a more avuncular image than the stentorian performances of the European dictators. Radio was the ideal medium for Roosevelt: crippled by polio, he also insisted on not being photographed in his wheelchair. Thirty years later, after the arrival of television, journalists would no longer be so accommodating in their treatment of politicians.

Television eroded the distinctions between the worlds of politics and entertainment, and obliged politicians to become performers in a way radio never had, particularly in the United States. In 1952 Democratic presidential candidate Adlai Stevenson refused to change his style of presentation to accommodate the new medium, saying that his opponent Dwight Eisenhower's commercials were "selling the Presidency like cereal. How can you talk seriously about issues with one-minute spots?" In 1960, John F. Kennedy's performance in the televised "Great Debates" was widely believed to have been responsible for his narrow victory over Richard Nixon. The impact of Kennedy's assassination was undoubtedly increased by the fact that the President had become a television "personality" whom the viewing public had been encouraged to feel they knew through the intimacy of the medium.

By providing daily coverage of presidents and prime ministers, television news has enhanced the stature of political office, but the image presented by politicians is scrutinized as intensely as their policies. In most democratic countries, radio and television maintain their own political credibility through a notion of "balance", giving equal time to opposing views. But television simplifies and dramatizes politics into a contest of sloganizing and opposing personalities. The media set the agenda around which elections are contested; they tend to reinforce and crystalize opinion rather than to change it.

▶ Hullabaloo at the US Republican Convention, 1988.

▶ The United States president Jimmy Carter was in part a victim of media image-building. Having come to the White House in 1976 as a "new-broom" untainted by the scandals of Washington, he projected an image of healthy informality. This image was summed up in his daily jog around the grounds of the White House. By 1979, however, when he was photographed in a state of collapse and near exhaustion while running, the world concluded how much he had suffered from the burdens of his office.

▲ Britain's Mrs Margaret Thatcher has tailored her image for maximum appeal. Top, a rigid hairstyle and her own teeth in 1961; above, in 1985, softer hair and a new smile.

▼ Libyan leader Colonel Qadhafi has been presented as a demon by the Western press. Below as "eminence grise" in 1985, and, bottom, as an "Arab fanatic".

BIOGRAPHIES

Abdul Rahman, Tunku 1903–

Malaysian prime minister. In 1951, Abdul Rahman became president of the United Malays' National Organization, which he later allied with the Malayan Chinese Association and the Malayan Indian Congress. The alliance won the elections of 1955, and Abdul Rahman became chief minister. He secured internal self-government in 1956, and independence from Britain in 1957. He cooperated closely with the British, and in 1963 became prime minister of the federation of Malaysia. He resigned in 1970 after ethnic rioting.

Acheson, Dean 1893–1971

US politician. A Democrat, Acheson was under secretary of state from 1945 to 1947. He gained the Senate's approval for UN membership, was instrumental in formulating the policy of Soviet containment and the Truman Doctrine, and helped shape the Marshall Plan. In 1949 he became secretary of state, and was involved in the formation of NATO. He also helped to arrange the Japanese peace treaty of 1951. His Asian policy was attacked by Republicans, particularly when the Korean war broke out.

Adenauer, Konrad 1876–1967

First chancellor of the West German Federal Republic. A member of the Catholic Center Party, Adenauer served as mayor of Cologne (1917–33), and from 1918 as a member of the Prussian State Council. Dismissed from both posts by Hitler in 1933, he was sent to a concentration camp. He was a founder member of the Christian Democratic Union, becoming its leader in 1946. In 1948 he was elected president of the Parliamentary Council for the three Allied zones of occupation, and drafted the constitution for the German Federal Republic. In 1949 he became chancellor of the German Federal Diet. In 1951, now foreign minister also, he achieved for West Germany full membership of the Council of Europe and of the European Coal and Steel Community, and in 1952 membership of the Project for European Defence Community. In 1954–55 he won West Germany recognition as a sovereign state, and brought it into NATO and in 1957 into the EEC. He achieved postwar reconciliation with France by his retirement in 1963. In working for his country's reconstruction, Adenauer aligned it firmly with the West and steadfastly refused to recognize the German Democratic Republic.

Allende, Salvador 1908–73

President of Chile. A founder member of Chile's socialist party in 1933, in 1943 Allende became its leader. Elected to the Chamber of Deputies in 1937, he served in a coalition government before being voted on to the Senate in 1945, later becoming its president (1965–69). In 1970, in his fourth contention for the presidency, Allende was elected

as the Popular Unity candidate. The Christian Democrats agreed to his ratification on condition that he preserve Chile's multiparty democracy. He antagonized the United States by nationalizing American property without compensation. He brought most of the mining and manufacturing industry under state control and gave over farmland to peasant cooperatives. He increased wages, froze prices and, to overcome the ensuing fiscal deficit, printed money. By 1972 Chile faced rising inflation and food shortages. Allende continued to enjoy working-class support, but middle- and lower-middle-class unrest showed itself in strikes and demonstrations. In 1973 Allende was deposed and killed in a US-backed military coup.

Amin (Dada), Idi 1925–

Ugandan dictator. An officer in the Ugandan army, Amin led a successful coup against Milton Obote in 1971, installed himself as president and head of the armed forces, and dissolved parliament. In 1972, he expelled all Asians from the country. He reversed the pro-Israeli policy in favor of the Palestinians and Libya, and was accused of involvement in the hijacking of an airliner carrying Israelis in 1976. Border disputes strained relations with Tanzania and Kenya. He is alleged to have persecuted members of tribes other than his own, and it has been estimated that 100,000–300,000 people were tortured and killed during his presidency. In 1978 he launched an attack on Tanzania, and Uganda was then invaded by Tanzanian troops and exiles. Amin escaped abroad in 1979.

Arafat, Yasir 1929–

Chairman of the Palestine Liberation Organization. In 1956, Arafat helped to found the resistance group al-Fatah ("the victory"), later becoming its leader. In 1969 al-Fatah gained control of the recently established Palestine Liberation Organization, and Arafat became its chairman. In 1973, as head of the PLO's political department, he began to place less emphasis on military action. He gained widespread recognition for the PLO, and in 1974 addressed the United Nations General Assembly. After the Israeli invasion of the Lebanon in 1982, he temporarily lost overall control of the PLO. In the late 1980s he condemned terrorism, and, after the declaration of a Palestinian state, seemed to recognize the state of Israel.

Asquith, Herbert H. 1852–1928

British prime minister. In 1886, Asquith was elected to the House of Commons as a Liberal. A barrister by profession, in 1887 he defended the Irish nationalist Parnell. He served as home secretary from 1892 to 1895, but was in opposition from 1895 to 1905. During this period, he

advocated free trade, and sided with the imperialist wing of the party during the Boer War (1899–1902). He became Chancellor of the Exchequer in 1905, and prime minister in 1908. In 1911, he abolished the House of Lords' right of veto, after they had rejected a radical budget. In 1912, he introduced an Irish Home Rule Bill. Both unionists and nationalists then joined paramilitary organizations in Ireland, and army officers at the Curragh near Dublin declared that they would not coerce Ulster into becoming a self-governing dominion. The bill was suspended when World War I broke out. In 1915, he became head of a coalition government, and shortly after, a succession of crises occurred. The Dardanelles campaign failed, and there was still no breakthrough on the western front. 1916 saw both the Easter Rising in Dublin and the battle of the Somme, in which the British lost 500,000 men, and Asquith resigned. He entered the House of Lords in 1925, and resigned the party leadership in 1926.

Atatürk, Mustafa Kemal 1881–1938

Soldier, and first president of modern Turkey. During World War I Atatürk commanded the Turkish forces at the Dardanelles and opposed German control of Turkey. After the war, he opposed the Sultan's surrender to the Allies and the intended partition of Turkey and in 1919 organized resistance against the Greek occupation of Smyrna. In 1920 he became head of a new National Assembly he had helped to form, and virtual head of state. In 1922 he abolished the sultanate and replaced the pro-Allied government with a new republic. He expelled the Greeks from Asia Minor and, by the 1923 Treaty of Lausanne, gained recognition for Turkey from the Allies. He was elected president in 1923, and created a dictatorship. He modernized Turkey, adopting the Latin alphabet, Western-style surnames and Western dress, and reformed the legal and educational systems. Under Atatürk, Turkey joined the League of Nations.

Attlee, Clement 1883–1967

British Labour prime minister. Elected to parliament in 1922, in 1924 Attlee became under secretary of state for war. Appointed Postmaster General in 1931, he became Labour party leader in 1935. In 1939 he refused to form a coalition with Chamberlain, but supported Churchill's accession in 1940. During World War II, Attlee served as Lord Privy Seal, deputy prime minister, dominions secretary, and Lord President of the Council. Immediately after the war he attended the San Francisco Conference, at which the UN charter was drafted, and the Potsdam Conference. In 1945 he was elected prime minister, defeating Churchill decisively. During Attlee's premiership, Britain joined NATO and the Council of Europe, granted

▲ Mrs Bandaranaike

▲ David Ben-Gurion

▲ Zulfikar and Benazir Bhutto

independence to India and the newly-formed Pakistan, Ceylon and Burma, and ceded control of Palestine and Egypt. In Britain he nationalized the railways, transport and communications, coal, gas and electricity, iron and steel, and the Bank of England. He also set up the welfare state system of social security including the free National Health Service. After his defeat in the election of 1951, Attlee was granted an earldom and entered the House of Lords.

Ayub Khan see **Khan**

Balfour, Arthur J. 1848–1930
British prime minister. In 1874, Balfour was elected to parliament as a Conservative. From 1878 to 1880 he acted as aide to the foreign secretary Lord Salisbury at the Berlin Congress, and served as secretary for Scotland during 1886–87. He was secretary for Ireland from 1887 to 1891, and strongly opposed Home Rule, which he attempted to "kill by kindness", whilst crushing any potential uprisings. In 1891, he became First Lord of the Treasury and leader of the Commons, and in 1902, prime minister. Domestically, he introduced reforms in education, defense and Irish absentee landlordism, and internationally he secured the Anglo-French Entente in 1904. The party had split, however, in 1903 over the question of tariff reform versus free trade, and this led to Balfour's resignation as prime minister in 1905, though he remained party leader until 1911. In 1915 he became First Lord of the Admiralty in Asquith's coalition. As foreign secretary (1916–17), in 1917 he issued the Balfour Declaration, expressing British support for a Zionist homeland in Palestine, and in 1919 was involved in the Versailles settlement. He represented Britain at the first congress of the League of Nations in 1920, and the Washington Naval Disarmament Conference in 1922. Also in 1922 he was granted an earldom. He served during 1925–29 under Baldwin, and was involved in the negotiations which led to the Statute of Westminster (1931), whereby self-governing dominions of the empire gained autonomy, but continued to owe allegiance to the Crown.

Bandaranaike, Sirimavo 1916–
Sri Lankan prime minister. After the assassination of her husband the prime minister in 1959, the Sri Lankan Freedom Party (SLFP) won a majority in the elections, and Mrs Bandaranaike became the new SLFP leader, and the world's first woman prime minister. She improved health and educational facilities, promoted native religion and culture, and brought private schools into the state sector. But because she also nationalized some of the rubber industry and the western-controlled oil industry, the United States stopped aid to Sri Lanka, whose economy was weak. The SLFP split over a coalition with a Marxist group, and lost

power in 1965, but regained it in 1970 as the senior partners in the United Front coalition. Abroad, Mrs Bandaranaike resumed her policy of nonalignment. Domestically, she expelled the US Peace Corps, and announced more nationalization. The pace of this was slow, however, and unemployment was rising. In 1971 she withstood an attempted leftist coup, but left office in 1977.

Begin, Menachem W. 1913–
Israeli prime minister. Born in Poland, in 1938 Begin headed the Zionist Betar youth movement, demanding a homeland on both banks of the Jordan. After the German invasion of 1939 Begin fled to Lithuania, and in 1940 the Russians deported him to Siberia. Upon his release in 1941 he joined the Free Polish Army, and in 1942 was sent to Palestine. He left the army in 1943 and became leader of the Irgun until 1948, when they disbanded, and he founded the Herut party, seeking Israeli sovereignty on both banks of the Jordan, no Palestinian state, and economic laissez-faire. In 1977, Begin came to power as head of the Likud coalition. He took a hard line on the return of territories occupied in 1967, and began the Israeli colonization of the West Bank. He did, however, withdraw from the Sinai peninsula as part of the peace treaty signed in 1979, with President Sadat of Egypt, for which they were jointly awarded the Nobel Peace Prize in 1978. In 1982, Israeli troops invaded the Lebanon and bombed Beirut in an attempt to destroy PLO bases. The PLO withdrew, and whilst under Israeli occupation, hundreds of Palestinian civilians in Beirut were massacred by Lebanese Christians. Begin resigned in 1983.

Ben-Gurion (Gruen), David 1886–1973
First prime minister of Israel. Having left Poland to work as a farmer in Palestine, Ben-Gurion, an active Zionist, was expelled by the ruling Turks as a subversive at the outbreak of World War I. He returned in 1917 to fight for the Allies after the British publication of the Balfour Declaration, promising the Jews a "national home". During British postwar rule he advocated massive Jewish immigration into Palestine. In 1930 he was a founder member and effective head of the Israeli Labor Party, the Mapai, and in 1935 became head of the influential Jewish Agency, which was equivalent to being head of state. He led a guerrilla war against the British, achieving victory in 1948, when the UN partitioned Palestine and created the state of Israel. Elected prime minister in 1949, he fused the various resistance movements into an army and repelled Arab attempts at invasion. In 1953 he resigned and went to the desert, but was called back 14 months later, and became prime minister again late in 1955. During the Suez crisis of 1956 he ordered the Israeli army to occupy the Sinai peninsula, but withdrew after an assurance

of peace along the Egyptian border and guaranteed access to the Strait of Tiran. In Israel Ben-Gurion brought about the unification of Jews from widely differing cultures, created settlements in desert areas, and founded a public education system. In his later years he devoted his energies to the task of establishing peace in the Middle East. He resigned in 1963.

Bethmann-Hollweg, Theobald 1856–1921
German imperial chancellor. In 1905, Bethmann-Hollweg was appointed Prussian minister of the interior. In 1907 he was state secretary in the imperial interior office, and in 1909, he became chancellor. He failed to end naval rivalry with Britain, and Germany's actions in the third Moroccan crisis of 1911 led to a a British guarantee of military assistance to France. Bethmann-Hollweg did, however, in conjunction with Britain, manage to prevent the escalation of the Balkan wars into a confrontation between Austria-Hungary and Russia. He expanded the army, and did not oppose the Austro-Hungarian action against Serbia in 1914, which was followed by World War I. The war was conducted largely by the military, but Bethmann-Hollweg opposed the introduction of unrestricted submarine warfare and in 1916 tried to obtain US mediation. In 1917, he announced plans for electoral reform and was forced to resign.

Bhutto, Zulfikar Ali 1928–79
President and prime minister of Pakistan. Appointed commerce minister in 1958, Bhutto was foreign minister from 1963 to 1965, forming a closer link with China at the expense of the West. In 1966 he resigned in protest over the peace reached with India after the Kashmir war, and in 1967 founded the Pakistani People's party. He spent two years in prison for accusing Ayub Khan of being a dictator. In elections held in 1970, after Ayub Khan had been deposed by Yahya Khan, the People's party won in West Pakistan, but lost in the East to the separatist Awami League, with whom Bhutto refused to form a coalition. In 1971 Bhutto succeeded Yahya Khan as president, following a civil war in which East Pakistan, assisted by India, became the independent state of Bangladesh. Bhutto nationalized major industries and taxed landed families. In 1973 he became prime minister under a new constitution transferring power to this post. Bhutto maintained martial law and strengthened Pakistan as an Islamic state. In the 1977 election his party won a large majority, but was accused of electoral fraud. That same year General Zia al Haq, the head of the army, seized power and arrested Bhutto for allegedly conspiring to murder a political opponent in 1974. He was found guilty, and executed in 1979, although several world leaders sent messages urging General Zia to spare his life.

▲ Willy Brandt

▲ Leonid Brezhnev

▲ Prince von Bülow

Blum, Léon 1872–1950

French prime minister. In 1919, Blum was elected to parliament as a Socialist. He rebuilt the party after the 1920 split with the Communists, and came to power in 1936 as head of the Popular Front coalition. France's first Socialist premier, he introduced radical measures, including a 40-hour week, paid holidays and collective bargaining and the nationalization of the Bank of France and the defense industries. Preparations for war against Germany were begun, but a policy of nonintervention in the Spanish Civil War alienated Communist coalition members. Blum resigned in 1937, after he had been refused emergency powers to deal with economic problems. He served again as prime minister for a brief period in 1938. He was arrested in 1940 and tried in 1942 by the Vichy government on charges of neglecting France's interests, but defended himself so effectively that the trial was abandoned. He was then imprisoned in a concentration camp from 1943 to 1945. Returning to politics after the war, in 1946 he secured a US loan for the reconstruction of France. In the same year he briefly headed a caretaker government, and was vice-premier for a short time in 1948. He then became France's chief representative to UNESCO.

Botha, Pieter W. 1916–

South African prime minister. He entered parliament in 1948 as a member of the National Party, serving in several ministerial posts before becoming prime minister in 1978. Nationalist activities in neighboring countries led to increasing black unrest in South Africa, and renewed demands for the abolition of apartheid. Botha strengthened the armed forces, which raided these countries regularly, and he funded antigovernment groups within them. At home, he abolished some minor apartheid laws, granted nominal independence to black homelands, and reformed the constitution, allowing limited political rights to Asians and coloreds, though not to blacks. As a result of this, the right wing of the party broke away in 1982 to form the Conservative party. After a cabinet revolt he was forced to resign in 1989.

Brandt, Willy 1913–

West German chancellor. Returning to Germany after the fall of Hitler, Brandt was elected to the federal parliament in 1949. In 1957 he became the Social Democratic mayor of West Berlin and an international figure, described as the "German Kennedy", during the building of the Berlin wall. Having run three times for the chancellorship, in 1966 he became vice-chancellor and foreign minister in a coalition with the Christian Democrats. He was elected chancellor at his fourth attempt in 1969 in the new Social Democrat–Free Democrat coalition, and remained in office until

1974. A signatory to the nuclear nonproliferation treaty, in 1970 Brandt joined with the Soviet Union in calling for the rejection of military force and the recognition of current European boundaries. He signed a nonaggression pact with Poland in 1970 establishing a mutually acceptable border, and in 1971 was a party to the "big four" treaty to determine the status of Berlin. He helped to expand the European Economic Community, and after his resignation headed the Brandt Commission, demanding a redistribution of wealth between the northern and southern hemispheres.

Brezhnev, Leonid Ilyich 1906–82

Leader of the Soviet Union. Benefiting from Stalin's purges and Khrushchev's favor, Brezhnev rose steadily in the Ukrainian party hierarchy. After World War II he was the Moldavian party leader (1950–52), served on the CPSU (Soviet Communist party) central committee and in the Politburo (1952), before his demotion on Stalin's death. He became once more a member of the Presidium (ex-Politburo) in 1957. Titular head of state from 1960, he finally became a party leader in 1964, briefly sharing power with Kosygin after the fall of Khrushchev. Brezhnev delegated much responsibility and concentrated his attention on foreign affairs and the suppression of internal dissent. Although opposed to liberalization at home he increased the emigration of Soviet Jews and tried to improve conditions for farmers and consumers. Abroad, he pursued a policy of détente while amassing conventional forces and using the Red Army to uphold Communist regimes in neighboring countries (Czechoslovakia 1968, Afghanistan 1979).

Bulganin, Nikolai A. 1895–1975

Russian politician. In 1931 Bulganin, who had been a secret policeman and a factory manager, became chairman of the Moscow soviet, then premier of the Russian Republic (1937–38), state bank chairman (1938–41), and deputy Soviet premier (1938–41). In 1939, he became a full member of the central committee, and during the war he was a political commissar on the Western front, a member of Stalin's war cabinet, and deputy defense minister. In 1947 he returned to his post as deputy premier, was made a marshal of the Soviet Union, and war minister (to 1949). In 1948 he became a full member of the Politburo (later Presidium). He served as defense minister under Malenkov from 1953 to 1955, and after Khrushchev's rise to power, Bulganin became Chairman of the Council of Ministers (premier) in 1955. He was closely associated with Khrushchev, accompanying him on several foreign visits; but in 1957 was involved in an unsuccessful coup against him, and in 1958 lost his place on the Presidium and his rank as marshal, and sank into obscurity.

Bülow, Bernhard H. 1849–1929

German politician. In 1897 Bülow, a diplomat, became foreign secretary under Kaiser Wilhelm. He secured territories in the Pacific, and extended German influence in the Middle East. In 1900, he was promoted to chancellor, overseeing the formation of the Triple Entente between France, Britain and Russia. Germany alienated Britain, adopting a proBoer stance in the South African War, and the German navy was enlarged to rival that of Britain. In an attempt to break the Anglo-French Entente of 1904, Germany supported Moroccan independence from the French in 1905. Russia allied with Britain and France in 1907, and Russo-German relationships were irrevocably damaged when Bülow forced Russia to accept the Austro-Hungarian annexation of Bosnia-Herzegovina. He was dismissed in 1909, after failing to vet the transcript of the Kaiser's interview with the British newpaper the *Daily Telegraph*, in which he had made remarks about anti-English opinion in Germany. During World War I he returned to the diplomatic service.

Carter, James Earl ("Jimmy") 1924–

39th US president. Democratic governor of Georgia from 1971 to 1975, in 1976 Carter was elected president. He attempted wide-ranging internal reforms, which were largely blocked by Congress. In 1977, he agreed to cede control of the Panama Canal by the year 2000. In 1978, his mediation ended the official state of war existing between Egypt and Israel since 1938. In 1979, he broke off relations with Taiwan and opened full diplomatic relations with China, in the same year signing the SALT II treaty with the Soviet Union, which the Senate refused to ratify. Also in this year, militant Iranian students occupied the US embassy in Tehran, holding 66 hostages. The Iranian government refused to negotiate for their release, and Carter suspended relations with Iran. In 1980, a military operation to free the hostages failed. Meanwhile, Carter applied economic sanctions against the Soviet Union in response to its invasion of Afghanistan, whose communist regime was faltering, and called for a boycott of the 1980 Moscow Olympics. At home, inflation rose, and unemployment remained high, and in 1980 Carter lost the presidency to Ronald Reagan.

Castro, Fidel 1926–

Revolutionary leader, prime minister and president of Cuba. In 1947 Castro joined the Cuban People's party, and in 1953 launched a guerrilla war against the Batista dictatorship. Having overthrown Batista, Castro became prime minister in 1959. Aligning Cuba with the Soviet Union, he began a program of mass nationalization, including the takeover of US properties, and in 1961 repelled a US-backed invasion at the Bay of Pigs. He gave support to

revolutionaries in Venezuela and Bolivia against the wishes of local pro-Soviet Communists, and was critical of Khrushchev's handling of the Cuban missile crisis in 1962. In the late 1960s, under pressure from Moscow, he moderated his confrontational style and followed the Soviet line more closely. He continued to export revolution, particularly assisting pro-Soviet forces in Angola and Ethiopia, and by the 1980s had 40,000 troops stationed in some twenty-five countries. Under Castro, hundreds of thousands of middle-class Cubans left for the United States, and tens of thousands of political prisoners were taken (many of whom were later released in a failed attempt at rapprochement with the Americans). In 1979, despite Cuba's close ties with the Soviet Union, Castro became the leader of the nonaligned countries' movement. He did not support the *perestroika* policies of political and economic reform advocated by Soviet premier Gorbachev in the late 1980s.

Ceauşescu, Nicolae 1918–

Romanian political leader. Ceauşescu joined the Communist party in 1933, and sided with its nationalist wing. He was imprisoned in 1936 and 1940 for antifascist activities. In 1945 he became secretary of the Budapest party branch, and in 1948 was elected to the central committee. From 1948 to 1950 he was deputy minister of agriculture, and from 1950 to 1954 deputy minister for the army. He then joined the secretariat of the central committee, and in 1955, the Politburo. In 1957 he became deputy leader, and in 1965 succeeded Gheorghiu-Dej as general secretary. In 1967 he became head of state, and in 1974 assumed the post of president. Domestically, he accelerated industrialization, maintained the orthodox Communist regime, and fostered a personality cult around himself. At the same time, he improved living standards and worked for economic independence from the Soviet Union. Abroad, he remained within the Warsaw Pact, but asserted Romanian sovereignty. He condemned the Russian occupation of Czechoslovakia in 1968, while remaining neutral in the Sino-Soviet conflict. He developed good relations with First and Third World countries but in the late 1980s his foreign policy was compromised, and his rule overshadowed by harsh and cruel legislation, the nepotism and high Stalinist character of his personal regime and the destruction of the once stable economy by irrational policies.

Chamberlain, Neville 1869–1940

British prime minister. Director general of national service in 1916 and 1917, in 1918 Chamberlain was elected to parliament as a Conservative. He served as Postmaster General (1922–23), Paymaster General (1923), health minister (1923, 1924–29, 1931), Chancellor of the Exchequer (1923–24,

1931–37), and finally prime minister (1937–40). As a minister he introduced social reforms, but his premiership was largely concerned with foreign policy. He ceded control of naval bases in Eire, pursued a policy of nonintervention in the Spanish Civil War, and one of appeasement towards the Axis nations. He dropped the sanctions which had been introduced against Italy after its occupation of Ethiopia, and in 1938 approved at Munich the German occupation of western Czechoslovakia, meanwhile increasing the pace of British rearmament. In 1939, Hitler occupied all of Czechoslovakia, and Chamberlain reversed his policy. He introduced conscription, and promised armed assistance to Poland, Romania and Greece. He declared war on Germany in 1939, after it invaded Poland. After the British defeat in the 1940 Norwegian campaign, Chamberlain resigned. He then became a member of Churchill's cabinet, as Lord President of the Council, but died soon after.

Churchill, Winston 1874–1965

British prime minister. After a period as a soldier and war correspondent, Churchill entered parliament as a Conservative in 1900. In 1904 he broke away over tariff reform to join the opposition Liberal party, and in 1906 was appointed Colonies Undersecretary, going on to become President of the Board of Trade in 1908 and Home Secretary in 1910. In 1911 he moved to the Admiralty, but resigned in 1915 after the failure of the Dardanelles expedition. Elected to parliament as an Independent in 1916, he served as munitions minister during 1917 and 1918. He rejoined the Conservative party in 1924, and was involved in breaking the General Strike of 1926. He was war secretary (1918–21), colonial secretary (1921–22), and Chancellor of the Exchequer (1924–29). As a backbencher from 1929 to 1939 he campaigned against Indian independence and constantly warned against the appeasement of Nazi Germany. Returning to the Admiralty in 1939, he became prime minister in 1940. During World War II Churchill's outstanding leadership qualities, oratorical skills and determination rallied and inspired the British people. He worked tirelessly to forge closer wartime alliances between Britain, the United States and the Soviet Union, holding meetings with both Roosevelt and Stalin. After the war he campaigned vigorously against Soviet power. Surprisingly defeated in the 1945 postwar election, he was reelected in 1951 at the age of 77, and resigned in 1955.

Clemenceau, Georges 1841–1929

French prime minister. In 1902, Clemenceau was elected to parliament as a member of the Radical party. In 1906, he became minister for the interior, breaking with the left when he ordered out troops against striking miners; he then became prime minister. In 1909 a tense situation was resolved

when he signed an agreement with Germany recognizing French rule in Morocco, while acknowledging Germany's economic interests there. He then resigned, after being criticized for not expanding the navy. He was reelected to the Senate in 1911, sat on the foreign affairs and military commissions, and campaigned for military preparedness. He became the leading internal critic of France's conduct of World War I, and called for American intervention. He assumed the premiership again in 1917, and served also as war minister. In 1917 he was instrumental in the US's entry into the war, and in 1918 secured a unified Allied command under the French officer, Ferdinand Foch. He presided autocratically over the Paris Peace Conference in 1919. The concessions made by France to Germany in the Treaty of Versailles were seized upon by the right wing, and in 1920, having failed to gain the presidency, Clemenceau resigned.

Coolidge, Calvin 1872–1933

30th president of the United States. Republican governor of Massachusetts in 1919, Coolidge came to national attention when he called out the state guard to restore order during a police strike. In 1921 he became vice-president, and on the death of Harding in 1923, president, then winning the elections of 1924. He reduced government intervention in the economy (although high, protectionist tariffs remained), cut taxes and paid off a large proportion of the national debt. Coolidge successfully opposed farm relief, but his opposition to bonuses for World War I veterans was defeated by Congress. He retired in 1929.

Curzon, George 1859–1925

British politician and Viceroy of India. Elected to parliament as a Conservative in 1886, Curzon became under secretary for India in 1891, and under secretary for foreign affairs and a privy councillor in 1895. From 1898, as Baron Curzon, and Viceroy of India (the youngest ever), he reformed taxation, created the Northwest Frontier Province, partitioned Bengal and restored the Taj Mahal, although there was personal rivalry and intrigue between him and his military commander, Lord Kitchener. In 1905 Curzon tendered his resignation, as a gesture. It was accepted, however, and, now an Earl, he entered the House of Lords, and in 1915 became Lord Privy Seal in Asquith's coalition government. He went on to become a member of Lloyd George's war cabinet in 1916, and from 1919 to 1924 served as foreign secretary under Lloyd George, Bonar Law and Baldwin. In 1919, he proposed the "Curzon Line" across Poland, which formed the basis of the Polish-Soviet border after World War II. He was instrumental in the conclusion in 1923 of the Treaty of Lausanne, and he helped to rebuild Anglo-German relations after World War I.

231

▲ Eamon de Valera

▲ Alexander Dubček

▲ Dwight D Eisenhower

de Valera, Eamon 1882–1975

Founder and prime minister of Eire (Republic of Ireland). In 1916 de Valera was a commander of the Irish Volunteers in the unsuccessful Easter Rising in Dublin, and was imprisoned until 1917, when he was elected president of the separatist party Sinn Fein ("We ourselves"). He was voted into parliament at the 1918 elections when Sinn Fein won three-quarters of the Irish seats, but was then imprisoned again. He escaped to the United States and in 1919 was elected president of the Irish Republic. Returning to Ireland toward the end of the Anglo-Irish War of 1919–21, he unsuccessfully opposed the partition of Ireland, and created a self-governing dominion of the British Empire in the south. In the ensuing civil war (1922–23), he fought for the Republicans against the Free Staters, who, on coming to power, imprisoned him. Released in 1924, he broke away from Sinn Fein, and in 1926 founded the alternative republican party Fianna Fail ("Soldiers of destiny"), and reentered the Dail. Head of government in 1932, he refused to pay land annuities to Britain, and started an economic war that lasted until 1938. In 1937 he created the state of Eire, and claimed sovereignty over all Ireland, while remaining within the British Commonwealth. In 1939, he outlawed the Irish Republican Army (IRA). During World War II he remained neutral. He was defeated in the 1948 elections, when a coalition renamed the state the Republic of Ireland. He was prime minister again from 1951 to 1954 and from 1957 to 1959, and president from 1959 to 1973.

Deng Xiaoping 1904–

Chinese politician and head of state. In 1953 Deng, a military man, became secretary general of the Chinese Communist party and, in 1955, a member of the Presidium. He was demoted in 1967 during the Cultural Revolution, but reinstated as deputy premier in 1973. He rejoined the Presidium (now Politburo) in 1975, and became vice-chairman of its central committee, and chief of general staff. Demoted again through the influence of the Maoist Gang of Four, he returned after Mao's death in 1976. After a power struggle, Deng was effective leader of the government by 1978. He removed Maoists from high offices and undertook a program of wide-ranging reforms. He introduced self-management for peasant farmers and financial rewards for industrial efficiency. He installed highly trained managers and technicians to run industry and the economy, and initially increased personal freedom. Internationally, Deng continued to develop relations with the West, establishing diplomatic relations with the United States in 1978. In 1989, his credibility as a reformer was severely damaged after prodemocracy demonstrations in China were crushed with savage force, leaving thousands dead, and alleged ringleaders rounded up and shot following summary show trials.

Dubček, Alexander 1921–

Czechoslovakian politician. A member of the resistance movement in World War II, Dubček rose through the Communist party hierarchy, attaining the Slovakian party leadership in 1963. He was voted Czechoslovakian party leader in 1968. Adopting the slogan "Socialism with a human face", Dubček's administration increased freedom of speech, removed Stalinists from high office and published a complete program of reform, "Czechoslovakia's Road to Socialism". However, the pace of change alarmed the Soviets, who feared the polarization of the Eastern bloc. After talks in which Dubcek made only minor concessions, the Soviet army invaded Czechoslovakia on 20–22 August 1968. Dubček was taken to Moscow, and forced to abandon his policies. He resigned as party secretary in 1969, and was expelled from the party in 1970.

Dulles, John Foster 1888–1959

American politician. At the end of World War I Dulles was appointed US legal advisor at the Paris Peace Conference, and represented the United States on the War Reparations Commission. He was a senior advisor at the San Francisco United Nations Conference in 1945, and a UN delegate in 1946, 1947 and 1950. In 1951, as advisor to the secretary of state, he negotiated the Japanese peace treaty. Appointed secretary of state in 1953, in 1954 he helped to set up SEATO (Southeast Asia Treaty Organization), and to draft the Trieste agreement (finalizing the Italian-Yugoslavian boundary). He also helped to draft the 1955 Austrian State Treaty, and in 1956 supported West Germany's admission to NATO. Prominent in the Cold War, he pursued uncompromising policies, threatening "massive nuclear retaliation" against any Soviet aggression. In 1956, he opposed the Anglo-French attempt to occupy the Suez Canal.

Ebert, Friedrich 1871–1925

German president. Elected to the Reichstag in 1912, in 1916 Ebert became chairman of the Social Democratic party (SPD). His support of World War I led to the breaking away of the left wing. In November 1918, revolution broke out, and the Kaiser was deposed. Ebert was made chancellor, but immediately transferred power to the Council of People's Representatives, where an SPD-USPD coalition formed a provisional government. In 1919, elections under the Weimar constitution were held. The SPD formed a coalition with the Center party and the Democrats, known as the black-red-gold coalition, and Ebert became president. He engaged in a civil war with revolutionary socialists. Due to the harsh terms of the Treaty of Versailles the coalition lost their majority in 1920. In 1923, when German payment of war reparations to France ceased, French troops occupied the Ruhr. A general strike

followed in the area, severely damaging the Germany economy, and Hitler led an attempted coup in Munich. The reparations question was eventually settled, and inflation was brought under control, but Ebert still took much of the blame, and was accused of treason, technically speaking, for supporting a munitions strike during the war. He died in 1925.

Eden, (Robert) Anthony 1897–1977

British prime minister. Elected to parliament as a Conservative in 1923, Eden was appointed under secretary for foreign affairs in 1931, Lord Privy Seal and minister for League of Nations affairs in 1934. He was foreign secretary from 1935 until 1938, when he resigned in protest at the appeasement of Germany and Italy. In 1939, after the declaration of war, he returned to government as dominions secretary, and in 1940 he served first as war secretary, then as foreign secretary (1940–45). He attended the San Francisco conference in 1945. He was then in opposition for six years, and returned to the foreign office in 1951, also assuming the post of deputy prime minister. In 1954 he helped to end the oil dispute with Iran and the Italian-Yugoslav dispute over Trieste. He also attended the Geneva Conference, which ended the Indochina War, and he helped to create the Southeast Asia Treaty Organization (SEATO). In 1955, he became prime minister, soon afterwards receiving Khrushchev and Bulganin. In 1956, there was unrest in Cyprus, and President Nasser of Egypt nationalized the Suez Canal, in which Britain was a major shareholder. Britain, France and Israel attacked Egypt, but withdrew under US and Soviet pressure. The canal remained under Egyptian control, and Eden resigned, owing to ill health, in 1957. In 1961 he was given an earldom.

Eisenhower, Dwight D. 1890–1969

World War II commander of the Allied forces in Europe, and 34th US president. In 1942, Eisenhower took charge of US troops in Europe, and led the successful invasions of North Africa and Italy, 1942–43. Appointed commander of the Allied forces in 1943, he was in overall charge of the landing of 1,000,000 troops across the English Channel to Normandy on 6 June 1944 (D-Day). After the Germans surrendered, on 7 May, 1945, Eisenhower was appointed chief of staff and oversaw the process of demobilization. He became NATO supreme commander in 1950. In 1953 Eisenhower became US president as a Republican. In office, he tended to delegate responsibility, presiding over some taxation reforms, the deregulation of prices, rents and wages and a reduction in federal powers. Under Eisenhower, the Civil Rights Act was passed in 1957, and the minimum wage and social security payments were increased. In his foreign policy Eisenhower helped end the Korean War in 1953, and the following

▲ Francisco Franco

▲ Mohandas Gandhi

▲ Charles de Gaulle

year assisted in the formation of SEATO. The International Atomic Energy Agency was set up in 1957 at his instigation for the purpose of sharing nuclear materials and information. He also introduced the Eisenhower doctrines, following the Suez crisis of 1956, offering military assistance to Middle Eastern countries perceived to be under Communist threat. In 1959 Eisenhower was visited by Khrushchev, but the invitation to a return visit was withdrawn after a US spy plane was spotted (and shot down) over Soviet territory.

Foch, Ferdinand 1851–1929
French general. During World War I, Foch helped stop the German advance at the first battle of the Marne (1914), and was at the battle of Ypres (1915). He coordinated French troops at the battle of the Somme (1916), and in 1918 he was given command first of Allied troops on the Western Front, and then of all Allied troops. After the war, Foch was made Marshal of France, and England made him an honorary field marshal. He broke with the prime minister Clemenceau, by insisting on French control of the Rhineland.

Franco, Francisco 1892–1975
Spanish dictator. An army officer, in 1927 Franco was appointed head of the military academy at Zaragoza. In 1931, the monarchy was replaced with a republic, and Franco was successively appointed to posts in the Balearic Islands and Morocco. In 1933 the center-right came to power, and in 1935 Franco became the army's chief of staff. However, after the radical Popular Front had gained a majority in 1936, he was demoted and posted to the Canary Islands. Anticipating revolt, he went to Morocco, from where he launched an attack on Spain; this was the beginning of the Civil War. He obtained aid from the Fascist governments of Italy and Germany, and was declared commander-in-chief and head of state. In 1937 the Falange and Carlist parties were merged, creating the State party, and in 1939 the republicans were finally defeated. A single-party state was established, and a short time later, Spain joined the anti-Comintern pact. Franco remained neutral in World War II, although he was openly sympathetic to the Axis nations. Afterwards the West at first ostracized, then gradually rehabilitated Spain as the Cold War progressed. In 1947 the monarchy was restored, with Franco as effective regent. In 1953, he permitted the establishment of US bases on Spanish soil in return for economic aid, and in 1955, Spain obtained membership of the United Nations Organization. Economic problems improved, and the country became somewhat more liberal, although there was some domestic unrest. In 1969 Franco named Prince Juan Carlos as his successor. He resigned as premier in 1975, but remained party leader, head of state and commander-in-chief.

Gandhi, Indira P. 1917–84
Indian prime minister. The daughter of Nehru, Mrs Gandhi became president of the Congress party in 1959, and minister for information and broadcasting in 1964. In 1966, she became prime minister, but the party split in 1969 over her nationalization of major banks and she lost her overall majority, regaining it in 1971. In the same year, West Pakistan lost the war against India and East Pakistan, which subsequently became the independent state of Bangladesh. Domestically, the economy and law and order declined, and in 1975, the High Court ruled that Mrs Gandhi had breached election laws. She declared a state of emergency, and centralized power in herself, curtailed civil liberties and arrested political opponents. In 1978 she founded the new Congress-I party, as a member of which she was elected to parliament, but later expelled. In 1980, Congress-I won a majority, and Mrs Gandhi became prime minister once again. Abroad, she worked to develop India's role among the developing nations, and remained on good terms with the Soviet Union, although she opposed the occupation of Afghanistan. At home, she introduced social and economic reform, but several Indian minorities were demanding more independence, particularly Punjabi Sikhs, some of whom used violence. In 1984, the army attacked the Golden Temple of Amritsar, and nearly 500 Sikhs died. In the same year, Mrs Gandhi was killed by Sikhs.

Gandhi, Mohandas K. 1869–1948
Indian nationalist leader. Born in India, in 1893 Gandhi went to work as a lawyer in South Africa, where he campaigned vigilantly against the discrimination suffered by his fellow Indians, developing the concept and using the technique of *satyagraha* (nonviolent resistance). Returning to India in 1914, Gandhi identified himself with the plight of the poor. During World War I he recruited Indians into the armed forces, but became disillusioned with British rule after the war when civil liberties were still restricted. In 1919 he began the first Indian campaign of nonviolent noncooperation and called a strike, which he called off after the British had massacred unarmed demonstrators at Amritsar. In 1920 Gandhi, now India's foremost leader, called for Indians to boycott British cloth, and in 1921 supervised the burning of imported goods. Once again he ended the campaign, in 1922, after the eruption of violence. That year he was imprisoned until 1924, when for a short time he was president of the Congress party. From 1924 to 1927 he campaigned for the rights of untouchables and of women, for unity with the Muslims, for cottage industries and for education. In 1928 he demanded dominion status for India. In protest against the salt tax, in 1930 he walked more than 300 kilometers to the

sea and there illegally distilled salt. The salt tax was lifted in 1931. In 1932 he was again imprisoned, and fasted in protest at the new constitutional status of untouchables. In 1934 he resigned from the Congress party. Gandhi launched his last campaign in 1942, calling on the British to quit India. Imprisoned again from 1942 to 1944, he was involved, in 1946, in independence negotiations. He opposed the partition of India. When rioting broke out in Bihar and East Bengal, Gandhi traveled there in an effort to bring peace. After partition, he fasted to appeal for an end to rioting. He was assassinated by a Hindu nationalist on 30 January 1948.

de Gaulle, Charles 1890–1970
Leader of the Free French during World War II, military strategist, and first president of the Fifth Republic. De Gaulle was mentioned in dispatches three times during World War I, and between the wars was promoted to the National Defense Council. In 1940, a brigadier general, he entered the Raynaud government but left for England when Pétain came to power. He formed and led the Free French Army, and in 1943 was elected president of the French Committee of National Liberation. Returning to France in 1944, he headed two provisional governments. He was elected provisional president in 1945 but resigned in 1946, believing that he could rebuild France effectively only if given more extensive powers. A consistent campaigner in parliament against the Fourth Republic of 1946, he was asked, in 1958, to form a temporary administration to avoid the impending chaos caused by unrest in Algeria. He reformed the constitution, and in 1958 was elected president and established the Fifth Republic. As president, he strengthened the economy, gave independence to 12 African colonies, withdrew France from NATO and acquired an independent nuclear deterrent. Regarded as a difficulty abroad and an autocrat at home, de Gaulle received a boost for his waning popularity after the student-worker riots of 1968, but this success was short-lived. Having lost in a national referendum, de Gaulle resigned in 1969.

Giap, Vo Nguyen 1912–
Vietnamese soldier and politician. A member of the Indochinese Communist Party, in 1945 Giap led the nationalist Vietminh forces to victory against the French colonial government at Hanoi, and served as a member of the new provisional government. He commanded the Vietminh during the Indochina War (1946–54), thwarting French attempts to reoccupy the country. After Vietnam was partitioned, he became North Vietnamese defense minister. His troops played a major part in the defeat of South Vietnam, in 1975. He then became defense minister and deputy prime minister of a united Vietnam.

Goebbels, P. Joseph 1897–1945

Nazi politician. Goebbels joined the Nazi party in 1925, and became head of the Berlin branch in 1926. In 1929 he was made responsible for party propaganda and in 1930 elected to the Reichstag. He was heavily involved in the Nazis' rise to power, and in 1933 was made government minister for propaganda. With control of the entire media, he used his position to justify policies such as the persecution of the Jews. In 1944 he successfully aroused the public appetite for total war, and was appointed minister for total war. He committed suicide in 1945.

Gomulka, Wladyslaw 1905–82

Polish political leader. Gomulka joined the Communist party in 1926. He was a union activist, and was imprisoned several times before World War II. He then moved to the Soviet-occupied east of the country, and organized resistance against the Germans after they had invaded the Soviet Union in 1941. In 1942, he became a member of the central committee of the newly formed Polish Workers' party, and in 1943 was made its general secretary. In 1945 he was deputy premier of the provisional government in Lublin, and went on to serve as minister for the recovered territories. In the same year, he became a member of the Politburo and general secretary of the central committee. He suppressed the Peasants' party, and supported a forced merger with the Socialist party. At the same time, he remained skeptical about the collectivization of agriculture, and in 1947 opposed the creation of the Cominform. In 1948 Stalin engineered his dismissal as party secretary and Politburo member, and in 1949 his expulsion from government and the party. He was imprisoned from 1951 to 1954, but rehabilitated by Khrushchev in 1956. Now a national hero, he was installed as first secretary in the same year. He curbed the role of the secret police, and abandoned the persecution of the Catholic Church and the collectivization of agriculture. However, he did not introduce freedom of speech or economic reform, and came to be regarded by many as still ultimately under the control of Moscow. In 1968, intellectuals spoke out against the regime, and students rioted in major cities. Gomulka then attempted to introduce economic reforms, but in 1970 a drastic increase in food prices led to more rioting, and he resigned.

Gorbachev, Mikhail 1931–

Leader of the Soviet Union and reformer. Gorbachev became a member of the Communist party's central committee in 1971 and a full member of the Politburo in 1980. In 1985 he succeeded Chernenko as general secretary, adopting a policy of *perestroika* (restructuring). He encouraged the growth of private-sector cooperatives and competition, and he traveled the Soviet Union extensively, speaking out against alcoholism and economic inefficiency. He introduced *glasnost* (openness), allowing greater freedom of speech and information, and in 1989 he allowed independent candidates to stand for election. They fared particularly well in nonRussian Soviet republics where there was considerable nationalistic unrest. Abroad he withdrew the Red Army from Afghanistan, developed the warmest relations with the West since World War II, and, after initial disagreement over Reagan's SDI policy, signed the INF treaty with the United States, agreeing to dismantle some of the nuclear weapons stationed in Europe. He became president of the Soviet Union in 1988.

Göring, Hermann W. 1893–1946

German politician. Göring joined the Nazi party in 1922, and in 1923 he took part in the unsuccessful coup in Munich, and then escaped abroad. He returned in 1927 and in 1928 was elected to the Reichstag (parliament), becoming its president in 1932. After the Nazi takeover of the country in 1933, Göring became Hitler's effective deputy, and commanded the Luftwaffe (airforce), until 1945. In 1933 he became interior minister for Prussia, organizing the local Gestapo and establishing concentration camps. Appointed aviation minister in 1933, Göring was given charge, in 1936, of a Four-Year Plan to make Germany self-sufficient and a great military power. In 1938 he became a field marshal; in 1939 he chaired the Council for the Defense of the Reich, playing a major role in the preparation for war, and was named as Hitler's successor. In 1940 he took control of economic policy. During World War II he became very rich by plundering Jewish communities. His fall from grace began after the Luftwaffe's defeat in the Battle of Britain of 1940, and ended in his expulsion from the Nazi party in 1945. He surrendered to the Allies in 1945 and was condemned to death at the Nuremberg war crimes trials, but committed suicide before his scheduled execution.

Gromyko, Andrei A. 1909–89

Soviet politician. A Communist party member from 1931, Gromyko was appointed to the People's Commissariat of Foreign Affairs in 1939, and became counselor at the Soviet embassy in Washington. In 1943 he was appointed Soviet ambassador to the United States. He attended the Tehran, Yalta and Potsdam conferences, and in 1946 sat on the UN Security Council, where he used his veto 25 times. Promoted to deputy foreign minister in 1946, he became chief Soviet representative in the UN General Assembly in 1949, and in 1952–53, was ambassador to the UK. He became a full member of the Communist party central committee in 1956 and foreign minister in 1957. In 1962 he took part in talks with President Kennedy to resolve the Cuban crisis, and in 1967 his diplomatic efforts paved the way for the nuclear nonproliferation treaty. He was a member of the Politburo by 1973. He remained foreign minister until 1985, when he became President (titular head of state), an office taken over by Gorbachev a short time later. Although a major figure in the Cold War, Gromyko was widely regarded as the principal engineer of Gorbachev's rise to power. Nevertheless, Gorbachev did not attend his funeral.

Guevara, Che (Ernesto) 1928–67

Professional revolutionary. Born in Argentina, Guevara mixed with revolutionaries throughout Latin America. He became Castro's advisor and trained his guerrillas. When Castro came to power in 1959, he conferred Cuban citizenship on Guevara and gave him a series of important posts, including directorship of the National Bank. As minister of industry in 1961 Guevara implemented mass nationalization and in the same year wrote an influential manual on guerrilla warfare. In 1965, after writing *Man and Socialism in Cuba*, he disappeared. It was revealed in 1967 that he had been captured and executed while leading revolutionaries in Bolivia. His works inspired many student-radicals in the late 19602.

Haig, Alexander M. 1924–

US general. An army officer, Haig was appointed military aide to Henry Kissinger in 1969. He then went on to become the chief deputy of the National Security Council, and in 1973 Nixon made him the army's vice-chief of staff. Now a four-star general, Haig advocated a harder line in Vietnam, and also in 1973 he became chief of White House staff. He is believed to have helped persuade Nixon to resign, and to have effectively ruled the country toward the end of the administration. It has been alleged that he was involved in wiretapping, and in plans to overthrow Allende in Chile and bomb Cambodia. During 1974–79, he was supreme commander of the NATO forces in Europe, and from 1981 to 1982 served as secretary of state under Reagan.

Haile Selassie 1892–1975

Ethiopian emperor. A member of the Ethiopian nobility, in 1916 he was instrumental in deposing Lij Yasu; when Zaudita became empress in 1917 he was regent and heir apparent. A progressive, in 1923 he gained membership for Ethiopia of the League of Nations. He became king in 1928, and emperor in 1930, taking the name Haile Selassie. In 1931 he introduced a new constitution, concentrating power in himself and making parliament redundant. In pursuit of centralization, he strengthened the police and abolished feudal taxation. After Italy invaded Ethiopia in 1935, Haile Selassie went into exile in 1936, addressing

the League of Nations conference in the same year. In 1941, Ethiopia was liberated with British assistance, and he resumed his position. He westernized Ethiopia, and extended educational facilities. Internationally, he aligned himself with the United States, and in 1963 was a founder member of the Organization for African Unity. He was deposed by a military coup in 1974, after mismanagement during the previous year's famine, and eventually replaced by a Marxist, Major Mengistu.

Hammarskjöld, Dag H. A. C. 1905–61

Swedish secretary general of the UN. In 1951, Hammarskjöld, a minister without portfolio, became Swedish delegate to the UN, and in 1953 he was elected UN secretary general, a role he considerably expanded. In 1955, he obtained the release of UN troops from China, and in 1956, during the Suez crisis, sent a force to Egypt. In 1958 he stationed troops in Lebanon and Jordan, and in 1959 sent an observer to Laos. In 1960 he sent a force to the Belgian Congo, which was suffering a great deal of internal conflict after independence. This decision was controversial, and the Soviet Union called for his resignation and replacement with a triumvirate representing the West, the Communists and the neutrals. Hammarskjöld was killed in a plane crash on his way to the Congo, and posthumously awarded the Nobel Peace Prize.

Himmler, Heinrich 1900–45

German politician. Himmler joined the Nazi party in 1923, and in 1928 became its deputy propaganda officer. In 1929 he took charge of the SS, originally Hitler's bodyguard, which by 1933 numbered 50,000. After Hitler came to power in 1933, Himmler was appointed head of the Gestapo (secret police) in Bavaria, and by 1934 he controlled the organization nationwide. In the same year, he drew up a list of Hitler's opponents in the SA (stormtroopers) and had them murdered by the SS. From 1936 he commanded all police forces. Using the SS and the Gestapo, he set up 17 concentration and extermination camps. In 1943 during World War II, he became minister of the interior, and in 1944 head of the German home forces and effective second in command. Toward the end of the war, Himmler, believing Hitler was lost, secretly proposed surrender to the Western allies. Captured by the Allies, he committed suicide before he was identified.

Hindenburg, Paul von 1847–1934

German general and president. A general during World War I, Hindenburg commanded the German Eighth Army, his forces defeating the Russians at Tannenburg and at the Masurian Lakes in 1914. He then went on to invade Poland. A field marshal by 1916, he was appointed chief of general

staff and transferred to the western front. In 1918, having been defeated at Amiens and at the second battle of the Marne, he pulled back his forces behind what became known as the Hindenburg line. Its penetration by the Allies virtually signaled Germany's defeat in the war. In 1925 Hindenburg was elected as the rightwing candidate for the presidency. In 1930, when no party held an overall majority in the German parliament, he held the power of veto to Brüning's government by decree; he then tried to operate a nonparty government under Von Papen. In 1932 he was re-elected in a contest against Hitler, but in 1933, acting on Von Papen's advice, Hindenburg appointed Hitler as chancellor of a coalition government.

Hirohito, 1901–89

124th Japanese emperor. Crown prince in 1916, Hirohito visited Europe in 1921, the first of his rank to do so. On his return to Japan, he became regent, and in 1926 succeeded to the throne. Under Hirohito, Japan began a large military buildup, and engaged in wars against China (1931–32 and 1937–45). From 1941 to 1945 Japan fought in World War II, beginning with the bombing of the US naval base at Pearl Harbor, and ending with the US atomic bombs dropped on the Japanese cities of Hiroshima and Nagasaki. Hirohito's role in the war, however, has never been clearly established. In 1945 he publicly announced Japan's acceptance of the Potsdam declaration (demanding Japan's unconditional surrender) and in 1946 accepted a new constitution granting the emperor only theoretical powers. In the same year, he addressed the Japanese people, denying that as emperor he had any divine status. Hirohito's influence on the Japanese royal family drew it closer to the people, and in 1959 Prince Akihito broke tradition by marrying a commoner. In 1971 Hirohito visited Europe again and briefly met President Nixon in Alaska, before making an official tour of the United States in 1974. An accomplished marine biologist, Hirohito published several works on the subject.

Hitler, Adolf 1889–1945

Austrian-born dictator and leader of Germany. By 1920 Hitler had come to dominate the German Workers' party, which he re-christened the National Socialist German Workers' (Nazi) party, becoming its leader in 1921. In 1923 he inspired their unsuccessful coup in Munich. Although in 1932 he failed to win the presidency of the Weimar Republic from Hindenburg, in 1933 he became chancellor. When the Reichstag burned down, the Communists were falsely blamed and soon afterwards Hitler assumed dictatorial powers. He ordered the establishment of the Gestapo (secret police) and concentration camps for political opponents. A magnetic orator, he preached a doctrine of German racial supremacy, and blamed

Germany's problems on the Jews, who were ruthlessly persecuted, most until they died in extermination camps. He rebuilt the armed forces, leading to economic recovery and raised morale. In 1934, he had potential enemies in the SA (storm-troopers) massacred, and in the same year he succeeded Hindenburg and took the title *Führer*. He then set about the complete restoration of national pride by avenging the Treaty of Versailles. In 1936, Germany occupied the demilitarized Rhineland, and made a pact with Italy, and in 1937, with Japan. In 1938, Hitler's troops invaded Austria, and occupied German-populated areas of Czechoslovakia. Hitler declared that he had no more territorial ambitions, but then occupied the rest of Czechoslovakia, and, after signing a nonaggression pact with Stalin, invaded Poland, bringing Britain and France into the war. In 1940, he invaded Denmark, Holland, Norway, Belgium and France, and reached the peak of his popularity in Germany. In 1941, Germany attacked the British in North Africa, supporting Mussolini, and turned on Russia, reaching, but not taking, Moscow. In 1942, Rommel's forces invaded Egypt but lost to Montgomery at El Alamein, and during 1942–43 the Allies drove them out of Africa. On the Eastern front, the Russians began gradually to repulse Hitler's troops. By 1944, members of the military had begun to plot against Hitler, and tried to assassinate him. Germany was now invaded from both sides, and on 30 April 1945, Hitler committed suicide.

Ho Chi Minh 1890–1969

Vietnamese revolutionary and president. In 1911, Ho fled a background of poverty to become a seaman. In 1917, he settled in France, where he joined the newly-formed French Communist party (PCF). He went to Moscow in 1923 and attended the 1924 Communist International there, and spoke on the importance of the peasantry in revolution. From 1923 to 1924 he was in the Soviet Union, and then, as a representative of Comintern, in China until 1927. He helped to found the League of Oppressed Peoples, the Vietnamese Revolutionary Youth League, and, in 1930, the Indochinese Communist party. He returned in 1940 to Japanese-occupied Indochina, and formed a resistance force, the Vietminh. He later established a government in Hanoi with himself as president. In 1946 he waged a war against the French, who had occupied southern Vietnam, finally defeating them at Dien Bien Phu in 1954, and so bringing about the partition of Vietnam. Abroad, Ho maintained good relations with China and the Soviet Union. In 1959 he agreed to help the Vietcong guerrillas in South Vietnam to overthrow their own government. In the same year, Ho resigned as party secretary, but remained president.

Enver Hoxha ▶

Mohammed Ali Jinnah ▶

Juan Carlos (right) ▶

Honecker, Erich 1912–

East German politician. Honecker joined the German Communist party in 1929, and in 1935 was imprisoned for antiNazi activities. Freed by the Russians in 1945, he joined the Communist party's central committee. He was chairman of the Free German Youth movement from 1946 to 1955. He helped to found the Socialist Unity party (SED), whose central committee he joined in 1946, and in 1958 he became a member of the Politburo. He supervised the building of the Berlin Wall in 1961. Party secretary in 1971, he became head of state in 1976, pursuing the hardline policies of his predecessor Ulbricht, more responsive to Moscow but opposed to détente. He resigned in 1989.

Hoover, Herbert C. 1874–1964

31st US president. In 1914, Hoover was appointed head of Allied Relief in London, and head of the Commission for Relief in Belgium. After the United States' entry into the war, he became national food administrator, coordinating the distribution of goods in both the United States and Europe. He was also on the War Trade Council, and helped to negotiate the Treaty of Versailles. In 1921, he became US secretary of commerce. He was also chairman both of the Colorado River commission and of the St Lawrence Waterways commission, and brought about the construction of the Hoover Dam and the St Lawrence Seaway. In 1929 he became president, but shortly after, the Depression began. He rejected the use of federal powers to deal with the economy, and instead attempted to persuade charities, businessmen and state governments to act. This was not successful and he later created the Federal Farm Board and the Reconstruction Finance Corporation, though he still refused to undertake a major program of public works, or to give direct relief to the unemployed. He was defeated in the 1932 election by Franklin D. Roosevelt. After World War II, Hoover was involved in famine-relief work in Europe.

Hoxha, Enver 1908–85

Albanian politician. In 1941 Hoxha was a founder member of the Albanian Communist party. In 1943 he took charge of the party's military wing, leading the resistance against the Germans and Italians. In 1946 he deposed King Zog, and Albania became a Communist state, effectively under Yugoslav control. Hoxha served as prime minister (1945–54), and minister of foreign affairs (1946). In 1954 he became first secretary of the central committee. In 1948, after the Soviet–Yugoslav split, Albania broke away from Yugoslavia and in 1961 Hoxha severed relations with the Soviet Union, and aligned his country more closely with China. However, he criticized the Chinese too, on ideological grounds, in 1977, and in 1978 China severed ties with Albania.

Jiang Jieshi 1887–1975

Chinese politician, leader of the Nationalist party, and soldier. Jiang fought in the overthrow of the Manchu dynasty, and then during 1913–16 against the would-be dictator, President Yuan Shikai. In 1918, he associated himself with the Nationalists (Guomindang), and in 1925, took control of the Nationalist Army. In collaboration with the Communist Party in 1926 he undertook a campaign against the Northern Warlords, achieving victory in 1928 by taking Beijing. Jiang then headed a new government at Nanjing. Meanwhile, in 1927, he purged the party of leftwingers, and began a civil war against the Communists which was suspended only during 1937–46 to make common cause against the Japanese. By 1946, the party was riddled with corruption and the army demoralized, and in 1949, Jiang was finally defeated by the Red Army of China. He fled to Taiwan (then Formosa), and formed a government in exile. He at first enjoyed US support, and so was able to begin the modernization of Taiwan's economy, but relations cooled with the rapprochement between China and the US in the 1970s.

Jinnah, Mohammed Ali 1876–1948

First governor general of Pakistan. Jinnah joined the Indian Congress party in 1906, and the Muslim League in 1913. In 1916 he negotiated the Lucknow Pact, a joint call with the Congress party for constitutional reform. In 1920, disagreeing with the policy of nonviolent noncooperation, he resigned from the Congress party and the Indian Home Rule League, which had both come to be dominated by Gandhi. Jinnah attended the Round Table Talks in London (1930–32), where he proposed, among other things, federalism and power-sharing. In 1935 he became president of the Muslim League. In the 1937 elections which followed the Government of India Act of 1935, Congress won majorities in many areas, and did not bring League politicians into governments. Jinnah now exchanged his policy of cooperation with the Hindu-dominated Congress for one of the creation of an independent Muslim state. When Congress ministers resigned their posts in 1939, Jinnah called for celebration, and in 1940, the Muslim League demanded partition. Jinnah was then involved in extensive negotiations, and in 1947 became governor-general and effective leader of Pakistan.

Johnson, Lyndon B. 1908–73

36th US president. In 1937, Johnson entered the House of Representatives as a Democrat and strong supporter of Roosevelt. In 1948, he was elected to the Senate, where from 1951 to 1953 he was majority whip, and party leader from 1953 to 1961, ensuring the smooth passage of the first civil rights bills of 1957 and 1960. In 1960 he unsuccessfully challenged Kennedy for the presidential

nomination. He became Kennedy's running mate, and was elected vice-president in 1960. He oversaw equal employment opportunities and space research, and in 1961 toured Southeast Asia. He became president in 1963 after Kennedy's assassination and ensured continuity, passing Kennedy's civil rights and voting rights bills. Reelected by a large majority in 1964, he undertook a large program of social legislation, including health care, housing, education, the environment and immigration, aimed at creating what he termed the "Great Society". His popularity waned when American involvement in the Vietnam war escalated. In 1968, he announced he would not seek reelection, and he stepped down in 1969.

Juan Carlos 1938–

Spanish king. The grandson of Alfonso XIII, Juan Carlos was groomed for the monarchy by Franco, who in 1969 nominated him as his successor. Juan Carlos came to power in 1975, and worked to obtain a democratic constitution and an amnesty for political prisoners. He adopted the role of a constitutional monarch. In 1981, Francoist members of the military occupied parliament, and held its members hostage. Juan Carlos denounced this action, so saving the new constitution. In the same year, he visited the Americas and China. In 1982, his promise to accept any freely elected government was upheld when the Socialist party came to power. Also in 1982, Spain joined NATO, and Juan Carlos was awarded the International Charlemagne Award, for furthering the cause of European unity.

Kaunda, Kenneth 1924–

Zambian president. Kaunda joined the ANC in 1949, and became secretary for Northern Rhodesia (Zambia) in 1952. He became head of the organization in 1953, but broke away in 1958 to found the Zambian ANC. He began a campaign of civil disobedience against the federation by Britain of Northern Rhodesia, Southern Rhodesia (Zimbabwe), and Nyasaland (Malawi). The federation was eventually abandoned. Kaunda was imprisoned in 1959 and released in 1960. Now regarded as a national hero, he headed the rapidly growing United National Independence party (UNIP) and in 1960 helped negotiate independence for Northern Rhodesia. The large European and Asian populations attempted to delay the process, and Kaunda managed, by and large, to defuse the ensuing tension. UNIP was victorious in the 1962 elections, and in 1964 Kaunda became chief minister. Zambia gained independence in 1964, and President Kaunda averted civil war. From 1965, he provided bases in Zambia for the anticolonial forces of Southern Rhodesia (Zimbabwe) and Namibia, and boycotted the former's railways. In 1972, Zambia became a single-party state.

▲ Jiang Jieshi

▲ Jomo Kenyatta

▲ Ruhollah Khomeini

Kennedy, John F. 1917–63

35th US president. A naval officer in World War II, in 1947, as a moderately liberal Democrat, he entered the House of Representatives, where he campaigned for the underprivileged and supported the Cold War. In 1952 he was elected to the Senate, and in 1960 he was selected as the Democratic presidential candidate campaigning for internatioalism and civil rights. In 1961, he became the youngest ever and first Roman Catholic US president. Domestically he introduced a program of radical reform, and spoke of the "New Frontier". Abroad, he established the Alliance for Progress between the USA and several Latin American countries for the development of the latter, and the Peace Corps, through which volunteers supplied Third World countries with skilled labor. In 1961, exiles attempted a US-backed invasion of Cuba, planned during the previous administration, but were routed at the Bay of Pigs. Kennedy accepted full responsibility. In 1961, he had a meeting in Vienna with Khrushchev. Kennedy's firmness prevented Khrushchev from signing a separate peace treaty with East Germany. In 1962 Kennedy demanded the removal of Soviet nuclear bases being installed in Cuba, the US navy blockaded Cuba, and the world seemed close to nuclear war. The Soviet Union agreed to remove the weapons in return for an American assurance that Cuban territorial integrity would be respected. Relations between the two superpowers improved, and in 1963 at Kennedy's initiative the United States, the Soviet Union and Great Britain signed a limited nuclear test ban treaty. On 22 November 1963, Kennedy was assassinated while campaigning in Dallas, Texas.

Kenyatta, Jomo 1890s–1978

First prime minister of independent Kenya. In 1922, Kenyatta joined the campaign for the return of Kikuyu tribal lands from the British, conducted by an organization called from 1926 the Kikuyu Central Association. In 1928, Kenyatta became its general secretary. He spoke in London against the proposed union with Uganda and Tanganyika and in 1930, in a letter to *The Times*, he demanded the return of tribal lands, representation in the legislature, educational opportunities, and freedom to follow tribal customs. In 1932, he got some compensation for the loss of lands. He then traveled extensively, writing and studying. In 1946, he attended the fifth meeting of the Pan-African Congress, and became its president. He returned to Kenya in 1946, became president of the Kenya African Union (KAU) in 1947, and made it into an influential power. In 1952, falsely accused by the British of leading the Mau Mau terrorist organization, he was imprisoned. In 1960, the British agreed to majority rule, and in 1961, Kenyatta was released, became president of the Kenya African National Union (KANU) and

negotiated a new constitution. KANU won the 1963 elections, and Kenyatta became prime minister. In 1964, Kenya became a single-party state. Domestically, Kenyatta developed the economy and attracted foreign investment, though there remained much inequality. Internationally, he pursued a policy of nonalignment, but was always sympathetic to the West.

Kerensky, Aleksandr 1881–1970

Russian prime minister. A member of the Socialist Revolutionary party, Kerensky was elected to the Duma in 1912, and he later supported World War I. After the February Revolution of 1917, he became vice-chairman of the Petrograd soviet and minister for justice, introducing universal suffrage, freedom of speech and of religion, and women's rights. Later in the year, he became minister of war and the navy, and suffered a disastrous military defeat. Shortly afterward he was elected prime minister. A dispute with his military commander Kornilov exposed the essential weakness of his position as a member of both the government and the soviet, he antagonized his military, the Bolsheviks came to power in the October Revolution of 1917, and Kerensky fled abroad. He finally settled in the United States, where he pursued a career as a writer and lecturer.

Khan, Mohammad Ayub 1907–74

Pakistani president. In 1951, Ayub Khan was appointed commander-in-chief of the army, and went on to serve as defense minister during 1954–55. In 1958, after a military coup, he became chief administrator under martial law, and later in the same year replaced Mirza as president. In 1959, he created the electoral college of Basic Democracies, and in the same year was promoted to field marshal. He also pursued economic reforms, and attempted to improve relations with East Pakistan. In 1962, he introduced a new constitution, with a powerful president and assemblies elected by the college of Basic Democrats. Martial law was lifted, and two years later he was returned as president. His support declined, however, particularly in East Pakistan, after the war with India in 1965 and during the increasing severity of his rule which followed it. He resigned in 1969, and martial law was reintroduced.

Khomeini, Ruhollah 1900–89

Iranian Shiah Moslem leader. In 1963 Khomeini denounced the Shah's policy of land reforms, and in 1964 the Shah exiled him. He lived abroad in Turkey, Iraq and France, coordinating strikes and campaigning for the Shah's overthrow. In 1979 Khomeini returned to Iran to great popular acclaim and launched the Islamic revolution. The Shah's caretaker government was overthrown, new ministers appointed, and a constitution

establishing an Islamic state and granting Khomeini wide-ranging powers approved by referendum. Western music and alcoholic beverages became illegal, women were obliged to wear veils, and Islamic punishments were reintroduced. Khomeini's foreign policy was marked by aggression and acts of terrorism, waging war on neighboring Iraq from 1980 to 1988 and attacking the United States on every opportunity, with rhetoric and terrorism. In 1989 he declared the book *The Satanic Verses* to be blasphemous, and shocked the Western world by ordering the death of its British author, Salman Rushdie. Khomeini also gave support to Islamic revolutionaries in other Middle Eastern countries.

Khrushchev, Nikita 1894–1971

Soviet political leader. Khrushchev joined the Communist party in 1918, and rose rapidly until becoming a member of the Politburo in 1939. After the outbreak of World War II, he consolidated Soviet power in eastern Poland, and after the German invasion in 1941 he organized the Ukrainian resistance movement. In 1944, he reasserted Soviet control of the Ukraine and presided over its reconstruction. In 1949 he resumed his post as first secretary of the Moscow City party, and became a specialist in agricultural matters, but was unsuccessful in his plan to create agricultural towns. In 1953 Khrushchev replaced Malenkov as first secretary of the all-union party, and in 1955 ousted him as chairman of the council of ministers, installing his own protégé Bulganin in his place. In 1955, on a visit to Yugoslavia, Khrushchev apologized to Tito for Stalin's condemnation of the Yugoslovian brand of Communism. In 1956 Khrushchev condemned Stalin, and argued for peaceful coexistence with the West. He introduced a degree of liberalization into Soviet society, and allowed the eastern bloc parties more independence. However, he resorted to military intervention in Hungary, after Imre Nagy had announced withdrawal from the Warsaw Pact. In 1957 Khrushchev survived an attempt to oust him, and in the following year succeeded Bulganin as chairman of the council of ministers (head of state). Khrushchev traveled widely throughout his career, and in 1959 met Eisenhower during a tour of the United States. A proposed summit was abandoned, though, after an American aeroplane was shot down over Soviet airspace. In 1961 he met Kennedy, but they failed to solve the Berlin problem, and later that year Khrushchev ordered the building of the Berlin Wall. In 1962 he attempted to install nuclear missiles in Cuba, and this led to a major confrontation with the United States. In 1963, the Soviet Union, the United States and Britain agreed the nuclear test ban treaty. Relations with China had deteriorated. The Soviet Union also suffered agricultural failures, and he was ousted in 1964.

Henry Kissinger

Bela Kun

Vladimir Ilych Lenin

King, Martin (Michael) Luther Jr 1929–68
US clergyman and civil rights leader. While studying for a PhD in theology, King was profoundly influenced by Gandhi's principle of *satyagraha*. In 1955–56 he led a boycott against racial segregation on local buses. After a year, this segregation was abandoned, and King became a national figure. He then helped to found and became president of the Southern Christian Leadership Conference, which oversaw civil rights organizations throughout the area. In 1960 he returned to his native Atlanta, supported demonstrations and was imprisoned. The civil rights movement under King was at its height during 1960–65, orchestrating generally successful demonstrations against localized examples of racial discrimination. In 1963 while in jail, King wrote his famous Letter from Birmingham, spelling out the principles of nonviolent noncooperation. In the same year, he helped to organize the March on Washington of more than 200,000 people, after which he delivered his "I have a dream" speech. In 1964, the Civil Rights Act was passed, and King was awarded the Nobel Peace Prize. In 1965 the Voting Rights Act was passed. King's campaign then moved to the turbulent north, where the Black Power movement was attracting support, and was marginally successful in protesting against segregated housing in Chicago. King broadened the civil rights agenda, and in 1967 publicly condemned the Vietnam War, tried to unite the poor of all races, and committed himself to the restructuring of society. In 1968 he planned a Poor People's Campaign, but was assassinated on 4 April.

Kissinger, Henry (Heinz) A. 1923–
US politician. In 1957 Kissinger wrote *Nuclear Weapons and Foreign Policy*, advocating a strategy of graduated "flexible response". He was security advisor to Eisenhower, Kennedy and Johnson. In 1969, Nixon appointed Kissinger assistant for national security and executive secretary of the National Security Council, and he became the architect of both Nixon's and Ford's foreign policies. He specialized in diplomacy, and pursued a policy of détente with the Soviet Union, culminating in the SALT 1 treaty in 1972. He also restored relations with China. In the Vietnam War, Kissinger ordered the bombing and invasion of Cambodia, oversaw the process of "Vietnamization" (the replacement of US combat troops with South Vietnamese), and in 1973 helped to negotiate a ceasefire and was awarded the Nobel Peace Prize. In the same year, he became Secretary of State, mediated a ceasefire in the Arab-Israeli "Yom Kippur" war, and restored US relations with Egypt. Kissinger also backed CIA operations to destabilize Allende's socialist government in Chile, and to give support to anti-Cuban forces in Angola. He resigned in 1977.

Kohl, Helmut 1930–
West German chancellor. In 1969 Kohl gained a place in the national parliament. In the same year, he became national deputy chairman of the Christian Democrat Union, and in 1973, party leader. He ran unsuccessfully for the chancellorship of West Germany in 1976, but acceded to power in 1982 in coalition with the Christian Social Union and the Free Democrats, after the fall of Schmidt's government. They won a majority in the 1983 elections, and Kohl pursued policies of moderate economic conservatism at home, and strong commitment to NATO abroad.

Kosygin, Aleksey 1904–80
Soviet politician. Kosygin fought in the Russian civil war, and joined the Communist party in 1927. In 1938 he was elected to the Supreme Soviet. In 1939, he became textiles minister, and joined the party's central committee. From 1940 to 1953, he was deputy chairman of the Soviet of People's Commissars. He was also premier of the Russian Republic during World War II, finance minister in 1948 and light industry minister (now including his old ministry of textiles) (1948–53). He became a full Politburo member in 1948. After the death of Stalin, however, Kosygin lost both his place on the Politburo and his position as deputy chairman. He regained the latter position a short time later, lost it again in 1956, but returned in 1957. During 1959–60 he was chairman of Gosplan. In 1960, he was restored as a full member of the Presidium (Politburo), and was also appointed as first deputy chairman of the Council of Ministers (head of state). In 1964, after the fall of Khrushchev, he became chairman of the Council of Ministers, and the moderate influence in the dual leadership comprised of himself and Brezhnev. Kosygin traveled widely, meeting Lyndon Johnson in 1967, and Zhou En Lai in 1969, after the Sino-Soviet border conflicts. In the mid-1970s, Brezhnev became more prominent, and in 1980 Kosygin retired on grounds of ill health.

Kun, Béla 1886–1937
Hungarian politician. Imprisoned by the Russians during World War I, Kun was converted to communism, and trained in revolutionary methods. He returned to Hungary in 1918, and founded the Hungarian Communist party. He was imprisoned until 1919, when the government resigned, after the Allies had ordered them to cede more territory to Romania. The Communist party then formed a revolutionary government in coalition with the Social Democrats. Technically foreign minister, Kun in fact exercised overall control. He was involved in the creation of a Red Army, which proceeded to attack Romania and Czechoslovakia, in the expectation of imminent assistance from the Soviet Union. This failed to materialize, however, and the collectivization of

agriculture angered farmers. Distribution of food deteriorated, and the army mutinied. The government fell, and Kun fled abroad. He eventually settled in Russia, where he became a member of the Third International and agitated for world revolution. He died in one of Stalin's purges.

Laval, Pierre 1883–1945
French politician. Laval joined the Socialist party in 1903, and in 1914 was elected to the Chamber of Deputies. He advocated compromise in World War I, and so lost his seat in 1919. He left the party in 1920, and began to move gradually to the right. Elected a deputy in 1924 and to the Senate as an independent in 1926, he served in four ministerial posts, and finally, in 1931, as prime minister. He lost the premiership a short time later, but regained it in 1935. He fell from power in 1936, after attempting to appease Mussolini with the Hoare-Laval pact, by which Abyssinia would have been partitioned. He helped to create the Vichy government after the fall of France, and in 1940 became its foreign minister. He was dismissed by Pétain in the same year, however, after the discovery of a plan to take power himself. In 1942, the Germans forcibly installed Laval as effective head of government, and he pursued a policy of open collaboration. In 1944 he fled to Spain, but in 1945 on his return to France was convicted of treason and executed.

Lenin, Vladimir Ilych 1870–1924
Marxist theorist, leader of the Russian October Revolution and founder of the Soviet Union. In 1895 Lenin was imprisoned as an agitator, and in 1897 exiled to Siberia. In 1900 he went to Western Europe, where he became involved with the Russian Social Democratic Labor party. In 1903 he split the party, forming the Bolshevik (majority) wing. He returned to Russia during the unsuccessful revolution of 1905, and left again in 1906. In 1912, he founded the breakaway Bolshevik party, coordinated the infiltration of Russian unions and increased the publication of propaganda. In 1914 he denounced World War I as imperialist and called on workers everywhere to transform the war into civil war. He returned to Russia in 1917, after the overthrow of the czar, and in October of that year used the Red Guard in a successful coup to replace the liberal-controlled Constituent Assembly with the Soviet of Peoples' Commissars, of which he became chairman. While in power, Lenin began the process of nationalization, though in his later years his New Economic Policy allowed some small-scale private enterprise. He created a secret police and was absolutely intolerant of opposition. A prolific writer with a powerful intellect, Lenin is regarded as probably the greatest-ever exponent of Marxism.

David Lloyd George

Patrice Lumumba

Douglas MacArthur

Litvinov, Maksim Maksimovich 1876–1951

Soviet politician. Litvinov joined the Russian Social Democratic Labor party in 1898, and was exiled to Siberia in 1901. He escaped in 1902, and eventually settled in England. In 1903 he sided with the Bolsheviks, and after the October Revolution of 1917, he became Soviet representative in London. He was not formally recognized in this role by the British, and a short time later he was arrested and deported to the Soviet Union, in exchange for the freedom of a British diplomat. In 1921 he was appointed deputy commissar for foreign affairs. In 1924, he gained recognition of the Soviet Union from Britain, and in 1928 signed the Kellogg-Briand pact, condemning the use of force to settle international disputes. He also spoke strongly in favor of disarmament at the preparatory commission of the League of Nations' World Disarmament Conference (1927–30). In 1931, Litvinov became commissar for foreign affairs. He was chief Soviet representative at the World Disarmament Conference (1932) in Geneva, and in 1933 led the Soviet delegation to the World Economic Conference in London. In 1934, he gained official recognition from the US and brought the Soviet Union into the League of Nations. From 1934 to 1938, he campaigned for the military isolation of Germany and Japan, and concluded pacts with France and Czechoslovakia. He was dismissed in 1939, and the Hitler-Stalin nonaggression treaty was signed. Litvinov was rehabilitated after the German invasion, and served as ambassador to the United States during 1941–43. He then became deputy commissar for foreign affairs, and retired in 1946.

Lloyd George, David 1863–1945

British prime minister. In 1890 Lloyd George was elected to parliament as a Liberal, and later opposed Britain's role in the Boer War. In 1905, he joined the cabinet as president of the Board of Trade, and in 1908 was appointed Chancellor of the Exchequer. He inspired the Old Age Pensions Act in the same year, and the National Health Insurance and Unemployment Insurance Acts in 1911. In 1909, he introduced the People's Budget, which proposed supertax and tax on land values. The House of Lords rejected it, however, and this precipitated a constitutional crisis. Their right of veto was removed in 1911. In the same year, Lloyd George confronted Germany over the third Moroccan crisis. He originally opposed British intervention in World War I, but reversed his views after the invasion of Belgium. In 1915, as munitions minister, he mobilized the war industries. In 1916 he served briefly as war minister, and replaced Asquith as prime minister. He introduced merchant shipping convoys to defeat the U-boat blockades, and subverted the influence of General Haig by securing a unified

Allied command under Foch. In 1918–19, Lloyd George was one of the three principal negotiators of the Treaty of Versailles. There then followed the Anglo-Irish war of 1919 to 1921, after which he partitioned Ireland, creating a self-governing dominion (the Irish Free State) in the south. This was very unpopular with Conservative members of his coalition, and after the Anglo-Turkish crisis at Chanak in 1922, they withdrew their support. Lloyd George left office in 1922.

Ludendorff, Erich von 1865–1937

German general. Ludendorff joined the army in 1883, and the general staff in 1894, in 1908 becoming head of its operations section. In 1914, he became Hindenburg's chief of staff in the east, and his planning led to victory at Tannenburg. In 1916, as First Quartermaster General, he was given equal responsibility with Hindenburg, and was sent to the west after the failure of the Verdun offensive. Several unsuccessful operations ensued, and the ineffectual chancellor, Bethmann-Hollweg, was brought down by Ludendorff, who then planned the last major German attack of the war, which was defeated by Foch in 1918. Ludendorff insisted on negotiation rather than surrender, and a short time later resigned his commission. In the same year, he fled to Sweden, but later returned to Germany. In 1920, he was involved in the Kapp putsch, and in 1923, in Hitler's Munich putsch. Ludendorff was a member of parliament during 1924–28, and in 1925 was the Nazi presidential candidate. He broke with Hitler after failing to gain the presidency, and founded a small party of his own.

Lumumba, Patrice H. 1925–61

Congolese prime minster. A Liberal party and union activist, Lumumba founded the Congolese National Movement (MNC) in 1958. In 1959 the Congo's Belgian rulers announced a five-year buildup to independence, beginning with local elections, which the nationalists, however, boycotted. A Belgian clampdown ensued, culminating in a violent confrontation, and Lumumba's imprisonment for incitement to riot. In 1960, Lumumba was released to attend a Round Table conference in Belgium, to set a date for independence. The MNC won the general elections of the same year, and Lumumba became prime minister. A short time later, a section of the army mutinied, the Katanga province seceded, and Belgian troops returned. UN troops arrived at Lumumba's request, but would not intervene in Katanga. Lumumba turned to the Soviet Union for help, alienating the West. He prepared to invade Katanga, and was then dismissed by President Kasavubu, but disputed the legality of this action. The army intervened against him, and the UN recognized Kasavubu's government. Lumumba was killed by Katangan secessionists in 1961.

MacArthur, Douglas 1880–1964

US general. MacArthur graduated from West Point Military Academy in 1903, and served with distinction in France during World War I. From 1919 to 1922 he was superintendent of West Point, and from 1922 to 1925 US commander in the Philippines. From 1930 to 1935, now a general, he was chief of staff, and from 1935 to 1937 head of the US military mission in the Philippines, building up their defensive capacity. He retired in 1937, but was recalled in 1941 to head US forces in the Far East. He fought a delaying action against the Japanese in the Philippines, retreated to Australia in 1942, and became Supreme Commander in the Southwest Pacific. After a successful Allied campaign in 1943–44, MacArthur became a five-star general. In 1945, as Supreme Allied Commander, he formally accepted the Japanese surrender in Tokyo. From 1945 to 1951, as the commander of Allied occupation, he was responsible for the demilitarization, democratization, and economic regeneration of Japan. In 1950, he became UN commander in Korea, leading troops against the Communist forces and twice invading the north, but he was relieved of his duties in 1951 when he publicly disagreed with President Truman over policy extending the war into China.

Macmillan, (Maurice) Harold 1894–1986

British prime minister. Macmillan was elected to parliament as a Conservative in 1924, and opposed appeasement of Hitler and Mussolini in the 1930s. In 1940 under Churchill he joined the ministry of supply, and was colonial under secretary in 1942. At the end of that year he became minister resident in North Africa, where he worked for good relations with other Allied powers. In 1943 he was head of the Allied Commission in Italy, and in 1945, minister for air. After 1945 he was in opposition until becoming housing minister in 1951, effecting the construction of 300,000 houses in a year. He was then defence minister (1954), foreign secretary (1955), Chancellor of the Exchequer (1955–57), and prime minister (1957–63). He continued many of the postwar policies of social reform, and prosperity grew. Abroad, he dismantled much of the British empire in Africa, and worked to improve relations with the US after Suez, meeting Eisenhower and Kennedy. He also pursued rapprochement with the Soviet Union, and met Khrushchev in 1959. In accordance with the Nassau agreement of 1962, the US supplied Britain with Polaris nuclear missiles, and the French consequently vetoed British membership of the EEC in 1963. At home, economic difficulties had led to a decline in popularity, and the Profumo scandal broke out in 1963. Although in the same year Macmillan helped negotiate the Partial Nuclear Test Ban Treaty, he retired a short time later, owing to ill health.

Mandela, Nelson R. 1918–

Black South African leader. In 1943 Mandela, a lawyer, joined the African National Congress, and helped to found its Youth League in the Transvaal. In 1952 he organized nonviolent resistance to apartheid and in 1953, now a member of the National Executive, was barred from public speaking until 1961 when, having become a leading figure in the ANC, he was acquitted of treason after a long-running trial, and coordinated a general strike. In 1962 he was imprisoned for encouraging industrial unrest. After the Sharpeville massacre (1960) the ANC was banned, and Mandela began to advocate armed struggle. He helped to found Umkonto We Sizwe (Spear of the Nation), the ANC's military wing, and in 1963 was charged with treason, following the discovery of an arms cache. At his trial he made a four-and-a-half-hour speech in his own defense and in 1964 was sentenced to life imprisonment. The South African authorities maintained that there would be no possibility of Mandela's release until he renounced the use of violence, which he refused to do, becoming an international figure and the symbol of black resistance.

Mao Zedong 1893–1976

Chinese head of state, revolutionary leader, and Marxist thinker. In the 1911 revolution, Mao fought with Sun Yat Sen's nationalist forces in the overthrow of the Manchu dynasty, and in 1919 became politically active with the May Fourth Movement. In 1921 he was a founder member of the Chinese Communist party (CCP), and later its leader. In 1927 he led the Communists in a civil war against the forces of Jiang Jieshi, and in the following year founded a soviet republic in southeast China. In 1934 to 1935, the period of the Communists' Long March and relocation in the northwest, Mao emerged as leader. After this he wrote his chief works of political philosophy. He finally achieved victory in 1949, and became chairman both of the CCP and of the newly founded People's Republic of China. Maoism differs from Marxism–Leninism in its emphasis on the peasantry as the driving force of the revolution, in its fight against the rise of bureaucratic and technocratic elites. These ideological differences with the Soviet Union, and Khrushchev's lack of support in China's 1962 border war with India, damaged Sino-Soviet relations, and Mao later cultivated the United States. In 1959 he resigned as chairman of the Republic, after failing to reconstruct the economy. He remained however as party chairman, and in 1966 launched the Cultural Revolution, a violent attempt to halt ideological revisionism. Soon after his death, Mao's theories of mass revolutionary fervor as a spur to economic growth, and of a paramilitary way of life, were replaced by an emphasis on managerial competence.

Marcos, Ferdinand E. 1917–89

Philippine president. In 1939, Marcos was convicted of the assassination of a political opponent of his father, but was acquitted on appeal a year later. He escaped from Japanese capture during World War II, but there is no evidence for his claim that he then became a Philippine resistance leader. He was elected to the House of Representatives in 1949, and to the Senate in 1959. He left the Liberal party in 1964, after failing to gain the presidential nomination, and in the same year, was elected president as the Nationalist party candidate. He introduced economic and social reform, but growing political unrest led him in 1972 to impose martial law, and imprison opposition leaders, including Benigno Aquino. The Catholic Church opposed his regime, and guerrilla warfare was waged against it by Maoists and Muslim separatists. In 1973 a new constitution was introduced, further extending the president's powers. In 1981, the constitution was amended, martial law lifted, and Marcos reelected. During the next two years, government corruption, the poverty gap, and Communist guerrilla activities all increased, while the economy declined. Opposition to Marcos grew, and in 1983 Aquino returned, to be shot dead on arrival. The government were widely believed to have been responsible, and Marcos's support fell still further. He was opposed in the presidential elections of 1986 by Aquino's widow, Corazon Aquino, and though Marcos was officially declared the winner, he was suspected both at home and abroad of having perpetrated massive electoral fraud. The army split, and later that year Marcos fled to Hawaii.

Marshall, George C. 1880–1959

US General. Marshall served in France during World War I, and in 1939 became US chief of staff. He attended many wartime conferences, and pressed for invasion across the Channel. He attempted unsuccessfully to mediate in the Chinese civil war. As secretary of state (1947–49), Marshall was the principal architect of the European Recovery Program, "the Marshall Plan", and saved thousands from starvation. Also during his term of office, the state of Israel was recognized, aid was given to Greece and Turkey, and preparations made for the formation of NATO. In 1950, Marshall became defense secretary, and prepared for intervention in the Korean War. He retired in 1951 and in 1953 became the first soldier to be awarded the Nobel Peace Prize.

Masaryk, Tomas G. 1850–1937

Czechoslovakian president. In 1890, Masaryk, a professor of philosophy, joined the Young Czech Party, and in 1891 was elected to the *Reichsrat* in Vienna, where he campaigned for Czech autonomy. In 1900, he founded the Realist party,

and was reelected to the *Reichsrat* in 1907. As leader of the left Slav opposition, he spoke against Austro-Hungarian encroachment upon the Balkans, and the alliance with Germany. In 1914 he fled to Western Europe, and helped to found the Czech National Council, of which he became president. Unlike most of his colleagues, he presented the case for Czech independence to Britain and France, rather than to Russia, which he visited after the overthrow of the czar. In 1918, he visited the USA, and received support both from Slovak immigrants and from President Wilson. Later the same year, the Allies recognized the republic of Czechoslovakia, and Masaryk became president. He held together the different nationalities, and was one of the first to express concern over Hitler's rise. He resigned in 1935.

McCarthy, Joseph R. 1908–57

US politician. Elected to the Senate as a Republican in 1946, McCarthy declared in 1950 that 205 Communists had infiltrated the state department. He failed to name any, but nevertheless embarked on a highly publicized crusade. In 1952, he accused the Democrats of "20 years of treason", and became chairman of the Permanent Subcommittee on Investigations of the Government Committee on Operations of the Senate. Although he interrogated large numbers of government employees, he failed to construct one reasonable case. Many people were victimized, however, and some forced from their jobs. McCarthy then attacked major political figures, including Eisenhower, but his popularity declined after a hearing was televised. He was dismissed in 1954, and later officially censured by the Senate.

Meir, Golda (Goldie Myerson) 1898–1978

Israeli prime minister. Born in Russia and brought up in the United States, in 1921 Meir emigrated to Palestine, where she held various executive positions in the Histadrut. During the war, she helped negotiate independence from the British, and in 1946 became head of the Jewish Agency's political department. She worked for the release of illegal immigrants and political prisoners. In 1948, after independence, Meir became ambassador to Moscow, and in 1949 was elected to parliament as a member of the Mapai party. From 1949 to 1956 as labor minister, she organized the building of houses and roads. From 1956 to 1966, as foreign minister, she worked to develop good relations with nonaligned African countries. In 1966 she became general secretary of the Mapai party, and after the six-day war in 1967 was involved in the creation of the Labor party. She became prime minister in 1969, traveled widely, tried to negotiate peace in the Middle East, and in 1973 received Willy Brandt, the West German Chancellor. Israel found itself unprepared for the Yom Kippur war in 1973, and in 1974, Meir resigned.

▲ Golda Meir

▲ François Mitterrand

▲ Robert Mugabe

Mitterrand, François M. 1916–

French president. Mitterrand was captured by the Germans during World War II, but escaped and became a resistance leader. He was elected to the National Assembly in 1946, and between 1947 and 1957, held cabinet posts in 11 different governments. He ran for the presidency in 1965. In 1971, as First Secretary of the Socialist party, he considerably increased its popularity. He ran unsuccessfully against Giscard d'Estaing in 1974, but defeated him in 1981 to become president. After a socialist majority in the general election, Mitterrand formed a government. He then began a program of nationalization, increased welfare payments and the minimum wage, and gave more power to local governments. He later moderated his economic policies when worldwide recession occurred. In his foreign policy, his tough but realistic attitude to the Soviet Union encouraged détente in the later 1980s.

Molotov, Vyacheslav 1890–1986

Soviet politician. Molotov joined the Bolshevik party in 1906, and was a member of the military revolutionary committee during the Bolshevik revolution. He joined the central committee in 1921, and the Politburo in 1925, when he also became chairman of the Moscow party committee, and in 1930 was selected as chairman of the Soviet of People's Commissars (premier). In 1939 as commissar for foreign affairs he negotiated the nonaggression pact with Hitler. In 1941 Stalin replaced Molotov as chairman of the council of ministers, and he then became first deputy chairman. He also joined the state defense committee (war cabinet), helped to form alliances with Britain and the US, and attended all the conferences of Tehran, Yalta, Potsdam, and San Francisco. After the war, he made extensive use of the Soviet veto in the United Nations. He retired as foreign minister in 1949, but then served again in this capacity during 1953–56. In 1956 he was appointed state control minister, but after participating in the attempted coup against Khrushchev in 1957, he was posted to Mongolia. He retired in 1962 and was reinstated in 1984.

Montgomery, Bernard L. 1887–1976

British general. Mentioned in dispatches during World War I, after the outbreak of World War II Montgomery led the British Third Division in France, and, after the evacuation of Dunkirk, commanded the Southeastern army in England. In 1942, as commander of the British Eighth Army in North Africa, he defeated Rommel's troops at El Alamein. The Axis forces were then driven across North Africa, and surrendered in the following year in Tunisia. Montgomery then led the Eighth Army in the invasions of Sicily and Italy. In 1944, he was given command of the ground troops in the

offensive across the English Channel, and a short time later he led the Twenty-first Army Group through Western Europe. He was then made a field marshal. Immediately after the war, he commanded the British army of occupation, and during 1946–48 was chief of the imperial general staff. He then served from 1948 to 1951 as chairman of the commanders-in-chief of the Western alliance, and from 1951 to 1958 as NATO deputy supreme commander in Europe.

Morgenthau, Henry Jr 1891–1967

US politician. In 1934, Morgenthau, then governor of the federal Farm Board, was appointed secretary for the Treasury. He financed Roosevelt's New Deal, and ran the US war economy. He was the principal architect of the International Monetary Fund and the World Bank. He resigned in 1945, after Truman's rejection of the Morgenthau Plan to prevent the re-industrialization of Germany.

Mountbatten, Louis 1900–79

British sailor and viceroy of India. Having joined the Royal Navy as a cadet in 1913, in 1942 Mountbatten became chief of combined operations, and joined the chiefs-of-staffs committee. During 1943–45 he was Supreme Allied Commander in Southeast Asia, and liberated Burma from the Japanese. In 1947, he was appointed viceroy of India, and oversaw the partition of the subcontinent and its peaceful transition to independence; also in this year he was created Earl. At Nehru's request, he served as governor general of India until 1948 and helped to unify the princely states with India and Pakistan. He was later commander-in-chief of the Mediterranean fleet (1952–54), first sea lord (1955–59), and chief of the UK defense staff (1959–65). He was killed by the IRA in 1979.

Mugabe, Robert G. 1924–

Zimbabwean president. In 1963, Mugabe broke away from Nkomo's Zimbabwe African People's Union (ZAPU), and helped to found the Zimbabwe African National Union (ZANU) fiighting for independence and black majority rule. He was imprisoned in 1964, and in 1965 Rhodesia's white elite made a unilateral declaration of independence from Britain. Mugabe became the leader of ZANU in 1974, and was freed in 1975. In the ensuing civil war (1975–79), Mugabe and Nkomo led the Patriotic Front against the government forces. ZANU gained a majority in the 1980 elections, and Mugabe became prime minister. He successfully encouraged the European community to remain, and introduced social reform. In 1982, he clashed with Nkomo, when he announced that only policies approved by ZANU would be implemented. He later expressed an intention eventually to institute a single-party state.

Mussolini, Benito 1883–1945

Italian dictator. In 1914, Mussolini was expelled from the Socialist party for advocating Italian intervention in World War I. He joined the armed forces in 1915 and became a fervent antisocialist. In 1919 he founded the Fascist movement, entered parliament in 1921, and in 1922 his supporters embarked on their March on Rome. The king asked Mussolini to form a government. He became prime minister in a multi-party coalition, but by 1928 had created a single-party state with the Fascist Grand Council in control. Whilst using terror tactics against his opposition and curtailing civil liberties, Mussolini restored self-respect to Italy and began a large program of public works. In 1929 he agreed the Lateran Treaty with the Papacy, by which the latter, in return for the establishment of the Vatican State, considerable compensation and the position of official religion of Italy, abandoned claims to land elsewhere in the country. Mussolini reached the height of his popularity with the invasion of Abyssinia (Ethiopia) in 1935–36; he supported Franco in the Spanish Civil War. In 1936 he formed the Rome–Berlin axis with Hitler, and in 1940 entered World War II, in which Italian troops acted principally as auxiliaries to the Germans. Italy gained control of Albania in 1939, and went on to a series of military débâcles, regularly requiring German assistance. In 1943, the Allies invaded Sicily, and Mussolini was voted out of office by the Grand Council of Fascism, and imprisoned, to be freed by the Germans, who set him up in a puppet Fascist state in the north, where he executed several members of the Grand Council who had voted for his dismissal. The Allies advanced north, and as the Germans withdrew, the partisans began to take control. In 1945, they captured Mussolini disguised as a German soldier, and shot him.

Nagy, Imre 1896–1958

Hungarian prime minister. Captured by the Russians during World War I, Nagy was converted to Communism and joined the Red Army. He returned to Hungary in 1921, and joined the revolutionary government. Imprisoned in 1927, he left for the Soviet Union in 1929, and returned again to Hungary in 1944. He served as minister of agriculture (1945), minister of the interior (1945–46), and speaker of the Hungarian parliament (1947–49). In 1953 he became premier, but was ousted in 1955 for his liberal policies. He was reinstated in 1956 after the outbreak of revolution, and promised a multi-party state and Soviet withdrawal. He also withdrew Hungary from the Warsaw Pact. Soviet troops invaded Hungary, and Nagy made a fruitless appeal to the West for help. He took refuge in the Yugoslavian embassy, but left with guarantees of safety from the Soviets, who then, however, transported him to Romania, and later executed him in Hungary.

▲ Gamal Nasser

▲ Jawaharlal Nehru

▲ Nicholas II

Nasser, Gamal A. 1918–70

Egyptian soldier, prime minister and president. While in the army Nasser helped to found the Free Officers' movement to overthrow British rule. He fought in the Arab–Israeli war (1948), and masterminded the coup which ousted King Farouk in 1952. As minister of the interior, Nasser then effectively took power. In 1954 he became prime minister, and in 1956 president. He created a single-party police state, westernized society, and made Islam the official state religion. Abroad, he pursued a policy of nonalignment, and became an international figure after the Bandung conferences in 1955. In the same year, he became effective leader of the Arab League. In 1956, Britain and the US canceled aid for the building of the Aswan dam, and the Suez Canal was nationalized to provide funds. The Aswan dam was completed in 1968, with Soviet aid. In 1958, Egypt and Syria formed the United Arab Republic. Nasser intervened in the Yemeni civil war from 1962–68, and in 1967 Israel defeated Egypt in the Six-Day War, after which Nasser nonetheless received a vote of confidence. Egypt was rearmed by the Soviet Union and in 1970 Nasser agreed to negotiations with Israel.

Nehru, Jawaharlal (Pandit) 1889–1964

President of the Indian Congress party, close associate of Gandhi, and first Prime Minister of the Republic of India. Educated at Harrow and Cambridge, and called to the Bar, Nehru returned to India, and in 1919 became involved with the Congress party. He spent more than nine of the next 21 years in prison. In 1929, having twice served as party general secretary, Nehru was elected president, and switched the party's aim from home rule to total independence. At the outbreak of war in 1939, he refused to support the Allies unless India was free, and in 1942 rejected the British offer of dominion status. In 1947, against the wishes of his mentor Gandhi, he agreed to the partition of the Indian subcontinent, and became prime minister. His policies combined a desire for a modern, secular, democratic socialist state with an assertion of Indian nationalism, exemplified by his determination to keep Kashmir within India, his forcible expulsion of the Portuguese from Goa in 1961, and his border dispute with China in 1962, disastrous because it compromised his nonaligned stance. Internationally, he kept India in the Commonwealth, but adopted a neutralist role, making India into a major Asian power, and often acted as a go-between in the disputes of other countries. He remained prime minister until his death in 1964.

Nicholas II 1868–1918

Russian czar. Nicholas, who took the throne in 1894, was an autocratic and repressive ruler, and in 1905 created the Duma to deal with revolutionary insurgence. Contrary to his promise, however, it was limited to a consultative role. In 1907, Russia formed an entente with Britain, and early in World War I, which Nicholas had tried his utmost to prevent, he appointed himself commander-in-chief. During his absence the country was effectively ruled by Rasputin, and the government's authority collapsed. Nicholas was forced to abdicate after the revolution of February 1917, and after the October Revolution of the same year he and his family were shot by Bolsheviks.

Nixon, Richard M. 1913–

37th US president. In 1946 Nixon was elected as a Republican to the House of Representatives, where he was a member of the Un-American Activities Committee. He was elected to the senate in 1950, and in 1953 became vice-president. He ran unsuccessfully for the presidency in 1960 and for the governorship of California in 1962, and in 1968 was elected president. He cut federal expenditure, twice devalued the dollar, and then introduced the New Economic Policy, instituting wage and price controls. He reestablished relations with China, which he visited in 1972, in the same year visiting the Soviet Union, and agreeing the SALT I treaty. In Indochina he followed the Nixon Doctrine of US disengagement from foreign wars, and by 1973 had withdrawn from Vietnam. He was criticized when it was later revealed that Cambodia had been secretly bombed during 1969–70. His political career came to an end with the Watergate affair. After an order of the Supreme Court, transcripts of conversations between Nixon and his staff were made public. They revealed that Nixon had tried to cover up a break-in to Democratic headquarters by several of his close aides. Threatened with impeachment, he resigned in 1974 and was succeeded by Gerald Ford, who granted him a pardon.

Nkrumah, Kwame 1909–72

Ghanaian president. In 1945, Nkrumah helped to organize the Fifth Pan-African Congress, and in 1947 he became general secretary of the proindependence United Gold Coast Convention (UGCC). In 1949 he helped to found the more radical Convention People's party, and in 1950 he initiated a campaign of nonviolent noncooperation. He was then imprisoned for encouraging strikes, and in 1951, while still in prison, he was elected to parliament. Upon his release, he became Leader of Government Business, and in 1952 was made prime minister. In 1957, the Gold Coast gained independence as Ghana. Nkrumah introduced social reforms, while taking a hard line on potential subversives. In 1960, Ghana became a republic, and Nkrumah its president. Economic recession led to social unrest, to which Nkrumah responded by increasing the

authoritarianism of his rule, and by turning to the Communist nations for assistance. He survived several assassination attempts. In 1964, a single-party system was installed, and in 1966, while Nkrumah was on his way to help negotiate a settlement of the Vietnam War, the military seized power. He was given asylum in Guinea, and dedicated the rest of his life to writing.

Pahlavi, Mohammad Reza 1919–80

Shah of Iran from 1941. In 1951, Mosaddeq, a nationalist opponent of the Shah, nationalized the British-owned petroleum industry, and became premier. The Shah made an unsuccessful attempt to dismiss him in 1953, and left the country. He returned a few days later and assumed full power, probably with US help. He denationalized the petroleum industry, and with US aid, embarked upon a process of westernization and modernization, which became known as the White Revolution. Some Iranians criticized the pace of change as being too slow, while others opposed westernization for religious reasons. Government corruption, the secret police, and the concentration of oil revenue in a few hands were also causes of controversy. Widespread rioting occurred in 1978, and the Shah fled abroad in 1979.

Palme, Olof 1927–86

Swedish prime minister. Palme entered parliament as a Social Democrat in 1958, and in 1963 he became minister without portfolio. In 1969, after two ministerial posts, he became party leader and prime minister. A pacifist, he spoke against US policy in Vietnam, and permitted the immigration of deserters, though he would not grant them refugee status. During 1976–82, while out of office, he chaired both the Nordic Council and the Independent Commission on Disarmament and Security (in Geneva), and was UN mediator in the Gulf War. He returned to power in 1982, and was assassinated in 1986.

Peron, Juan D. 1895–1974

Argentinian politician. In 1943, a group of profascist army officers staged a coup, among them Peron, who then became secretary for labor and social welfare, building up a following among the laboring classes. In 1944 he became minister for war and vice-president. Democracy was restored in 1945, but he was released from prison after two weeks when his supporters flooded into Buenos Aires, creating a potential riot situation. In 1946, after so-called free elections, he became president. He accelerated the pace of industrialization, increased public spending, nationalized utilities and increased welfare payments. This program was funded by wealth accumulated during the war, and by a state monopoly on the purchase of agricultural produce, which was subject to state price control. He also exiled political opponents,

▲ Richard Nixon

▲ Pol Pot

▲ Ronald Reagan

suppressed freedom of speech, allegedly interfered with the legislature and considerably curtailed civil liberties. Argentina became more influential in Latin America. An economic downturn, coupled with a public attack by Peron on the Catholic church, led to his deposition in 1955. He fled abroad, and finally settled in Spain. His supporters remained active, and won the 1973 elections, after which Peron returned and was himself elected president. He died in 1974.

Pétain, H. Philippe 1856–1951

Soldier and president of Vichy France. A general, Pétain led the French defense of Verdun in 1916. In 1917 he became French commander-in-chief, restoring morale after mutinies, and in 1918 he became marshal of France. He later entered politics, in 1934 became war minister, and in 1939–40 was ambassador to Spain. In 1940 he became head of state after the fall of France, and signed an armistice with the Germans. He relocated his government in Vichy, with any effective control only in the south, and pursued a secret policy of neutrality. He dismissed his openly pro-German foreign minister Laval in 1940, sent a secret emissary to London, tried to persuade Franco not to give the Germans access to North Africa, and maintained relations with the US. In 1942 Laval was forcibly reinstated as prime minister, and the Germans occupied southern France. After this, Pétain's powers became only nominal, but in 1942, while officially denouncing the Allied landing in North Africa, he issued secret orders for Vichy troops to join them. After the 1944 Allied landing in Normandy, he fled to Germany, but later returned voluntarily to France, where in 1941 he received a death sentence for collaboration; this was later commuted to life imprisonment.

Pilsudski, Jozef K. 1867–1935

Polish revolutionary and politician. In 1887, Pilsudski was falsely accused of plotting to assassinate the Russian czar, and was exiled to Siberia. On his return he joined the Polish Socialist party, of which he later became leader. Having failed to overthrow the government during the Russo-Japanese war (1904–05) and the Russian revolution which followed it, he formed the Polish Legion in Austria. Technically under Austro-Hungarian command, he led the legion against the Russians during 1914–16, but then disbanded it, sure that Germany and Austria-Hungary would not grant Polish independence. He was imprisoned 1917–18, and then became provisional head of state of an independent Poland, as well as commander-in-chief of the Polish army. He was promoted to Marshal of Poland in 1919, and defeated a Soviet invasion in 1920. He did not stand in the subsequent general election; he served as chief of staff until 1923. In 1926, during an economic crisis,

he staged a military coup. He then served as defense minister (1926–35) and prime minister (1926–28, 1930). From then on he effectively ran the country, and in 1930 had 18 opponents arrested. In 1934, he signed a nonaggression treaty with Hitler, after the French had refused to join forces against Germany, and extended his treaty with the Soviet Union. He later refused to meet Hitler, and rejected his proposals for an anti-Soviet alliance.

Poincaré, Raymond 1860–1934

French prime minister and president. In 1887, Poincaré was elected to the Chamber of Deputies as a Republican. He served in several ministerial posts, was elected to the senate in 1903, and in 1912, became prime minister, reaffirmed the alliance with Russia, and strengthened that with Britain. In 1913 he was elected president. He tried to unite France during the war years, appointing his adversary Clemenceau as prime minister in 1917. He left office in 1920, and returned to the Senate, where he chaired the reparations committee. He regained the premiership in 1922, and, claiming that Germany had defaulted on war reparations, in 1923 ordered the French occupation of the Ruhr. Fiscal problems resulted, and he lost the premiership in 1924, but regained it in 1926, and solved the economic crisis he then inherited. He retired in 1929.

Pol Pot (Saloth Sar) 1925–

Kampuchean political leader. A member of Ho Chi Minh's resistance movement, in 1946 Pol Pot joined the Communist party, which in Cambodia was an underground movement. After studying radio-electronics in Paris, he returned in 1953 to Phnom Penh and joined the leftwing group Pracheachon. He led the Khmer Rouge in the revolution of 1975, and the following year became prime minister. Under his rule between one and three million people died from neglect and brutality. In 1979, Vietnam invaded Kampuchea and Pol Pot was ousted. He fled to the mountains with the Khmer Rouge, to wage guerrilla warfare. The government refused to negotiate while Pol Pot was leader, and in 1985 he was officially removed from leadership of the Khmer Rouge.

Pompidou, Georges 1911–74

French president. As de Gaulle's aide, in 1958–59 Pompidou helped to draw up the constitution of the Fifth Republic, and to make plans for economic recovery. In 1961, he helped to negotiate a ceasefire in Algeria, and in 1962 became prime minister. In 1968, he helped end the student-worker revolt, and then resigned. De Gaulle resigned in 1969, and Pompidou was elected president. He strengthened the economy, maintained good relations with Arab nations, kept the French military independent of NATO, and reversed de Gaulle's veto on British membership of the EEC.

Primo de Rivera, Miguel 1870–1930

Spanish dictator. Primo served as military governor of Cadiz during 1915–19, and then became captain general of Valencia. In 1922, he was appointed military governor of Barcelona. He led a military coup in 1923, and then established a dictatorship, through his leadership of the Union Patriótica. He began a program of public works and improved labor relations, but failed to introduce land reforms and curtailed civil liberties in Catalonia. In 1926, he defeated three attempts to overthrow him. Abroad, in 1927 he ended the Moroccan war. By 1929 the economy had seriously deteriorated and Primo lost the support of the army. He resigned in 1930.

Qadhafi, Muammar 1942–

Libyan revolutionary and president. A captain in the Libyan army and leader of the Free Officers movement, Qadhafi led a military coup and proclaimed a republic. In 1970 he closed down British and US military bases, later deported ethnic Italians and Jews, and in 1973 nationalized foreign-owned sections of the oil industry. In 1977, as president, he installed a single-party system, blending his own interpretation of Islam with revolutionary socialism. Internationally, he first allied Libya with Egypt, and sought a pan-Arab federation between Libya, Egypt and Syria. He gave unqualified support to the Palestinians and opposed the Egyptian President Sadat's peace initiatives. He gave a lot of money to revolutionary organizations abroad. In 1986, following accusations of Qadhafi's involvement in several major European terrorist incidents, the US airforce bombed Libya. Qadhafi himself escaped unharmed, but his one adopted child was killed in the raid.

Reagan, Ronald 1911–

40th US president. After a long career as a screen actor, during which he aided McCarthy (q.v.), Reagan was Republican Governor of California from 1967 to 1975. He was elected president in 1980, standing on the ticket of traditional American values and military strength. Reagan greatly raised military spending at the expense of nonmilitary spending, and lowered taxes, doubling the national debt in five years. He initially reverted from détente to cold war, but, after some difficulty concerning his Strategic Defense Initiative policy, his most notable achievement was the signing in 1988 of the INF Treaty with the Soviet Union, the first ever agreement to dismantle nuclear weapons. The latter years of the Reagan administration were overshadowed by the Iran-Contra scandal in which it was alleged that members of the administration had sold arms to Iran hoping to obtain the release of hostages in the Lebanon, and that some of the profits had been diverted to the rightwing Contra forces in Nicaragua. Reagan retired in 1988.

▼ Franklin D Roosevelt (center)

▼ Theodore Roosevelt

Rhee, Syngman 1875–1965

South Korean president. In 1896, Rhee helped to form the Independence Club, and in 1898 he was imprisoned until 1904, when he went to the US, and in 1910 he returned to Korea, shortly after the Japanese occupation. He returned to the US in 1912 as an international campaigner for Korean independence. President of the government in exile from 1919 to 1939, he returned again to Korea after World War II, and, after the assassination of his principal opponents, was elected president in 1948. He outlawed the major opposition party, had its leader executed for treason, and ruled in a dictatorial fashion, although he also introduced educational and land reforms. In the early 1950s, he attempted unsuccessfully to prolong the Korean War with the Communist North, by releasing anti-Communist prisoners of war against the terms of the proposed truce. In 1960, electoral fraud by Rhee led to rioting, and the National Assembly called for his resignation. He complied, and spent the rest of his life in Hawaii.

Roosevelt, Franklin D. 1882–1945

32nd US president, who was elected for four successive terms. In 1910, Roosevelt entered the New York Senate as a Democrat, and in 1932, he was elected president. His "New Deal" effected a partial economic recovery from the Depression. He made an unsuccessful attempt to reform the Supreme Court, after it had declared some of this legislation unconstitutional. This, together with another bout of recession in the late 1930s, lost him much popularity. In the 1930s he tried to avert war while maintaining neutrality. In 1940 he concluded the Destroyer Deal, thus supporting Britain. In 1941 the Lend Lease Act was passed, enabling the US to sell war supplies to the Allies on credit, and Roosevelt defined the Four Freedoms he saw as essential to world peace – freedom of speech and of worship, and freedom from want and fear. Later in 1941 he and Churchill drew up the Atlantic Charter, which defined any postwar settlement, and Roosevelt asked Congress to revise the Neutrality Act. In late 1941 the Japanese attacked Pearl Harbor, and the US entered World War II. Roosevelt became one of the three major Allied leaders, and in 1943 met with Churchill and Stalin in Tehran. They met again in Yalta in 1945 to devise plans for the final defeat of the Axis forces and for postwar reconstruction, in particular the establishment of the United Nations Organization.

Roosevelt, Theodore 1858–1919

26th US president. Roosevelt, a moderate Republican, became leader of the New York legislature in 1884. In 1897 he became assistant secretary for the navy and when war was declared on Spain, he helped to form a volunteer regiment, the Rough Riders, which he went on to lead in Cuba. He returned home a national hero, and in 1898 became governor of New York. In 1900 he became vice-president, and in 1901, after the assassination of McKinley, took over as president. He described his domestic policies as providing a "square deal" for all groups in the nation. He pursued a policy of "trust-busting" under the Sherman Anti-Trust Act, intervened on behalf of public interest in a coal strike in 1902, introduced the Hepburn Act to regulate railways in 1906, and in the same year introduced the Pure Food and Drug Act. Internationally, he based his policies on the principle "speak softly and carry a big stick". He supported a revolution against the Colombians in Panama, and consequently gained a lease on the canal zone, and began construction. He undertook to ensure that Latin American countries met their international obligations. As a mediator he was instrumental in 1905 in bringing the Russo-Japanese war to a close, for which he was awarded the Nobel Peace Prize in 1906, and he intervened in the first Moroccan crisis between European Powers in 1906. He retired in 1908, but, regarding his successor Taft as too conservative, stood again, unsuccessfully, for the Republican nomination in 1912, and then founded the progressive Bull Moose party, but lost that year's election. He advocated neutrality in 1914, but then came to favor intervention.

Sadat, Muhammad Anwar el- 1918–81

Egyptian president. During World War II, Sadat cooperated with the Germans and was imprisoned twice. In 1950, he joined Nasser's Free Officers movement, and was involved in the military coup two years later. He was then general secretary of the National Union party (1957–61), and vice-president (1969–70). Although he soon resigned this post he became president by default on Nasser's death in 1970, and began a process of social and economic liberalization, expelling many Soviet advisors in 1972. In 1973, he ordered an unsuccessful attack on the Israeli-occupied Sinai Peninsula. After the ceasefire, Sadat restored relations with the United States, and worked to attract Western aid and investment. He later repudiated the 1971 friendship pact with the Soviet Union. He also began to adopt a more conciliatory attitude towards Israel, and in 1975 consented to a mutual policy of nonbelligerency, and the reopening of the Suez Canal. In 1977, he visited Israel and presented a peace plan in the Knesset (Israeli parliament). In 1978, he met with Begin at Camp David, and agreed in principle to a treaty in return for Egyptian control of the Sinai Peninsula. Later the same year, he and Begin were awarded the Nobel Peace Prize, and in 1979 they signed the peace treaty. At home, there were economic problems, and the treaty proved unpopular with some sections of Egyptian society. Sadat responded with repression, and was assassinated in 1981.

Salazar, Antonio de Oliveira 1889–1970

Portuguese dictator. In 1921, Salazar helped to found the Catholic party, and served briefly as a member of parliament. After a military coup in 1926, he was appointed finance minister, but resigned five days later. He was restored to the post in 1928, and proceeded to balance the national budget. Appointed premier in 1932, in 1933 he introduced a new constitution, concentrating power in himself. He later created a single-party state. He supported Franco in the Spanish Civil War, and was neutral during World War II. He obtained Portuguese membership of NATO in 1949, and of the UN in 1954. He showed great determination to maintain the Portuguese empire, but was unable to prevent the return of Goa to India in 1961. Later in the 1960s, his domestic program suffered from his substantial diversion of resources to suppress independence movements in the African colonies. He retired in 1968 after suffering a stroke.

Schmidt, Helmut 1918–

West German chancellor. Awarded the Iron Cross during World War II, in 1946 Schmidt joined the Social Democratic party. Between 1949 and 1969 he served twice alternately in the Hamburg municipal government and the Bundestag. He served as defense minister from 1969 to 1972, and as finance minister from 1972 to 1974, consolidating what was known as the "economic miracle". He became chancellor in 1974, and worked to defuse international tension with the Communist states. He also enjoyed good relations with the United States, and supported the EEC. Economic problems at home resulted in the collapse of the coalition with the Free Democrats, and after a vote in the Bundestag, Schmidt resigned the chancellorship in 1982.

Sihanouk, Norodom 1922–

Cambodian monarch and prime minister. Sihanouk ascended to the throne in 1941, under French control. In 1944, the Japanese, who had recently invaded Cambodia, endorsed his declaration of independence, but French rule resumed in 1945. In 1952 Sihanouk began a campaign for independence, which was effectively granted by the Geneva agreements in the following year. In 1955, he founded the People's Socialist Community party and abdicated in favor of his father. His party then won the elections, and Sihanouk became prime minister. He also served as representative to the UN, and became head of state in 1960, after the death of his father. Although Cambodia remained neutral in the Sino-Soviet conflict, relations with China improved, and in 1965 relations with the US were terminated. Sihanouk's government followed a policy of nonintervention in the Vietnamese war, but the Vietcong established bases in Cambodia.

Consequently, the United States backed Lon Nol's coup in 1970, and Sihanouk fled abroad. He supported the Khmer Rouge, and returned after their victory in 1975. He was arrested, and released in 1979 in an attempt to gain UN support after the Vietnamese invasion, which he condemned, at the same time refusing to give support to the Khmer Rouge. In 1982 he became president of a government in exile.

Smith, Ian D. 1919–

Rhodesian prime minister. In 1948, Smith was elected to the South Rhodesian Assembly as a member of the rightwing Liberal party. In 1953 he joined the governing Federal Party. Representation for blacks was proposed, and in 1961 Smith broke away to found the ultra-rightwing Rhodesian Front, who won a majority in the 1962 elections; in 1964 Smith became premier of Southern Rhodesia. He opposed majority (black) rule, and called for immediate independence from Britain. Negotiations failed, and in 1965 Smith made a unilateral declaration of independence. A further round of talks broke down, and the United Nations applied economic sanctions. Smith extended discriminatory legislation and in 1970 declared an "apartheid-style" republic. Protest and guerrilla war escalated, forcing Smith to attempt to incorporate blacks into government, without however, conceding to effective majority rule. He resigned as prime minister in 1979 and attended the Lancaster Constitutional Conference, which conceded the principle of majority rule.

Smuts, Jan (Christian) 1870–1950

South African prime minister. Smuts was given charge of a commando group in the Boer war, and in 1902 invaded the Cape Colony. He later advocated peace. The Boers lost their two independent republics, and Smuts, together with General Botha, demanded Boer rights. In 1906, the British granted white self-government to the Transvaal, and Smuts was elected to the House of Assembly in 1907. In 1910, four British colonies were merged into the Union of South Africa with Botha as its premier and Smuts as his right-hand man. During World War I, they conquered German-controlled Southwest Africa. Smuts also commanded Allied troops in East Africa, and in 1917 he became Lloyd George's minister for air. He opposed the harshness of the Versailles Treaty, and helped pave the way for the establishment of the League of Nations. Smuts then served as prime minister from 1919-24, and as deputy prime minister in a coalition from 1933–39, when he regained the premiership and declared war on Germany. The South African army helped to overthrow the Axis forces in North Africa, and in 1945 Smuts attended the San Francisco conference at which the United Nations Organization was founded. He lost in 1948 to the National party.

Stalin (Djugashvili), Joseph V. 1879–1953

Leader of the Soviet Union. In 1898 Stalin gave up studying for the priesthood, and soon after joined the Russian Social Democratic Labor party. In 1903 he sided with the Bolshevik wing of the party and was appointed to their central committee. He also became one of the first editors of *Pravda*. In 1913 he was exiled, but returned in 1917. After the Bolsheviks seized power in the October Revolution, Stalin was appointed to the Soviet of People's Commissars. He was Commissar for Nationalities (1917–23), Commissar for State Control (1919–23), and a political commissar during the civil war of 1918–20. In 1922 he became general secretary of the party's central committee, and after Lenin's death (1924) engaged in a power struggle, from which he emerged the victor in 1928. Under a series of Five-Year Plans, Stalin massively accelerated the industrialization of the Soviet Union, and collectivized agricultural production with brutal force, at the cost of many thousands of lives. In the 1930s he conducted a reign of terror, purging potential rivals. In 1939 Stalin and Hitler signed a nonaggression pact, whereby the Soviet Union occupied eastern Poland and the Baltic states. However, after Germany had attacked the Soviet Union without warning in 1941, Stalin appointed himself commander-in-chief and premier, and became one of the three major leaders of the Allies. When, by 1943, the Soviets, after suffering enormous losses, finally began to drive the Germans back, Stalin secured agreement for the opening of a second front in the west at a meeting with Roosevelt and Churchill in Tehran. He met with them again for postwar planning in 1945 at Yalta. During the late 1940s he increased his influence in eastern Europe, making most of the countries Soviet satellites, and conducted a cold war against the Western bloc countries headed by the United States. At home, he increased political repression and tightened the hold of the Communist party.

Stresemann, Gustav 1878–1929

German politician. In 1907, Stresemann was elected to the Reichstag as a member of the National Liberal party, and became its leader 10 years later. During World War I he advocated expansionism and unlimited submarine warfare, and was also involved in the overthrow of the moderate chancellor Bethmann-Hollweg. In 1918, Stresemann founded the German People's party, which although monarchistic was prepared to work within the existing framework. In 1923, Stresemann was appointed chancellor, but resigned later that year, and then became foreign secretary. In 1924, he negotiated the Dawes' Plan to reduce reparations, and led the evacuation of the Ruhr. In 1925, he negotiated the Locarno Pact with the Allies. In 1926, he made a treaty with Russia, gained for Germany membership of the League of

Nations, and together with Briand was awarded the Nobel Peace Prize. In 1928, Stresemann signed the antiwar Kellogg-Briand Pact, and in 1929 he negotiated the Young Plan and received assurances of the total evacuation of the Rhineland.

Sukarno, Achmed 1901–70

Indonesian president. In 1927, Sukarno helped to found the Indonesian Nationalist party. He was imprisoned during 1929–31, and in 1932 he became leader of the Indonesia party. He was interned in the following year, but was released in 1942 by the Japanese, with whom he then cooperated until 1945, when he declared an independent republic, and then defeated attempts by the Dutch to regain control of the country. As president, Sukarno introduced social reforms and encouraged Indonesian culture, but there was also government corruption and very high inflation. Frequent attempts were made on his life, and in 1958 rioting broke out in the provinces. In 1959, he imposed the system of Guided Democracy, actually a dictatorship. In his foreign policy, he withdrew from the UN in 1965, and by the end of his presidency was on bad terms with both the United States and the Soviet Union. In 1965, the Communists attempted to seize power, but were decisively defeated by the army, under the command of General Suharto. Suharto then became effective ruler of the country, and officially succeeded Sukarno as president in 1968.

Sun Yat-sen 1866–1925

Revolutionary and "Father of Modern China". In 1894, Sun helped to found the Revive China Society and worked for the overthrow of the Manchu dynasty. In the following year he fled abroad, where he organized uprisings and promoted the revolutionary cause. In 1905 he became head of the Tokyo-based Alliance Society, a pro-republican coalition, based on 3 principles: People's Rule, People's Authority, and People's Livelihood (often interpreted as nationalism, democracy, and socialism), and in 1911, after 10 unsuccessful uprisings, the Manchus were overthrown. Sun returned to China to become president of the new republic, but soon resigned in favor of the powerful Yuan Shikai. Sun then denounced Yuan's dictatorial ambitions, tried unsuccessfully to overthrow him in 1913, and fled abroad to reorganize the Guomindang (Nationalist Party, founded 1912). After Yuan's death in 1916 China deteriorated into warlordism and the Peking government fell into dictatorial hands. In 1920 he became president of a regime in Guanzhou and later cooperated with the Soviet Union and the Chinese Communist party to work for national unification. He reorganized the Guomindang on Soviet lines, though it remained dedicated to Sun's three principles. Sun died in Beijing after a long winter trek to attend a National Assembly.

Josip Broz Tito

Leon Trotsky

John Vorster

Thatcher, Margaret Hilda 1925–

British prime minister. Mrs Thatcher became Conservative party leader in 1975 after 16 years in parliament, and in 1979 she became prime minister. She brought down the inflation rate by drastically cutting public expenditure and limiting the printing of money, but unemployment nearly tripled during her first two terms, and in the early 1980s Britain lost 20 percent of its manufacturing industry. Mrs Thatcher restricted trade unions, privatized state-owned industries, and allowed the purchase of council homes. The income of the average family increased by 30 percent during 1979–89, but unemployment remained high, homelessness increased by approximately 60 percent between 1981 and 1987, and the social security reforms of 1988 reduced payments to many poor people. Her handling of the National Health Service was also unpopular. In her foreign policy, she oversaw the transition to majority rule in Zimbabwe in 1980, and in 1982 she used military action to end the Argentinian occupation of the Falkland Islands. In 1985 she signed the Anglo-Irish agreement. She developed a warm relationship with US president Reagan, and allowed the use of British bases for the US bombing of Libya in 1986. She was also cultivated by President Gorbachev. In Europe, she supported the European Community's principle of free trade, but was wary of the accompanying political implications.

Tito (Josip Broz) 1892–1980

Yugoslavian president. Captured by the Russians in World War I, Tito lived in Russia from 1915 to 1920, became a Communist, and fought in the Russian Civil War. On his return home he was imprisoned for conspiracy from 1928 to 1934. He then fought in the Spanish Civil War. In 1934 he joined the central committee of the Yugoslavian Communist party, and in 1936 visited Moscow as a member of the Balkan secretariat. In 1937, he became party general secretary and greatly increased membership. In 1941 Tito formed and led the resistance to the invading Axis forces. Made a marshal in 1943, in 1945 he became president. In 1948, Yugoslavia was expelled from the Cominform, because of Tito's objection to Stalin's interference in the country's affairs. Attempts at rapprochement with Khrushchev ultimately failed, and Tito became unpopular with the Chinese. He emerged as a major neutralist leader, and visited nonaligned states. In the decade preceding his death, he established a collective leadership to succeed him.

Trotsky, Leon 1879–1940

Russian revolutionary and Marxist thinker. Trotsky joined the Russian Social Democratic Labor party in 1896, and was banished to Siberia in 1900. He escaped abroad in 1902, and in 1903 sided with the Mensheviks against Lenin, whom he criticized as a potential dictator. Trotsky returned to Russia, and was prominent in the 1905 revolution. Banished again, he escaped to Europe, and tried to reunite the two wings of the party. He campaigned against World War I, and so was deported from France. He returned to Russia after the February Revolution, joined the Bolsheviks and was appointed to their central committee. During the October Revolution, as chairman of the Petrograd soviet, he organized the seizure of power in St Petersburg. From 1917 to 1918 he was commissar for foreign affairs, negotiated with Germany at Brest-Litovsk, but resigned over the conclusion of the treaty. From 1918 to 1925 he was war commissar, founded the Red Army, and led them in the civil war of 1918–20, afterwards using them as labor in economic reconstruction. He was also a Politburo member from 1919 to 1927. After Lenin's death in 1924, Trotsky seemed his most likely successor. He argued a theory of "permanent revolution" as opposed to Stalin's "socialism in one country", forming the left "combined opposition" with Zinoviev and Kamenev. They were defeated by Stalin and his new comrades on the right, and in 1929 Trotsky was banished abroad. He continued to propagandize against Stalin, who successfully represented him to the Soviet people as a monster. Trotsky attempted unsuccessfully to create a Fourth International to fight fascism and replace the Comintern. He was assassinated in 1940, probably by a Stalinist agent.

Truman, Harry S. 1884–1972

33rd US president. Elected as a Democrat to the US Senate in 1934, Truman rose to prominence as chairman of the Committee Investigating National Defense. He became vice-president in 1944, and president in 1945. He prepared at once for the San Francisco conference at which the UN was founded, helped to arrange the German surrender, met with Stalin and Churchill at Potsdam, and gave the order to drop atomic bombs on Hiroshima and Nagasaki. After the war, he developed the policy of containment of Soviet influence, and the Truman Doctrine of aid to countries vulnerable to Communism (Greece and Turkey, 1947). In 1948 he approved the four-year Marshall Plan for the economic reconstruction of Western Europe, and organized an airlift to defeat the cold-war Soviet blockade of Berlin. In 1949 he made America a founder member of NATO, and introduced the Point Four Program of aid to Third World countries. In 1950 the US developed the hydrogen bomb, and sent troops under General MacArthur to Korea. MacArthur expressed a desire to attack China, and Truman dismissed him in 1951. Domestically, Truman created the CIA in 1947, and in 1949 attempted unsuccessfully to institute a radical program of legislation, known as the Fair Deal. He left office in 1953.

Tshombe(-Kapenda), Moise 1919–69

Congolese politician. In 1959 Tshombe became president of the Katangan Conakat party, who supported a federalist system, which was not adopted. In the 1960 elections, Conakat won a majority in the Katanga provincial assembly, and Tshombe declared independence from the rest of the Congo. Lumumba was ousted as premier by the military, and Tshombe was allegedly involved in his subsequent murder. After unsuccessful negotiations with President Kasavubu, the Katangan secessionists were finally defeated in 1963 by UN forces, and Tshombe fled abroad. He was rehabilitated in 1964, and appointed premier to subdue leftwing insurrectionists. He achieved this with the use of white mercenaries, but was sacked in 1965 amid rumors of a plot to overthrow Kasavubu. He went abroad again, and after rumors of his imminent return, he was kidnapped in 1967 and taken to Algeria, where he remained for the rest of his life under house arrest.

Ulbricht, Walter 1893–1973

East German head of state. A member of the Social Democratic party, in 1919 Ulbricht helped found the German Communist party. He joined its central committee in 1923, and was elected to the Reichstag in 1928. After Hitler's rise to power in 1933, Ulbricht fled abroad and worked as a Comintern agent. He settled in Russia, and during World War II was involved in propaganda work with German prisoners of war. He returned to Germany in 1945, and helped to form an administration in the Soviet zone. He was also involved in the forced merger with the Social Democrats. In 1949 he became deputy premier of East Germany, and in 1950 general secretary of the ruling Socialist Unity Party (SED). A harsh ruler, in 1953 he resisted, with Soviet help, attempts to overthrow him. In 1960 he was elected chairman of the council of state, a newly created post which replaced the presidency. He successfully resisted pressure for reform after Stalin's death, but permitted some liberalization after the construction of the Berlin Wall at his behest in 1961. The East German economy became highly developed. In his foreign policy he regarded West Germany with deep suspicion, and opposed détente. In 1968 he was one of the chief advocates of military intervention in Czechoslovakia. He retired as general secretary in 1971, but held his post as chairman of the council of state until his death.

Vorster, John (B. Johannes) 1915–83

South African prime minister. During World War II, Vorster was a member of the neo-Nazi Ossewa Brandwag (Oxwagon Guard), and was imprisoned in 1942. In 1953 he was elected to parliament as a member of the Nationalist party, and promoted in 1960 to minister for justice, police and prisons. He took a hard line in the drafting of the apartheid

▲ Chaim Weizmann

▲ Wilhelm II

▲ Zhou En Lai

system, created a new security police force, and introduced the power of detention for 90 days without trial in cases of suspected subversion. Having gained the premiership in 1966, he introduced minor reforms to apartheid and severely restricted antiapartheid movements. Abroad, he pursued dialogue with black African leaders, but in 1975 sent troops to ppose the Angolan liberation movement. He was later instrumental in persuading Ian Smith to share power in Rhodesia, but totally rejected a similar policy for South Africa. He resigned the premiership in 1978, and assumed the principally ceremonial position of president. He resigned in 1979, after it became known that he had tried to cover up the Muldergate scandal, in which large amounts of government money had been misappropriated.

Walesa, Lech 1943–

Polish trade unionist and politician. An electrician in the Lenin shipyard in Gdansk, in 1980 Walesa led an unofficial strike after a sharp rise in food prices. Industrial action escalated, and Walesa became head of an inter-factory strike committee, which succeeded in having many of its demands met, and was then renamed Solidarity. In 1981, however, martial law was imposed, Solidarity outlawed, and Walesa interned for a year. In 1983, martial law was lifted, and he was awarded the Nobel Peace Prize. In 1989 Solidarity was again legalized and its representatives, including Walesa, were allowed to contest some parliamentary seats and won a majority; Poland thus became the first Eastern bloc country since World War II to have a nonCommunist leader, Solidarity member Tadeusz Mazowiecki.

Weizmann, Chaim Azriel 1874–1952

Russian-born Zionist leader. Weizmann, a prominent Young Zionist, strongly opposed the British offer for a homeland in Uganda at the 1903 Zionist Congress. In 1904 he was elected to the General Council, and from 1914 was involved in negotiations which led to the 1917 Balfour Declaration. In 1917 he became president of the English Zionist Federation, and in 1920 was elected president of the World Zionist Organization. As principal advocate of cooperation with Britain, Weizmann was criticized when the British began to distance themselves from the Zionist cause in the 1920s. In 1930 he resigned the presidency of the now expanded Zionist Organization and Jewish Agency. He worked to help German Jews, and was reelected in 1935. In 1937 he supported a British proposal for the partition of Palestine. After the war, he condemned Zionist guerrilla activities, and in 1946 he again lost his presidency. In 1948 he was sent to Washington for talks with President Truman, secured American recognition of the state of Israel, and negotiated a substantial loan. Soon

after he became president of the provisional state council, and in 1949 president of Israel. Ill health prevented extensive involvement in public affairs, and he died three years later.

Wilhelm II 1859–1941

German emperor. Wilhelm succeeded to the throne in 1888, and in 1890 forced Bismarck to resign as chancellor. In the same year, Germany refused to renew the Reinsurance Treaty with Russia, which then strengthened its ties with France. In 1896, Wilhelm damaged relations with Britain by congratulating the South African President Kruger on the defeat of the British-inspired Jameson raid; and also by building up the German navy. In 1905, he attempted unsuccessfully to subvert the Franco-British Entente (1904) by siding with Britain against French domination of Morocco. The Triple Entente of France, Britain and Russia was formed in 1907, and in 1908 Wilhelm again caused alarm in Britain by telling a newspaper reporter that many Germans were antiEnglish. In 1911 he tried to intervene in Morocco once more, as a consequence of which Britain agreed to send troops to the French front in the event of war with Germany. Wilhelm delegated all major decision-making during World War I. A few days before the armistice was signed, he was forced by internal unrest to abdicate, and fled to the Netherlands.

Wilson, (James) Harold 1916–

British prime minister. During World War II Wilson worked at the ministry of fuel and power, where he produced the basic plan for the nationalization of the coal industry. He became a Labour member of parliament in 1945 and in 1947 became president of the Board of Trade, introducing a degree of deregulation and negotiating a trade agreement with the Soviet Union. He resigned in 1951, in protest over the introduction of medical prescription charges. He was elected party leader in 1963, and promoted Labour as the party of technology and efficiency. In 1964, he became prime minister, and failed to prevent Southern Rhodesia's unilateral declaration of independence in 1965; and subsequent negotiations and economic sanctions proved ineffective. Wilson was returned with a greatly increased majority in 1966, but soon met with economic problems; and in 1967 the pound was devalued. In 1968, he visited both the United States and the Soviet Union, in a vain attempt to help solve the crisis in Vietnam. In 1969, he abandoned plans to introduce trade union reform. The economy began to recover and Wilson's popularity revived, but Labour lost the elections of 1970. Wilson regained the premiership in 1974, during a period of rising inflation and a miners' strike. Inflation rose sharply, and in 1976 Wilson resigned as prime minister and party leader.

Wilson, (Thomas) Woodrow 1856–1924

28th US president. Wilson rose to prominence as the reforming Democratic governor of New Jersey, and in 1913 became president. He immediately embarked upon a program of radical domestic legislation, to achieve what he had described as the New Freedom. He passed the Underwood Tariff Act, and, to regulate the currency, the Federal Reserve Act. In 1914 the Federal Trade Commission was established to promote competition, and later the same year came the Clayton Anti-Trust Act. Abroad, Wilson abolished US exemption from Panama Canal tolls. The Mexican situation presented him with a longstanding problem, and he failed to end the civil war there. Adopting a neutral stance in World War I, he offered to mediate. In 1916 he issued an ultimatum to Germany over the dangers their submarines posed to American shipping, and a short time later Germany promised the abandonment of submarine warfare. However in 1917 they reneged on this, and a proposal for an antiAmerican alliance of Germany, Mexico and Japan was revealed. Wilson declared war later in the same year. This year also saw the passing of the 18th amendment, the beginning of the "Prohibition" legislation fully enforced in 1920. In 1918 Wilson listed his Fourteen Points necessary to a lasting peace. In 1919 he attended the Paris Peace Conference, which undertook notably the establishment of the League of Nations on his recommendation. He was a signatory to the Treaty of Versailles, and was awarded the 1919 Nobel Peace Prize. He left office in 1921.

Zhou En Lai 1898–1976

Chinese politician. Zhou was active in the Chinese Communist party in Paris from 1921, and fought with Jiang Jieshi in China against the warlords, but was sentenced to death in 1927 during Jiang's purge of the Communists. Now a Politburo member, he continued to spread revolutionary propaganda until 1931, when he became political leader of the Chinese Red Army. After the Communists' Long March, he became their chief negotiator, and in 1936 saved Jiang from execution by his own generals by securing his promise to make war against the Japanese his first priority. In the ensuing Communist–Nationalist coalition Zhou was Jiang's military advisor.. In 1949, on the foundation of the People's Republic of China, Zhou became prime minister and foreign minister. In 1950 he secured the Sino–Soviet alliance, and at the 1954 Geneva conference negotiated concessions for Korean and Indochinese Communists. He attended the Bandung Conference of neutral countries in 1955, and in 1971 engineered President Nixon's visit to China. Zhou was a stabilizing influence during the Cultural Revolution, and helped to suppress the Red Guards.

247

GLOSSARY

Allies
The states allied against the Central Powers in World War I or the Axis Powers in World War II.

Anarchism
A political theory founded on the principle of the freedom and innate goodwill of the individual, and denying the validity of any form of government.

Anarcho-syndicalism
A movement deriving from the ideas of Sorel in the late 19th century, advocating cooperation through trade unions in order to overthrow the state.

Antisemitism
Prejudice against Jews arbitrarily rationalized and frequently used to justify persecution and discrimination.

Apartheid
(Lit "apartness".) A system, established in 1948 in South Africa, of legalized discrimination against the black majority resulting in oppression and severe deprivation.

Appeasement
The procedure of making concessions to another power in response to a direct or implicit threat.

Armistice
The suspension of hostilities between two or more states preceding the negotiation of a peace settlement.

Authoritarianism
Advocacy of a system of government by a source of authority wielding absolute or inflexible power.

Axis
The coalition headed by Germany, Italy and Japan, that fought the Allies in World War II; the name came from the announcement in 1936 of a Rome-Berlin "axis".

Bolshevism
The advocacy of violent revolution derived from the policies of the majority (Bolshevik) wing, led by V.I. Lenin, of the Russian Social Democratic Labor party.

Bourgeois
A term used by Marxists to denote those who supported and profited from the development of capitalism, now loosely used to refer to anyone seen as having an investment in its perpetuation.

Capitalism
A politico-economic system based on the accumulation and retention of capital by private individuals, with others working for them for fixed wages.

Centrism
The pragmatic advocacy of a policy which is a compromise between the left- and the rightwing.

Civil rights
The rights accorded by law to a citizen to be treated fairly and equitably by the state regardless of race, color or creed.

Client
A state which is depended on another economically or for defense to the point where it is also politically submissive.

Coalition
The cooperation of two or more parties in government, usually because no party has an electoral majority, or in a national emergency.

Cold War
The state of hostility between the Western and Soviet blocs, characterized by political and economic, but not military, acts of aggression.

Collectivization
The action of bringing property into collective ownership, especially as in the Soviet agricultural system under Stalin in the 1920s and 1930s.

Colonialism
The practice, common among European countries in the late 19th century, of settling in and imposing a system, economic, political and, to some extent, social, on other less politically unified nations in order to exploit their resources or people.

Commonwealth
The free association of sovereign states which were once part of the British Empire, connected by similar systems and ideals but not bound by any common rules.

Communism
The political philosophy expounded by Karl Marx and now practiced primarily in Eastern bloc countries, characterized in theory by the abolition of private property and the development of harmonious anarchy. In practice it involves the nationalization of major property, a planned economy and a comprehensive welfare system.

Conservatism
Politically, the tendency to value and maintain tradition and to promote organic and gradual rather than revolutionary change.

Consumerism
A political view that emphasizes the priority of acquisition and consumption.

Cooperativism
The advocacy of ownership by cooperatives of commercial enterprises, so that workers, as coowners benefit from their profitability.

Corporatism
A form of social organization in which independent corporations function as intermediaries between their members and the state.

Coup d'état
The overthrow of a government by force, usually by or with the support of the military.

Decentralization
The process of transferring political and executive power from a central authority to local organizations.

Decolonization
The withdrawal of colonial rule, and the transfer of government to the natives of the ex-colony.

Democracy
In the Western bloc, rule by all of the people, now usually translated into one of various electoral systems. In the Eastern bloc, it is interpreted as rule for the good of all, not necessarily by common consent or choice.

Depression
An extended period of cessation or stagnation of economic activity, with high unemployment. The Great Depression was the worldwide occurrence of this in 1929-35.

Despotism
Tyrannical and capricious government, with no legal limitation or effective opposition.

Détente
(Lit: releasing.) An easing of tensions between two major powers or power blocs.

Determinism
The doctrine that there are forces beyond those manifest in historical events which shape them, regardless of conscious human choice.

Development
The process of economic growth in a nation, usually measured in terms of per capita income, but taken as involving industrialization, urbanization and the increase in investment.

Dictator
A ruler with absolute power.

Dominion
An autonomous member nation of the British Commonwealth that regards the British monarch as the head of state.

Duma
The Russian state assembly from 1906 to 1917, established by Czar Nicholas II as a legislative body.

Ecology
As a political ideology, one based on the need to construct a political system that can sustain the biosphere. Ecologists believe that economic growth per se is undesirable and, in the long term, impossible.

Elite
(Lit: chosen.) A small and self-perpetuating group of people holding power and special privileges in a society.

Empire
The territory or rule of an emperor; the authority of a dominant nation or culture over others, usually achieved by conquest or maintained by a degree of coercion.

Entente
(Lit: understanding.) An agreement between states which is publically affirmed but not formalized; notably the Anglo-French entente of 1904, and the Anglo-Russian entente of 1907.

Ethnic
Belonging to a racial group or traditional culture.

Fascism
A political ideology usually embracing extreme nationalism and rejection of liberalism, seeking national regeneration through a mass movement via a single-party state with strong leadership.

Feminism
A movement seeking for women's equal rights and status with men.

First World
Generic term usually taken to mean the industrial, developed countries of the "West" (Western Europe, North America, Japan etc). The Second World is usually taken to mean the industrialized planned economies of the Eastern bloc. The term First World is sometimes used to apply, before 1945, to the industrial countries of Europe, in distinction to the New World of North America, Australasia, etc.

Free market
An economy in which prices are determined only by supply and demand, with little or no government intervention.

Genocide
The crime of attempting to destroy a national, cultural or ethnic group by killing or persecuting its members or destroying conditions of life.

Glasnost
(Lit: having a voice.) The innovative policy of political openness, internally and internationally, introduced in the Soviet Union in the 1980s.

Gradualism
The view that political and social change must take place slowly and steadily, rather than through violent revolution.

Hegemony
The influence of one state over others.

Humanism
The view that the needs of human beings should form the basis of ethical and moral values, and thus of political organization.

Imperialism
The policy of extending an empire, usually through military means, but sometimes through cultural hegemony or economic domination.

Independence
The ability of a state to govern itself by law without any other state encroaching on its internal affairs.

Individualism
The view that the needs and rights of the individual have priority over those of any group.

Intelligence
Information gathered, usually by espionage, by one state about another, viewed as an actual or potential enemy.

International
Any of a series of international leftwing federations of workers. The first, founded in 1864, was led by Marx. The second, founded in 1889, expelled anarchists. The third issued in 1919 from the splitting of the second, and was also called the Communist International, or Comintern. The fourth was founded in 1938, with the involvement of Trotsky.

Interventionism
The policy of government intervention in an economy in pursuit of economic or social ends; this might embrace price controls, subsidies, nationalization, etc.

Isolationism
The declared practice of a state of refraining from intervention in the affairs of any other, unless and except insofar as it judges itself to be threatened in some way.

Leftwing
With a political bias toward government for the good of all, with common ownership of vital resources; of a socialist or radical tendency.

Liberalism
A political doctrine supporting the freedom of the individual above all, along with a humanist tendency; it is marked by tolerance, and a wish to make society fairer, without losing the right of self-determination.

Market economy
An economy governed by the movement of supply and demand.

Marshall Plan
The post-World War II economic recovery plan for Europe, instituted in 1947 by the US secretary of state George Marshall. Large sums in dollars were offered, on condition that Europe would cooperate economically.

Marxism-Leninism
The form of Communism practiced in the Eastern bloc. Marxism is characterized by a belief in the fundamental power of economic forces, that private property is manifest of an exploitative society, and the people, not an elite, must establish a truly free society. Lenin identified "the people" as the Communist party; he also advocated the concentration of power in the hands of a few held to be operating in the interests of the people.

Materialism
The doctrine that as only matter exists, material values are paramount, and material causes underlie all processes – mostly promulgated in Marxism, along with the repudiation of religion.

Nation
A body of people with a sense of common identity in terms of history, culture, and geography, to varying extents. The term is often used in place of "nation-state"; that is, a nation united geographically under one system of government.

Nationalism
The belief that the needs, rights and privileges of one's nation take priority over individual or wider interests.

Pacifism
The belief that war is unjustifiable, and that disagreement should be resolved by negotiation.

Partition
The establishment of two separate autonomous states in what was one territory; this can be effected by another power, or arise from internal unrest.

Perestroika
(Lit.: "restructuring".) Mikhail Gorbachev's policy of reorganising Soviet society along less repressive lines.

Planned economy
An economy which is controlled by the actions of a central administration, not by the mechanism of price.

Plebiscite
A device which allows the whole population to give its opinion on an issue; a referendum.

Power
A state viewed as a military and economic force of substance in world affairs.

Racism
The belief that people of specified other races are inferior or worthless, usually used to justify personally, soically, or politically hostile and destructive means.

Radicalism
The advocacy of profound and wide-ranging social and political change. Also used loosely to indicate a leftwing political tendency.

Referendum
The referral of a point at issue to the people, to be decided by their vote.

Reformism
The doctrine that reform is preferable to revolution as a mode of social and political change.

Refugee
A person who has fled his or her home territory as a result of social, political or military acitivity, such as war, attrition or tyranny, and who no longer has the protection of a government.

Revolutionary socialism
A form of socialism advocating revolution as the necessary means of achieving an equitable society.

Rightwing
Politically and socially conservative, tending toward the authoritarian, valuing the individual before the collective, and espousing free enterprise.

Satyagraha
(lit.: "truth force".) MK Gandhi's name for the practice of openness and nonviolence in pursuing social justice and harmony.

Secession
The quitting of one state of a political federation, in an attempt to become independent.

Socialism
A political doctrine based on the equality of individuals, with the state as the administrator and protector of equal rights, and the removal of systems through which individuals can dominate others. In Marxist theory, it signifies a stage of transition between capitalism and Communism.

Soviet
Any of the adminstrative councils that form the basic unit of government in the Soviet Union, existing at all levels, from village to national (the Supreme Soviet).

State
The political system of a country, effectively defining its international identity. The state is the administrative and internal political system of a country, as viewed from within.

Status quo ante bellum
The state of affairs existing in a nation prior to a specific war.

Suffrage
The right to vote in local and national elections.

Superpower
Term used since 1945 to describe the United States of America or the Soviet Union, in that their economic resources and military capability are by far in excess of those of their nearest rivals. Other nations, principally China, may yet achieve this status.

Technocracy
As a concept, government by those who have greatest access to and greatest expertise in the products of modern information and communications technology.

Terrorism
The policy of carrying out random attacks, often on civilian targets, in order to force governments to initiate political or social change.

Third World
The group of countries also known as "developing", mostly politically or economically damaged as a result of colonialism, and the investment of the First World in acquiring their produce at low prices, and whose populations on the whole are engaged in a struggle for physical survival. These include the countries of Africa south of the Sahara, with the exception of white South Africa, most East Asian countries, and those of South America.

Totalitarianism
A society governed in every detail of life by the political ruler. For example, Nicolae Ceauşescu decreed in the late 1980s that every Romanian woman must bear six children.

Treaty
A formal negotiated agreement between two states, for example, to affirm the ending of a war. Treaties must usually be ratified (endorsed) by a majority of members of the government of the signatory states.

Truce
A cessation of hostilities, usually temporary, between parties involved in a war.

Truman Doctrine
US President Truman's doctrine, asserted in 1947, that the United States would act in support of peoples whose freedom was threatened.

Universalism
A belief in one's political ideology as universally applicable, found on a view of human nature as universally the same.

Utopianism
The belief in the existence of a model of an ideal society, whose construction in reality is the proper goal of politics.

Voluntarism
The view that the human will is the predominant factor in the shaping of history.

Welfare State
A state which provides the basic needs of all its citizens, protecting the disadvantaged against total destitution.

Zionism
The Jewish movement enshrining the aspiration for a homeland (often identified as Israel) where they will be safe from persecution.

FURTHER READING

General

Aldcroft, DH *The European Economy, 1914–1970* (London, 1978)

Berghahn, VR *Modern Germany, Society, Economy and Politics in the Twentieth Century* (Cambridge, 1982)

Brogan, Hugh *Longman History of the United States of America* (London, 1985)

Carr, AR *Spain 1808–1939* (Oxford, 1966)

Craig, Gordon, A *Germany, 1866–1945* (Oxford, 1978)

Joll, James *Europe Since 1870, An International History* (London, 1973)

Kennedy, Paul *The Rise and Fall of the Great Powers* (New York, 1988)

McNeill, William *The Pursuit of Power* (Oxford, 1982)

Storry, Richard *A History of Modern Japan* (London Penguin, 1976)

The Origins and Course of the First World War

Fischer, Fritz *Germany's Aims in the First World War* (London, 1967)

Hart Liddell, BH *History of the First World War* (Revised edn, London, 1970)

Joll, James *The Origins of the First World War* (London and New York, 1984)

Keiger, John FV *France and the Origins of the First World War* (London, 1983)

Kennedy, Paul M *The War Plans of the Great Powers, 1880–1914* (London, 1979)

Kennedy, Paul M *The Rise of the Anglo-Saxon Antagonism 1860–1914* (London, 1980)

Macartney, CA *The Habsburg Empire, 1790–1918* (London, 1968)

Pulzer, PGJ *The Rise of Political Anti-Semitism in Germany and Austria* (New York, 1964)

Seton-Watson, Hugh *The Russian Empire, 1801–1917* (Oxford, 1967)

Steiner, Zara K *Britain and the Origins of the First World War* (London, 1983)

Taylor, AJP *The Struggle for Mastery in Europe, 1848–1918* (Oxford, 1954)

Winter, JM *The Experience of World War I* (London and New York, 1988)

Zeman, ZAB *A Diplomatic History of the First World War* (London, 1971)

The Inter-War Period and the Second World War

Addison, P *The Road to 1945: British Politics and the Second World War* (London, 1975)

Best, G *Humanity and Warfare: The Modern History of the International Law of Armed Conflicts* (London, 1980)

Bracher, Karl-Dietrich *The German Dictatorship. The Origins, Structure and Effects of National Socialism* (London, 1971)

Bullock, Alan *Hitler. A Study in Tyranny* (London Penguin, 1962)

Calvocoressi, Peter; Wint, Guy and Pritchard, John *Total War: The Causes and Courses of the Second World War* (London, Penguin revised edn, 1989)

Campbell, John (ed.) *The Experience of World War II* (London and New York, 1989)

Carr, William *Poland to Pearl Harbour: the Making of the Second World War* (London, 1985)

Conquest, Robert *The Great Terror, Stalin's Purge of the Thirties* (London Penguin, 1971)

Duus, Peter *The Cambridge History of Japan, Vol VI* (Cambridge, 1989)

Gathorne-Hardy, G *A Short History of International Affairs* (London, 1950)

Feis, Herbert *Churchill, Roosevelt, Stalin* (London, 1957)

Gilbert, Martin *The Second World War* (London, 1989)

Hinsley, Francis, H *British Intelligence in the Second World War: its Influence on Strategy and Operations* (London, 1979)

Hosking, Geoffrey *A History of the Soviet Union* (London, 1985)

Keegan, John *The Second World War* (London, 1989)

Kershaw, Ian *The "Hitler Myth": Image and Reality in the Third Reich* (Oxford, 1987)

Kershaw, Ian *The Nazi Dictatorship, Problems and Perspectives of Interpretation* (2nd ed, London, 1989)

Kershaw, Ian *Popular Opinion and Political Dissent in the Third Reich: Bavaria 1933–1945* (Oxford, 1983)

Kindleberger, CP *The World in Depression, 1929–1939* (London, 1973)

Macdonald, CA *The United States. Britain and Appeasement, 1936–1939* (London, 1980)

Marrus, MR *The Unwanted: European Refugees in the Twentieth Century* (New York, 1985)

Milward, Alan S *War, Economy and Society, 1939–1945* (London, 1977)

Mommsen, Wolfgang and Kettenacker, Lothar *The Fascist Challenge and the Policy of Appeasement* (London, 1983)

Nelson, Harold I *Land and Power. British and Allied Policy on Germany's Frontiers, 1916–1919* (London, 1963)

Nicholls, AJ *Weimar and the Rise of Hitler* (London, 1979)

Overy, Richard and Wheatcroft, Andrew *The Road to War* (London, 1989)

Robertson, Esmonde M (ed.) *The Origins of the Second World War: Historical Interpretations* (London, 1971)

Seaton, Albert *The Russo-German War, 1941–45* (London, 1971)

Seton-Watson, Christopher *Italy from Liberalism to Fascism, 1870–1925* (London, 1965)

Taylor, AJP *The Origins of the Second World War* (London, 1971)

Thorne, Christopher *Allies of a Kind: the United States, Britain and the War Against Japan, 1941–45* (London, 1978)

Thorne, Christopher *The Approach of War, 1938–1939* (London, 1967)

Watt, Donald Cameron *How War Came* (London, 1989)

Weinberg, Gerhard L *The Foreign Policy of Hitler's Germany* (2 vols. Chicago, 1970 and 1980)

Wheeler-Bennett, John W and Nicholls, Anthony *The Semblance of Peace: The Political Settlement after the Second World War* (London, 1972)

The World Since 1945

Chen, J *Mao and the Chinese Revolution* (Oxford, 1965)

Crockatt, Richard and Smith, Steve (eds.) *The Cold War Past and Present* (London, 1987)

Feis, Herbert *From Trust to Terror: the Onset of the Cold War, 1945–1950* (London, 1970)

Fleming, D *The Cold War and its Origins* (London, 1961)

Hargreaves, JD *Decolonization in Africa* (London, 1988)

Knapp, Wilfred *A History of War and Peace* (Oxford, 1967)

Luard, Evan *The Blunted Sword: the Erosion of Military Power in Modern World Politics* (London, 1984)

Milward, Alan S *The Reconstruction of Western Europe, 1945–51* (London, 1984)

Robertson, Charles L *International Relations since World War II. A Short History* (2nd edn. New York and London, 1975)

Rothwell, Victor *Britain and the Cold War, 1941–1947* (London, 1982)

Rubinstein, AZ *Soviet Foreign Policy Since World War II: Imperial and Global* (Cambridge, Mass, 1981)

Urwin, DK *Western Europe since 1945. A Short Political History* (London, 1981)

ACKNOWLEDGEMENTS

Picture credits
1 LC 2–3 M/H. Cartier-Bresson 4 IWM 6 M/Erich Lessing 9 E.T. Archive 10–11 National Archives, Washington D.C. 13 M/Robert Capa 15 M/B. Glinn 16 M/Philip Jones-Griffeths 19 FSP/F. Lochan 25 CP/IWM 26tl Edimedia 26br MEPL 26–27 Royal Commonwealth Institute, London 27br Staatsgalerie, Stuttgart 28t MEPL 28b UB 28–29 Culver Pictures, N.Y. 31tl DKC 31tr Victoria and Albert Museum, London 31br Picturepoint 32 JH 34t LC 34b IWM 34–35 Bibliothèque Nationale, Paris 35t Alexander Meledin 35b P 37 HDC 38–39t BPK 38–39b SV 40–41t JH 40b TPL 41 MEPL 42–43 SV 43t TPL 44t, 44–45 IKON/USPG 45tl, 45cr MEPL 45bl RF 47 P 48 *Illustrated London News* 49 DKC 50l LC 51t HDC 51b MEPL 52 LC 59 HDC 61t IWM 61b The Tank Museum, Bovington 62 Bibliothèque de Documentation Internationale Contemporaine, Paris 63 National Museum, Dresden 65 IWM 66t National Museum of Ireland, Dublin 66b P 67t DKC 67cr New York Public Library 67b Roger-Viollet, Paris 68l Lenin Museum, Moscow 68r DKC 70t Equinox Archive 70b Mayakovsky, 20 years of work, Museum of Modern Art, Oxford 71t DKC 71c JH/Marc Riboud 71b Universidad Autónoma de Chapingo, Chapel 73l National Archives, Washington D.C. 73r, 74 IWM 75t David Low 75b UB 76–77 HDC 77 Bettmann Archive 78t HDC 78b TPL 79 P 81, 82 DKC 83 Alexander Meledin 84 HDC 85 Equinox Archive 86–87 Alexander Meledin 86 inset t International Museum of Photography, N.Y. 87t Roger-Viollet 87c IKON 87b M/Robert Capa 93 P 94–95 HDC 95t Arthur Lockwood 95c David Low 96 Alexander Meledin 97t ICP Library of Photographers, N.Y. 97b, 98–99 IKON 98t HDC 98b,99t IKON 99c FSP 99b CP 101 M/David Seymour 102tl HDC 102tr IKON 102br IWM 103t M/René Burri 103b HDC 104 P 104–105 M/Robert Capa 105tr Centro Internacional de la Historia, Barcelona 105br M/Robert Capa 107 AP 108 HDC 108–109 SV 111t HDC 111b, 112t UB 112–113 IWM 114t John Erikson 114b TPL 114–115 DKC 115r BPK 116 RF 119t Robert Hunt Library 119b Alexander Meledin 120b National Archives, Washington D.C. 120–121, 121b IWM 122t Wiener Library, London 122c, 122–123 Lee Miller Archives 122b Alexander Meledin 123t JH/Sygma 123b RF/Kraipit 129, 132b P 133t TPL 133b, 134 P 137t TPL 137b USIS 138 M/Henri Cartier-Bresson 139 Edimedia 140t, 140b P 140–141 Science Photo Library/US Department of Energy 141t IKON 141c HDC 141b U.S. Air Force 143 M/Erich Lessing 144, 144–145 CP 145t, 146 P 149 Cas Oorthuys 150b, 150t P 150–151 Government of India 152t, 152b, 153t, 153b P 154t JH/Ernest Cole 154–155, 155l M/Ian Berry 158t HDC 158b FSP 158–159 UNRWA/Myrtle Winter-Chaumeny 159t M/Burt Glinn 159c M/Alex Webb 159b UN Photo/John Isaac 165 M/Henri Cartier-Bresson 166, 167b CP 167c *Chicago Sun-Times*, Mauldin 168t P 168b AP 169t, 169b, 171 CP 172–173 JH/Marc Riboud 173 CP 175t M/Philip Jones-Griffeths 175b JH/Marc Riboud 176t, 176b M/Ian Berry 177t, 177b M/Don McCullin 178 M/Leonard Freed 179 M/Micha Baram 180t M/Robert Capa 180b M/F. Scianna 180–181 AP 181bl, 181bc RF 181br AP 183 M 184t IKON 184b M/Roger Malloch 185 M/Bruno Barbey 186t P 186b M/Elliott Erwitt 187t P 187b *Los Angeles Times* 188–189 M/Philip Jones-Griffeths 188b M/Don McCullin 189 IKON 190t, 190b P 190–191 M/Don McCullin 192t IKON 192b RF 192–193 M/Bruno Barbey 193tl Arthur Lockwood 193tr AP 193br RF 199b, 199t RF 200–201 Network Photographers/Peter Jordan 201t CP 201b FSP 202l Format/Raissa Page 202r Format/ Brenda Prince 203t FSP 203b P 205 RF 206 M/C. Steele-Perkins 207b RF 207t *Observer Magazine* 208, 209, 210t FSP 210b CP 211l TPL 211r Anti-Apartheid Movement, London 212–213 RF 213tr M/Raghu Rai 213br M/Abbas 214l Katz Eyes/J.B. Pics, J. Nordel 214r CP 215l RF 215r, 216t FSP 216b, 216–217 P 217tl, 217tr CP 217bl AP 217br Greenpeace/Miller 219t M/Peter Marlow 219b FSP 220l Greenpeace/Walker 220r FSP 221 Network Photographers/Sturrock 222t M/Jean Gaumy 222b, 223b RF 222–223, 224l RF 224r, 225t, 225b RF 226bl CP 226br FSP 226–227 M/Costa Manos 227t, 227tc, 227bc, 227b, 228l P 228c, 228r HDC 229l P 229c TPL 229r M/Abbas 230l, 230r P 230c, 231l HDC 231r IKON 232l P 232c M/JK 232r IWM 233l, 233c P 233r IWM 234l P 234c Lucien Aigner 234r, 235l, 235r, 236l P 236c HDC 236r, 237c, 237r P 237l M/Robert Capa 238l P 238c, 239l, 239c HDC 239r P 240l International Defence & Air Fund for South Africa 240c RF 240r CP 241l, 241c P 241r HDC 242l, 242c, 242r P 243l M/Elliott Erwitt 243c CP 243r M/Peter Marlow 244l Arthur Lockwood 244r, 245l, 245r P 245c HDC 246l IWM 246c P 246r CP 247l HDC 247c P 247r JH/Marc Riboud

Abbreviations
AP   Associated Press
BPK   Bildarchiv Preussischer Kulturbesitz, W. Berlin
CP   Camera Press, London
MEPL   Mary Evans Picture Library, London
JH   John Hillelson Agency, London
HDC   Hulton Deutsch Collection, London
IWM   Imperial War Museum, London
DKC   David King Collection, London
LC   Library of Congress, Washington D.C.
M   Magnum Photos, London
P   Popperfoto, London
RF   Rex Features, London
FSP   Frank Spooner Pictures, London
SV   Süddeutscher Verlag, Munich
TPL   Ullstein Bilderdienst, W. Berlin
UB   Topham Picture Library, Edinbridge

Part Openers
20–21   Funeral of Queen Victoria HDC
54–55   Battle of Passchendaele IWM
88–89   Nuremburg rally FPG International, N.Y.
124–125   Atomic bomb test, Nevada FPG International, N.Y.
160–161   Antiwar demonstration, Washington JH/Charles Harbutt
194–195   Civil war, Beirut FSP/F. Demulder

Editorial and research assistance
Monica Byles, Steve Chapman, Jackie Gaff, Jane Higgins, John Horgan, Louise Jones, Andy Overs, Maria Quantrill, Graham Speake, Michelle Von Ahn, Elaine Welsh

Artists
Alan Hollingbery, Ayala Kingsley, Colin Salmon, Dave Smith

Photographs
Shirley Jamieson, Alison Renney

Cartography
Maps drafted by Euromap, Pangbourne; Alan Mais (Hornchurch). Sarah Rhodes

Typesetting
Brian Blackmore; OPUS Ltd, Oxford

Production
Clive Sparling

Color origination
J. Film Process, Bangkok

Index
Ann Barrett

251